Perspectives in Cultural-Historical Research

Founding Editor

Fernando González Rey

Volume 9

Series Editors

Marilyn Fleer, Peninsula Campus, Monash University, Frankston, Australia

Mariane Hedegaard, University of Copenhagen, Copenhagen, Denmark

Nikolai Veresov, Faculty of Education, Monash University, Frankston, Australia

There is growing interest in the work of LS Vygotsky internationally, but also in finding new ways and perspectives for advancing cultural-historical theory for solving contemporary problems. Although Vygotsky has become one of the most influential scholars in education and psychology today, there is still a need for serious studies of his work because so much remains unexamined.

The books in this series draw on the collected works of Vygotsky as a primary source of authority. They go beyond secondary sources and discuss Vygotsky's original ideas in the context of a system of concepts or through the elaboration and theorisation of research findings so that contemporary problems can be addressed in new ways.

This series collectively brings together under one umbrella a more equal representation of works from scholars across both the Northern and Southern continents. In the context of a large volume of contributions to cultural-historical theorisation and the empirical work from North America, there is an urgent need for making visible the works of scholars from countries who reside in countries other than North America.

More information about this series at http://www.springer.com/series/13559

Daniel Magalhães Goulart ·
Albertina Mitjáns Martínez · Megan Adams
Editors

Theory of Subjectivity from a Cultural-Historical Standpoint

González Rey's Legacy

Editors
Daniel Magalhães Goulart 🆔
Faculty of Education
University of Brasilia
Brasilia, Brazil

Albertina Mitjáns Martínez 🆔
Faculty of Education
University of Brasilia
Brasilia, Brazil

Megan Adams 🆔
Faculty of Education
Monash University
Clayton, VIC, Australia

ISSN 2520-1530   ISSN 2520-1549   (electronic)
Perspectives in Cultural-Historical Research
ISBN 978-981-16-1419-4   ISBN 978-981-16-1417-0   (eBook)
https://doi.org/10.1007/978-981-16-1417-0

This Springer imprint is published by the registered company Springer Nature Singapore Pte Ltd.
The registered company address is: 152 Beach Road, #21-01/04 Gateway East, Singapore 189721,
Singapore

Foreword

Festschrift in Honour of the Lifework of Fernando González Rey

It is 2002 and the rooms surrounding the auditorium are filling up as delegates attending the Congress of *The International Society of Cultural-historical Activity Research* (ISCAR) congregate. There is a feeling of anticipation in the air, as delegates greet each other, and await the forthcoming keynotes and papers to be presented at VU University in Amsterdam. All of a sudden, an explosion of hugs, kisses, and laughter attracts the attention of delegates. Who is this man that is so warmly greeted? One person after another makes their way towards him, and each greets him in the same way. Clearly, he is someone of note, someone who is highly regarded, and a scholar well known to many in the ISCAR community.

ISCAR is the key association for scholars interested in promoting multidisciplinary theoretical and empirical research on societal, cultural, and historical dimensions of human practices. The Congress is their major international event. It brings members together every three years. According to the Standing Orders, ISCAR supports the interchange of information related to research among its members and with other Associations throughout the world (Article 3; https://www.iscar.org/about/legal-information/). With so much attention directed to one delegate at this ISCAR Congress, it becomes possible to see how interchange of more than research is taking place. This person is so personable and fun to be around. This person must be a scholar of great importance. Therefore, it is not surprising that 19 years later, a *Festschrift* is dedicated to him by members of this community.

This volume celebrates the lifework of Fernando González Rey. It is not just a book within the Series published by Springer—*Perspectives in Cultural-Historical Research*—but it is a *Festschrift*. A *Festschrift,* as a collection of papers, is prepared by scholars to honour a respected member of their research community. The work of Fernando González Rey is honoured in this volume through the writings of different academics who each pay tribute to his brilliance, to his scholarship, and to the person. Qualities that were clearly on display at the ISCAR Congress in 2002 in Amsterdam.

This image of Fernando González Rey as an esteemed and personable scholar is refracted through the words of each author of this volume. Authors bring out his seminal ideas and concepts by plotting their place in relation to his key works (Chapter 1), through showcasing how they have used his work to amplify and theorise their own research (Chapters 3, 5–7, 9–17), by engaging in dialogue with his ideas through critique (Chapters 4 and 8), and by bringing together the contributions made by others in celebration of the lifework of Fernando González Rey (also Chapter 1).

This *Festschrift* is also a memorial to our esteemed scholar Fernando González Rey who sadly passed away before the volume could be completed. Therefore, this volume could also have been called a *Gedenkschrift*.

The 2002 Congress in the Netherlands was one of many moments in the life of Fernando González Rey. Members' responses to him were also indicative of the esteem in which he was held. Many prestigious scholars enthusiastically clapped at his closing keynote address. What did so many take away from his presentation? The terms subjectivity, subjective senses, subjective configurations, symbolic processes, and the concept of unity were dotted over the pages of any delegate recording his presentation. But the complexity of the concepts being introduced could not be reduced to a word, but rather, they had to be experienced through a cacophony of historical moments, cultural-emotional refractions, reported research results, and a deep theorisation of the human condition. Like all those early in their career, or first to hear the insights from a great scholar like Fernando González Rey, it is difficult to synthesise and report on what is heard within a 60-minute period. But one term came through in the words heard, in the manner of the presentation, and in the person himself, and that was *emotions*.

Zaporozhets (1986/2002), in drawing upon Lange (1914), drew attention to the lack of scholarship into emotions, stating, the metaphor of Cinderella best describes the unfair share of research attention that the study of emotions had in favour of her older sisters—Thinking and Will (paraphrased; p. 46). Vygotsky (1925/1971, 1933/1999) was unable to fully elaborate his theory of the unity of cognition and emotion, leaving much to be done by post-Vygotskian researchers, such as Fernando González Rey (1999, 2009, 2011). Fernando González Rey brought forward for many, this area of research—arguing that we should not be blind to it.

Fernando González Rey also took us back to *The Psychology of Art*, Vygotsky's Ph.D. thesis, to reclaim and reintroduce to the broader ISCAR community the different periods in Vygotsky's writing where emotions as a concept was embedded, developed, or absent (González Rey, 2016). Having spent time in the lab of L.I. Bozhovich, Fernando González Rey knew the importance of simultaneously understanding the historical and the contemporary as foundational for progressing his work. Fernando González Rey always located his concepts and research within a historical critique of the conception and development of cultural-historical theory within the Soviet and later Russian tradition of philosophy and psychology. The cultural-historical development of the concept of emotions was but one of his major theoretical and empirical contributions.

Fast forward from the 2002 ISCAR Congress in the Netherlands and on to a series of symposia in Australia in 2013. Fernando González Rey's personality and unwavering commitment to developing the original works of Vygotsky and his contemporaries was heard as he presented the established concept of sense. Characteristic of Fernando González Rey was how he began his presentation—no matter how large or small the audience was—with words such as these:

> *I have entered into the topic of subjectivity within a cultural-historical framework, because it was a topic of historical and ideological reason that was overlooked by the Soviet psychological tradition, but was taken forward by Zinchenko through the matter of consciousness....* (https://www.youtube.com/watch?v=HNsGiyDdxsc)

Wading through the historical complexities of cultural-historical theory in 2013 to discuss his own work, a passionate plea was made by Fernando González Rey to not disaggregate the human mind, the person, society, human relationships, and more, when undertaking research. The concepts he developed are testimony to this unity:

> *The concept I extend is the concept of subjective sense and subjective configuration – that I try to work them as the inseparable relationship between emotional and symbolical processes, in a way that emotions always appear; implies symbolical as inseparable, and they configure a kind of unity.* (see https://www.youtube.com/watch?v=HNsGiyDdxsc)

Daniel Goulart, Albertina Martínez, and Megan Adams in the introductory chapter of this volume note that Fernando González Rey suggested that "the concept of subjectivity implies the rejection of any universal principle as its theoretical basis". In Australia, Fernando González Rey brought forward the concept of subjective sense as part of a symbolic-emotional system that was foundational for the empirical and theoretical development of his work, and the work of others interested in using his system of concepts. His scholarship brought together many research groups, including those from Brazil and Australia, who are both represented in the editorship of this volume, and the chapters within the book. In many respects, he lived his theory in dialogue with others:

> *Subjective sense are processes that practically can be identified with human experience, we live our life through subjective sense, our conversations ... it's a symbolical sense production, which may meet the individual in a very particular way, that have a lot to do with my content at the moment, with my history, and with my own culture. Subjective configurations are such a complex organisation of subjective sense, that organise the ongoing human experience, of the ongoing human action, it's a way to represent a unique system, processes subjective senses which flow one into another....* (https://www.youtube.com/watch?v=HNsGiyDdxsc)

Another concept Fernando González Rey was pivotal in developing was the Russian term *Perezhivanie*. A volume of Mind, Culture and Activity dedicated to this concept is forever stamped with his contribution (González Rey, 2016), and the 2014 ISCAR Congress in Sydney, Australia, where he was an invited keynote speaker, brings out how this concept could be further developed. Once again, Fernando González Rey made important contributions to better understanding the concept of *Perezhivanie* in examining *The Problem of the Environment* (Vygotsky, 1994), noting that reflection acted as a mirror, whilst refraction as a metaphor better captured the human experience and condition.

Fernando González Rey's passion and scholarship are held into perpetuity in this volume. The chapters in this volume show the complexity of his work, but do so in ways that demonstrate the significance of his concepts for research and for furthering scholarship. The dialogue with Fernando González Rey continues in each moment we discuss his ideas, use his concepts, and theorise our work. Fernando did not want scholarship to stop or to stay as a replication of those who had written in the past, but he wanted to keep it alive, to grow it, and to use it to develop new ideas. The concepts he introduced into the ISCAR community are testimony to this theoretical and conceptual development and his genius as a scholar. This *Festschrift* captures his original contribution to cultural-historical theory, at the same time as honouring the legacy he has left for others to take forward.

Marilyn Fleer
Australian Research Council Laureate Fellow
Monash University, Clayton, Australia

References

González Rey, F. (1999). Personality, subject and human development: The subjective character of human activity. In S. Chaiklin, M. Hedegaard, & U. J. Jensen (Eds.), *Activity theory and social practice* (pp. 523–275). Aarhus, Denmark: Aarhus University Press.

González Rey, F. (2009). Historical relevance of Vygotsky's work: Its significance for a new approach to the problem of subjectivity in psychology. *Outlines, 1,* 59–73.

González Rey, F. (2011). A re-examination of defining moments in Vygotsky's work and their implications for his continuing legacy, *Mind, Culture and Activity, 18,* 257–275.

González Rey, F. (2016). Vygotsky's concept of Perezhivanie in the psychology of art and at the final moments of his work: Advancing his legacy. *Mind, Culture and Activity, 23*(4), 305–314.

Lange, N. N. (1914). *Psikhologiia* [Psychology]. Moscow.

Vygotsky, L. S. (1971). *The psychology of art.* Cambridge, MA: MIT Press (Original work published 1925).

Vygotsky, L. S. (1994). The problem of the environment. In J. Valsiner & R. vander Veer (Eds.), *The Vygotsky reader* (pp. 347–348). Oxford: Blackwell.

Vygotsky, L. S. (1999). The teaching about emotions: Historical–psychological studies. In *Scientific legacy. The collected works of L.S. Vygotsky* (Vol. 6, M. J. Hall, Trans., & R. W. Rieber, Ed.; English trans., pp. 69–235). New York, NY: Plenum (Original work published 1933).

Zaporozhets, A. V. (1986/2002). Toward the question of the genesis, function, and structure of emotional processes in the child. *Journal of Russian and East European Psychology, 40*(2), 45–66. ISSN 1061–0405/2003.

Contents

Editors and Contributors

About the Editors

Daniel Magalhães Goulart is an Assistant Professor at the Department of Theory and Foundations of the Faculty of Education of the University of Brasilia. He is also a Collaborating Professor at the Master's in Psychology of the University Center of Brasilia. He graduated as a psychologist from the University of São Paulo and completed his Ph.D. at the Faculty of Education of the University of Brasilia (CAPES), Brazil. He is the current coordinator of the Reading and Research Group "Subjectivity: Theory, Epistemology and Methodology". His latest books are: (1) Subjectivity within a cultural-historical approach: theory, methodology and research (Ed., Springer, 2019), (2) Subjectivity and critical mental health: lessons from Brazil (Routledge, 2019), and (3) Saúde mental, desenvolvimento e subjetividade: da patologização à ética do sujeito [Mental health, development and subjectivity: from pathologization to the ethics of the subject] (Cortez, 2019).

Albertina Mitjáns Martínez is a Research Professor of the Faculty of Education at the University of Brasilia, Brazil. She obtained her Ph.D. qualification in psychological sciences at the University of Havana, Cuba, and concluded post-doctoral studies at the Faculty of Psychology of the Autonomous University of Madrid. Her research interests focus on education and psychology from a cultural-historical approach in three specific fields: (1) creativity and innovation in education; (2) subjectivity in human development and learning; (3) disabilities and school inclusion. Her latest books are: (1) Subjectivity within cultural-historical approach: theory, methodology and research (Ed., 2019, Springer); (2) Subjetividade: teoria, epistemologia e método [Subjectivity: theory, epistemology and method] (Alínea, 2019); (3) Psicologia, educação e aprendizagem escolar [Psychology, education and school learning] (Cortez, 2019).

Megan Adams is a Senior Lecturer of Inclusion at Monash University, Melbourne, Australia. She obtained her Ph.D. qualifications in Education at Monash University. Her main research interests are focused on education from a cultural-historical approach using subjectivity to investigate (1) families with young children moving countries (2) identity, curriculum, and pedagogy (3) preservice teacher's perceptions about working with students displaying challenging behaviours in classrooms.

Contributors

Megan Adams Faculty of Education, Monash University, Melbourne, Australia

Juan Balbi Cetepo (Post-Rationalist Center of Psychotherapy), Rome, Italy

Ole Dreier University of Copenhagen, Copenhagen, Denmark

Moisès Esteban-Guitart University of Girona, Girona, Spain

Marilyn Fleer Conceptual PlayLab, Monash University, Melbourne, VIC, Australia

Fernando González Rey Faculty of Health and Education Sciences, University Center of Brasilia, Brasilia, Brazil

Daniel Magalhães Goulart Faculty of Education, University of Brasilia, Brasilia, Brazil

Cristina M. Madeira-Coelho Faculty of Education, Universidade de Brasília (UnB), Brasília, Brazil

Luiz Roberto Rodrigues Martins University of Brasilia, Brasilia, Brazil

Albertina Mitjáns Martínez University of Brasilia, Brasilia, Brazil

Valéria Deusdará Mori Center of Brasilia, Brasilia, Brazil

Ian Parker University of Manchester, Manchester, UK

Gloria Quinones Monash University, Melbourne, VIC, Australia

Wanda C. Rodríguez Arocho University of Puerto Rico, San Juan, Puerto Rico

Maristela Rossato University of Brasilia, Brasilia, Brazil

David Subero University of Girona, Girona, Spain

Maria Carmen Villela Rosa Tacca University of Brasília, Brasília, Brazil

José Fernando Patino Torres Faculty of Psychology, Federal University of Tocantins, Miracema, Brazil

Nikolai Veresov Monash University, Clayton, VIC, Australia

Chapter 1
Theory of Subjectivity Within Cultural-Historical Perspective: Presenting González Rey's Legacy

Daniel Magalhães Goulart, Albertina Mitjáns Martínez, and Megan Adams

Abstract This chapter presents González Rey's legacy in the context of Cultural-Historical Psychology and situates this book as a celebration of his academic contributions to various contexts and fields. The central concepts introduced through his study of subjectivity include the dynamic relations between social, individual, institutional, and political perspectives, where symbolic-emotional processes and formations feature. This introductory chapter outlines the collection of chapters and brings together examples of how these concepts are employed and developed in the study of subjective processes, as well as their contribution to different contexts and fields. González Rey's foundational concepts and his creative epistemological and methodological approach are discussed in brief. Finally, some questions and theoretical challenges that direct future pathways are proposed by the authors through their commitment to the open and always-in-development character of the Theory of Subjectivity.

1.1 Introduction

This edited volume examines key ideas related to the academic contributions made by Professor Fernando González Rey (1949–2019), emphasizing his Theory of Subjectivity within a Cultural-historical approach. It acknowledges and honors González Rey's contribution to the Perspectives in Cultural-Historical Research Series by Springer, both as a founding editor and as an author.

D. M. Goulart (✉) · A. M. Martínez
Faculty of Education, University of Brasilia, Brasilia, Brazil
e-mail: danielgoulartbr@gmail.com

A. M. Martínez
e-mail: amitjans49@gmail.com

M. Adams
Faculty of Education, Monash University, Melbourne, Australia
e-mail: megan.adams@monash.edu

González Rey's first coedited book in the series was *Perezhivanie, emotions and subjectivity: Advancing Vygotsky's legacy* (Fleer et al., 2017), in which Vygotsky's ideas of perezhivanie, emotions, and imagination were discussed in depth, and González Rey's Theory of Subjectivity was explored as a way to advance this legacy, presenting a new understanding of human development. The aforementioned edited volume is an expression of González Rey's critical and innovative interpretation of Soviet psychology, which has historically challenged mainstream approaches (González Rey, 2009, 2011a, 2016a, 2017).

Departing from the historical and current significance of Cultural-historical psychology, the edited volume (Fleer et al., 2017) acknowledges the dissemination of Soviet psychology in Western countries has been relatively limited and mistakenly associated with a partial reading of a few authors, mainly L. S. Vygotsky, A. N. Leontiev, and A. R. Luria (González Rey, 2009, 2011b, 2014, 2020; Yasnitsky, 2012; Zavershneva, 2010). However, the readings provide different understandings for important and historically less well-known concepts of Vygotsky's, such as *perezhivanie*, the social situation of development and sense. Also, they advance this legacy through the focus on subjectivity.

1.2   Historical Inspirations

Other authors in Cultural-historical psychology have explicitly addressed the topic of subjectivity, such as Abuljanova (1980), Chudnovsky (1988), and Lomov (1984). In these pioneering works by disciples of Rubinstein, Bozhovich, and Ananiev, it is possible to see the potential that the dialectic legacy of previous generations of Soviet psychology has for the development of subjectivity (Mitjáns Martínez & González Rey, 2017). However, at the time of writing, the authors did not conceptually define subjectivity, nor turn the focus toward a research project (González Rey, 2011a, 2014).

González Rey was inspired by these authors, and especially by the initial attempts of Vygotsky and Bozhovich "to advance a representation of human psyche as a generative, and not an assimilative system" (González Rey et al., 2019, p. 8). Based on his initial works with a focus on the concept of personality, González Rey elaborated a Theory of Subjectivity from a Cultural-historical standpoint. He presented the related concepts and the basic pillars of subjectivity in 1997, in the book titled *Qualitative Epistemology and Subjectivity* (González Rey, 1997). From this theoretical perspective, a programmatic research design was developed, which also demanded new epistemological and methodological constructions (González Rey et al., 2019). As González Rey explained:

> It was not easy at all to advance on subjectivity as such within a psychology dominated by a theoretical imagery, the Marxist character of which was defined by an objective representation of human psyche, and which developed itself within a political context in which idealism was defined as a political enemy. (…) [This psychology was] centered on explaining

human psyche as determined by something external, and on replacing psyche by something different. (González Rey et al., 2019, p. 4)

Importantly, Marxist's inaugural perspective was at the foundation of González Rey's theorization throughout the years. Especially in the need to examine any human process within the social network in which human life takes place, and on dialectics as a continuous process of change in contradictory relationships. Marx's concept of working class was also an important step to a different understanding of the social subject (González Rey, 2015). However, according to González Rey, as an author from the nineteenth century, Marx:

> (…) fails to transcend, in the alternative view of history he presents us, the rationalism of his time, and presents society as a system subject to laws that define the progressive evolution of history – in a representation that leaves no space for the subject in this production. The subject is guided by laws that go beyond his possibilities of action. (González Rey, 2012, p. 150)

With regard to Marxists' different approaches, González Rey takes a critical view of what he considers "anti-individualist Marxists" (González Rey, 2012, p. 154), who are usually closed and authoritarian elites and control and repress the exercise of criticism, producing processes of subjectivation that deny the principles at the basis of the renewing social action. Also, González Rey was historically critical of the institutionalized Marxist tradition when it praises the materialist conception of human being and society, creating difficulties to understand the active character of the subject and his productive capacity in the most diverse social scenarios. As a result, the dialectic defended by Marx was often neglected (González Rey, 2012, 2015).

1.3 González Rey's Contributions

In the volume *Perezhivanie, emotions and subjectivity: Advancing Vygotsky's legacy* (Fleer et al., 2017), the Theory of Subjectivity was presented as a way to advance a complex theory of human functioning with theoretical, epistemological, and methodological implications. Also, in this volume, the consequences of the Theory of Subjectivity for a new understanding of human development were explored. Subjective development is defined as "the development of new subjective resources that allows the individual to make relevant changes in the course of a performance, relations or other significant lived experiences" (González Rey et al., 2017, p. 222). The complex interrelation between the main concepts of the Theory of Subjectivity, including, individual and social subjectivity, subjective sense, subjective configuration and subject, subjective development represents a way to overcome absolute and universal criteria, emphasizing the singularity of this process, the generative character of individuals and social groups, as well as the dialectic between individual and social.
González Rey's second coedited book in the Springer series Perspectives in Cultural-Historical Research was *Subjectivity within Cultural-Historical approach: Theory,*

methodology and research (González Rey et al., 2019). This volume deepened the contributions of González Rey's Theory of Subjectivity, Qualitative Epistemology, and Constructive-Interpretative Methodology across different research fields. Also, the volume highlighted the implications of the theoretical, epistemological, and methodological approach for professional practice, by presenting different case studies conducted in various countries. In the volume, González Rey conceptualized subjectivity as follows:

> Subjectivity as an ontological domain specifies a new kind of process, that is qualitatively different from all the processes involved in its genesis. As such, subjectivity is ontologically defined by the integration of emotions and symbolical processes, forming new qualitative units: subjective senses. Such subjective senses are "snapshots" of symbolic emotional flashes that unfold in a chaotic movement, from which subjective configurations emerge as a self-regulative and self-generative organization of subjective senses. (González Rey, 2019, p. 28)

From this perspective, an effective professional practice demands the understanding of this dynamic and contradictory system through the construction of conjectures, indicators, and hypothesis that represent possible interpretations that become the basis of both research and professional strategies and actions. Indeed, research and professional practice share the same attributes and are developed hand in hand. They are based on dialogical systems oriented toward the emergences of singular subjective processes, which gain relevance for the production of knowledge on the studied topic (González Rey & Mitjáns Martínez, 2017b, 2019). On the other hand, the constructed knowledge on singular cases, understood as theoretical models, are the basis for generating new strategies, instruments, and dialogical spaces that provoke the emergence of agents and subjects capable of opening up alternative paths of individual and social subjective development. González Rey and Mitjáns Martínez explain:

> The only difference between practice and scientific research is in the intention of the professional who develops them: the practice is oriented to the change of people, groups and concrete institutions, and the research aims to produce knowledge with a capacity for generalization that transcends the participants of their current moment. A good practice implies, in fact, research and the production of knowledge about the particular question that guides it. (González Rey & Mitjáns Martínez, 2017b, p. 15)

From this perspective, theory is not "applied" as preexistent content in concrete situations. According to González Rey (2019b), static theories are converted into dogmas, which are frequently turned into ideologies lacking reflexivity. In his view, theories are lively systems in development. They are analytical devices for constructing knowledge about singular phenomena, which are always unexpected and dynamic (González Rey, 2019b). When explaining the Theory of Subjectivity, González Rey explains that there are two different levels, a macro-theory and a micro-theory.

> The macro-theory has a set of concepts that make up a complex system, which produces multiple ways of intelligibility and new representations; it even generates new problems for science, new fields of theoretical significance that we had not previously noticed. (González Rey & Patiño-Torres, 2017, p. 122)

The macro-theory level of the Theory of Subjectivity is not related to a conception of metatheory whose subject matter is itself a theory. It represents a general theory of human functioning based on broad generalizing concepts that have been gradually developed through programmatic research. The micro-theory is represented by theoretical models in development, which are the theoretical meanings researchers are able to construct based on the diversity of emerging information in research fields, according to their researched topic (González Rey & Patiño-Torres, 2017). Based on Qualitative Epistemology, both micro-theory and macro-theory are in a lively process, while representing different levels of theoretical generalization. The micro-theory is permanently in tension and may gradually lead to the development of the macro-theory (González Rey, 2019b). As we explained elsewhere:

> Theory of Subjectivity, while supported by an ontological, epistemological and methodological basis, is a macro-theory that has an impact on understanding and acting in different fields such as health, education, psychotherapy and community practices, among others. (…) The Theory of Subjectivity is a genuine way of understanding human behaviour and motivation. (Goulart et al., 2020, p. 16)

This view can be understood as an alternative to positivistic epistemology, which culminated in a mechanistic understanding of research as a data collection process that, in the end, reach general conclusion via statistics or experimental demonstrations (González Rey & Mitjáns Martínez, 2019). Even in qualitative methodologies, significant aspects of the positivistic epistemology are present today (González Rey & Mitjáns Martínez, 2017a). This dominant point of view in science led to the exclusion of theory from its own constructions, as if the complexity of the studied topic was secondary in relation to the so-called "scientific method".

In 2020, a new volume, entitled *Cultural-Historical and Critical Psychology: Common ground, divergences and future pathways* (Fleer et al., 2020), was published after the passing of González Rey and was dedicated to his works. Marilyn Fleer and Peter Jones, his friends and collaborators, acknowledged him as the one who "initiated and inspired this project" (Fleer et al., 2020, p. V). This book opened up a critical dialogue within and across the theoretical traditions of Cultural-historical psychology and critical psychology, with a view to finding new ways for cooperation and productive discussion between these two important standpoints in contemporary psychology. We have previously located González Rey's Theory of Subjectivity as a way to advance Cultural-historical psychology, based on the unfinished legacy of different authors, such as L. S. Vygotsky, L. Bozhovich, Chudnosvki, and Lomov. Nevertheless, we could also locate this theory as a way to advance Critical Psychology.

Different traditions in Critical Psychology have emphasized the narrow and problematic way in which psychology has historically dealt with human processes, such as the Critical Discursive Psychology (Burman, 2017; Foucault, 1978, 1987; Parker, 2015), Social Constructionism (Gergen, 1994; Harré, 1995), the German Critical Psychology (Dreier, 2008, 2020; Holzkamp, 1991; Teo, 2017), and the Latin American Critical Social Psychology (Martín Baró, 1987; Montero, 1994; González Rey, 1987). Essentialism, individualism, universalism, and different forms of alienation have been pointed out as characteristics of mainstream psychology by all these tradi-tions. Through different theoretical approaches, Critical Psychology "[has] emerged as politically engaged and as critical investigations of societal processes and insti-tutions, focusing on such topics as discrimination and exclusion in terms of gender, race and class and the exercise of power through ideological means" (Fleer et al., 2020, p. 3). These different theoretical approaches have emphasized different and, sometimes, contradictory concepts and ideas, such as the unity individual-social, subject, discursive practices, power, language, and ideology.

These different approaches that conform to Critical Psychology have been impor-tant in advancing the understanding of human actions as inseparable from social symbolical construction. However, in many cases, they have neglected the indi-vidual as intricately interacted with these constructions (González Rey, 2016b). In this way, individual processes, such as imagination, emotions, human motivation, and subjectivity have become often associated with metaphysics and romanticism without bearing in mind the possibility of exploring them through different theoret-ical paths. These individual processes began to be understood as epiphenomena of dominant discourses separating from individuals and social groups the capacity for agency and creativity (González Rey, 2018).

It is precisely in relation to this gap that González Rey's Theory of Subjectivity can be understood as a way to advance current challenges of Critical Psychology. From this perspective, subjectivity is a qualitatively differentiated production from human beings within the cultural, social, and historically situated conditions in which we live, which cannot be reduced to any of the processes implied in its genesis (González Rey & Mitjáns Martínez, 2017a).

Defined as a symbolic-emotional system, the concept of subjectivity implies the rejection of any universal principle as its theoretical basis. Importantly, in this perspective, the social is not conceived of as external, but as a complex constituent dimension of the subjective system. González Rey (2018) explains that subjectivity is not opposed to the concepts of discourse or power, but complementary to them, as it allows, along with the other concepts of Theory of Subjectivity, new paths of intelligibility regarding how these socially engendered processes affect individuals and social groups and may become a source of motivation within their life contexts. In other words, the Theory of Subjectivity allows the understanding of the generative capacity of individuals and social groups within shared symbolical realities.

Subjectivity represents a generative system, which, although has a socially, cultur-ally, and historically located genesis, is not an epiphenomenon of other dimensions. This condition allows the emergence of individuals and social groups as agents of subjects. As explained by González Rey and Mitjáns Martínez (2017a), the agent represents the individual or social group that is actively situated in the becoming of events in the current field of a specific experience. On the other hand, the concept of subject represents the individual or social group that opens an alternative path of subjectivation to a normative social space.

This explains why González Rey's Theory of Subjectivity should be understood as a way to advance Critical Psychology: it inaugurates a new theoretical avenue to explain the productions and actions of individuals and social groups as inseparable from broader social dynamics (González Rey, 2019b). This aspect allows advancing the research and practice on several topics that Critical Psychology has historically claimed as important and neglected by dominant psychology. Examples include individual change in the face of normative institutions, differentiated aspects that institutions develop within a broader social context, implicit conservative productions related to forms of institutionalization within progressive movements, deep social changes beyond formalities and explicit intentions, gender, race, social exclusion, and ideology.

1.4 The Context of the Book

This new edited volume, entitled *Theory of Subjectivity from a Cultural-Historical Standpoint: González Rey's legacy*, advances these series of publications and puts forward González Rey's academic contributions toward understanding human subjectivity in different contexts and fields, such as psychological research, cultural-historical psychology, critical psychology, education, psychotherapy, and human health. Different from the previously mentioned works, González Rey is not, of course, one of its editors, but the collection of chapters composes a tribute to his legacy. It brings together chapters by colleagues and former students, who used González Rey's body of work either as a platform for their research projects or as an important reference for a productive dialogue throughout the years.

Notably, all authors contributing to this volume have shared not only vibrant academic discussions with González Rey, but have also been deeply touched by his energy, generous enthusiasm, and friendship. Among us, who constructed this book based on this academic and life bond with him, Fernando is not only remembered by his fruitful and productive legacy, but also by his passionate thinking, which was permanently intermingled by loud laughter and affectionate slaps on our backs.

Fernando passed away on March 26, 2019, in the midst of dozens of life and academic projects, after fighting an aggressive cancer for seven years. It was striking to see how he could live with this difficult and inevitably deadly experience through his philosophy of life, keeping several plans, continually writing, teaching, and contributing to his life projects, as if he had 50 years ahead of him. A good example of his philosophy of life is an extract of a dialogue with him on January 31, 2019, when he said:

> Today, I have many projects, because paradoxically I have an intellectual lucidity like never before. But we must get out of our anthropocentrism of thinking that we are the center of the world. No, we are not. I believe I have lived a good, productive and happy life with a happy family, full of experiences of all kinds. I had a life that was so intense, that sometimes a person who lives 90 years does not have. I could write a book of my life like the one Neruda wrote: "Confieso que he vivido" (I confess I have lived). Then, when death comes, as it must, I would write I am privileged to have reached the age of 70 like this. (Goulart, 2019, p. 106)

It has not been easy to deal with this loss. We are writing to celebrate his presence and lively legacy among us.

1.5 Presenting the Book Content: Sections, Chapters, and Topics

The contributions of this edited volume are ordered in two broad sections: (1) Fernando González Rey: life and work, and (2) Dialogue and contribution for different contexts and fields. The first section emphasizes the genesis, development, and main concepts of González Rey's theoretical, epistemological, and methodological proposal, the second section addresses possible dialogues and contributions for different contexts and fields.

The first section starts with a historiographical chapter by Mitjáns Martínez. She explains: "González Rey's work: Genesis and development", his work is characterized by its breadth, depth, and creativity. González Rey's academic legacy comprises of twenty-nine books, ten edited or coedited books, ninety book chapters, and one hundred and thirty-two scientific articles published in five languages (Spanish, Portuguese, English, Russian, and French). Mitjáns Martínez characterizes González Rey's body of work in two closely linked moments. The first, the Personality Moment, starts shortly after his graduation as a psychologist in 1973 and lasts until the first half of the 1990s. The second, the Theory of Subjectivity and Qualitative Epistemology Moment, comprises his works from 1997 until his last publications in 2020. Mitjáns Martínez explains the importance of crucial contexts and experiences that were articulated in González Rey's thinking, such as the Cuban Revolution, his studies in the former USSR, his participation in the Latin American Critical Social Psychology movement, and his last years living in Brazil.

Secondly, a scientific article by González Rey (2017) is republished. It is entitled "The topic of subjectivity in psychology: Contradictions, paths and new alternatives" and draws a picture of how the topic of subjectivity has appeared in different psychological theories. In this paper, González Rey argues that subjectivity has been mainly used to refer to specific phenomena without advancing a general theory. In this paper, he highlights his proposal of a Theory of Subjectivity based on Cultural-historical traditions in psychology.

This scientific article is an expression that, in the development of Theory of Subjectivity, not only the legacy of Cultural-historical psychology was relevant, but also the critical dialogue with different theoretical approaches, such as Humanism (Allport, 1967, 1978), Gestalt (Dembo, 1993), Psychoanalysis (Guattari, 1996; Castoriadis, 1995; Elliott, 1992; Frosh, 2010; Parker, 2011), Social Representation Theory (Moscovici, 1967; Jodelet, 1989; Markova, 1996), and Social Constructionism (Gergen, 1985; Harré, 1995; Shotter, 1995). Also, González Rey's philosophical incursion was fundamental for his theoretical and epistemological advances. Authors like Marx (1976, 1992), Merleau-Ponty (1964), Foucault (1978, 1987), Cassirer (1953), and Dewey (1920) were particularly important in this process (González Rey, 2019).

In the chapter entitled "A cultural-historical theory of human subjectivity", Dreier presents González Rey's Theory of Subjectivity through his analytical gaze, addressing the background inspirations, its core concepts, the advantages, and key issues in Cultural-historical psychology it aims to resolve. Overcoming a descriptive approach, Dreier also presents his ideas on some steps toward the future development of this theory based on his main theoretical reference: A science of the subject founded by Holzkamp.

Goulart and Patiño-Torres conclude the first section of the book with their chapter entitled "Qualitative epistemology and constructive-interpretative methodology: contributions for research in social sciences and humanities". They discuss the contributions of González Rey's Qualitative Epistemology and Constructive-Interpretative Methodology for research in social sciences and humanities. They present the indissoluble articulation between Theory of Subjectivity, Qualitative Epistemology, and Constructive-Interpretative Methodology, and explain how this proposal contributes toward a qualitative approach that considers human creativity and emotionality crucial dimensions of scientific construction.

The second section of the book addresses different topics articulated to present specific contexts and fields for which González Rey's legacy contributes. Three chapters are dedicated to discuss González Rey's authorial and creative reading of Cultural-historical psychology, with emphasis on how he transcends and opens new paths in this tradition: (1) "A Theory of Subjectivity in the context of critical currents trends in the cultural-historical approach" by Rodríguez-Arocho, (2) "Understanding and developing Vygotsky's legacy through the work of González Rey" by Esteban-Guitart and Subero, and (3) "Advancing Vygotsky's legacy: interrupted argument with Fernando González Rey" by Veresov.

Rodríguez-Arocho's chapter examines, in the light of González Rey's biographical, institutional, and sociocultural contexts, Theory of Subjectivity as an example of development within the Cultural-historical approach. Along a similar line, Esteban-Guitart and Subero's chapter emphasizes González Rey's new interpretative framework, not only to better understand Vygotsky, but also to go beyond his works. On the other hand, Veresov presents agreements and disagreements with González Rey's considerations about the main stages of development of Cultural-historical theory.

Following, is the chapter "The impact and diffusion of Fernando González Rey's in Brazil", where Rossato, Mitjáns Martínez, and Martins present an analytical description of the impact and diffusion of González Rey's academic works in Brazil, as the country where he lived the last two decades of his life and where he is most known and influential. Then, Adams and Quinones, in their chapter "Social relations and friendships: Pathways to study motive, motivation and subjectivity" address González Rey's contribution to a new understanding of human motivation. They discuss how this view may provide a framework for the study of friendship, as families with children transition to live in a new country.

Learning and development are topics addressed as subjective processes based on González Rey's legacy by Madeira-Coelho and Tacca in their respective chapters: "Dialogue as a subjective process: impacts on learning and development in school contexts" and "Theory of Subjectivity and learning: possibilities and perspectives". Madeira-Coelho emphasizes dialogue as a subjective process as a way to shed light on the individual's active and complex role in his/her learning and developmental process. She explains how this perspective overcomes linguistic-discursive approaches on dialogue, which do not consider the role of individual subjective production in their teaching and learning experiences in the context of classroom. Tacca explores the subjective dimension of the learning process, which considers relations, events, and processes that are far beyond what happens in the classroom. She argues that the teaching-learning process should be structured by pedagogical strategies that consider cultural dimensions in a network of experiences that need to be understood in their constitutive complexity. Following this, Parker highlights links and contradictions between psychology and Marxism through a reading of current critical debates in the discipline in his chapter "Subjectivity, psychology, Marxism and Critical Realism: eleven thesis". He approaches the task of taking subjectivity seriously through Marx's Eleven Theses on Feuerbach.

Goulart presents his chapter "Human health and subjectivity: History, development and unfolding", discussing González Rey's contribution to the field of human health. He argues that González Rey's whole body of work represents a valuable proposal for advancing a representation of human health as a culturally and historically organized process affected by (1) the subjective production of individuals and social groups in a certain moment of life, (2) the action of individuals, social groups, and institutions, (3) current interactive situations, (4) bio-somatic processes, as well as (5) social and natural ecology in which one lives. These processes are permanently articulated constituting a configurational definition of human health.

The field of psychotherapy is discussed through the lens of Theory of Subjectivity both in Balbi's and Mori's chapters. Balbi, in his chapter "Subjectivity and psychotherapy: contributions of Fernando González Rey", presents the advancements of the study of subjectivity and its consequences in psychotherapy. He presents a dialogue between González Rey's perspective and other approaches, such as Social Constructionism, Psychoanalysis, Systemic Family Therapy, Dialectical Constructivist Model and Post-Rationalist Therapy. On the other hand, Mori, in her chapter "Reflections on the challenges of psychotherapy and the processes of social subjectivity", discusses the implications of psychotherapy from the perspective of the Theory of Subjectivity to professional practice and its implication to produce knowledge in psychology. In this discussion, Mori emphasizes the concept of social subjectivity as an important dimension in psychotherapy for understanding the organization of different configurations that take shape in institutions and social groups.

Fleer authors the last chapter of the book, which is entitled "Subjectivity and children's play: The conceptual legacy of Fernando González Rey in early childhood". She contributes to the now well-trodden pathway created by González Rey by discussing imagination, emotions, and play in relation to early childhood education. Fleer emphasizes González Rey's concepts of subjective senses and subjective configurations through studying how development in play can be conceptualized as a dynamic system within social relations rather than as a collection of psychological functions.

1.6 An Open Theory: Discussions and Future Pathways

This edited collection presents González Rey's Theory of Subjectivity and discusses its implication for different contexts and fields. In this introductory chapter, we argued this theoretical proposal represents an expression of current developments within Cultural-historical psychology, by advancing in relation to the classics from this perspective in the effort to understand human psychology in its complex, Cultural-historical, and singular constitution. In this sense, a new ontological definition for human subjectivity was proposed by emphasizing it as a symbolical-emotional system. Moreover, we argued that González Rey's Theory of Subjectivity contributes to the construction of a critical psychology that, on the one hand, crucially considers symbolical constructions within the historical, social, and cultural constitution of humanity. On the other hand, it provides a theoretical pathway to explain, and therefore favors, the fundamental role of individuals and the generative character of subjectivity for social change.

Notably, the collection of chapters that integrate this volume not only presents and discusses González Rey's academic contributions, but also highlights divergences, open discussions, and possible future pathways. This is in line with González Rey's theoretical construction process, which, as Mitjáns Martínez explains in her chapter, was permanently open to confrontation, and change to overcome itself. The open character of the Theory of Subjectivity is expressed by its historical development, expansion, and the permanent refining of its concepts, as well as by the permanent dialogue González Rey kept alive with other authors from various theoretical approaches.

These divergences, open discussions, and future pathways are brought to light in this book so that other researchers can develop them in the face of new theoretical challenges. An example of that is Veresov's arguments regarding what he considers as "the new reality with Vygotsky's legacy", which partially agree and partially disagree with González Rey's critical interpretations on the contradictory development of Soviet psychology. These different perspectives on the history and current moment of Cultural-historical psychology, along with other interpretations and even new historical archives that have been emerging in the last decades in relation to Vygotsky's legacy, represent an important open theoretical discussion.

Parker also problematizes the fraught relationship between Marxism and psychology through a reading of current critical debates in the disciplines. He claims the importance of not only providing an innovative basis for working inside psychology, but also, most significantly, for working against psychology. In his arguments, psychology is geared toward interpreting the world, whereas Marx highlights the importance of its change. His critique of dominant psychology coincides with González Rey's, especially when tackling its essentialism, methodological reification, universalism, and alienation. On the other hand, González Rey argues that critical approaches within psychology, such as Theory of Subjectivity, may also provide new theoretical models that sustain alternative practices to dominant psychology. (González Rey & Mitjáns Martínez, 2017a). In this sense, instead of denying psychology as a whole, González Rey (2018) proposes that, in order to solve the problems involved in its theories and practice, it may be more useful to address these problems through new theoretical constructions.

Also, Dreier, in his chapter, brings several challenging and insightful aspects "directed at those who are involved in carrying this work further". They are based on Dreier's theorizing of subjects in social practices within Holzkamp's tradition. One of them is a more precise definition of the relation between psychic functions and subjectivity in action. Dreier argues that a more careful specification of the psychic and/or subjective nature of experience is needed within the Theory of Subjectivity. This may avoid the risk of regarding psychic functions as fixed and general processes so that they could be better conceptually integrated with human subjectivity.

González Rey and Mitjáns Martínez (2017c) have previously addressed this challenge pointed out by Dreier and emphasized the differentiation between psychic development and subjective development. However, the interrelation between psychic and subjective processes represents indeed an open field for future research and further theorizations. This research line is closely linked to another one that is also in need of further development, the process of constitution of subjectivity in its ontogenesis. Research projects that interpret and understand further the initial development of subjectivity in early childhood have been already happening in an initial stage, and may be a fruitful way to address some of these open questions.

Another important aspect to be further theorized, according to Dreier's critical reading, is the conceptual status of nonsymbolic social realities within the Theory of Subjectivity. He explains: "González Rey's theory, and empirical projects based on it, primarily include society and social practices as social realities and empirical facts but not as concepts integrated with the theory of subjectivity". Historically, González Rey (1997, 2012, 2016b, 2018) has been vigorously opposed to the idea of external determinism of individuals and social groups. He also has consistently defended the ontological status of subjectivity, which implies not reducing it to any of the conditions implied in its genesis. Still, subjectivity is historically, culturally, and socially situated. How could we, therefore, conceptually explain these nonsymbolic social realities that are important for individual and social subjective production? This is another question to be further developed. This might be a fruitful theoretical avenue to advance and overcome the subject–object split, which was one of González Rey's historical objectives and which his concept of subjectivity itself allows advancing.

By exploring this collection of chapters, the readers are invited to find other questions and opened pathways related to the Theory of Subjectivity to reflect upon. The continuing dialogue with other theoretical perspectives, with its challenges, questions, and provocations, as well as the reflexive and critical work from within González Rey's Theory of Subjectivity, are essential to develop theoretically and keep thinking further. Maintaining this dialogue alive, along with diving into different emerging current critical—and noncritical—approaches is fundamental for pursuing González Rey's aim of constructing Theory of Subjectivity as an open and developing conceptual system.

Any theory or practice runs the risk of becoming a reified and preestablished set of contents and, therefore, a type of dogma. Nothing could be more against González

Rey's effort. Generating alternatives to this temptation implies taking responsibility to think and to construct along the emerging research projects, societal changes, and theoretical challenges. We hope this book can become a contribution to this always-ongoing purpose.

References

Abuljanova, K. A. (1980). *Deyatelnocti i Psikjologia Lichnosti* [Activity and theory of personality]. Moscow: Nauka.

Allport, G. (1967). *La Personalidad. Su configuracion y desarrollo* [Personality. Its configuration and development]. Habana, Cuba: Editora Revolucionaria.

Allport, G. (1978). Lo individual y lo general en el estudio de la personalidad [The individual and the general in the study of personality]. In C. S. Hall & G. Lindzey (Eds.), *Temas de la Personalidad* (pp. 163–176). Mexico DC: Limusa.

Burman, E. (2017). *Deconstructing developmental psychology* (3rd ed.). London and New York: Routlegde.

Cassirer, E. (1953). *Language and myth*. New York: Dove Publications.

Castoriadis, C. (1995). Logic, imagination, reflection. In A. Elliott & S. Frosh (Eds.), *Psychoanalysis in context* (pp. 15–35). United Kingdom: Routledge.

Chudnovsky, V. E. (1988). Problema subjektivnosti v svete sobremennyx zadach psykjologii vospi-taniya [The problem of subjectivity in the light of the current tasks of the education]. *Voprocy Psykjologii, 4*, 5–24.

Dembo, T. (1993). Thoughts on qualitative determinants in psychology. A methodological study. *Journal of Russian and East European Psychology, 31*(6), 15–70.

Dewey, J. (1920). *Reconstruction in philosophy*. New York: Henry Holt & Company.

Dreier, O. (2008). *Psychotherapy in everyday life*. New York, NY: Cambridge University Press.

Dreier, O. (2020). Critical psychology–Subjects in situated social practices. In M. Fleer, F. González Rey, & P. E. Jones (Eds.), *Cultural-historical and critical psychology–Common ground, divergences and future pathways*. Singapore: Springer Nature.

Elliott, A. (1992). *Social theory and psychoanalysis in transition*. United Kingdom: Blackwell.

Fleer, M., González Rey, F., & Veresov, N. (Eds.). (2017). *Perezhivanie, emotions and subjectivity: Advancing Vygotsly's legacy*. Singapore: Springer.

Fleer, M., González Rey, F., & Jones, P. (2020). Introduction: advancing dialogues between critical psychology and cultural-historical theory. In M. Fleer, F. González Rey F., & P. Jones (Eds). *Cultural-historical and critical psychology: Common ground, divergences and future pathways*. Singapore: Springer. https://doi.org/10.1007/978-981-15-2209-3_1.

Foucault, M. (1978). *The History of sexuality* (Vol. 1). New York: Pantheon Books.

Foucault, M. (1987). *A Arqueologia do Saber* [*The archaeology of knowledge*]. Rio de Janeiro: Forense Universitaria.

Frosh, S. (2010). *Psychoanalysis outside the clinic. Interventions in psychosocial studies*. United Kingdom: Pallgrave Macmillan.

Gergen, K. (1985). The social constructionist movement in modern psychology. *American Psychologist, 40*(3), 266–275.

Gergen, K. (1994). *Realities and relationship*. Cambridge: Cambridge University Press.

González Rey, F. (1987). Psicología, ideología y política: Un marco conceptual para su análisis en América Latina [Psychology, ideology and politics: A conceptual framework for its analysis in Latin America]. In M. Montero (Ed.), *Psicología Política Latinoamericana* [Latin American political psychology] (pp. 105–130). Caracas: Panapo.

González Rey, F. (1997). *Epistemología cualitativa y subjetividad* [Qualitative epistemology and subjectivity]. São Paulo: Educ.

González Rey, F. (2009). Historical relevance of Vygotsky's work: Its significance for a new approach to the problem of subjectivity in psychology. *Outlines, 1,* 59–73.

González Rey, F. (2011a). *El Pensamiento de Vigotsky: Contradicciones, Desdoblamientos y Desarrollo* [Vygotsky's thought: Contradictions, unfolding and development]. Mexico DF: Trillas.

González Rey, F. (2011b). A re-examination of defining moments in Vygotsky's work and their implications for his continuing legacy. *Mind, Culture and Activity, 18,* 257–275. https://doi.org/10.1080/10749030903338517.

González Rey, F. (2012). *O Social na Psicologia e a Psicologia Social: a emergência do sujeito* [Social in psychology and social psychology: The emergency of the subject]. Petrópolis: Vozes.

González Rey, F. (2014). Advancing further the history of Soviet psychology: Moving forward from dominant representations in Western and Russian psychology. *History of Psychology, 17*(1), 60–78.

González Rey, F. (2015). Marxism, subjectivity and cultural-historical psychology: moving forward on an unfinished legacy. *Annual Review of Critical Psychology, 12,* 27–35.

González Rey, F. (2016a). Vygotsky's concept of perezhivanie in the psychology of art and at the final moment of his work: Advancing his legacy. *Mind, Culture and Activity, 23,* 305–314.

González Rey, F. (2016b). Advancing on the topics of the social and subjectivity from a cultural-historical approach: Moments, paths and contradictions. *Journal of the Theoretical and Philosophical Psychology, 36,* 175–189. https://doi.org/10.1017/CCOL0521831040.

González Rey, F. (2017). The topic of subjectivity in psychology: Contradictions, paths and new alternatives. *Journal for the Theory of Social Behaviour, 47,* 502–520. https://doi.org/10.1111/jtsb.12144.

González Rey, F. (2018). Subjectivity and discourse: Complementary topics for a critical psychology. *Culture & Psychology, 25*(2), 178–194. https://doi.org/10.1177/1354067X18754338.

González Rey F. (2019a). Subjectivity as a new theoretical, epistemological, and methodological pathway within cultural-historical psychology. In: F. González Rey, A. Mitjáns Martínez, Goulart, D M. (Eds.), *Subjectivity within cultural-historical approach: Theory, methodology and research* (pp. 21–36). Singapore: Springer. https://doi.org/10.1007/978-981-13-3155-8_2.

González Rey, F. (2019b). Methodological and epistemological demands in advancing the study of subjectivity from a cultural-historical standpoint. *Culture & Psychology, 0,* 1–16. https://doi.org/10.1177/1354067X19888185.

González Rey, F. (2020). The two pathways of Vygotsky s legacy: The critical and noncritical coexisting positions in Vygotsky's thought. In: M. Fleer, F. González Rey, & P. Jones. *Cultural-historical and critical psychology: Common ground, divergences and future pathways* (pp. 175–191). Singapore: Springer.

González Rey, F., & Mitjáns Martínez, A. (2017a). *Subjetividade: epistemologia, teoria e método* [*Subjectivity: epistemology, theory and method*]. Campinas: Alínea.

González Rey, F., & Mitjáns Martínez, A. (2017b). Epistemological and methodological issues related to the new challenges of a cultural–historical-based psychology (pp 264–296). In M. Fleer, F. González Rey, N. Veresov (Orgs.), *Perezhivanie, emotions and subjectivity: Advancing Vygotsky's legacy* (pp. 264–296). Singapore: Springer.

González Rey, F., & Mitjáns Martínez, A. (2017c). El desarrollo de la subjetivide: una alternativa frente a las teorias del desarrollo psíquico [The development of subjectivity: na alternative to the theories of psychic development]. *Papeles de Trabajo sobre Cultura, Educación y Desarrollo Humano, 12*(2), 3–20.

González Rey, F. & Mitjáns Martínez, A. (2019). The constructive-interpretative methodological approach: orienting research and practice on the basis of subjectivity. In F. González Rey, A. Mitjáns Martinez, & D. M. Goulart. *Theory of subjectivity: New perspectives within social and educational research* (pp. 37–60). Singapore: Springer. https://doi.org/10.1007/978-981-13-3155-8_3.

González Rey, F., Mitjans Martinez, A., Rossato, M., & Goulart, D. M. (2017). The relevance of subjective configurations for discussing human development (pp. 217–243). In M. Fleer,

F. González Rey, & N. Veresov (Eds.), *Perezhivanie, emotions and subjectivity: Advancing Vygotsky's legacy*. Singapore: Springer.

González Rey, F., Mitjáns Martínez, A., & Goulart, D. M. (2019a). The topic of subjectivity within cultural-historical approach: Where it has advanced from and where it is advancing to. In F. González Rey, A. Mitjáns Martínez, & D. Goulart (Eds.), *Subjectivity within cultural-historical perspective: Theory, methodology and research* (pp. 3–19). Singapore: Springer. https://doi.org/10.1007/978-981-13-3155-8_1.

González Rey, F., Mitjáns Martínez, A., & Goulart, D. M. (Eds.). (2019b). *Subjectivity within cultural-historical perspective: Theory, methodology and research*. Singapore: Springer. https://doi.org/10.1007/978-981-13-3155-8.

González Rey, F., & Patiño-Torres, J. F. (2017). La epistemología cualitativa y el estudio de la subjetividad en una perspectiva cultural-histórica: Conversación con Fernando González Rey [Qualitative epistemology and the study of subjectivity in a cultural-historical perspective: Conversation with Fernando González Rey]. *Revista de Estudios Sociales, 60*, 120–127.

Goulart, D. M. (2019). Subjectivity and life: In memory of Fernando González Rey. *Mind, Culture, and Activity* (Online) http://doi.org/ https://doi.org/10.1080/10749039.2019.1619775.

Goulart, D., Mitjáns Martínez, A., & Esteban-Guitart, M. (2020). The trajectory and work of Fernando González Rey: Paths to his theory of subjectivity. *Studies in Psychology, 41*(1), 9–30.

Guattari, F. (1996). *Micropolítica: cartografias do desejo* [Micropolitics: cartographies of desire]. Petrópolis: Vozes.

Harré, R. (1995). Discursive psychology. In J. A. Smith, R. Harre, & L. Van Langenhove (Eds.), *Rethinking psychology* (pp. 143–160). London: Sage Publication.

Holzkamp, K. (1991). Societal and individual life processes. In C. Tolman & W. Maiers (Eds.), *Critical psychology: Contributions to an historical science of the subject* (pp. 50–64). New York: Cambridge University Press.

Jodelet, D. (1989). *Madness and social representation*. Hemel Hempstead, UK: Harvester Wheatsheaf.

Lomov, B. F. (1984). *Teoretishie e metodologuiskeskie problemy psykjologii* [Theoretical and methodological problems of psychiology]. Moscow: Nauka.

Markova, I. (1996). Toward an epistemology of social representations. *Journal for the Theory of Social Behavior, 26*, 177–196.

Martín Baró, I. (1987). Del opio a la fe liberadora [From opium to liberating Faith]. In M. Montero (Ed.), *Psicología Política Latianoamericana* [Latin American political psychology] (pp. 229–268). Caracas: Editorial Panapo.

Marx, K. (1976). Theses on Feuerbach. In F. Engels & K. Marx (Eds.), *Ludwig Feuerbach and the end of classical German Philosophy* (pp. 61–65). Peking: Foreign Language Press.

Marx, K. (1992). *Early writings*. London: Penguin.

Merleau Ponty, M. (1964). *Signs*. Chicago: Northwestern University Press.

Mitjáns Martínez, A., & González Rey, F. (2017). *Psicologia, educação e aprendizagem escolar: avançando na contribuição da leitura cutural-histórica* [Psychology, education and school learning: Advancing the contribution of cultural-historical reading]. São Paulo: Cortez.

Montero, M. (Ed.) (1994). *Construcción y crítica de la psicología social* [Construction and critique of social psychology]. Anthropos: Barcelona.

Moscovici, S. (1967). Communication processes and the properties of language. In L. Berkowitz (Ed.), *Advances in experimental social psychology* (Vol. 3) (pp. 225–270). New York: Academic Press.

Parker, I. (2011). *Lacanian psychoanalysis. Revolutions in subjectivity*. United Kingdom: Routledge.

Parker, I. (2015). *Critical discursive psychology*. London: Palgrave Macmillan.

Shotter, J. (1995). Dialogical psychology. In J. A. Smith, R. Harre, & L. Van Langenhove (Eds.), *Rethinking psychology*. United Kingdom: SAGE Publications.

Teo, T. (2017). From psychological science to psychological humanities: Building a general theory of subjectivity. *Review of General Psychology, 21*(4), 281–291.

Yasnitsky, A. (2012). Revisionist revolution in Vygotskian science: Toward cultural historical Gestalt psychology. *Journal of Russian & East European Psychology, 50,* 3–15. https://doi.org/10.2753/rpo1061-0405500400.

Zavershneva, E. (2010). Vygotsky's familiar archive: New findings. Notebooks, notes and scientific journals of L. S. Vygotky (1912–1934). *Journal of Russian and East European Psychology, 48*(1), 34–65.

Daniel Magalhães Goulart is an Assistant Professor at the Department of Theory and Foundations of the Faculty of Education of the University of Brasilia. He is also a Collaborating Professor at the Master's in Psychology of the University Center of Brasilia. He graduated as a psychologist from the University of São Paulo and completed his Ph.D. at the Faculty of Education of the University of Brasilia, Brazil. He is the current coordinator of the Reading and Research Group "Subjectivity: Theory, Epistemology and Methodology". His latest books are: (1) Subjectivity within a cultural-historical approach: theory, methodology and research (Ed., Springer, 2019), (2) Subjectivity and critical mental health: lessons from Brazil (Routledge, 2019), and (3) Saúde mental, desenvolvimento e subjetividade: da patologização à ética do sujeito [Mental health, development and subjectivity: from pathologization to the ethics of the subject] (Cortez, 2019).

Albertina Mitjáns Martínez is a Research Professor of the Faculty of Education at the University of Brasilia, Brazil. She obtained her Ph.D. qualification in psychological sciences at the University of Havana, Cuba, and concluded post-doctoral studies at the Faculty of Psychology of the Autonomous University of Madrid. Her research interests focus on education and psychology from a cultural–historical approach in three specific fields: (1) creativity and innovation in education; (2) subjectivity in human development and learning; (3) disabilities and school inclusion. Her latest books are: (1) Subjectivity within cultural-historical approach: theory, methodology and research (Ed., 2019, Springer); (2) Subjetividade: teoria, epistemologia e método [Subjectivity: theory, epistemology and method] (Alínea, 2019); (3) Psicologia, educação e aprendizagem escolar [Psychology, education and school learning] (Cortez, 2019).

Megan Adams is a Senior Lecturer of Inclusion at Monash University, Melbourne, Australia. She obtained her Ph.D. qualifications in Education at Monash University. Her main research interests are focused on education from a cultural-historical approach using subjectivity to investigate (1) families with young children moving countries (2) identity, curriculum, and pedagogy (3) preservice teacher's perceptions about working with students displaying challenging behaviours in classrooms.

Part I
Fernando González Rey: Life and Work

Chapter 2
González Rey's Work: Genesis and Development

Albertina Mitjáns Martínez

Abstract Fernando González Rey (1949–2019) had an extensive and creative scientific production, expressed in twenty-nine books, ten edited or coedited books, ninety book chapters, and one hundred and thirty-two scientific articles. This chapter presents the genesis and development of the Theory of Subjectivity—his main scientific contribution associated with the contexts and circumstances that favored its emergence. A detailed study of González Rey's work allows for it to be characterized in two closely linked moments. The first moment, called Personality Moment, ranges from his first works—shortly after his graduation as a psychologist in 1973— until his work in the first half of the 1990s. His conception of personality was his main scientific contribution at this stage. The second moment, the Theory of Subjectivity and Qualitative Epistemology Moment, comprises his works from 1997 until his last publications in 2020. This moment is characterized by the transition from the concept of personality to that of subjectivity, represented as a new ontology of human processes—both social and individual—under the conditions of culture. The analysis of his production in this second moment shows the complex, critical, subversive, and open character of his theory, its epistemological and methodological implications, as well as its value for research and professional practice in different fields.

2.1 Introduction

González Rey's work, the fabric of its history and configuration, is an example of the way in which the historical and sociocultural context, as well as the author's personal characteristics, are expressed in scientific production. Contexts, circumstances, and personal characteristics that, in his case, favored a scientific production that encompasses twenty-nine books, ten edited or coedited books, ninety book chapters, and one hundred and thirty-two scientific articles, published in 5 languages

A. M. Martínez (✉)
Faculty of Education, University of Brasilia, Brasilia, Brazil
e-mail: amitjans49@gmail.com

(Spanish, Portuguese, English, Russian, and French). A work that is characterized by its breadth, depth, and creativity.

González Rey was born in Havana, Cuba, in 1949. He intensely experienced the revolutionary process initiated by the Cuban Revolution in 1959 and its subsequent institutionalization and rigidification. His identity as a Cuban, and his active immersion in a process of profound economic and social change had a significant place in the configuration of his work.

This was a decisive context for the development of his scientific, professional, political, and social interests, as well as for his nondogmatic appropriation of Marxism.

His childhood as an only child of a lower middle-class family and remarkable experiences during his adolescence contributed to the development of personal characteristics without which his work would not have been possible: a profound interest in the complexity of human psychological functioning, the capacity for reflection and conceptualization, critical spirit, independence, audacity, disciplined work ethic, and persistence. These characteristics were already expressed at the time of his university studies in Psychology and were consolidated in the subsequent years with his immersion in different spaces of action and interrelations. Of great importance to such development was his participation in the Union of Young Communists, in the Student University Federation and the Communist Party of Cuba, as well as his academic-scientific activity as a professor at the University of Havana, an institution in which he was head of Department, Director of the Psychology College, and Vice Rector. His personal characteristics were consistently and singularly expressed in other contexts that were especially significant for the constitution of his work: his doctoral studies in the former Soviet Union, his participation in the Latin American Critical Social Psychology Movement, and his academic-scientific activity in Brazil.

González Rey's main scientific contribution is, without a doubt, the Theory of Subjectivity from a cultural-historical perspective and, related to it, an epistemological conception necessary for the production of knowledge regarding subjectivity: Qualitative Epistemology and its unfolding in the Constructive-Interpretative Methodology. This chapter's objective is to present the genesis and development of González Rey's main scientific contribution based on the two moments that a historical analysis of his work allow it to be characterized in: The Personality Moment and the Theory of Subjectivity and Qualitative Epistemology Moment.

2.2   The Personality Moment

The Personality Moment comprises González Rey's production from his first works on personality—shortly after graduating as a psychologist in 1973—to the works he published on the subject in the first half of the 1990s. González Rey's reflections on personality began as a Psychology student at the University of Havana, in which he became an avid, critical, and reflective reader. He studied psychoanalysis and humanistic psychology in depth and reflected acutely upon the complexity of human psychological functioning, which led to questioning the fragmented, reductionist, and universalizing way in which it was conceived. Gordon Allport's (1967, 1978) critical work on hegemonic psychology and particularly the work of L. I. Bozhovich (1965, 1972, 1981) on motivation and personality had a particular influence on his reflections and research at that time.

His first studies expressed the articulation of phenomena traditionally treated separately: morality and professional choice. They were the basis of his thesis for obtaining his doctoral degree in Psychological Sciences in 1979, entitled Роль нравственных идеалов в профессиональных намерениях школьных подростков [The Role of Moral ideals in the formation of professional intentions in school adolescents], at the Moscow Institute of General and Pedagogical Psychology. In this thesis, his integrative perspective in understanding human action was already evident. He chose to carry out his doctoral studies at this Institute in order to work in the Laboratory dedicated to the study of personality formation created and led by L. I Bozhovich—whose work had been significant for him as a student and for whom he always felt a profound admiration.

His period of studies in the former Soviet Union was a decisive context for the consolidation of his scientific training, especially because it allowed him to advance and consolidate his conception of personality and conduct a reflective, critical, and creative study on the work of the cultural-historic perspective's main representatives, which had important consequences in his subsequent scientific production. It was a stage in which he consolidated his work and study discipline, to which he devoted daily, a great number of hours. It also consolidated his persistence, expressed in the mastery of the Russian language in a short period of time and in the process of meeting his study and production goals that, with time urging, he had set for himself. These qualities were thereafter expressed in the self-taught study of the English language, one of the elements that underpinned the breadth and scope of his scientific production.

His audacity, critical spirit, and creativity, combined with a deep cultural insertion in psychological science, philosophy, and social sciences in general, allowed him to perceive critical aspects of Soviet Psychology upon which he could advance, both theoretically and methodologically. These advances were expressed in a new conception of personality, considering it as a complex configured system constituted culturally and historically, which does not linearly determine behavior, but constitutes one of the elements that take part in it. We can mention as representative works of the Personality Moment the following:

- Motivación Moral en Adolescentes y Jóvenes. Habana: Editorial Científico-Técnica, 1982. [Moral Motivation in Adolescents and Youth].
- Motivación Profesional en Adolescentes y Jóvenes. Habana: Editorial de Ciencias Sociales, 1983. [Professional Motivation in Adolescents and Youth].
- Psicología de la personalidad. Habana: Ciencias Sociales, 1984. [Personality Psychology].
- Psicología: principios y categorías. Habana: Editorial de Ciencias Sociales, 1986. [Psychology: principles and categories].
- La personalidad: su educación y desarrollo. Habana: Editorial Pueblo y Educación, 1989. [Personality: education and development].

- Personalidad, Salud e Modo de vida. Universidad Autónoma de México 1993. [Personality, health and way of life].
- Comunicación, Personalidad y Desarrollo Habana Editorial Pueblo y Educación 1995. [Communication, Personality and Development].

In this last work, González Rey presents his most advanced conception of personality, expressed in the concept of psychological configurations of personality. Still, in the book Personalidad, Salud y Modo de Vida [Personality, Health and Way of Life], the author stated:

Personality is the systemic, living and relatively stable organization of the different psychological formations, their systems and functional integration of their contents that actively participate in the regulatory and self-regulatory functions of behavior, being the subject who exercises such functions. (González Rey, 1993 p. 63)

In Personalidad, Comunicación y Desarrollo [Personality, Communication and Development], he argues:

At the present moment, in the configurational approach, we emphasize even more the dynamic character of personality, understanding configuration as the integration of multiple dynamic elements around a specific psychological sense, so that one configuration can be included within another, not as different elements that integrate, but as a new qualitative level of psychic organization. (González Rey, 1995 p. 59)

The leap from the concept of systemic organization to the concept of configuration, emphasizing its dynamic character, constitutes a significant advance with important consequences for his subsequent Theory of Subjectivity. This work also expresses more clearly an idea that, preserving its essence, will be developed and occupy a central place in the Theory of Subjectivity: the idea that the diversity of the social world is expressed in a unique way in personality.

In this sense, he says:

Understanding the meaning of the social environment in the configuration of personality, implies breaking with the representation of the social as external and objective and the subjective as internal, since the former is contained in subjectivity, the only reality in which its personalized historical syntheses is expressed and the latter defines the aspects and relations of the social in its psychological sense for man (González Rey, 1995, p. 77)

His complex and dynamic conception of personality, linked to his understanding of the role of communication—very well developed in the work previously highlighted—allowed him to defend, in 1987, at the Institute of Psychology of the Academy of Sciences of the former Soviet Union, the degree of Doctor in Sciences,[1] title that constitutes, up until today, the maximum scientific degree granted in the scope of Russian science, with González Rey being the only Latin American psychologist to have obtained it (Goulart et al., 2020).

Also in this first moment of his work are his first productions regarding the epistemological and methodological problems of Psychology. It is interesting to mention

---

[1] There is a difference in relation to the Doctorate, being that the Doctorate in Sciences corresponds to a much higher level than the common Doctorate, and implies the defense of a thesis that expresses the body of an entire work in a specific line of scientific research.

that, being a Psychology student, González Rey already questioned the dominant forms of psychological diagnosis. He wondered how the uniqueness and complexity of the psychological world of young people admitted to the Center for the Rehabilitation of Minors, with whom he worked with as an intern, could be "apprehended" by the psychological tests used. These critical reflections were expanded in his work as a researcher as he confronted the dominant ways of undertaking research in Psychology and, especially, as he faced the challenges that research on personality, understood as configuration, presented him with. Significant productions on this theme are:

- Algunas cuestiones metodológicas sobre el estudio de la personalidad. Habana: Editorial Pueblo y Educación, 1982. [Some methodological inquiries regarding the study of personality].
- Relación entre la metodología, la teoría y la investigación empírica en el estudio de la personalidad. Journal de Psicología, v. 10, n.6, 1989. [Relations between methodology, theory and empirical research in the study of personality].
- Problemas Epistemológicos de la Psicología. México: Colegio de Ciencias y Humanidades. UNAM, 1993. [Epistemological issues in Psychology].

In the above, the critique of the concept of dominant science and the objectivity of scientific knowledge is clearly presented. Also, a new way of seeing the interrelations between the theoretical and the methodological in research and the consideration of professional practice as a space for the production of scientific knowledge are presented. These last two ideas will later be further developed and consolidated in his characterization of Qualitative Epistemology and of the Constructive-Interpretative Methodology.

For his contributions in the field of personality and for his production on epistemology and methodology, González Rey quickly gained visibility in Latin America, being invited to teach courses and give lectures at different academic institutions and scientific events. In 1991, he received the Inter-American Psychology Award for his contribution to the development of Psychology in the Americas.

2.3 The Theory of Subjectivity and Qualitative Epistemology Moment

We call the second moment in González Rey's work the Theory of Subjectivity and Qualitative Epistemology Moment, as this is the period in which his two most significant scientific works take place. This moment represents, simultaneously, a continuity and a break with the previous moment and comprises the period that starts in 1997, until his last publications in 2020, one year after his death. This second moment is characterized by the transition from the conception of personality to the development of a Theory of Subjectivity (González Rey, 1997, 2003, 2004, 2005a, 2007, 2014a, 2016a, 2017a, 2017b, 2019a, 2019b, 2019c; González Rey & Mitjáns Martínez, 2017a).

Subjectivity, the central concept of his theory, implies a new ontology[2] of human processes—both social and individual—under cultural conditions, considering emotions as intrinsic to subjective functioning. Also during this period, his methodological and epistemological reflections—already present in the previous moment—are consolidated and expanded, which is expressed in the elaboration of Qualitative Epistemology and its unfolding in the Constructive-Interpretative Methodology (González Rey, 1997, 2002, 2005b, 2009a, 2013, 2014b, 2019d, 2019e; González Rey & Mitjáns Martinez, 2016, 2017a, 2017b, 2019). His conception of personality was the fundamental antecedent for the elaboration of the Theory of Subjectivity. In a previous publication, he stated:

> (…) the concept of subjective personality configuration represented the theoretical and epistemological link between personality theory and the emergence of the theme of subjectivity, going beyond the idea that it is only situated in the individual, and arriving at a definition of subjectivity as the quality of a type of process, either social or individual, specific to human development under cultural conditions. (González Rey & Mitjáns Martínez, 2017a, p. 27)

In the transition from the consolidated conception of personality to the Theory of Subjectivity, two contexts were profoundly significant. The first was his stay in the former Soviet Union, whose importance in elaborating and consolidating his conception of personality was already highlighted in the previous topic.

However, also during this stay, his philosophical and political interests, constituted in his participation from a very young age in the Cuban revolutionary process, were expanded and consolidated, contributing to his critical reflections on how Marxism was expressed in cultural-historical psychology (González Rey, 2011a, 2015a). The in-depth study of the main exponents of this psychology allowed him to question the reductionist and mechanistic way in which, in Soviet Psychology, the participation of the social and of culture was understood in the constitution of the human being, with the social being primarily conceived as external, concrete, and immediate, as well as essentially as a mediator of psychic processes through sign systems, of which language is the main one (González Rey, 2011a, 2011b, 2014b, 2016a; González Rey & Mitjáns Martínez, 2017a). Also, his stay in the former Soviet Union made it possible for him to engage with the work of B.F. Lomov, director of the Institute of Psychology of the Academy of Sciences of the Soviet Union at the time, who stood out for considering communication "(…) not just as another category of psychology, but as a new principle by means of which themes that until that moment had not yet found expression in Soviet Psychology began to develop" (González Rey, 2016b, p. 245). Lomov also played an important role in the development of social psychology, advancing the understanding of social psychic processes beyond individuals and recognizing a dialectical relationship between the social and the individual (González Rey, 2016b). All the elements aforementioned contributed to González Rey conceiving the place the social holds in human functioning from a different perspective.

---

[2] We understand ontology not in terms of a reality of being independent of human knowledge, but as those different phenomena that find a specific theoretical expression in science, allowing for new practices that other knowledge did not enable (González Rey, 2013, p. 27).

The other important context for the transition from personality to subjectivity was his active participation in the Latin American Critical Social Psychology movement in the 1980s. His social and political interests, his proximity to social psychology during his stay in the former Soviet Union, in addition to the stance taken by representatives of said movement, aimed at the development of another type of social psychology that would contribute to the social problems of Latin America, to which he was particularly sympathetic to, led him to join this group.

Referring to his participation in this movement, González Rey expresses:

> These years represented a great intellectual vitality in the management of a psychology erected by our own continent, when we had the opportunity to share congresses, symposia and joint papers that ended up contributing to a large extent to the group's visibility in the continent. In my particular case, these discussions strongly led me to the field of social psychology, which was one of the important influences in my transition from a personality psychology to the study of subjectivity. Such transition led me to consider personality and social subjectivity as recursive systems that are integrated in the same ontological definition supported by the emergence of symbolic emotional processes that qualitatively define a new quality of human processes: their subjective character. (González Rey, 2018a, pp. 82–83)

This participation was decisive for his reflections on the way in which the social appears constituted in individuals and groups, not functioning as something external to them. And also, his reflections on the way in which individuals and groups are constituents of the social, and not only constituted by it, acquired special relevance.

While his works on personality essentially pointed to the individual dimension of human functioning, the concept of subjectivity, central to the Theory of Subjectivity, expresses an original articulation between the individual and the social, enabling the understanding of the mutual constitution of both dimensions. Subjectivity represents a system in which social subjectivity—a concept that he had already formulated in 1991[3]—and the individual are reciprocally configured, thus overcoming the reductionist tendency to think of subjectivity only as an individual phenomenon, which has characterized both science and the common sense (González Rey, 1997, 2003, 2004, 2016a, 2019a, 2019c; Mitjáns Martínez & González Rey, 2019). Based on the notion that theories are "systems of concepts, representations and paths that, articulated among themselves, represent channels of intelligibility on the central issue that constitutes their focus" (González Rey, 2014b, p. 16), we can say that before us lies, not just a conception of subjectivity, but a theory. It is integrated by a set of articulated concepts, namely, subjectivity—individual and social, subjective senses, subjective configurations, and subject and is focused on generating intelligibility regarding the complexity of human processes in cultural conditions, with a specific ontological definition.[4]

Pinpointing his definition, González Rey states:

---

[3]This concept was first presented at the Magistral Conference given at the time of receiving the Inter-American Psychology Award, at the Inter-American Psychology Congress in San José, Costa Rica, in 1991.

[4]In Chap. 3, González Rey profoundly discusses essential concepts and ideas of the Theory of Subjectivity.

Subjectivity as an ontological domain specifies a new kind of process, that is, qualitatively different from all the processes involved in its genesis. As such, subjectivity is ontologically defined by the integration of emotions and symbolical processes, forming new qualitative units: subjective senses. Such subjective senses are "snapshots" of symbolic emotional flashes that unfold in a chaotic movement, from which subjective configurations emerges as a self-regulative and self-generative organization of subjective senses. (González Rey, 2019a, p. 28)

The author thus presents a new ontological definition, different from the "five main ontological definitions of what psyche is: behavioral, cognitivist, semiotic operational, linguistic, and discursive, with emotions being understood as epiphenomena within each of these representations" (González Rey, 2019d, p. 562). The essence of this new ontology lies in considering emotion as intrinsic to subjectivity, expressed by its essential unit: the subjective senses. In this new ontology, the subjective senses, as symbolic-emotional units, represent a new qualitative level for the accounting of the emotional in the human psyche.

The central concepts of the Theory of Subjectivity and the principles of Qualitative Epistemology, together with their background and foundation, are systematized in the book Epistemologia Cualitativa y Subjetividad [Qualitative Epistemology and Subjectivity], published simultaneously in Cuba and Brazil in 1997. Also, in this work, by means of the analysis of different lines of research, the heuristic value of the Theory of Subjectivity, as a general theory of human functioning, for understanding the action of individuals and groups in the fields of health, education, and development, is made evident. For this reason, this book inaugurates the second moment of González Rey's work, who will develop, elaborate, and consolidate his ideas throughout his subsequent scientific production.

While his stay in the former Soviet Union and his participation in the Critical Latin American Social Psychology Movement were decisive for the transition from personality to subjectivity, for his continuous development and consolidation of Theory of Subjectivity and Qualitative Epistemology, his academic-scientific work in Brazil as of the late 1990s was decisive. After working as a visiting professor from 1995 to 1999 at the Institute of Psychology of the University of Brasilia, González Rey was forced to stay in Brazil, when, for political reasons, he was not allowed to return to Cuba to reinstate his work as a professor at the University of Havana, as he had wished. Thus, as of the year 2000, González Rey worked as a professor and researcher at different Brazilian universities where he led productive workgroups, consolidated lines of research—which he was already developing during his work in Cuba—and created new ones. The results of this work were very important for the advancement of the Theory of Subjectivity, which was being developed in conjunction with the different lines of research he coordinated.

Significant works from this second moment are:

- Epistemología Cualitativa y Subjetividad. São Paulo: EDUC, 1997. [Qualitative Epistemology and Subjectivity].
- Sujeito e subjetividade: uma aproximação histórico-cultural. São Paulo: Thomson, 2003. [Subject and Subjectivity].

- O social na psicologia e a psicologia social: a emergência do sujeito. Petrópolis: Vozes, 2004. [The social in Psychology and Social Psychology: the subject's emergence].
- Pesquisa qualitativa e subjetividade: os processos de construção da informação. São Paulo: Thomson, 2005. [Qualitative research and subjectivity: the process of constructing information].
- Psicoterapia, subjetividade e pós-modernidade: uma aproximação histórico-cultural. São Paulo: Thomson, 2007. [Psychotherapy, subjectivity and post-modernity: a cultural-historical approach].
- Subjetividade e saúde: superando a clínica da patologia. São Paulo: Cortez, 2011. [Subjectivity and health: overcoming the pathology practice].
- El pensamiento de Vigotsky: contradicciones, desdoblamientos y desarrollo. México: Trillas, 2011. [Vygotsky's work: contradictions, unfoldings and development].
- Subjetividade: teoria, epistemologia e método. Campinas: Alínea, 2017. [Subjectivity: theory, epistemology and method].
- Subjectivity within cultural-historical perspective: Theory, methodology and research: Springer, 2019.

As a comprehensive theory of human functioning under cultural conditions, the Theory of Subjectivity presents a set of important characteristics to be highlighted: its complex, critical, subversive character, its unfolding of change processes—both individual and social, its open character and, especially, its epistemological character—this last characteristic having been essential for the genesis of Qualitative Epistemology.

The complex character of the Theory of Subjectivity (Mitjáns Martínez, 2005) is substantiated by the Epistemology of Complexity (Morin, 1995, 1998, 2002, 2015), insofar it subverts the four pillars of simplifying thinking: (1) the principle of order, by recognizing the singular and deeply contradictory character of human subjectivity; (2) the separability principle, by presenting subjectivity as a configured system; (3) the principle of reduction, due to the ontological condition of subjectivity, whose specificity resides in the unity of the symbolic and the emotional, irreducible to other segments of the reality; and (4) the principle of inductive-deductive-identity logic, by demanding a configurational logic in studying it and for its "construction", in correspondence with the configurational character of its constitution.

Although the Theory of Subjectivity was not explicitly defined by the author as a critical psychology, we could undoubtedly consider it as part of the wide range of so-called Critical Psychologies. Its critical character is emphasized in the way in which its postulates regarding the understanding of human phenomena are opposed to hegemonic conceptions—marked by neutrality, universalization, and a-historicity and, especially, by its contribution to the understanding of the subjective dimension of many social phenomena that have not been historically considered in their complexity by the hegemonic conceptions of psychology, such as social inequality, power relations, ideology, and politics, among others. In the case of the Theory of

Subjectivity, its critical character includes a propositional dimension, as it constitutes a new way of understanding human processes that provides a basis for new professional and social practices.

With regard to the subversive character of the Theory of Subjectivity, we can state that subjectivity is "a subversive concept, because its definition allows for the theoretical explanation of how resistance and confrontation with the hegemonic social order emerged historically, opening a theoretical path to explain this resistance" (González Rey & Mitjáns Martínez, 2020 p. 50). On the other hand, the production of subjective senses and their organization in generative subjective configurations, escape the conscious control of individuals and groups, such that no external influence has a direct impact on their processes or actions. This impact always derives from the singular subjective productions of individuals or groups in face of external influences. This explains that no form of absolute external control based on power relations is truly possible (González Rey, 2002, 2004, 2007, 2015b; González Rey & Mitjáns Martínez, 2017a).

Associated with its subversive character, the Theory of Subjectivity is also characterized by its repercussions for understanding significant change processes, both individual and social. The concept of the subject as "(…) one who opens a path of subjectivity, which transcends the normative social space within which his/her experiences take place, exercising creative options in the course of his/her experience, which may or may not be expressed in action" (González Rey & Mitjáns Martínez, 2017, p. 73) is particularly important for understanding the possibility of individuals and groups to subvert the dominant order in the contexts in which their action is organized—an essential element for significant institutional and social changes.

A very significant feature of the Theory of Subjectivity is its open character. The historical analysis of the works that correspond to this second moment shows how the author develops ideas and refines definitions and concepts, which shows a theory in constant process of development and expansion. González Rey has always defended theories as systems in motion. In that sense, he stated:

> Theories are living systems that have in the empirical a constant source of confrontation, which compels the researcher to generate new concepts and to give singular definitions to categories that already exist in the theory, which represents an intrinsic process theory development. When a theory loses its capacity to signify new situations, it loses its heuristic value and turns into dogma. (…) The relevance of the theory lies in its movement, in its generative capacity in face of the challenges to which the empirical moment and the researcher's new ideas constantly expose them to. (González Rey, 2013, p. 25)

An example, among many others, of the Theory of Subjectivity being in a constant process of development, is the conceptualization of subjectivity that appears in the inaugural work of 1997, in which it was defined as:

> The constitution of the psyche in the individual subject, which also integrates the processes and characteristic states of that subject in each moments of his social action, which are inseparable from the subjective senses that such moments will have for him. Simultaneously, subjectivity is expressed at the social level as a constituent of social life, a moment we have called social subjectivity. (González Rey, 1997, p. 83)

In this definition, three aspects that characterize the Theory of Subjectivity already appear clearly: the regard of subjective senses as a unit of subjectivity, the dual and simultaneous condition of subjectivity—individual subjectivity and social subjectivity—and the way in which the social integrates subjectivity.

However, in a subsequent work, he emphasizes subjectivity as "a symbolic-emotional system oriented toward the creation of a particularly human reality – culture - of which subjectivity itself is a condition for its development and within which it has its own, socially institutionalized and historically situated, genesis" (González Rey & Mitjáns Martínez, 2017, p. 27). While maintaining the central idea of the unity between the symbolic and the emotional as a defining feature of subjectivity, the author provides vast visibility to one of subjectivity's characteristic aspects: its generative character—in this case, in relation to culture, which appears as a subjective production and not just as a scenario for the constitution of subjectivity. The generative character of subjectivity was one of the aspects enhanced by the author in his process of continuous research and theoretical production.

The in-depth study and the author's reflections regarding other theoretical concepts, not only of psychology, but of human sciences in general—a process that marked his entire scientific trajectory—had an important role in the process of development, consolidation, and evolution of the Theory of Subjectivity. The dialogue with the Theory of Social Representations, with Social Constructionism, with the work of representatives of contemporary Psychoanalysis and Critical Psychology was fruitful in highlighting similarities and differences, in order to consolidate his creative proposal. Also, his reflection and his extensive scientific production on the legacy of the Soviet Psychology classics, as well as its appropriation in the West (González Rey, 1996, 2009b, 2011a, 2011b, 2014d, 2015a, 2016a, 2016c, 2016d, 2018b, 2020) were channels for strengthening and consolidating the Theory of Subjectivity.

The epistemological character of the Theory of Subjectivity, due to its significance in the genesis and development of Qualitative Epistemology,[5] is particularly relevant. The author states:

> The development of Qualitative Epistemology was the result of my inability to solve the problems that appeared in my research, as I delved into theoretical categories that represented theoretical constructions that generate a possible intelligibility option, but that did not guarantee this intelligibility a priori, but that facilitated this intelligibility in the course of the research. These categories upon which my current research on subjectivity is founded are not prone to be constructed directly from the meanings and representations of the research participant's intentional speech. (González Rey, 2013, pp. 29–30)

Qualitative Epistemology is characterized by three strongly articulated principles: the constructive-interpretative character of scientific knowledge, the dialogical character of the knowledge construction process, and the recognition of the singular as a legitimate locus for the production of this knowledge (González Rey, 1997, 2005b, 2009a). These principles unfold a specific methodological conception, the Constructive-Interpretive Methodology, which is characterized by:

---

[5]In Chap. 4, an excellent characterization of Qualitative Epistemology and the Constructive-Interpretative Method is presented, as well as its foundations and scope.

(a) the consideration of research as a relational-dialogical process and not as a set of instrumental acts; (b) the inseparability of the instrument application phase and the production and construction of information during research; (c) the interrelation of the instruments used in the investigation that unfold from each other in the course of the investigation and which are inseparable in the process of information construction; (d) the guiding character of ideas in the development of the theoretical model that guides the research's general process; the empirical is regarded as theoretical moment and not an external instance that legitimizes the theoretical and (e) the consideration of both researcher and participants as subjects of the research process, although with different functions and interests in the course of research. (González Rey & Mitjáns Martínez, 2016, p. 10)

Many of the author's epistemological and methodological reflections expressed in the foundation and elaboration of Qualitative Epistemology were already present in regard to personality. Important elements that also contributed to the formulation and foundation of his epistemological proposal were his closer approach to the Philosophy of Science, his mastery of hegemonic epistemological conceptions in social sciences and psychology, as well as his critical reflections on the growing production of qualitative research in psychology in the 1980s and 1990s.

From the critical movements monopolized by social constructionism to the epistemological fragility of qualitative research that strongly emerged as of the 1980s, Qualitative Epistemology is a creative alternative to the traditional way of doing science in psychology. Even though it was conceived for the production of knowledge on subjectivity, Qualitative Epistemology—and its unfolding in the Constructive-Interpretative Methodology—provides visibility and substantiates aspects to be taken into account in conducting research that provides for an alternative quality for qualitative research that does not specifically focus on the study of subjective processes (Mitjáns Martínez, 2019). This is the reason for its increasing use in qualitative research in different fields.

In the same way that González Rey's ideas on the Theory of Subjectivity have been enhanced and developed, Qualitative Epistemology has followed a process of refinement and evolution, especially in relation to its unfolding in the Constructive-Interpretive Methodology (González Rey, 2019d, 2019e; González Rey & Mitjáns Martínez, 2017b, 2019). In the inaugural work of 1997, the methodological proposal for the research of subjectivity was still relatively unprecise in relation to Qualitative Epistemology principles that are at its base. A clear differentiation and articulation between Qualitative Epistemology as epistemology and Constructive-Interpretative Methodology as methodology was outlined throughout the author's production, especially with an emphasis on the place the dialogical holds in research, the channels through which research constitutes itself as theoretical and the articulation between research and professional practice.

The author's conceptions with regard to the place theory holds in the production of knowledge and in regard to research as theoretical production (1997, 2002, 2005a, 2013, 2014b, 2014c, 2019d, 2019e) are emphasized by the permanent articulation between the theoretical, the epistemological, and the methodological (González Rey, 2013, 2019d; González Rey & Mitjáns Martínez, 2017a, 2017b) which characterizes his scientific production in this second moment of his work. The Theory of

Subjectivity itself, in its construction and development process, is an expression of the principles and developments of Qualitative Epistemology.

Even if the Theory of Subjectivity is associated with psychology as a disciplinary field, due to the way in which scientific knowledge is currently organized, on account of its nature—an alternative for the understanding of human, individual, and social phenomena, under the conditions of culture—it poses a broad scope. It is a general psychological theory that opens new comprehensive possibilities for human, individual, and social phenomena in different fields and, consequently, for necessary changes in professional and social practices. The Theory of Subjectivity, as the basis of research and practices, has shown its heuristic value in understanding teaching-learning processes, human development, professional training, health processes, sexuality, psychotherapy, school inclusion, diagnosis, evaluation, institutional functioning, innovation processes, legal expertise, community work, political processes, and violence, among others.

The Theory of Subjectivity is not only increasingly widespread in the Brazilian context, as expressed in this book's ninth chapter, but it has acquired significant visibility and recognition in the international scenario, especially as of the author's increasing publications in English in the last 10 years. González Rey's work is an example of the fact that relevant scientific theory can be produced from Latin America, an idea that he always defended in face of what he considered the frequent uncritical importation of theories developed in the United States and Europe.

González Rey died of cancer on March 26, 2019, at a time of increasing and intense intellectual productivity. He faced the disease with optimism, serenity, and strength and it was yet another stimulus for his scientific production in the last years of his life.

2.4   Final Remarks

González Rey's vast and creative work was the product of a complex fabric of culturally and historically situated contexts and unique personal characteristics that marked his reflections and actions in all of the said contexts. His transit through different contexts allowed him unique experiences that were configured in his scientific production in multiple ways. In the formulation of his Theory of Subjectivity and Qualitative Epistemology, his main scientific contributions, his critical and creative reflection on important hegemonic and counter-hegemonic theoretical, epistemological and methodological concepts in the field of psychology and social sciences in the twentieth and twenty-first centuries are also reflected. His international activity as a professor and guest researcher in several academic institutions in Latin America and Europe and as a lecturer in many significant scientific events was marked by permanent spaces for dialogue, which, in turn, impacted his production.

His work can be divided into two articulated moments: the Personality Moment, in which his research and theoretical contributions focused on the theme of personality and the Theory of Subjectivity and Qualitative Epistemology Moment, in which he founds and develops a general theory of human functioning, with subjectivity as its central concept, as well as an epistemological and methodological conception for its study and comprehension. This second moment represents a continuity with the previous moment, in the sense that his conception of personality was an essential antecedent of his conception of subjectivity, as were his epistemological and methodological reflections related to the investigative process. But this second moment simultaneously implies a break because it expresses a leap away from the focus on the individual—even if socially constituted—toward a broader conception of human functioning that also integrates social functioning. The construction of a theory, as a set of articulated concepts, which represents a new ontological conception in the understanding of human functioning as based on the unity of the symbolic and the emotional, is made evident.

As a general theory "capable of keeping up with the ambiguous, relative and contradictory world of human existence" (González Rey & Mitjáns Martínez, 2017, p. 74), the Theory of Subjectivity has enabled us to advance in the understanding of individual and social human phenomena in different fields: education, health, psychotherapy, development, institutional functioning, and community work, among others. The Qualitative Epistemology and Constructive-Interpretative Methodology principles have not only been used in research and professional practice focusing on subjectivity, but have also inspired a wide range of qualitative research. González Rey leaves us a solid and open work, whose continuity is a challenge for his disciples and followers. In an interview conducted on January 31, 2019, less than two months before his death he stated:

I am very confident that my work will continue to open paths. Its purpose becomes part of others, which continue it, change it, metamorphose it. That's life. A work are creations that come to life. (…) My wish is for it to continue to move forward, to open new horizons, to continue finding good creators capable of taking its creations into consideration. That's the most important.

References

Allport, G. (1967). *La Personalidad: Su configuración y desarrollo* [Personality: Its configuration and development]. Havana: Editora Revolucionaria.

Allport, G. (1978). Lo individual y lo general en el estudio de la personalidad [The individual and the general in the study of personality]. In C. S. Hall & G. Lindzey (Eds.), *Temas de la Personalidad* (pp. 163–176). Mexico DC: Limusa.

Bozhovich, L. I. (1965). *Psicología de la personalidad del niño escolar* [Psychology of the personality of the school child]. Havana: Editora Universitária.

Bozhovich, L. I. (1972). El problema del desarrollo de la esfera de las motivaciones del niño [The problem of developing the sphere of motivations of the child]. In L. I. Bozhovich & L. Blagonadiézhina (Eds.), *Estudio de la motivación de la conducta de los niños y los adolescentes* [Study of the motivation of the behavior of children and adolescents]. Pueblo y Educación: Havana.

Bozhovich, L. I. (1981). *La personalidad y su formación en la edad infantil - Investigaciones psicológicas* [Personality and its formation in childhood—Psychological investigations]. Havana: Pueblo y Educación.

González Rey, F. (1993). *Personalidad, salud y modo de vida* [Personality, health and way of life]. Mexico: UNAM Iztacala.

González Rey, F. (1995). *Comunicación, Personalidad y Desarrollo* [Comunication, personality and development]. Havana: Editorial Pueblo y Educación.

González Rey, F. (1996). L. S. Vygotsky: presencia y continuidad de su pensamiento en el centenario de su nacimiento [L. S. Vygotsky: presence and continuity of his thought in the centenary of his birth]. *Psicologia e Sociedade, 8*(2), 63–81.

González Rey, F. (1997). *Epistemología cualitativa y subjetividad* [Qualitative epistemology and subjectivity]. São Paulo: Educ.

González Rey, F. (2002). *Pesquisa qualitativa em psicologia: caminhos e desafios* [Qualitative research in psychology: Paths and challenges]. São Paulo: Thomson Learning.

González Rey, F. (2003). *Sujeito e subjetividade: uma aproximação histórico-cultural* [Subject and subjectivity: A cultural-historical approach]. São Paulo: Pioneira Thomson Learning.

González Rey, F. (2004). *O Social na Psicologia e a Psicologia Social: A emergência do sujeito* [The social in psychology and social psychology: The emergence of the subject]. Petrópolis: Vozes.

González Rey, F. (2005a). O Valor Heurístico da Subjetividade na Investigação Psicológica [The heuristic value of subjectivity in psychological research]. In F. González Rey (Ed.), *Subjetividade, Complexidade e Pesquisa em Psicologia* [Subjectivity, complexity and psychology research] (pp. 27–52). São Paulo: Pioneira Thomson Learning.

González Rey, F. (2005b). *Pesquisa qualitativa e subjetividade: Os processos de construção da informação* [Qualitative research and subjectivity: The processes of construction of information]. São Paulo: Cengage Learning.

González Rey, F. (2007). *Psicoterapia, subjetividade e pós-modernidade: Uma aproximação histórico-cultural* [Psychotherapy, subjectivity and post modernity: A cultural-historical approach]. São Paulo: Pioneira Thomson Learning.

González Rey, F. (2009a). Epistemología y Ontología: un debate necesario para la Psicología hoy [Epistemology and ontology: A necessary debate for psychology today]. *Revista diversitas - perspectivas en psicología, 5*(2), 205–224.

González Rey, F. (2009b). Historical relevance of Vygotsky's work: Its significance for a new approach to the problem of subjectivity in psychology. *Outlines, 11,* 59–73.

González Rey, F. (2011a). *El Pensamiento de Vigotsky: Contradicciones, Desdoblamientos y Desarrollo* [Vygotsky's thought: Contradictions, unfolding and development]. Mexico DF: Trillas.

González Rey, F. (2011b). A re-examination of different moments in Vygotsky's work and their implications for his continuing legacy. *Mind, Culture and Activity, 18,* 257–275.

González Rey, F. (2013). O que oculta o silêncio epistemológico da psicologia? [What hides the epistemological silence of psychology]. *Pesquisas e Práticas Psicossociais* [Researches and psychosocial practices], *8*(1), 20–34.

González Rey, F. (2014a). Human motivation in question: Discussing emotions, motives and subjectivity from a cultural-historical standpoint. *Journal for the Theory of Social Behavior, 45*(4), 419–439. https://doi.org/10.1111/jtsb.12073.

González Rey, F. (2014b). Ideias e modelos teóricos na pesquisa construtivo-interpretativa [Ideas and theoretical models in constructive-interpretive research]. In A. Mitjáns Martínez, M. Neubern, & V. D. Mori (Eds.), *Subjetividade contemporânea: discussões epistemológicas e metodológicas* [Contemporary subjectivity: epistemological and methodological discussions] (pp. 13–34).). Campinas: Alínea.

González Rey, F. (2014c). A imaginação como produção subjetiva: as ideias e os modelos da produção intelectual [Imagination as subjective production: the ideas and models of intellectual production]. In A. Mitjáns Martínez & P. Álvarez (Eds.), *O sujeito que aprende. Diálogo entre a psicanálise e o enfoque histórico-cultural* [The learning subject. Dialogue between psychoanalysis and the historical-cultural approach] (pp. 35–61). Brasília: Liber Livro.

González Rey, F. (2014d). Advancing further the history of Soviet psychology: Moving forward from dominant representations in Western and Soviet psychology. *History of Psychology, 17,* 60–78.

González Rey, F. (2015a). Marxism, subjectivity and Cultural-historical psychology: Moving forward on an unfinished legacy. *Annual Review of Critical Psychology, 12,* 27–35.

González Rey, F. (2015b). A new path for the discussion of social representations: advancing the topic of subjectivity from a cultural-historical standpoint. *Theory & Psychology, 25*(4), 494–512. https://doi.org/10.1177/0959354315587783.

Gonzalez Rey, F. (2016a). Advancing on the topics of the social and subjectivity from a cultural-historical approach: Moments, paths and contradictions. *Journal of the Theoretical and Philosophical Psychology, 36,* 175–189. https://doi.org/10.1017/CCOL0521831040.

González Rey, F. (2016b). Vida e Obra de Boris Fedorovich Lomov: o "giro" da psicologia soviética nos anos setenta do século XX [Life and Work of Boris Fedorovich Lomov: the "turn" of Soviet psychology in the seventies of the twentieth century]. In R. Valdes Puente & A. Maturano Longarezi (Eds.), *Ensino desenvolvimental: vida pensamento e obra dos principais representantes russos* [Developmental education: life thought and work of the main Russian representatives] (pp. 239–266). Uberlandia: EDUFU.

González Rey, F. (2016c). Vygotsky's concept of perezhivanie in the psychology of art and at the final moment of his work: Advancing his legacy. *Mind, Culture and Activity, 23,* 305–314.

González Rey, F. (2016d). El pensamiento de Vigotsky: momentos, contradicciones y desarrollo [Vygotsky's thought: Moments, contradictions and development]. *Summa Psicológica, 13,* 7–17.

González Rey, F. (2017a). The topic of subjectivity in psychology: Contradictions, paths and new alternatives. *Journal for the Theory of Social Behaviour, 47*(4), 502–521. https://doi.org/10.1111/jtsb.12144.

González Rey, F. (2017b). Advances in subjectivity from a cultural-historical perspective: Unfolding and Consequences for cultural studies today. In M. Fleer, F. González Rey, & N. Veresov (Eds.), *Perezhivanie, emotions and subjectivity: advancing Vygotsky's legacy* (pp. 173–193). Singapore: Springer.

González Rey, F. (2018a). Silvia Lane: Caminhos de uma pioneira [Silvia Lane: Paths of a pioneer]. In: B. B. Sawaia, & G. T. Purin. (Eds.), *Silvia Lane: uma obra em movimento* [Silvia Lane: a work in motion]. (pp. 73-93). São Paulo: EDUC.

González Rey, F. (2018b). Vygotsky's "The Psychology of Art": A foundational and still unexplored text. *Estudos de Psicologia (Campinas), 35*(4), 339–350.

González Rey, F. (2019a). Subjectivity as a new theoretical, epistemological, and methodological pathway within cultural-historical psychology. In: González Rey, F., Mitjáns Martínez, A. & Goulart, D. (Eds). *Subjectivity within cultural-historical approach. theory, methodology and research* (pp. 21–36). Singapore: Springer.

González Rey, F. (2019b). Subjectivity in debate: Some reconstructed philosophical premises to advance its discussion in psychology. *Journal for the Theory of Social Behavior, 49,* 212–234.

González Rey, F. (2019c). The rescue of subjectivity from a cultural-historical standpoint. In R. Beshara (Ed.), *A critical introduction to Psychology* (pp. 9–25). New York: Nova Science Publishers.

González Rey, F. (2019d). Methodological and epistemological demands in advancing the study of subjectivity from a cultural-historical standpoint. *Culture & Psychology, 26*(3), 562–577. https://doi.org/10.1177/1354067X19888185.

González Rey, F. (2019e). Epistemologia qualitativa vinte anos depois [Qualitative epistemology twenty years later]. In A. Mitjáns Martínez, F. González Rey, R. Valdés Puentes (Eds.), *Epistemologia qualitativa e teoria da subjetividade: discussões sobre educação e saúde* [Qualitative epistemology and theory of subjectivity: discussions on education and health]. (pp. 21-45). Uberlândia: EDUFU.

González Rey, F. (2020). The two pathways of Vygotskys legacy: The critical and noncritical coexisting positions in Vygotsky's thought. In M. Fleer, F. González Rey, & P. Jones. *Cultural-historical and critical psychology: Common ground, divergences and future pathways* (pp. 175–191). Singapore: Springer.

González Rey, F., & Mitjáns Martínez, A. (2016). Una epistemología para el estudio de la subjetividad: sus implicaciones metodológicas [An epistemology for the study of subjectivity: its methodological implications]. *Psicoperspectivas (Online): Individuo y Sociedad* [Psicoperspectivas (Online): Individual and society], *15*(1), 5–16.

González Rey, F., & Mitjáns Martínez, A. (2017a). *Subjetividade: epistemologia, teoria e método* [Subjectivity: epistemology, theory and method]. Campinas: Alínea.

González Rey, F., & Mitjáns Martínez, A. (2017b). Epistemological and methodological challenges for the study of subjectivity from a cultural-historical perspective. In M. Fleer; F. González Rey, & N. Veresov (Eds.), *Perezhivanie, emotions and subjectivity: Advancing Vygotsky's legacy* (pp. 195–216). New York: Springer.

González Rey, F., & Mitjáns Martínez, A. (2019). The constructive-interpretative methodological approach: orienting research and practice on the basis of subjectivity. In F. González Rey, A. Mitjáns Martinez, & D. Goulart (Eds.), *Theory of subjectivity: New perspectives within social and educational research* (pp. 37–60). Singapore: Springer.

González Rey F., & Mitjáns Martinez, A. (2020). Looking towards a productive dialogue between cultural-historical and critical psychologies. In M. Fleer, F. González Rey, & P. Jones (Eds.), *Cultural-historical and critical psychology: Common ground, divergences and future pathways* (pp. 43–62). Singapore: Springer.

Goulart, D., Mitjáns Martínez, A., & Esteban-Guitart, M. (2020). The trajectory and work of Fernando González Rey: Paths to his theory of subjectivity. *Studies in Psychology, 41*(1), 9–30. https://doi.org/10.1080/02109395.2019.1710800.

Mitjáns Martínez, A. (2005). A teoria da subjetividade de González Rey: uma expressão do paradigma da complexidade na Psicologia [González Rey's theory of subjectivity: an expression of the complexity paradigm in Psychology]. In F. González Rey (Ed.), *Subjetividade, complexi-dade e pesquisa em Psicologia* [Subjectivity, complexity and research in psychology] (pp. 2–25). São Paulo: Thomson Learning.

Mitjáns Martinez, A. (2019). Epistemologia Qualitativa: dificuldades, equívocos e contribuições para outras formas de pesquisa qualitativa [Qualitative epistemology: difficulties, mistakes and contributions to other forms of qualitative research]. In M. Rossato, & V. L. A. Peres. *Formação de educadores e psicólogos. Contribuições e desafios da subjetividade na perspectiva cultural-histórica* [Training of educators and psychologists: Contributions and challenges of subjectivity in the cultural-historical perspective]. (pp. 47–69). Curitiba: Appris.

Mitjáns Martínez, A., & González Rey, F. (2019). A preparação para o exercício da profissão docente: contribuições da Teoria da Subjetividade [Preparation for the exercise of the teaching profession: contributions from the theory of subjectivity]. In M. Rossato, & V. L. A. Peres *Formação de educadores e psicólogos. Contribuições e desafios da subjetividade na perspectiva cultural - histórica* [Training of educators and psychologists: Contributions and challenges of subjectivity in the cultural-historical perspective]. Curitiba: Appris.

Morin, E. (1995). *Os meus demônios* [My demons]. Portugal: Europa-América.

Morin, E. (1998). *O método 4:as ideias* [Method 4: ideas]. Porto Alegre: Sulina.

Morin, E. (2002). *Religação dos saberes: os desafios do século XXI* [Reconnection of knowledge: the challenges of the 21st century]. Rio de Janeiro: Editora Bertrand Brasil.

Morin, E. (2015). *Introdução ao pensamento complexo* [Introduction to complex thinking]. Porto Alegre: Sulina.

Albertina Mitjáns Martínez is a Research Professor of the Faculty of Education at the University of Brasilia, Brazil. She obtained her Ph.D. qualification in psychological sciences at the University of Havana, Cuba, and concluded post-doctoral studies at the Faculty of Psychology of the

Autonomous University of Madrid. Her research interests focus on education and psychology from a cultural–historical approach in three specific fields: (1) creativity and innovation in education; (2) subjectivity in human development and learning; (3) disabilities and school inclusion. Her latest books are: (1) Subjectivity within cultural-historical approach: theory, methodology and research (Ed., 2019, Springer); (2) Subjetividade: teoria, epistemologia e método [Subjectivity: theory, epistemology and method] (Alínea, 2019); (3) Psicologia, educação e aprendizagem escolar [Psychology, education and school learning] (Cortez, 2019).

Chapter 3
The Topic of Subjectivity in Psychology: Contradictions, Paths, and New Alternatives

Fernando González Rey

Abstract This paper draws a picture of how topics related to subjectivity have appeared in different psychological theories, such as psychoanalysis, Gestalt and post-structuralist approaches, discussing in-depth a specific proposition from a cultural-historical standpoint. I argue that, in most of these theories, subjectivity has been used to refer to specific processes and phenomena without advancing a more general theory about it. The way in which subjectivity was treated within the Cartesian/Enlightenment tradition, taken together with the individualistic tradition of psychology, led critical psychological theories to reject the concept. In this way, such critical theories have omitted the heuristic value of subjectivity to study processes that can neither be exhausted by language, nor by discourse. A new proposal of subjectivity is highlighted, based on the cultural-historical tradition in psychology. From this perspective, subjectivity is defined by units of emotions and symbolical processes generated throughout the human experience. On the basis of such definition, I discuss how institutionalized orders can be subverted by subjective productions that represent new social pathways. Far from being a remnant of Modernity, in this way subjectivity is defined as a human production, capable of transcending the apparent objective limits of human existence.

González Rey F. (2017). The topic of subjectivity in psychology: contradictions, paths and new alternatives. J Theory Soc Behav. 2017; 1–20. https://doi.org/10.1111/jtsb.12144.

F. González Rey (✉)
Faculty of Health and Education Sciences, University Center of Brasilia, Brasilia, Brazil

3.1 Introduction

Throughout its history, psychology has avoided the ontological definition[1] of its concepts, replacing the specific nature of psychological phenomena with concepts that deal with other domains previously established by science (Abuljanova, 1973). Clear examples of this are concepts like system, behavior, reflex, energy, variables, language, and, more recently, the concept of discourse. All of these were generated in other sciences and in philosophy before being used within psychology. However, none of them highlights the specific subjective quality of human phenomena, as engendered within socio-culturally and historically located realities.

The failure of psychology in advancing new ontological definitions, on which new theoretical systems related to the systemic functioning of mind could be developed, has led to an extensive, empirical and descriptive taxonomy of categories that are mainly interrelated via statistical criteria, without any theoretical construction. Subjectivity, as treated in this paper, does not represent just another concept of psychology, but a new ontological definition of human phenomena. Subjectivity emerges as a new qualitative human phenomenon defined as the unit between symbolical processes and emotions. As discussed below, none of the psychological theories that refer directly or indirectly to subjectivity formulates a theory based on such a complex system.

Theory, as such, has been mistreated in psychology due to its subordination to empirical facts or its use as a dogma. In both cases, theory is reduced to labels or definitions used a priori, which are imposed on the information coming from the studied phenomenon, instead of being used as a general system of intelligibility, from which new meanings can be produced during professional and research practices.

The fragmentation of psychology in the twentieth century is rightly exemplified by Danziger:

> The story of twentieth-century academic Psychology is the story of an ultimately unsuccessful struggle against an ever more obvious fragmentation (…). Psychologists had gained an academic foothold by doing experiments on such topics as sensation, perception and memory. For some time, that remained the respectable core of the discipline, but how test intelligence related to this core was far from clear. It was much easier to annex such a field institutionally than to assimilate it intellectually. (Danziger, 1997, p. 85)

Empirical definitions are theoretically empty, leading to an understanding of practical and research activities as mere technical empirical and instrumental procedures. As a result, practices addressed by the quantitative measurement of psychological features have thus been extended in psychology.

Nevertheless, European psychology, unlike American behavioral psychology, took another path, one more influenced by philosophy and social sciences, within which theory was given more attention. Paradoxically, Soviet psychology in the

---

[1]Ontological definition is used in this paper as the specific theoretical constructions that permit the identification of any domain of science. On the basis of these constructions epistemological and methodological conceptions are defined which, together with the ontological definition that inspires them, form a core of scientific work.

1920s was closer to behaviorism than to other European theories, such as Gestalt's theory, despite the profound influence of Gestalt's theory on Vygotsky's work in the early 1930s.

The present paper aims to bring back subjectivity as a culturally, socially, and historically located human production, characterized by units of symbolical processes and emotions, which appear together as subjective singular configurations, both of which configure social and individual subjectivities in their complex interweaving. In contraposition to the individualistic psychology that had prevailed during the first half of the twentieth century, in the 1960s there was a turn toward social psychology focused on socially engendered psychological phenomena (Moscovici, 1967; Tajfel, 1965).

Since the 1980s, the most innovative and critical trends within psychology have been based on terms like discourse, deconstruction, relations of power, gender, and so on, omitting the different paths of subjectivation, through which those processes are subjectively produced by individuals and social groups. This gap does not imply rejecting those important concepts but implies complementing them by facing the complex challenges that come with the study of human phenomena. Subjectivity as discussed in this paper is an alternative to fill this gap.

The paper begins with a short overview of psychoanalysis and Gestalt theory, due to their relevance to the discussion in focus. Psychoanalysis, for instance, has been taken as the reference for the topic of subjectivity in culture, philosophy and social sciences in general, as a result of the theoretical vacuum associated with this topic in psychology and social sciences.

3.2 Psychoanalysis: Its Implications for Advancing the Topic of Subjectivity

This section does not aim to be a historical overview of psychoanalysis as such. It is, rather, a dialogue with a series of authors who made important advancements in topics that are relevant to the conception of subjectivity. The authors discussed below are revisionists of Freud, Klein, Winnicott, and Lacan, developing the cultural character of subjectivity from the works of these authors. In their attempt to overcome some of the universal principles upon which these authors built their works, many points of contact appear with the theoretical position sustained in the present paper in regard to a cultural-historical definition of subjectivity.

Despite the fact that subjectivity was never explicitly assumed by Freud as his theoretical focus, post-Freudian authors attempted to identify subjectivity in Freud's definition of representation, understanding it as an imaginary production capable of embodying the force of drives (Castoriadis, 1995; Elliott, 1992).

The use of Freud's definition of representation, despite the efforts of the afore-mentioned authors, remained very vague in its psychological nature. According to

Freud, drives have a somatic nature, leading to the emergence of the psychical apparatus only through representation which, according to Freud's understanding, cannot be identified as conscious. Representations were defined by Freud as living instances with functions that are beyond the individual consciousness. Elliott defines representation in Freud as "an indeterminable imaging of drives (…) there is no such thing as a drive in its pure state. Libidinal drives are mediated through the forming of images, by the 'representational process'" (Elliott, 1992, pp. 25–26).

That relation between drive and representation is a cornerstone of psychoanalysis, on which the libidinal drives are defined as foundational for the psychological; the motivational side of psychological functioning remains dependent on the original natural and universal drives. This fact makes it impossible for psychoanalysis to recognize the intrinsic dynamic character of new psychological phenomena that are organized on the basis of historically located ongoing socio-cultural engendered experiences.

The main obstacle for the revitalization of the topic of subjectivity in psychoanalysis is that its theoretical basis sets up in advance the situation it intends to explain, which is common to all versions of psychoanalysis. How could intelligibility be produced in research on the Oedipus complex, or on early sexual drives? How could research be advanced about the universal statement that children try to escape from the painfulness of "lack" through their imaginary fantasies? These universal claims are impossible to study; they are hermetical points of departure that have to be assumed in order to work within one or another version of psychoanalysis. These foundational and universal concepts are present even in the more advanced versions of psychoanalysis, those that emphasize the cultural genesis of subjectivity (Castoriadis, 1995; Frosh, 2002, 2010; Parker, 2011; Elliott, 1992, among others).

In Elliott's terms, those hermetic points of departure, previously referred to, appear as follows:

> In Freud's eyes, the fundamental condition for a drive to attain psychical expression is by means of a "delegation through representation". This involves primary repression, the fixation and sedimentation of drives to representational forms. The primary unconscious thus exists as a condition of subjectivity, from which "repression proper" and consciousness emerge… The primal representation of the unconscious is the affective anchor for the fulfillment of desire and, as a matter of definition, specifically resist being brought to consciousness. (Elliott, 1992, pp. 28–29)

It is difficult to know what the author's phrase, "delegation through representation," means. In any case, the absolute and universal character of the statement above must be either accepted or rejected, with no chance of confronting it during the research process. It is also difficult to accept that the "primary unconscious… exists as a condition of subjectivity." In my opinion, there is no primary unconscious; unconscious appears as a quality of subjectivity. Subjectivity as a cultural-historical formation is not anchored in a universal condition of individuals. These claims only assume meaning within the theoretical apparatus of psychoanalysis, which acts as an external constraint on research and practice.

Anyway, as we will discuss below, the abovementioned authors, among others who share some of these foundational principles, had also developed important critiques, advancing important new constructions that should be taken into account in discussing subjectivity on this new basis, as this paper aims to do.

3.3 The Premises for a Cultural-Historical Definition of Subjectivity

K. Lewin and his group, Vygotsky, and other Soviet psychologists, like Rubinstein and Bozhovich, also advanced important concepts oriented toward understanding psychological processes and personality as cultural, social, and historical phenomena, although they kept narrow definitions of social realities and culture (González Rey, 2016). Nonetheless, they advanced toward new definitions of emotions and motivation, taking an important step forward on the subjective character of psychological phenomena. For the first time in the history of psychology, K. Lewin and his followers broke down the primacy of social determinism in relation to psychological phenomena, emphasizing how human needs make the difference in the relevance of social environments for individuals.

Lewin strongly influenced Vygotsky's shift to emotions, motivation and consciousness between 1932 and 1934 (Yasnitsky, 2012, 2016; Zavershneva, 2010, 2016). He also highly influenced the work of Bozhovich and her team, the group within Soviet psychology which made the most notorious advances in the study of personality and motivation, in which the topic of subjectivity was embedded in the study of personality (Tolstyx, 2008).

One of the closest collaborators of Lewin, Tamara Dembo, made an interesting contribution related to a new comprehension of psychological concepts, giving attention to their qualitative character. She wrote: "I had to get away from properties, which were static notions (not affecting other units) that did not permit understanding of the nature of psychological qualities in their totality or in their manifestation as single entities and occurrences" (Dembo, 1993, p. 15).[2]

Dembo's turn toward the qualitative nature of psychological units led her to also advance on the qualitative nature of psychological research, articulating for the first time in history the idea that theory and methodology in psychology are two intermingled processes that must advance together in psychological research. The malleability and dynamic of such units fulfill an important theoretical demand for advances in the topic of subjectivity. These units were defined as psychological qualities in movement, simultaneously characterizing the quality of the system and its expressions

---

[2]The quotation is referenced to its year of publication. However, that was the year in which Dembo died at the age of 92 years, which makes me think that the paper, according to its contents, was written many decades before, when Dembo was actively involved in Lewin's research into motivation and personality.

as single entities, as stated by Dembo above. This definition is an important theoretical premise for understanding subjectivity as a cultural-historical production, as intended in this paper.

Advancing her definition of this new concept, she stated:

> I could no longer bear to deal with analysis of properties that were related to our senses yet unrelated from psychological unit to another. Finally, I called for a change! [...] But change also seemed to entail another more positive meaning; change indicated activity and thus was in contrast to properties understood in a static way. (Dembo, 1993, pp. 17–18)

The emphasis on change and movement as intrinsic to the qualitative units of psychological life permits progress toward a comprehension of the psychological system, not as an intra-psychical system, but as a system in action, as an open and dynamic system. This proposal by Dembo was close to Rubinstein's principle of the unity of consciousness and activity, as well as to the last concepts proposed by Vygotsky for the comprehension of psychological functioning, like sense and *perezhivanie*.

This emphasis on the qualitative character of psychological concepts was absent in cultural-historical psychology in terms of how it was developed during its Soviet period. Psychoanalysis, for a long time, was only related to clinical practice, and it passed unnoticed among psychoanalysts themselves that practice represents new epistemological premises for advancing new methodological pathways. Maybe this has been one of the reasons why psychoanalytic theory has kept many of its principles beyond the questioning of research.

Dembo proposed, following Lewin, a promissory theoretical-methodological articulation oriented toward understanding psychological functioning as inseparable from the course of individual social life. However, in advancing this articulation between social environment and psychological concepts, Lewin took the field as the ground within which psychological concepts and the environment are linked to each other, without advancing a definition of any psychological system.

Subjectivity, as proposed in this paper, implies transcendence of its comprehension as individual and intra-psychical essence and, at the same time, requires an advance beyond the social determinism that characterized Soviet psychology. Subjectivity displays a generative character, permitting individuals and groups to transcend, through their subjective productions, the immediate influences from their environments; subjective processes are based on the creation of new human, cultural environments. Having their genesis within culture, subjective processes are, at the same time, the basis for cultural development. As Cassirer stated:

> Consequently all schemata which science evolves in order to classify, organize, and summarize the phenomena of the real world turn out to be nothing but arbitrary schemes – airy fabrics of the mind, which express not the nature of things, but the nature of mind. (Cassirer, 1953, p. 7)

There are arbitrary symbolical schemes generated by culture to advance the topic of subjectivity, schemes which Cassirer referred to as the link still missing in the work of Lewin's group as well as in that of Vygotsky and the Soviet psychologists. These "arbitrary schemes – airy fabric of the mind" characterize the nature of mind and of culture, which are intermingled with each other in such a way that one is generated by the other.

Subjectivity, according to this definition, is a subversive concept, because its definition implies continuous resistance to and confrontation with the social hegemonic status quo throughout the history of mankind, opening a theoretical pathway to explain this resistance. At the same time, subjective phenomena are intrinsically polychromatic inside one culture, making impossible any attempt to standardize subjectivity or to submit it to control. Change and development are intrinsic to subjectivity, so any form of resistance is engendered from inside one structure of power, within new subjective productions that may lead to non-predictable changes and consequences, transcending the dominant established rationality. As well as culture, subjectivity is not anchored in ahistorical truths.

The model of functioning, which makes subjectivity different from any other ontological definition assumed by psychology in its history, first appeared in philosophy. Marx, Dewey, Sartre, Merleau-Ponty, and Edgar Morin, among others, contributed to the representation of such a complex phenomenon.

If modernism adhered to a rationality in which reasoning marginalizes emotions, post-structuralism, as one of the paths taken by the postmodern movement in social sciences, adopted rationality, reducing human phenomena to discursive practices. The hermeneutical shift inaugurated by Heidegger was continued by Gadamer, Foucault, Derrida, and Rorty who, despite their differences, agreed on replacing epistemology with hermeneutic. In doing so, they attempted to make knowledge a permanent flux that can never be taken as a theoretical system related to well-located questions in the way knowledge can be understood by natural sciences.

The understanding of discourse as practice led to the ignoring of the relevance of theoretical models as paths of intelligibility about realities that do not function as texts or as discursive processes. In their critiques of epistemology, the abovementioned authors referred specifically to representational epistemology. Despite Heidegger's later reconsideration of his initial critique of epistemology, Foucault, Derrida, and Rorty, in fact, rejected not only epistemology but all theoretical systems based on scientific knowledge. Nonetheless, subjectivity specified an ontological definition that was impossible to reduce to texts, discourses, or language.

The rejection of foundational epistemology led to a rejection of the kind of ontological presuppositions on which that epistemology lies, among which was subjectivity as it was understood by the philosophies grouped under the Cartesian/Enlightenment tradition. Neglecting subjectivity, in the way it was treated in that tradition, led to the disregarding of the heuristic value of subjectivity as a phenomenon to define qualities of human beings and human realities that could not be defined through concepts in fashion in post-structuralist thinking.

The opposition between text and nature was a dangerous precedent in the rejection of subjectivity as a topic in human sciences, not because subjectivity belongs to the domain of nature, but because the challenges that its study presents are very similar to those advanced today in the study of the natural sciences (Prigogine, 2004). This coincidence suggests orienting our attention again toward a new epistemology on which new methodological proposals can be based.

As Westphal stressed in relation to Rorty's radical rejection of epistemology: "By failing to distinguish the generic epistemological task from the specifically modern foundationalist projects, Rorty obscures the fact that hermeneutics is not the replacement of epistemology as such, but the replacement of one type of epistemology with another" (Westphal, 1999, p. 416).

The idea of discourse as practice (Foucault, 1987), as a network of symbolical processes, within which human practices take place, turns discourse into a universal ontological principle capable of explaining all human phenomena, instead of recognizing it as an important quality of all human phenomena, but which does not exhaust them.

Discursive practices were taken as emancipatory from a naturalistic and individualistic psychology, but by doing this some theories, such as social constructionism, for example, rejected the relation between theory, epistemology and methodology in favor of the construction of truth as conversational agreement. This extreme position is clearly stressed by Shotter:

> A central methodological assumption of social constructionism is that – instead of the inner dynamics of the individual psyche (romanticism), or the already determined characteristics of the external world (modernism) – we must study the continuous everyday flow of contingent communicative activity occurring between people. (Shotter, 1995, p. 160)

Once again, those authors inspired by post-structuralist discourse criticized the inner dynamics of the individual psyche due to the way it was constructed by romanticism. The proposal of subjectivity discussed in this paper is also far from the romantic understanding of the inner psychical world, and also differs from the concept of the psyche. However, unlike the constructionist position, this paper advances another proposal to understand individual subjectivity in such a way that the social is not represented as external and different, but as part of a complex recursive system that integrates social and individual subjectivities in different levels. Discourses do not represent the opposite of human subjectivity; on the contrary, discourse is subjectively configured in the complex interweaving between social and individual subjectivities.

The emphasis on social phenomena as symbolically constructed realities represented an important step forward in the comprehension of human actions as inseparable from social constructions. Nevertheless, the theories that take discourses, narratives, and social representations as their theoretical epicenters, instead of advancing a new conception of the individual inextricably intermingled with those social phenomena, replaced individuals with socially constructed realities (González Rey, 2015).

3.4   Some Constraints and the Advances Within Traditional Cultural-Historical Psychology Regarding the Study of Subjectivity

Cultural-historical psychology is a label widely used to define Vygotsky's instrumental period between 1926 and 1931 (Leontiev, 1984; Yasnitsky, 2009, 2012; González Rey, 2011, 2014, 2016). However, the reduction of this label to one period of Vygotsky's work seems to be a very narrow and reductionist use of the term. Instead, all of the main trends in Soviet psychology that recognized the cultural, social, and historical genesis of the human psyche can be considered as cultural-historical theories (González Rey, 2014b).

From the 1920s, Soviet psychology's dominant versions subscribed to a dogmatic social determinism, in which the genesis of the psychological processes was reduced in the extent to the internalization of external operations (González Rey, 2014b). However, that social determinism was subverted by different authors, among which I will focus on some of Vygotsky's theoretical concepts in the last period of his work, due to their relevance to advancing the discussion on subjectivity from a cultural-historical standpoint. The concepts of sense and *perezhivanie*, as developed by Vygotsky in 1933–1934, opened an interesting path toward a new comprehension of human consciousness as a psychological system involved in human actions (González Rey, 2009, 2011, 2014b).

The growing attention to *perezhivanie* (Fakhrutdinova, 2010; Fleer & Quinones, 2013; Mitchel, 2016; Veresov, 2017) in the last ten years has, to some extent, separated *perezhivanie* from sense. I have always attempted to interrelate these concepts to each other due to their complementary meanings and consequences, in order to advance on the topic of subjectivity (González Rey, 2009, 2011). In regard to sense, Vygotsky wrote: "A word's sense is the aggregate of all the psychological facts that arise in our consciousness as a result of the word [...] Meaning is only one of these zones of the sense that the word acquires in the context of speech" (Vygotsky, 1987, p. 276). Advancement on subjectivity requires the definition of such theoretical concepts that permit the integration of culture and subjectivity within the nature of their own action, without reducing one to the other. The concept of sense was an important premise in this direction.

The concept of *perezhivanie* somehow overlaps the concept of sense, but *perezhivanie* was specifically addressed toward specifying that social influences in themselves have no significance for human development. The concept of *perezhivanie* stressed the inseparable integration of the social environment and the child's personality. These concepts allowed Vygotsky to emancipate psychological development from the direct influences of the environment.[3]

---

[3]In the last period of his work, Vygotsky defined *perezhivanie* as the unit of consciousness capable of integrating the influences of the environment and the characteristics of the child's personality. The concept of unit was used by Vygotsky as the "cell" that embodies the quality of consciousness as a whole.

Vygotsky explicitly stressed his effort to understand human beings as a system capable of integrating multiple processes and functions in his discussions about thinking. So, in "Thinking and Speech" Vygotsky stated: "Thinking was divorced from the full vitality of life, from the motives, interests and inclinations of the thinking individual" (Vygotsky, 1987, p. 50).

This calls my attention to the fact that, in the same book in which sense was defined, Vygotsky defined thinking as intrinsically associated not only with speech but with the "full vitality of life," referring to this vitality as a concept that included motives, interests, and inclinations. Nonetheless, the concept of sense was not used by Vygotsky to transcend these more fragmented and traditional concepts which, in my opinion, resulted from his definition of sense within the domain of speech as "word sense." At that time, Vygotsky had still not assembled the advances in the concepts of sense and *perezhivanie* into a new representation of the psychological system.

Communication, as a specific and independent concept of psychology capable of integrating social and individual psychological processes, was only discussed by Soviet psychology at the end of the 1970s (Lomov, 1978). That was an important period in continuing to develop the premises for the study of subjectivity in Soviet psychology. Communication as a concept was completely replaced by the concept of based object activity under the theoretical hegemony of Activity Theory in Soviet psychology. The constraints created by Activity Theory to advance on the topic of subjectivity in Soviet psychology have been carefully discussed by me elsewhere (González Rey, 2002, 2009, 2011, 2014a, 2014b).

The last concepts developed by Vygotsky, taken together with the consideration of communication as a relevant and specific concept, were important premises in overcoming the constraints of Activity Theory, advancing the topic of subjectivity. However, the lack of an ontological definition of these concepts made it impossible for Soviet psychologists to advance a definition of subjectivity addressed toward understanding a new, properly human phenomenon as resulting from human cultural, social, and historical existence.

3.5 Some Important Approaches to the Matter of Subjectivity Today

Vygotskian studies is an area that appeared in Western psychology inspired by Vygotsky's legacy, the roots of which lie in pioneering American interpretations of Vygotsky's work (Bruner, Cole, Wertsch, among others). These interpretations were greatly influenced by Leontiev's group which, via Luria, monopolized contacts with American psychologists in the 1960s (González Rey, 2014a).

During Soviet times, Soviet psychology had its identity defined in contraposition with so-called "bourgeois theories," which explained the lack of dialogue between Soviet authors and representatives of other theories and fields of psychology, marking

Soviet psychology as the privileged expression of Marxism in psychology. Up to the present day, dialogue between Vygotskian studies circles and other theories has developed little. There have been important attempts to develop cultural, social, and historical psychology within other theoretical traditions, and to advance on the cultural genesis of the human mind (Castoriadis, Holzkamp, Frosh, Elliot, Parker, among others), which are rarely quoted by the representatives of Vygotskian studies.

Holzkamp's explicit assumption of subjectivity as a result of societal conditions is an important antecedent in advancing a cultural-historical definition of subjectivity. Assuming Marx as an important reference for his work, Holzkamp made explicit how the individual, as an active agent, has remained outside of Marx's dominant representation:

> As many futile attempts have shown, progress in this direction (the author refers to the comprehension of human nature as results of the societal conditions of life) by starting with the Marxist anatomy of bourgeois society and expecting somehow to arrive at a conception of the individual from the dissection and specification of the mode of production in particular capitalist societies. No matter how precise and detailed such an analysis may be, the "individual as such" remains somehow out of reach. (Holzkamp, 1991, p. 51)

Holzkamp opposed a definition of subjectivity as encapsulating intra-psychical structure, defending a specific definition of the individual as inseparable from societal conditions. He argued: "(...) human subjectivity, as the possibility of conscious control over one's own life conditions, always and necessarily requires moving beyond individuality toward participation in the collective determination of the societal process" (ibid., p. 58). Holzkamp, recognizing subjectivity as a phenomenon, did not make an important contribution to a new theoretical definition of subjectivity. He remained within the limits of Soviet psychology in his emphasis on the conscious character of psychological functioning and its function of control.

Holzkamp continued using traditional concepts, such as cognitive processes, motivation, and others, defining subjectivity as one more concept associated with two main attributes. These attributes were personal action potency as a "means of revealing the way in which individuals related to their possibilities" and the concept of "productive needs," used by him to define the "emotional aspect of psyche" (ibid., p. 58). Emotions continued to be referred to as psyche and have not been understood as intrinsic to the definition of subjectivity due to their subordination to rational processes. In his own words "(...) it became clear that with the objective necessity of having to participate in the social provisioning process in order to control individual life conditions, a subjective necessity also developed" (ibid., p. 59, author's emphasis).

Psychoanalysis, from its more critical positions, unlike Holzkamp, emphasized the generative capacity of the imagination beyond the conscious control of individuals. Authors such as Castoriadis, Frosh, and Elliot stressed the relevance of imagination as a distinctive non-rational attribute of the human psyche, something that, in my opinion, is essential for advancing a theoretical definition of subjectivity. As Castoriadis pointed out: "Man's distinguishing trait is not logic, but imagination, and, more precisely, unbridled imagination, defunctionalized imagination. As radical imagination of the singular psyche and as social instituting imaginary, this sort of imagination provides the conditions for reflective thought to exist" (Casto-riadis, 1995, p. 15). That association between imagination and reflective thought is very important in understanding thinking as a subjective function, because imagi-nation represents the creative character of thinking. At the same time, as Vygotsky defended in "The Psychology of Art," "[…] we see therefore, that emotion and imag-ination are not two separated processes; on the contrary, they are the same process" (Vygotsky, 1971, p. 210). Psychological functioning acquires its subjective character based on imagination, through which emotions are embedded in psychological func-tions, turning functions into subjective configured processes. As Castoriadis stated, "imagination (…) is always paired with the positing of new forms/figures of the thinkable, which are created by the radical imagination and are subject to the control of reflection" (ibid., p. 34).

Imagination is much more than this; it is a subjective production that transforms and integrates images into concepts and generates new concepts that lead to new models of the thinkable, turning emotions into symbolic processes, while symbolic processes become inseparable from emotions. From these processes emerge repre-sentations that, once formed, become sources of new concepts, images and other productions, leading to new imaginative creations. Imagination is intrinsic to the creation of new cultural realities in a path in which new forms of subjectivation are continuously emerging.

Individuals continuously produce conscious representations; they are producers of reflections that, at times, lead them to create a "(…) way to break the closure in which we are each time necessarily caught up as subject," as Castoriadis himself noted (ibid., p. 35). When this happens, individuals or groups may become subjects of their action, opening new paths within the social order, whether in action or imaginarily advancing new subjective resources. The subject also emerges actively organizing its resistance to a situation that cannot be changed with a personal or group action.

From my point of view, the understanding in Lacanian psychoanalysis of the symbolic, as depending on the social order in contraposition to the imaginary, preserves the dichotomy between conscious and unconscious that Freud unfruit-fully attempted to overcome with his structural model of the psychical apparatus. Elliott echoes this dichotomy as follows: "The symbolic, on the contrary (of the imaginary), depends upon the continual structuring of the imaginary, grasping as the transformation of the virtual order of 'phantasized objects' into a matrix of common, social forms" (Elliott, 1992, p. 246). This dichotomy between the symbolic and the imaginary is grounded in the primary split between the drive and the psychological.

Finally, in this picture of theories, it is possible to identify some positions that are closer to what subjectivity means in our proposal. So, for example, Parker made an interesting attempt to overcome the sexual reductionism of Freud. He sees sex as a human condition that is embedded in actions that apparently have nothing to do with sex:

> (…) we track in analysis how sex comes to attach itself into our representation of other things. Not so that sex appears as the bare ground on which the rest of our life is played out, but how sex comes to influence, by turns to enliven or ruin, the ground, the ground of being. (Parker, 2011, p. 16)

The way in which sex appears in Parker's definition has important points of contact with our understanding of sex as a subjective configuration. As well as sex becoming attached to our representations of other things, as Parker has said, other social symbolical constructions, such as morality, gender, and religion, become attached to the subjective configuration of sex as subjective senses. This is related to the way in which those social constructions have been experienced by individuals in other areas of life that apparently have nothing to do with sex, but that emerge through specific subjective senses in a sexual setting. This perspective understands sex, as well as all human experience, as inseparable from the network of lived experiences, in a process such that the cultural-historical comprehension of subjectivity reaches its maximum meaning. Social symbolical constructions, such as discourses, social representations, the normative institutional system of values, and other dominant symbolical social productions, are not external to individuals and groups; they appear subjectively and are singularly configured in them.

Following his position of attempting to relativize the universal claims of psychoanalysis related to an "internal psychological nature," Parker stated:

> There is then a series of consequences for diagnosis, for how psychoanalysis might tackle 'obsessionalising', 'psychoticising', 'hystericising', and 'perversionalising' strategies in the clinic. Our task is to trace how these categories are historically constituted and to engage with them as lived positions in relation to structures of power in capitalist society. (Parker, ibid., p. 40)

The idea of "mental pathology" is also alien to our proposal on subjectivity. Parker's call to understand these phenomena as "lived positions in relation to structures of power in capitalist society" goes in the direction of our comprehension of human phenomena, including suffering, as subjectively configured processes, in which individual biographies appear through the subjective senses, through one experience of life qualifying others, defining the subjective configurations within which the actual experience is lived. However, the structures of power in capitalism are associated with many different experiences, within which other processes are involved. In relation to these different experiences, the effects of those structures of power should be known by their expression in the subjective configuration that reveals the unique trajectories of lived experiences. The structures of power in capitalism are not an external determinant of human suffering; they act within unique networks of the individual social life from which the individual and social subjective configurations emerge. Within these subjective configurations, it is impossible to separate the structures of power in capitalism from the many occurrences of one individual or group life. Individuals and groups are not passive recipients of social influences.

It is not possible to reduce the emergence of subjective disturbance to political reasons only, or the functioning of normative repressive institutions. It is under these adverse conditions that individuals also emerge as subjects capable of resisting and of opening up new alternatives when facing the dominant institutional forces. Despite being configured within the interweaving of societal forces, within a historically located cultural order, subjectivity is always beyond the processes engaged in its genesis.

As Elliott pointed out:

> Such an analysis leaves no room for the autonomous action of acting subjects, which form
> the starting point for the progressive unfolding of social contradictions (…) this gives the
> impression that the connection between social power and the structure of modern work
> practices affect everyone in an equal manner. It thus completely ignores the intricate ways
> in which repressive work practices and industrial relations are produced, sustained and
> experienced by individuals in various social settings. (Elliott, 1992, p. 77)

The omission of the subject in current psychological and philosophical theories under the influence of "post-structuralist wings" has made it very difficult to understand a definition of a subject who, being subjectively configured within some circumstances emerges as an instance of active resistance to the dominant order within which that emergence takes place. The generative and active character of both subjectivity and subject assumes an important heuristic value in explaining that rupture.

One of the problems of psychoanalysis that limits its advances in the understanding of subjectivity as a cultural-historically engendered phenomenon is that all its classical tendencies represent a closed system, grounded on different hermetic beliefs which are impossible to reconcile with each other into one path capable of being confronted and developed in research and in professional practices. Facing this fact, Bollas defends the need for pluralism.

Bollas sharply states:

> Indeed, a risk faced by remaining in one of these schools (the author is referring to the
> classic school of psychoanalysis) is the scotomatic effect of a canalized vision. Rather than
> listening to the analysand with an open mind, they listen out for something in particular,
> whether it is the castration complex, the drive derivative or the ego position. Such selective
> listening makes psychic transformation in analysis possible so far as the analytical model is
> concerned. (Bollas, 2007, p. 6)

The pluralism claimed by Bollas stressed the limits inherent in psychoanalysis in its dominant practices. The theory of subjectivity has to imply openness to concepts of professional practice and research, and a capacity to change and develop in response to the confrontations that this implies.

3.6 Advancing the Topic of Subjectivity on a Cultural-Historical Basis

Despite the advances related to subjectivity by the aforementioned authors, subjectivity as such has not been the main focus for any of them. Due to this fact, none of these authors was explicitly oriented to subjectivity. Therefore, they made contributions that represent important premises on which to advance this topic from a cultural-historical standpoint. From our perspective, subjectivity implies a new system that characterizes human realities and processes. The advancement of a theory of subjectivity from a cultural-historical standpoint might address the next demands:

1. To advance a new ontological definition of what subjectivity is, making explicit the differences with other concepts that have characterized psychology, which has kept it restricted to individual phenomena. Subjectivity integrates processes and configurations, which are engendered within cultural-social life, but which, at the same time, do not reproduce cultural social life. Being generated within culture, subjectivity does not depart from any universal structured principle. Subjectivity is emancipated from the psyche as a natural system and, at the same time, is a resource for emancipation from the socially dominant institutionalized order;

2. The need to integrate a qualitative side of human phenomena, both social and individual, understanding each of these configured within the other through specific subjective senses resulting from the subjective configuration of the other. Despite one being configured within the other, social and individual subjectivities represent two different sites of subjective productions, maintaining tensional and contradictory relations between them;

3. An attempt to define integrative and dynamic concepts capable of advancing an understanding of how the systems of socio-cultural historical experiences and realities are configured into new kinds of subjective phenomena, whose generative character is the basis for the co-developed system of culture-subjectivity.

Our representation of subjectivity departs from the need to integrate symbolical processes and emotions as dynamic units, which characterize the ontological definition of subjectivity as a qualitative level of human phenomena, both social and individual. Subjectivity is not defined in opposition to objectivity; it refers to the objective character of human phenomena. Subjectivity is a specific quality of human phenomena within culture, and its functioning involves individual and social instances as agents who have active, generative, and creative character.

Our comprehension of subjectivity departs from concepts that embody the use of psychological units, as defended by Dembo and Vygotsky. Vygotsky used the idea of the psychological unit to define different psychological phenomena. At the very end of his work, he defined *perezhivanie* as the unit of consciousness (Vygotsky, 1984). However, the meaning of sense and *perezhivanie* began to overlap, for both concepts were similar in some of their attributes. They were both aimed at integrating consciousness and action through the interplay of dynamically interconnected elements, including those of a cognitive and affective nature.

Unlike Vygotsky's definition of "word sense," our theoretical proposal advances the concept of subjective sense as the most elemental unit that embodies the quality of subjectivity as a system. This unit integrates symbolic processes and emotions in such a way that the unit becomes a new ontological definition. This definition of subjectivity allows the transcendence of dichotomies, such as intellectual–emotional, external–internal and subjective–objective, which has historically characterized psychology. In Soviet psychology, symbolical processes were used in a very narrow way, as signs that mediate psychological functions (Zinchenko, 1993).

Any social experience becomes subjective through the emergence of subjective senses, which represent a subjective side of any living experience. Subjective senses always carry an imaginary character. They do not reflect objective processes of experience; they are individual and social productions based on how social symbolic constructions are experienced by individuals, groups, and institutions, depending on their own subjective configured histories. Subjective senses emerge, embedded in the complex context within which the actual experience is taking place. Attributes like race, gender, age, social status, pathological labels, and, in general, all the social symbolical constructions on which our cultural-social environment is constructed, are embedded in human experiences as subjective senses. These subjective senses are not ruled by the dominant manner in which this social symbolical environment appears in socially dominant discourses, social representations or other social symbolic productions. Only by studying the subjective level of experience, whether social or individual, will we be capable of knowing how individuals, groups and institutions are affected in their different experiences by social symbolical constructions.

Subjective senses have an ephemeral character. They emerge as snapshots of symbolic-emotional flashes that unfold in a chaotic movement, from which subjective configurations emerge as a self-regulative and generative organization of subjective senses. Subjective configurations are dynamic but have relative stability due to the congruency of the subjective senses that they generate. These are different but complementary in their effects on the subjective settings of individuals and groups in their ongoing actions.

The relative stability of the subjective configurations results from the resistance they offer to change in the face of the new processes that result from the actual moment of any ongoing activity. At the same time, this stability is relative, because paths and decisions taken by individuals and groups, as the agents of their own actions, lead to new subjective senses. Any new paths taken by the agents of actions will imply the emergence of new subjective senses, which would integrate, or not, into the subjective configuration in the process of one experience.

Subjective senses always imply different and simultaneous processes; one emotion evokes a perception that turns into a thought, which evokes new emotions that lead to the imagining of new paths in such an endless movement of subjective senses and configurations that characterizes the subjective functioning of individual and social instances. This dynamic, malleable, instantaneous, and transitory character of the subjective senses allows the representation of the "microcosmos of one life" as a unique subjective configuration in the different experiences lived by individuals, groups and other social networks, not as something given forever, but as a different living configuration in which that microcosm takes different forms, highlighting new angles of a lived history. Subjectivity is not a result; it represents an authentic human production that differentiates itself from all the processes engaged in its genesis.

Emotions are intrinsic and decisive in the way that symbolical social constructions appear as singular living processes. As Dewey brilliantly noted:

> It has been noted that human experience is made human through the existence of associations and recollections, which are strained through the mesh of imagination so as to suit the demands of the emotion.... The things most emphasized in imagination as it reshapes experience are things which are absent in reality. (Dewey, 1920, pp. 103–105)

It is impressive how Dewey intuitively integrated within the language of his epoch the unity of the symbolic and imaginary as parts of the same reality, underlying the role of imagination and emotions in the production of our reality. Despite not having explicitly spoken on subjectivity, Dewey's (2016) definition of experience is reflected in some key topics developed below in our proposal on subjectivity from a cultural-historical standpoint. It is impressive how the legacy of Dewey and that of M. Ponty have been crystalized in some of the dominant concepts within the main philosophical principles of their main philosophical affiliation, Pragmatism and Phenomenology, while omitting their important legacy in advancing a cultural-historical representation of human subjectivity.

The concepts assembled in this proposal about subjectivity are organized in such a way that the changes in one of them will imply changes in the others. These concepts represent a broad range of subjective units of different complexity, which are recursively integrated one into another. This theoretical proposal on subjectivity implies a system in movement that is configured by different ways of living different experiences. This is the basis of our definition of subjectivity as a configurational system. One subjective configuration embodies others through specific subjective senses that emerge during its course, and it is this endless process that characterizes subjective functioning.

This definition of subjectivity has the following theoretical implications:

1. Psychical functions, once they are subjectively configured, become self-generative subjective productions. This means that intellectual, motor, or any other operation become sources of subjective senses, transforming psychological functions into motives for their own functioning. Motivation becomes intrinsic to the psychical function itself. Personality, or any other concept used to refer to an individual subjective system, is configured in action, instead of being an a priori determinant of the action. In any case, subjective configurations of personality are responsible for a certain congruency that it is possible to perceive in individual trajectories. Subjectivity as a system is engaged in actions through the subjective configurations of those actions.

2. The definition of psychological functions and actions as subjectively configured processes allows the transcendence of psychological classification based on behavioral/symptomatic entities. This stresses the understanding of behaviors and psychological "pathological entities," such as those formulated via DSM III, IV, V, and other classifications, as subjectively configured processes. This comprehension breaks down any standardization of individuals or groups as carriers of those labels. The study of subjective configurations is always a singular process.

I experienced an example of the consideration of subjective configuration instead of disorders of any kind during research with a 13-year-old male adolescent. In one of the sessions, the teenager, who was trying to solve a problem used as a research tool, suddenly turned toward me in a very disrespectful way, shouting aggressively that the task he was doing was meaningless and absurd. After this episode, he left the classroom, pulling the door violently. Once the session had finished, I found him seated alone outside the classroom. I gently approached and asked: "Why were you so angry with me if I always treat you in a very respectful way?" As a reaction, the teenager began to cry in a very uncontrollable way, saying he was ashamed because he felt that he would fail in the task, making all his classmates laugh at him.

Subjective senses generated at that moment in our conversation had the same origin as those that configured his aggressive reaction during the research session. However, they were expressed in different ways in different contexts. In both cases, the aggressive reaction and his extreme sensitive reaction to my affective approach to him, these reactions were generated subjective senses related to his lack of affection, his lack of a social place in the classroom, his insecurity and anxiety related to social evaluation. These factors configured a theoretical explanation completely different to descriptive levels in use by psychology, for example, to classify him as an aggressive personality. The same subjective configuration, from which emerge low esteem, insecurity, fear, and shame in one context, was the source of completely different feelings in the other context, communication being the main device of that change. This example, as with many others discussed in our line of research (Goulart, 2013; Rossato, 2009; Bezerra, 2014), demonstrates that behaviors in educative work should be understood, not by their immediate contents, but by their subjective configurations.

Any human motivation understood as subjective configuration is dynamic, variable, and dependent on context; it is impossible to judge the motivation for one behavior by its explicit content. There are no motivational forces that can be understood outside the dynamic network of processes represented by the subjective configurations of one concrete experience.

3. Individual and social actions are simultaneously configured in individuals and in social scenarios within which individual actions take place, and are in tension with one another. The subjective system is not the actor of its own configurations; the actors are the individuals and social agents that actively and reflexively create their own paths, taking their own decisions during their experiences. The relevance of the concept of subject is stressed by Frosh as follows: "(…) human subjects may be ´socially constructed', but from that constructed position they exert choices which are never quite reducible to the forces that constructed them in the first place" (Frosh, 2002, p. 3).

The definition of individual and social subjects is essential to understand subjectivity from a cultural-historical standpoint. The subjective impacts of the paths, decisions, and plans of the subject's ongoing activities, whether social or individual, do not result from his/her own conscious assumptions, but from the flux of subjective senses that are configured during the action, embodying the subject's action beyond any conscious intention. Conscious and unconscious, in this theoretical account, are not two separated instances; they are processes organized in two different and simultaneous moments that define two different sets of the same system. The subject of the action and the subjective configuration of the subject's action are configured by each other in such a process that transcends conscious representations and intentions.

The emphasis on the subject leads to another distinctive attribute of this theoretical proposal; the subject's actions are always engaged within systems of communication and social networks of relations. Being part of a social subjective configuration is irreducible to the individual configurations of those who interact within those systems of communication.

4.   Overcoming the split between social and individual processes.

The proposal of subjectivity defended in this paper allows an advance in the comprehension of social reality, not as a blending of external influences acting on the individuals, but as multiple symbolical constructions subjectively configured in social and individual instances. The institutionalized social order exists within the living dynamic networks of individuals, groups and institutions, and is sensitive to the new forms of subjectivation generated in these networks. Subjectivity is not reduced to the individuals; it is a phenomenon that integrates all human reality, whether social or individual.

The intermingled configurations of social and individual subjectivities have been developed by me elsewhere (González Rey, 2014, 2015, 2017). My focus here lies in the fact that subjectivity, from this cultural-historical standpoint, is far from being reduced to any kind of individual intra-psychical apparatus or structure. Subjectivity's functioning and genesis is always in process and tension within the social networks. These networks' subjective configurations, in turn, are a source of subjective senses for individuals.

3.7   Some Final Remarks

Throughout the development of psychology, the topic of subjectivity has been a peripheral concept. However, as discussed above, different authors with different theoretical approaches have highlighted ideas and concepts that, taken together, represent an important premise for advancing toward a theory of subjectivity within a cultural-historical approach. In fact, subjectivity has largely been overlooked by philosophy, psychology, and the social sciences.

Subjectivity, from a cultural-historical standpoint, has an integrative function regarding the taxonomy of concepts traditionally used by psychology. At the same time, the definition of subjectivity proposed here permits an understanding of the individual subjective processes as part of cultural social realities, both of which are reciprocally configured.

This cultural-historical proposal about subjectivity essentially differs from all versions of psychoanalysis, among other things, by the fact that it recognizes human motivations as inseparable from symbolic processes and constructions. This makes it possible to advance a definition of human motivation in constant movement as an intrinsic part of current actions, performances and relations. Human motivation is intrinsic to the definition of subjectivity proposed in this paper.

This definition of subjectivity allows a transcending of the classical patterns of behavioral disorders, dysfunctional personalities or families, and psychopathological definitions on which the traditional individual and descriptive psychologies have operated. Subjectivity opens a new path to relate social symbolical productions with individuals in such a way that these two instances preserve their generative character and their dynamics. Nonetheless, social and individual subjectivities are configured one into the other through subjective senses which, embodying the other level of subjectivity, are themselves produced by the subjective configurations generated by each of these subjectivities.

The paper emphasizes the need to open a dialogue with authors from different perspectives who are advancing the cultural-historical definition of subjectivity by other means. Subjectivity, as defined in this paper, is configured within social-symbolical, institutional and social networks, including power relations and structures of power at macro- and micro-social levels, the impacts of which on society and individuals have to be defined through the subjective configurations of individuals and social instances. Subjectivity never results directly from any social and political attributes of social functioning.

References

Abuljanova, K. A. (1973). *O Subjekt psykjicheskoi deyatelnosti* [On the subject of psychical activity]. Moscow: Nauka.

Bezerra, M. S. (2014). Dificuldades de aprendizagem e subjetividade: Para além das representações hegemônicas do aprender [Learning difficulties and subjetivity: Beyond hegemonic representations of leraning]. Masters dissertation. Retrieved from: http://repositorio.unb.br/handle/10482/17772.

Bollas, C. (2007). *The Freudian moment*. United Kingdom: Karnac.

Cassirer, E. (1953). *Language and myth*. New York: Dove Publications.

Castoriadis, C. (1995). Logic, imagination, reflection. In A. Elliott & S. Frosh (Eds.), *Psychoanalysis in context* (pp. 15–35). United Kingdom: Routledge.

Danziger, K. (1997). *Naming the mind: How psychology founds its language*. United Kingdom: Sage.

Dembo, T. (1993). Thoughts on qualitative determinants in psychology: A methodological study. *Journal of Russian and East European Psychology, 31*(6), 15–70.

Dewey, J. (1920). *Reconstruction in philosophy*. New York: Henry Holt & Company.

Dewey, J. (2016). *Experience and nature*. New York: Dover Publications.

Elliott, A. (1992). *Social theory and psychoanalysis in transition*. United Kingdom: Blackwell.

Fakhrutdinova, L. R. (2010). On the phenomenon of "Perezhivanie". *Journal of Russian and East European Psychology, 48*(2), 31–47. https://doi.org/10.2753/RPO1061-0405480203.

Fleer, M., & Quinones, G. (2013). An assessment of perezhivanie: Building and assessment pedagogy for, with and of early childhood science learning. In D. Currigim, R. Gunstone, & A. Jones (Eds.), *Valuing assessment in science education: Pedagogy, curriculum, policy* (pp. 231–247). Dordrecht: Springer.

Foucault, M. (1987). *A Arqueologia do Saber* [The archaeology of knowledge]. Rio de Janeiro: Forense Universitaria.

Frosh, S. (2002). *After words*. New York: Palgrave.

Frosh, S. (2010). *Psychoanalysis outside the clinic: Interventions in psychosocial studies*. United Kingdom: Pallgrave Macmillan.

González Rey, F. (2002). *Sujeto y Subjetividad: un enfoque histórico-cultural* [Subject and subjectivity: A historical–cultural approach]. Thomson: México D.F.

González Rey, F. (2009). Historical relevance of Vygotsky's work: Its significance for a new approach to the problem of subjectivity in psychology. *Outlines: Critical Practical Studies, 11,* 59–73.

González Rey, F. (2011). A re-examination of defining moments in Vygotsky0s work and their implications for his continuing legacy. *Mind, Culture, & Activity, 18,* 257–275. https://doi.org/10.1080/10749030903338517.

González Rey, F. (2014a). Advancing further the history of soviet psychology: Moving forward from dominant representations in western and soviet psychology. *History of Psychology, 17*(1), 60–78. https://doi.org/10.1037/a0035565.

González Rey, F. (2014b). Human motivation in question: Discussing emotions, motives, and subjectivity from a cultural-historical standpoint. *Journal for the Theory of Social Behaviour, 45*(4), 419–439. https://doi.org/10.1111/jtsb.12073.

González Rey, F. (2015). A new path for the discussion of social representations: Advancing the topic of subjectivity from a cultural-historical standpoint. *Theory & Psychology, 25*(4), 494–512. https://doi.org/10.1177/0959354315587783.

González Rey, F. (2016). Advancing the topics of social reality, culture, and subjectivity from a cultural-historical standpoint: Moments, paths, and contradictions. *Journal of Theoretical and Philosophical Psychology, 6*(6), 175–189. https://doi.org/10.1037/teo0000045.

González Rey, F. (2017). Advances in subjectivity from a cultural-historical perspective: Unfoldings and consequences for cultural studies today. In M. Fleer, F. Gonzalez Rey, & N. Veresov (Eds.), *Perezhivanie, Emotions & Subjectivity: Advancing the Vygotsky's legacy.* Melbourne: Springer.

Goulart, D. M. (2013). *Institucionalização, subjetividade e desenvolvimento humano: abrindo caminhos entre educação e saúde mental* [Institutionalization, subjectivity and human development: Opening new paths between education and mental health]. Masters dissertation, University of Brasília. Retrieved from http://repositorio.unb.br/handle/10482/14958.

Holzkamp, K. (1991). Societal and Individual Life Processes. In C. Tolman & W. Maiers (Eds.), *Critical psychology: Contributions to an historical science of the subject* (pp. 50–61). Cambridge: Cambridge University Press.

Leontiev, A. A. (1984). The productive career of Aleksei Nikolaevich Leontiev. *Soviet Psychology, 13,* 6–56.

Lomov, B. F. (1978). Kategorii obtscheniya i deyatelnosti v psykjologii [The categories of communication and activity in psychology]. *Voprocy Filosofii* [Questions of Philosophy], *8,* 34–47.

Mitchel, M. (2016). Finding the "prism": Understanding Vygotsky's perezhivanie as an ontogenetic unit of child consciousness. *International Journal in Early Chilhood Education, 7,* 5–33.

Moscovici, S. (1967). Communication processes and the properties of language. In L. Berkowitz (Ed.), *Advances in experimental social psychology* (Vol. 3, pp. 225–270). New York: Academic Press.

Parker, I. (2011). *Lacanian psychoanalysis: Revolutions in subjectivity.* United Kingdom: Routledge.

Prigogine, I. (2004). ¿Tan solo una ilusión? Una exploración del caos al orden [Just an illusion? An exploration from chaos to order]. Barcelona: Tusquet Editores

Rossato, M. (2009). O movimento da subjetividade na superação das dificuldades de aprendizagem [The movement of subjectivity in the overcoming of learning disabilities]. Doctoral thesis, University of Brasília. Retrieved from: http://repositorio.unb.br/bitstream/10482/8800/1/2009_Mariste laRossato.pdf.

Shotter, J. (1995). Dialogical psychology. In J. A. Smith, R. Harre, & L. Van Langenhove (Eds.), *Rethinking psychology.* United Kingdom: Sage Publications.

Tajfel, H. (1965). Report of the conference in Frascati. *Social Sciences Information, 4,* 190–200.

Tolstyx, N. N. (2008). The formation of personality as the subject of development. *Voprocy Psykjologii, 5,* 134–140.

Veresov, N. (2017). The concept of *perezhivanie* in cultural-historical theory: Content and contexts. In M. Fleer, F. Gonzalez Rey, & N. Veresov (Eds.), *Perezhivanie, emotions & subjectivity: Advancing the Vygotsky's legacy*. Melbourne: Springer.

Vygotsky, L. S. (1971). *The psychology of art*. Cambridge: MIT Press.

Vygotsky, L. S. (1984). Krisis cemi let [The crisis at age seven]. In A. V. Zaporozhets (Ed.), *Sabraniye Sochinenii* (Vol. 5, pp. 376–385). Moscow: Pedagoguika.

Vygotsky, L. S. (1987). Thinking and Speech. In R. Rieber & A. Carton (Eds.), *The collected works of L. S. Vygotsky* (Vol. 1, pp. 43–287). New York: Plenum Press.

Westphal, M. (1999). Hermeneutics as Epistemology. In J. Greco & E. Sosa (Eds.), *The Blackwell guide to epistemology* (pp. 415–435). London: Blackwell Publisher.

Yasnitsky, A. (2009). *Vygotsky circle during the decade of 1931–1941: Toward an integrative science of mind, brain and education* (Unpublished doctoral dissertation). University of Toronto, Toronto, Canada.

Yasnitsky, A. (2012). Revisionist revolution in Vygotskian science: Toward cultural-historical gestalt psychology. *Journal of Russian & East European Psychology, 50*, 3–15. https://doi.org/ 10.2753/RPO1061-0405500400.

Yasnitsky. (2016). El arquetipo de la psicología soviética: del estalinismo de los años 1930 a la "ciencia estalinista" de nuestros días [The archetype of Soviet psychology: From the stalinism of the 1930s to the stalinist science of our days]. In: A. Yasnitsky, R. Van Der Ver, E. Aguilar, & L. Garcia (Eds.), Vygotski revisited: una historía crítica de su context y legado [Vygotsky revisited: A critical history of his context and legacy] (pp. 39–66). Buenos Aires, Argentina: Miño y Dávila Editores.

Zavershneva, E. (2016). El camino a la libertad: Vygotski en 1932 [The path to freedrom: Vygotsky in 1932]. In A. Yasnitsky, & R. Van der Veer (Eds.), Vygotsky revisitado: una historia crítica de su contexto y legado [Revisionist revolution in Vygotsky studies: the state of art]. España: Miño y Dávila Editores.

Zavershneva, E. (2010). The Vygotsky's familiar archive: New findings. Notebooks, notes and scientific journals of L. S. Vygotsky (1912–1934). *Journal of Russian and East European Psychology, 48*(1), 34–65.

Zinchenko, V. P. (1993). Kulturno-Istorisheskaya Psykjologia: Onyt amplifikatsii [Cultural-historical psychology: The experience of amplification]. *Voprocy Psykjologii, 4*, 5–19.

Fernando González Rey was a Full Professor of the Faculty of Education and Health Sciences of the University Centre of Brasília (Brazil) and Senior Associate Professor of the Faculty of Education of the University of Brasília (Brazil). He obtained his Ph.D. qualification at the Institute of General and Pedagogic Psychology of Moscow. He also obtained the title of Doctor in Science from the Institute of Psychology of the Sciences Academy of Moscow. His research interests focused on subjectivity, education, health, and psychology from a cultural-historical approach. Key recent publications are: (1) Cultural-Historical and Critical Psychology: Common Ground, Divergences and Future Pathways (Ed., 2020, Springer), (2) Subjectivity within cultural-historical approach: theory, methodology, and research (Ed., 2019, Springer), (3) González Rey, F. (2019). Subjectivity in debate: some reconstructed philosophical premises to advance its discussion in psychology. Journal for the Theory of Social Behaviour, 49, 212–234, and (4) González Rey, F. (2019). Methodological and epistemological demands in advancing the study of subjectivity from a cultural-historical standpoint, Culture & Psychology, 26(3), pp. 562–577.

Chapter 4
A Cultural-Historical Theory of Human Subjectivity

Ole Dreier

Abstract González Rey's highly original cultural-historical theory of subjectivity is the pinnacle of his scientific work. This chapter, first, briefly presents the background inspirations for the theory. Second, the theory is presented. Its core concepts and their interrelationships in the theory are characterized. The arguments behind the conceptual choices and definitions are laid out and it is made clear why and how González Rey regards a cultural-historical theory of subjectivity to be the cornerstone in psychological theorizing. The main advantages of the theory are mentioned as well as the key issues in cultural-historical theorizing in psychology it is aimed at resolving. In the third section of this chapter, some steps in the future development of the theory are proposed. They are inspired by my theoretical work on subjects in social practices based on the tradition of a science of the subject founded by Holzkamp. And they are presented in the course of going deeper into, and discussing, three areas in González Rey's theory. First, his position on psychic functions and subjectivity in action; second, issues about subjectivity in relation to culture, social reality, and social practice; and, third, his position on individual transcendence and critical theorizing.

4.1 Background

González Rey developed an outstanding cultural-historical theory of subjectivity over the last approximately twenty years and presented it in a series of publications (González Rey, 2009, 2014a, 2014b, 2015, 2016a, 2016b, 2017a, 2017b, 2018, 2019a, 2019b, 2019c, 2020; González Rey & Mitjánz Martínez, 2017; González Rey et al., 2018). But the roots of his theory go back to the beginning of his academic career.

He defended his doctoral thesis in the Soviet Union in 1979. It was about moral ideals, self-evaluation, motivation, and creativity. These concepts address higher

O. Dreier (✉)
University of Copenhagen, Copenhagen, Denmark
e-mail: ole.dreier@psy.ku.dk

order psychological formations which are crucial in understanding human development and the integrative role of human personality in relation to elementary psychological functions. His approach was profoundly inspired by the strong tradition of Soviet cultural-historical psychology in the work of Vygotsky, Boschovich, Rubinstein, and many others. He was deeply involved in discussions about this tradition and in its development. But his critiques and his theoretical resolutions are as relevant for theoretical psychology as a whole.

González Rey adopted the insight in Soviet cultural-historical psychology that the psychic processes of cognition, thinking, emotion, etc., do not function as firmly bounded and fixed elements. They interact and hang together in a systemic manner in the functioning of the human mind. They are also inextricably involved in the ongoing activity of a human being. So, he does not conceptualize a purely internal functioning of the human psyche—as in the traditional basic notion of the psyche, mind, or soul in religion and philosophy—which is merely triggered by an external stimulus and ends in launching a behavior. He is also critical of the prevalent tendency to prioritize cognition over emotion in the functioning of the mind and of the ensuing rationalism with the scientist and all-encompassing knowledge as guiding stars of individual human development. In addition, he is critical of Leontiev's version of activity theory conceiving a subject's psychic processes as his or her tools in his or her activity directed at an object. Lomov's Habermasian distinction between a subject's instrumental activity and communication between subjects, hence, inspired him—though, ordinarily, tools and other subjects are combined in a subject's activity. Finally, González Rey is critical of the widespread—and, in a cultural-historical approach, deeply paradoxical—trend not to include the sociocultural worlds and societies in theorizing about human psychological processes. Instead, he insists that a cultural-historical psychology must become a historically and culturally specific psychology.

4.2   Subjectivity as a Cultural-Historical Formation

Having mentioned the main backgrounds, in the legacy of Soviet psychology, of introducing human subjectivity as the core concept in González Rey's cultural-historical psychological theory, we turn to the main features of his theory of human subjectivity.

Subjectivity is traditionally regarded as an attribute in the mind, mostly as the subject of experience. Maintaining that the human mind unfolds across time in the activity of the subject, González Rey regards the subject as an agent and subjectivity and agency as inextricably intertwined. "Our relationship with our surroundings always implies that living activities existing within the intertwined flow of many unfolding avenues open themselves during the course of activity. This flow of endless avenues that characterize the realization of human activities implies the emergence, change, and development of thoughts, feelings, and other psychological functions" (González Rey, 2016a, pp. 178–179). Overcoming objective determinism is, therefore, a precondition for noticing and conceptualizing subjectivity.

Moreover, González Rey insists that human subjectivity is a cultural-historical formation. Social and cultural realities hold important subjective qualities in the complex symbolic networks of human cultures, such as symbolic social constructions of discourses, social representations, normative systems, and social symbolic institutional realities of religion, morals, science, and policy. These human productions establish sociocultural subjective realities. Subjectivity is, hence, intrinsic to the cultural character of human social life and culture incorporates a social subjectivity in relation to which the formation of individual subjectivity unfolds. The subjective character of both social and individual phenomena transcends the dichotomy between social facts and individual subjective processes and calls for focusing on the blending of social and individual subjectivities. Because individual subjectivity is created in culturally and historically located symbolic practices, it also changes from one generation to the next.

Recognizing the cultural, social, and historical genesis of individual subjectivity, González Rey defines subjective senses as the primary subjective processes of individual subjects. An individual subject encountering cultural symbols in his or her social, cultural-historical experiences combines them with his or her emotions in creating his or her individual subjective senses. This occurs in the course of his or her actions in concrete social networks where his or her emotions and cultural symbols continuously interweave. The concepts in González Rey's theory of subjectivity are, thus, about units of a psychological system engaged in ongoing human activity, and a subject's action is not reduced to being a result of his or her prior conscious intention. A human subjective sense, and with it the formation of human subjectivity, has a sociocultural quality—rather than a general natural quality—because it emerges as the subjective quality of a subject's social experiences.

According to González Rey, human subjectivity refers to processes of a higher order than psychic functions as traditionally defined. Inspired by Vygotsky and Bozhovich, he regards the processes of subjectivity as a new subjective psychological formation. The processes of individual subjective senses are functional units in a new subjective system rather than functional elements operating as homunculi in the psyche. Quoting Vygotsky, he states: "'Thinking itself became the thinker of thoughts. Thinking was divorced from the full vitality of life, from the motives, interest and inclinations of the thinking individual' (1987, p. 50). Vygotsky understood in that final moment of his work that psychological functions are functions of the subject" (González Rey, 2015, p. 505). The formation and dynamics of human subjectivity orchestrate the systemic functioning of human psychological processes. A subject's emotions and subjective senses evoke and conduct the psychic functions of perception, thinking, memory, etc., as auxiliary processes of the subject. The theory, thereby, moves beyond the rationalist impersonal grasp of cognition and consciousness in mainstream psychology.

Subjective senses are instantaneous emotional-symbolic units characterizing the flux of human experiences as life is lived subjectively. In the course of their endless movements, dynamic chains of subjective senses integrate to form subjective configurations. These subjective configurations become a self-regulating organization of subjective senses and they are relatively stable due to the congruency of the integrated subjective senses. They also become a generative open subjective system which is a source of new subjective senses in ongoing human activity. Subjective senses and configurations are inseparable aspects in the ongoing activity of individual subjects where the fleeting subjective senses and the more stable subjective configurations have different complementary impacts. To González Rey, "This system of subjective senses and configurations in process is what is defined ...as subjectivity" (2014b, p. 434). It includes the subjective configuration and dynamics of experience and psychic functions. An individual subject configures the social symbolic realities of social subjectivity he or she encounters—such as gender, race, beliefs, norms, and other social symbolic productions—in singular ways in his or her subjective senses and configurations.

An individual's subjective configurations integrate the subjective senses of his or her past experiences. Together with current subjective senses, the open dynamic system of subjective configurations establishes a mixture of stability and fluidity across a large time scale in the functioning of the individual subject. The subjective senses and configurations are able to comprise the present, past, and future of a human life due to their complex, interweaving, and malleable character. The integration in subjective configurations of the many persons, situations, and historical moments of an individual's history is an imaginary integration. Based on his conception of subjectivity, González Rey reconsiders the concept of personality arguing that personality is a dynamic system of subjective configurations expressing the most relevant individual experiences as they are subjectively configured. It represents the historical dimension in an individual subject's current action where it constrains the movements of subjective senses in ongoing experiences. But it is also a living system configured in a specific manner in the subjective configuration of action. This stability of functioning is not due to the causal effect of fixed universal traits but subjectively created and configured. Indeed, subjective stability is established without a fixed structure and with shifting and developing states of subjective coherence and insight.

González Rey regards subjectivity as primarily a motivational system because social realities and experiences can only engage individual actors when they are subjectively configured. He defines motivation as a subjectively configured process and a specific quality of the subjectively configured system. The motivational character of a human experience is defined together with other subjective senses in a complex subjective configuration of senses. So, a motive does not relate directly to a given object. It is an integrative expression of subjectivity as a system of subjective configurations. And it is the ongoing subjective configuration of an action which is not given as an intra-psychic reality prior to that action.

The emergence of diverse subjective senses with experiences from different times and places in the subjective configuration of a current activity is an imaginary subjective process. The malleability, speed, and dynamic character of subjective senses makes it impossible for conscious operations to apprehend such a generative process and for conscious intentions to exhaust such complex subjective configurations. The generative character of subjective configurations rather results from emotions embedded in them. So, subjectivity is a motivated system in which imagination is

the cornerstone of human creations. Imagination and fantasy are subjective qualities associated with all psychological processes emerging in a subjectively configured activity and subjective senses always have an imaginary character. Imagination
transforms and integrates images into concepts and generates new concepts leading
to new models of what is thinkable and new imaginative creations. Imagination is,
thus, intrinsic to the creation of new cultural realities and new forms of subjectivation.
Objects in social reality also incorporate a subjective, imaginative creation because
they are invented by psychological processes of emotion, fantasy, and imagination.
And the subjective potential for critique and change is grounded in subjective imagination and dealing with contradictions. Indeed, to González Rey, "Subjectivity is
not the reaction of our mind to a given world and reality; it is part of the complex
reality lived by human beings not as reactive beings but as creative generative ones"
(2014b, p. 432). His theoretical position emphasizing imagination and creative transcendence opposes positions of adaptation and determinism. The generative character of human subjectivity makes an individual able to transform him- or herself
and the world instead of just adapting to it. The fact that individual subjectivity
is subjectively configured, underlines the anti-determinist theoretical stance on the
relationship between individual subjectivity and cultural-historical social practice.
Referring to Dewey's similar position on the generative character of subjectivity
due to imagination and emotion, González Rey regards them as the "qualitative
expression of a new type of psychological phenomena typical of human beings"
and characterizes his position as "a definition of the subject as a subversive singular
position of a person or a group within a dominant social reality" (2015, p. 504). "Subjectivity is a subversive concept, because its definition implies continuous resistance
to and confrontation with the social hegemonic status quo throughout the history of
mankind, opening a theoretical pathway to explain this resistance" (González Rey,
2017b, p. 507).

4.3 To Be Continued

González Rey's cultural-historical theory of subjectivity holds many important, original, and inspiring insights. The open processual qualities of the psychological
subjective system in action readdress what was couched as a relationship between
consciousness and activity in a new productive way. It introduces a much more
concrete grasp of psychological processes unfolding in ongoing human, cultural-
historical activities instead of as fixed general properties in the psyche. This major
accomplishment illuminates the complex, dynamic, uncertain, unique, and contradictory character of the individual psyche and subjectivity. It leads to a new understanding of psychological processes and of the social functioning of human subjects
captured with new core concepts and redefinitions of other concepts. It is now up to
other researchers to continue this line of theorizing, all the more so because—in a
cultural-historical approach—a theory is an open system in development fueled by
new cultural, social practices. My arguments below are, first of all, directed at those

who are involved in carrying this work further. They rest on my theorizing of subjects in social practices (e.g., Dreier, 2008, 2016, 2019, 2020) in the tradition of a science of the subject founded by Holzkamp (1983, Schraube & Osterkamp, 2013). And they are proposals for opening up, broadening, and developing González Rey's critical, cultural-historical theory of human subjectivity to become more robustly grounded in social practice and, thereby, more powerful.

4.4   Psychic Functions and Subjectivity in Action

In González Rey's theory, subjectivity is a specifically human integrating formation distinguished from other psychic processes which it draws on as resources. Emotional responses to cultural symbols lead to the formation of subjective senses and subjectivity. Emotions, thus, have a generative capacity. He often writes that emotional responses to cultural symbols are based on experiences. The complete chain of processes should then be: cultural symbol, experience, emotion, sense, and configuration. But the theory does not specify the psychic and/or subjective nature of experience. González Rey's conception of emotions as self-generative processes inseparable from imagination is inspired by Vygotsky's (1971) work on the psychology of creative art. He sees it as an opening toward unpredictable, uncontrollable, emotional, and unconscious processes instead of predictable, controllable, rational, intellectual, and conscious processes. Recently, he added the body and embodiment to human subjectivity as a permanent source of sensations and emotions (González Rey, 2019c, p. 97).

To González Rey, the deeply interrelated processes of the human psyche and subjectivity are irreducible to one another due to their different genesis and functioning. Thus, a human perception is only a cognitive process, but it becomes a subjective process when emotions are involved as symbolic devices in it. A blending then occurs in which the emotional-symbolic has the upper hand: "Subjective senses always imply different and simultaneous processes; one emotion evokes a perception that turns into a thought, which evokes new emotions that lead to the imagining of new paths in …an endless movement of subjective senses and configurations" (González Rey, 2017b, p. 514). The dynamic, emotional-symbolic subjective senses orchestrate the subjective process which is not conducted by intellectual meanings and constructions. There is a functional primacy of subjective, emotional-symbolic processes using other psychic functions as subsidiary tools, and these other functions only become generative by being involved in the subjective system. Thus, in the subjective system imagination—not memory—extends the time dimension of the emotional, subjective senses allowing experiences from other times and places to emerge in imaginary productions in current configurations of activity. "The way in which experiences lived by persons in different places and temporal moments emerge through diverse subjective senses as part of today's subjective configurations of human performance represent an imaginary and subjective production" (González Rey, 2015, p. 505). Imagination also "transforms and integrates images into concepts, and generates new concepts that lead to new models of the thinkable, turning emotions into symbolic processes... Imagination is intrinsic to the creation of new cultural realities in a path in which new forms of subjectivation are continuously emerging" (González Rey, 2017b, p. 511). Imagination is not controlled by thinking seen as a process of instrumental logic—though I would argue that a different, co-creative notion of thinking as an analytic-synthetic process is also involved. Only the core properties of the subjective system are able to relate to the world of cultural symbols while, in themselves, other psychic processes are detached from the cultural world. The theory expresses an uneasy relation to cognitive and intellectual processes as merely formal and logical or only involved as auxiliary processes conducted by emotions and imaginations in a subjective system where motivation is subjective while thinking is not. González Rey calls them "intellectual operations" (2018, p. 12) and states that, "Pure cognitions only characterize formal activities without emotional involvement" (González Rey, 2016b, p. 313). However, the belief that a psychic function is an isolated element with its own general, internal essence, is a product of the methodology of variable-based experimental research. Such a notion of psychic functions must be carefully distinguished from understanding both psychic and subjective processes as variably involved in and contributing to the ongoing processes of a subject in his or her ongoing activity in the world (Dreier, 2019). All psychic functions and subjective processes must then be reconsidered accordingly. Emotional processes then not always hold the chair of the conductor of the process as a whole. That varies with the varying dynamics of the ongoing processes and activities. González Rey, sometimes, comes close to such an idea (e.g., González Rey, 2016b, pp. 306 and 311; 2018, p. 12) while, at other times, he holds back, in reaction against the prevailing notion of the predominance of cognition in psychology. The generativity of the subjective system is then only provided by emotions and subjective senses instead of by the varying dynamic functioning of the system as a whole.

González Rey regards psychic functions as fixed general processes. But the phylogeny of psychic processes and the emergence of specifically human psychic processes and subjectivity show that human psychic processes are involved in, and contribute to, the ongoing processes of a subject in varying ways in his or her ongoing activity in a social world (Holzkamp, 1983; Dreier, 2019). The phylogenetic evolution of psychic properties uncovers a transformation from elementary, fixed properties to modifiable properties in varying relations with other properties in an increasingly complex activity in an increasingly complex, changing, and—in human beings—socio-historical world. Human nature, then, holds natural potentials for living by participating in re-producing and changing a society with structural arrangements and cultural formations. Mutually related, specifically human psychic processes of cognition, thinking, memory, needs, emotion, motivation, and consciousness are involved in varying ways in the activity of human subjects in societal practices. This modifiability is the functional basis of human learning. In contrast, González Rey (2020, p. 18) characterizes the evolution of Homo sapiens by a broader use of symbolic devices leading to different kinds of interrelated human activities and forms of sociality. Without addressing the evolution of human psychic processes, he contends that symbolic processes merge with emotions in the formation of human subjectivity and that "subjectivity is emancipated from psyche as a natural system" (González Rey, 2017b, p. 514).

González Rey stresses the shifting ephemeral character of the key phenomena of human subjectivity. This makes it difficult to examine and define them and to capture how they are linked with other processes represented by other concepts in his theory. What, then, does a well-defined concept mean? How can we avoid committing violence on the phenomena we study by using a concept? And how can the idea of an accumulation of a general core of attributes be maintained as implied in the persistence of earlier configurations? A more robust anchoring of human subjectivity in social practice may strengthen our interpretations and determinations.

4.5   Culture, Social Reality, and Social Practice

In González Rey's theory, the relationship between individual subjects and the world is defined as a relationship between individual subjectivity and social subjectivity. It is not a relationship between a subject and an object in the world but within the quality of subjectivity as it exists in the world. Subjectivity is defined as the objective character of the specifically human, cultural life because it is intrinsic to the cultural character of human social life. This is a highly unusual position in psychology. It also differs from theories of discourse, social construction, and social representation in psychology which, to González Rey, focus on social subjectivity but reduce individual subjectivity to those social constructions. Social representations do not just flow into the individual subject but are "subjectively configured and reconfigured during the subjects' ongoing actions in a process in which persons, actions, and social contexts are reciprocally configured, one into the other, leading to different subjective configurations in each of those instances" (González Rey, 2015, p. 505). Indeed, he vigorously opposes any notion of external determinism of individual subjectivity— to the point, I would say, of evading other social realities than the symbolic ones and, thereby, "rescuing" a generative, imagining individual subject. According to the theory, the symbolic is all that human subjects sense in the world, also in their creative imaginations. It is then all that matters in the world to human subjects. This makes human subjectivity too free-floating, reduced, and arbitrary. González Rey's already broad conception of human subjectivity must become even broader.

To González Rey, culture and society are symbolic realities. Institutional orders, race, gender, illness, etc.—or at least what is relevant about them for psychology— are aspects of a symbolic cultural order. Living in a society is living in a symbolic order. These symbolic realities intermingle with "politics, education, health systems, religions, science and other institutionalized forms of social life" (2018, p. 4). But the social subjectivity of "normative systems of discourses and representations (…) in different ways rule the institutional systems of society and the diversity of social practices that take place in society" (2014b, p. 432). What else characterizes social practices and a society recedes into the background in this theory of human subjectivity. However, societies and social practices are too "unruly" to be ruled by symbolic realities—and so are cultures. The symbolic cultural order is not a homogenous consensual tradition, especially not in a glocalized world of cross-cutting cultures. The social subjectivity in relation to which individual subjects generate their subjective senses and configurations is ambiguous, contested, and contradictory. It offers no clear-cut and robust anchoring of the configuration of individual subjectivity. This affects its guidance of individual activity and generativity.

This issue about the relation between individual subjectivity and social realities/practices resurfaces in González Rey's core concept of emotion. It is not clear what emotions are about, why they matter for individuals, and what is at stake for individuals in having them. This elusiveness tips the dynamic balance in the formation of individual subjectivity towards the significance of the social subjectivity of given symbolic orders. Likewise, imaginary subjective productions are the core characteristics of individual subjective generativity. Referring to Castoriadis, González Rey regards imagination as unbridled and defunctionalized. But this reduces the significance of the world for a subject's generative imagining to getting at a distance from it rather than being inspired by it. Imagination as mind wandering and distraction can then not be distinguished from imagination as envisioning events and other possible situations and realities (Newby-Clarke & Thavendran, 2018). It is also hard to believe that imagination can be completely unbridled. How can imagination be unaffected by a subject's earlier life and responses to restrictions and problems or by his or her current aspirations?

González Rey's theory, and empirical projects based on it, primarily include society and social practices as social realities and empirical facts but not as concepts integrated with the theory of subjectivity. Conceptually, the theory does not say much about the cultural-historical, social practices in which the psychological phenomena are investigated in research projects based on it. That is surprising in a cultural-historical approach. In fact, González Rey launches another subject–object split instead of the dichotomy he wants to overcome with his theory: "(T)he subjective character of social and individual phenomena allows the overcoming of the dichotomy between social facts and individual subjective processes. Social realities and individual psychical processes are replaced by a new type of human reality, the subjective one, which integrates both into a new qualitative level" (2018, pp. 6–7). They are linked subjectively but not as parts of a common social reality in which the formation and circulation of symbols occurs in social practices. We must ask what is to count as the interface between subject and world in an interdisciplinarily grounded conception of human subjectivity—and re-raise this question as the theory develops. Just like we must grasp subjective processes as mattering for a subject's life in a social world, we must theorize what matters in the social world for the lives of individual subjects and how it matters. In González Rey's theory, the question about which aspects have a subjective character overshadows the question about their importance in the lives of human subjects. And it is not clear why human subjects do not, need not, or cannot sense other aspects of the world than the symbolic subjective ones.

The concept of social practice inextricably combines the subject, activity, and the social world in social practice. It comprises the objective as well as the subjective and grounds individual and social subjectivity in practice. Social subjective configurations are important aspects of social practices. The actions of individual subjects are also involved and grounded in ongoing social practices. Highlighting the ongoing dynamic relations between a subject's psychic processes and actions is an important strength in González Rey's theory. But actions are captured too narrowly by not grounding them in social practice. González Rey (2014a) leveled a similar critique at the Soviet cultural-historical psychology, but his theory does not inform us well about how courses of actions are involved in social practices. The links between individual actions and subjective processes are, then, captured one-sidedly. A similar issue characterizes González Rey's conception of imagination and thinking. He states that imaginations may be controlled by later reflections and the "association between imagination and reflective thought is very important in understanding thinking as a subjective function, because imagination represents the creative character of thinking" (González Rey, 2017b, p. 511). Here we see a broader notion of thinking which may be linked more closely with imagination. It could even lead to capturing other subjective qualities and sources of thinking than emotional-symbolic imaginations. But when González Rey defines unbridled, defunctionalized imagination as the generative character of subjectivity, imagination is not spurred by the possibilities—and necessities—of living. And if thinking is merely conceptualized as logical operations, analysis, and prediction, it is not theorized as capturing dynamic relations between aspects in the world in nexuses of social practice, including how these nexuses matter to the subject and how the subject may draw on and affect the dynamic nexuses in his or her actions (Holzkamp 1983). Thus understood, a subject's thinking and imagination may, in different but interrelated ways, address what is possible, can be brought about, is wanted, problematic, and restricting. They may also be involved in a subject's ongoing, varying, and open-ended pursuit in social practice of his or her concerns in a mix of imagining, deliberating, and valuing which involves and combines emotions, thinking, and imagination and is redirected, reconsidered, revalued, and reimagined as the pursuit unfolds.

González Rey warns against the prevalent notion in variable-based psychology of regarding the individual human being as determined by his or her environment and regarding his or her response as an adaptation to a pre-given environment. Instead, he grasps subjectivity nondeterministically by emphasizing the human subject's transcendence of the pre-given world spurred by imagination. But there is a nondeterministic alternative to that idea: The set of conditions in the social world of an individual human subject affords a certain scope of possibilities for acting and living by drawing on some of these possibilities (Holzkamp, 1983). A human subject's relation to his or her world is, then, a relation of possibility. We can even distinguish between conditions in the world which a subject is able to draw on as his or her possibilities and other conditions in relation to which the subject is (presently) in a state of dependence and powerlessness. Likewise, we can capture individual psychological and subjective processes as sources of a subject's influence on his or her worldly affairs.

Moreover, if we do not consider a subject's scope of possibilities, we risk lapsing into moralizing appeals to individual transcendence. And if our theory does not consider equalities and inequalities between the scopes of possibilities of different subjects, it loses a key source of critique. Furthermore, a human subject develops subjective abilities enabling him or her to realize certain possibilities (Holzkamp, 1983). In fact, these abilities turn conditions into possibilities for him or her. But González Rey's theory does not address the formation of subjective abilities. It focuses on the formation of subjective senses and, thus, grasps learning as the production of new subjective senses while it disregards the formation of new abilities.

In addition, as embodied beings, individual subjects always are situated in a local context of social practice. Possibilities, then, present themselves locally to subjects. Their state of mind, psychic/subjective functioning, senses, emotions, observations, etc., have a situated quality too. If we want to capture subjective configurations concretely, we must capture them situatedly. There are, therefore, limits to González Rey's claim that an overall synthesis of an individual's subjective configurations can cover the plurality of experiences of a singular life history.

Social practices hold a, larger or smaller, number of individual subjects and individual human subjects live as participants in social practices (Dreier, 2008, 2016, 2020). Together with their co-participants, they re-produce and change a social practice which they share unequally. This is where their subjective senses and configurations emerge and this is what they are a subjective response to. A society is a dynamic structural arrangement of social practices—a nexus in which these practices and their participants hang together. It also involves an arrangement of dynamic connections between its multiple local social practices. Local contextual practices serve various purposes and their practices are arranged in various ways, e.g., with various positions for participating in them. On their positions in them, individual subjects face different responsibilities, relations of power, contradictions, conflicts, and scopes of possibilities. In relation hereto, they pursue their concerns in this social practice. Individual subjects take part in several, local, contextual practices by moving into and across them. In doing so, they pursue other concerns, or the same concern in other ways, in other social practices together with other co-participants. At any given time in their lives, individual subjects take part in a particular set of local social practices. They conduct their lives, and pursue their concerns, in and across this bundle of social practices. There is a spatial composition to the lives of individual subjects in a structure of social practice across which their possibilities, concerns, etc., vary. Individual lives do not simply unfold and cohere in a dimension of time, as usually assumed in psychology and highlighted in González Rey's theory. Time and space are inseparable in practice. And due to the social arrangements and varying characteristics of social practices, subjects' movements in practice cannot be a mere "flux" (González Rey, 2015, p. 505).

In light of the above, González Rey's core concepts of subjective senses and configurations are not sufficiently grounded in a subject's life in social practice. They fall too much back on the subject him- or herself and hang too much in the air. So, therefore, does their interpretation. Working out the groundedness of subjectivity in practice supports and strengthens our interpretations of it. It makes a person's subjectivity more accessible and comprehensible to him- or herself. By contrast, González Rey regards subjective senses and configurations as ephemeral, fleeting, only visible in a subject's style of expression, and only accessible to a researcher (e.g., 2019b). The practical basis for supporting a particular interpretation over others is conceptually indistinct. So is the basis for characterizing subjects by which particular aspects and nexuses of practice they configure and address and which they do not capture and address, turn upside down, etc.

4.5.1 Individual Transcendence in a Critical Theory

My arguments and proposals so far have implications for considering how González Rey's theory captures individual transcendence and for considering its critical power. In psychology, individual transcendence is regarded as a strictly individual affair with an individual moving beyond his or her given state of development—sometimes also beyond his or her given situation. The individual is the yardstick of his or her transcendence. Vygotsky's (1971) notion of individual transcendence in his psychology of art follows this model. So does González Rey, arguing that how an individual subject senses and configures social subjective configurations, determines his or her transcendence as well as his or her resistance, subversion, or submission to a social order (e.g., 2017a, p. 185). It is then only up to each individual, with his or her history of configurations, whether he or she reacts generatively or adaptively. Indeed, González Rey's reaction against the notions of adaption and determinism in psychology affects his understanding of the generative and creative individual subject. The subject's generativity and creativity act as counterforce against adaptation and determinism. In that sense, subjectivity is "a subversive concept" (González Rey, 2017b, p. 507). But adaptive, restrictive, and suppressive subjectivity then fall out of focus and little is said about them. Important issues for a critical theory of subjectivity are, thereby, lost (Dreier, 2020). Emotions and imaginations are also theorized as creative and generative processes while other qualities of emotions, imaginations, and subjective symbolic processes are not conceptualized. González Rey does write that the generative subjectivity is not always realized and then exists as a potentiality of individual subjects which "might allow (them) to 'invent', to generate new subjective alternatives" (2015, p. 505). Subjectivity is then a potentiality which individuals only realize in their generative moments. In addition, he writes that some subjective productions are "compatible with our processes of institutionalization, development and socialization whereas others qualify as disorders that do not permit the integration of the individuals into a social life nor the development of the self by alternative paths of life" (2017a, p. 185). Human suffering is then also a subjectively configured process generating problematic subjective configurations (González Rey, 2017b, p. 512). And the subject overcomes his or her suffering by generating other subjective senses, configurations, and imaginations. But, again, the generative moments are in focus while the subjectivity of living as a suffering subject or restrictively or in an unchangeable situation are not.

However, the generativity and transcendence of individual subjects does not belong to themselves per se. It hangs together with their participation, with and against various others, in the varying structurally arranged social practices of their ongoing everyday lives. This affords subjects possibilities for generating and transcending these practices and their participation in them. But subjects must also take part in re-producing the practices which form the basis of their lives so that its basis does not collapse. Participation in social practices is a mixture of re-producing and changing, and of developing as an individual participant in and with the scopes of possibilities of his or her changing practices. The significance of the arrangements and positions, scopes of possibilities, conflicts and alliances, concerns, and abilities must then be recognized. It is insufficient to say that "some persons are capable of generating new manners of subjectivation ... whereas others remain submissive" (González Rey, 2017a, p. 185). Subjects' abilities are changeable potentialities. Their scopes of possibilities, alliances, conflicts, and social practices may change, and they may take part in bringing these changes about. And a subject does not overcome the conflicts and instabilities of his or her life and scopes of possibilities by pursuing generative changes of his or her own on the cost of his or her co-participants in their shared practices. The current and possible future influence of an individual subject on what goes on in his or her social practices is strangely absent in psychological theorizing, also of subjectivity. Transcendence then seems too innocent, as if it does not involve and lead to problems and conflicts. It is not only problematic to remain within the present boundaries of restrictive social practices. In the social worlds we know, human subjectivity is problematic in so many ways. A critical theory of subjectivity must guide our comprehension of these problematics.

Generative and critical practices take place in the given world. When subjects opt for "emancipation from the socially dominant institutionalized order" (González Rey, 2017b, p. 514), they do so by taking part in changing the given world. Relating to the world as it is given, is also involved in transcending it. Critical practices relate to the given world without accepting its state of affairs. Critique of a dominating social subjective configuration is part of the practice of transcending it. Subjects do not configure their individual subjective configurations just by relating to social subjective configurations. They are engaged in distinguishing between skewed, problematic, ideological social subjective configurations and others worth preserving and strengthening. That is also the case in the domains of practice where psychologists work. For instance, knowledge and expertise in education and health, learning, and psychotherapy are marked by positioned interests in the particular socio-historical arrangements of these practices with associated social-subjective configurations (Dreier, 2008). Indeed, social and cultural development is not reducible to individual transcendence because "Creative subjects as individuals are inseparable from social and cultural development" (González Rey, 2015, p. 504).

References

Dreier, O. (2008). *Psychotherapy in everyday life*. New York, NY: Cambridge University Press.

Dreier, O. (2016). Conduct of everyday life: Implications for critical psychology. In E. Schraube & C. Højholt (Eds.), *Psychology and the conduct of everyday life* (pp. 15–33). London: Routledge.

Dreier, O. (2019, August 19–23). *Subjectivity and?* Paper presented at the 18th biannual conference of the International Society for Theoretical Psychology, University of Aarhus, Copenhagen.

Dreier, O. (2020). Critical psychology–subjects in situated social practices. In M. Fleer, F. González Rey, & P. E. Jones (Eds.), *Cultural-historical and critical psychology–common ground, divergences and future pathways* (pp. 11–26). Singapore: Springer Nature.

González Rey, F. (2009). Historical relevance of Vygotsky's work: Its significance for a new approach to the problem of subjectivity in psychology. *Outlines: Critical Social Studies, 11*, 59–73.

González Rey, F. (2014a). Advancing further the history of Soviet psychology: Moving forward from dominant representations in Western and Russian psychology. *History of Psychology, 17*(1), 60–78. https://doi.org/10.1037/a0035565.

González Rey, F. (2014b). Human motivation in question: Discussing emotions, motives, and subjectivity from a cultural-historical standpoint. *Journal for the Theory of Social Behaviour, 45*(4), 419–439. https://doi.org/10.1111/jtsb.12073.

González Rey, F. (2015). A new path for the discussion of social representations: Advancing the topic of subjectivity from a cultural-historical standpoint. *Theory & Psychology, 25*(4), 494–512. https://doi.org/10.1177/0959354315587783.

González Rey, F. (2016a). Advancing the topics of social reality, culture, and subjectivity from a cultural-historical standpoint: Moments, paths, and contradictions. *Journal of Theoretical and Philosophical Psychology, 36*(3), 175–189. https://doi.org/10.1037/teo0000045.

González Rey, F. (2016b). Vygotsky's concept of *perezhivanie* in the psychology of art and at the final moment of his work: Advancing his legacy. *Mind, Culture, and Activity, 23*(4), 305–314. https://doi.org/10.1080/10749039.2016.1186196.

González Rey, F. (2017a). Advances in subjectivity from a cultural-historical perspective: Unfoldings and consequences for cultural studies today. In M. Fleer, F. González Rey, & N. Veresov (Eds.), *Perezhivanie, emotions & subjectivity: Advancing Vygotsky's legacy* (pp. 173–193). Singapore: Springer Nature.

González Rey, F. (2017b). The topic of subjectivity in psychology: Contradictions, paths and new alternatives. *Journal for the Theory of Social Behavior, 47*, 502–521. https://doi.org/10.1111/jtsb.1214.

González Rey, F. (2018). Subjectivity and discourse: Complementary topics for a critical psychology. *Culture & Psychology, 24*, 1–17. https://doi.org/10.1177/1354067X18754338.

González Rey, F. (2019a). Subjectivity in debate: Some reconstructed philosophical premises to advance its discussion in psychology. *Journal of the Theory Social Behavior, 49*, 212–234. https://doi.org/10.1111/jtsb.12200.

González Rey, F. (2019b). Methodological and epistemological demands in advancing the study of subjectivity from a cultural-historical standpoint. *Culture & Psychology, 25*, 178–194. https://doi.org/10.1177/1354067X19888185.

González Rey, F. (2019c). A dialogue with Holzkamp on the matter of subjectivity. *Annual Review of Critical Psychology, 16*, 80–101.

González Rey, F. (2020). The rescue of subjectivity from a cultural-historical standpoint. In R. K. Beshara (Ed.), *A critical introduction to psychology* (pp. 9–25). New York: Nova Science Publishers, Inc.

González Rey, F., & Mitjánz Martínez, A. (2017). Epistemological and methodological issues related to the new challenges of a cultural-historical-based psychology. In M. Fleer, F. González Rey, & N. Veresov (Eds.), *Perezhivanie, emotions & subjectivity: Advancing Vygotsky's legacy* (pp. 195–216). Singapore: Springer Nature.

González Rey, F., Mitjanz Martínez, A., & Goulart, D. M. (2018). The topic of subjectivity within cultural-historical approach: Where it has advanced from and where it is advancing to. In F. González Rey, A. Mitjánz Martinez, & D. M. Goulart (Eds.), *Subjectivity within cultural-historical approach: Theory, methodology, research* (pp. 3–19). Singapore: Springer Nature.

Holzkamp, K. (1983). *Grundlegung der Psychologie* [Foundation of psychology]. Frankfurt am Main: Campus Verlag.

Newby-Clarke, J. R., & Thavendran, K. (2018). To daydream is to imagine events: Conceptual, empirical and theoretical considerations. *Theory & Psychology, 28*(2), 261–268. https://doi.org/ 10.1177/0959354317752270.

Schraube, E., & Osterkamp, U. (Eds.). (2013). *Psychology from the standpoint of the subject. Selected writings of Klaus Holzkamp*. Basingstoke, UK: Palgrave Macmillan.

Vygotsky, L. S. (1971). *The psychology of art*. Cambridge, MA: MIT Press.

Vygotsky, L. S. (1987). Thinking and speech. In R. Rieber & A. Carton (Eds.), *The collected Works of L. S. Vygotsky: Vol. 1.* (pp. 43–287). New York, NY: Plenum.

Ole Dreier Ph.D., Dr. Habil., is a Professor Emeritus at the Department of Psychology, University of Copenhagen. Dreier introduced Leontiev's cultural-historical activity theory and Critical Psychology in the Scandinavian countries. Since then he has worked extensively with the development of Critical Psychology as a science of the subject. He has published widely on foundational issues of subjectivity in psychology especially in relation to social psychology, personality psychology, psychotherapy, health, and learning. He was a visiting professor at the universities in Berkeley, Irvine, Berlin, Leipzig, Lüneburg, Mexico City, and Lillehammer. Dreier has been a member of ISTP and ISCAR and of the editorial boards of *Theory & Psychology*; *Mind, Culture and Activity*; *Journal of Theoretical and Philosophical Psychology*; *Outlines*; Forum Kritische Psychologie and Nordiske Udkast. He is an approved specialist in psychotherapy and supervision.

Chapter 5
Qualitative Epistemology and Constructive-Interpretative Methodology: Contributions for Research in Social Sciences and Humanities

Daniel Magalhães Goulart and José Fernando Patino Torres

Abstract This chapter aims to discuss the contributions of González Rey's Qualitative Epistemology and constructive-interpretative methodology for research in social sciences and humanities. Firstly, some of the main epistemological problems that have sustained the history of social sciences and humanities are discussed. Secondly, epistemological principles of González Rey's proposal and the main definitions, characteristics and configurational logic of knowledge production of constructive-interpretative methodology are discussed as a consistent way to advance in the unity between research and professional action. We claim this approach revitalizes science as a living and creative production by considering the researcher as a subject of knowledge construction. Three epistemological principles sustain this proposal: (1) singularity as a legitimate source for scientific knowledge, (2) research as a dialogical process, and (3) the constructive-interpretative character of scientific knowledge. An important feature of this methodological approach is the rupture with the historical dichotomy between "data collection" and "data analysis". We argue that González Rey's epistemological and methodological proposal contributes towards a qualitative approach that considers human creativity and emotionality crucial dimensions of scientific construction.

Keywords Qualitative epistemology · Constructive-interpretative methodology · Subjectivity

D. M. Goulart (✉)
Faculty of Education, University of Brasilia, Brasilia, Brazil
e-mail: danielgoulartbr@gmail.com

J. F. P. Torres
Faculty of Psychology, Federal University of Tocantins, Miracema, Brazil
e-mail: jfpatinotorres@outlook.com

D. M. Goulart et al. (eds.), *Theory of Subjectivity from a Cultural-Historical Standpoint*,
Perspectives in Cultural-Historical Research 9,
https://doi.org/10.1007/978-981-16-1417-0_5

5.1 Introduction

This chapter aims to discuss central aspects of the contribution of González Rey's Qualitative Epistemology and constructive-interpretative methodology (González Rey, 1997, 2002, 2005, 2014, 2019a, 2019b; González Rey & Mitjáns Martínez, 2016, 2017a, 2017b, 2019) for research in social sciences and humanities. As we have discussed in previous work (González Rey & Patino, 2017; Patiño & Goulart, 2016, 2020; Goulart, 2018), a significant part of research in social and human sciences presents different philosophical, epistemological and methodological problems. One of these problems has been the repeated objectivist and instrumentalist claim that the dominant forms of scientific representation took, which did not allow to recognize culture, history and singularity in the complex human psychology.

Facing these scientific problems, González Rey's proposal for the study of subjectivity involved, in the first instance, defending that theory, epistemology and methodology were inseparable. This unity demanded the gradual construction of an epistemological and methodological perspective that was consistent with the complexity of the demands of the study of subjective processes (González Rey & Mitjáns Martínez, 2016, 2017a)".

As González Rey argues:

> Subjectivity as an ontological domain specifies a new kind of process, that is, qualitatively different from all the processes involved in its genesis. As such, subjectivity is ontologically defined by the integration of emotions and symbolical processes, forming new qualitative units: subjective senses. Such subjective senses are "snapshots" of symbolic emotional flashes that unfold in a chaotic movement, from which subjective configurations emerge as a self-regulative and self-generative organization of subjective senses. (González Rey, 2019a, p. 28)

González Rey and Mitjáns Martínez (2017a) explain that subjective processes are not exhausted in the current experience, but represent the quality of processes experienced in the present, articulated with life plots crossed by history, different spaces, and social relations. Subjective productions are inseparable from the symbolic constructions of culture within which they emerge. "In these productions, emotions are embedded within symbolic processes, which turn subjectivity into an intrinsic component of culture" (González Rey, 2017, p. 182).

González Rey developed three fundamental principles to elaborate his Qualitative Epistemology (González Rey, 1997, 2005), (1) the constructive-interpretative nature of knowledge, which implies to assume scientific knowledge as production of intelligibility, and not as a simple application of concepts to the studied topic; (2) singularity as a legitimate source of scientific knowledge, which implies to articulate singular information within a theoretical model[1] that allows theoretical generalization; (3) the scientific knowledge production as a dialogical communication process.

---

[1] A theoretical model "(…) represents a theoretical construction with capacity for development at the empirical moment and which is expressed in the progressive development of hypotheses and constructions of the researcher" (González Rey, 2009, p. 220).

Taking into account the aforementioned principles, González Rey and Mitjáns Martínez (2017a) argue that the study of subjectivity, through constructive-interpretative methodology, must go beyond the analysis of explicit information, as well as hermeneutics or discourse analysis, demanding the construction of inter-pretations about the theoretical articulation of different forms of expression of the research participants. González Rey and Mitjáns Martínez argue:

> Thus, the study of subjectivity is only possible by advancing through indirect pathways on the basis of complex systems of expression, which articulate postures, gestures, speech, emotions, and thoughts in one imperceptible order that can only be accessed through intel-lectual constructions capable of generating intelligibility throughout a sequence of human expressions. (González Rey & Mitjáns Martínez, 2019, p. 40)

Unlike theoretical frameworks of the social sciences and humanities that are still sustained by the dominant paradigm of modern science, Theory of Subjectivity does not work with concepts that express a priori content, demanding alternatives to the so-called "application of theory" to the information that comes from the research field. Qualitative Epistemology proposes a configurational logic of knowledge production characterized by the generation of developing conjectures, indicators and hypotheses, which gain consistency throughout the field research process. In this chapter, we discuss that this logic implies revitalizing the researchers' ability to imagine, to create and to produce new ideas. This process involves considering field research as a theoretical path in permanent development towards the construction of theoret-ical models that allow new spaces of intelligibility for the understanding of studied phenomena.

5.2 Epistemological Problems in Humanities and Social Sciences: A Critical Vision

In dialogue with authors like Danziger (1990, 1997), Koch (1999), Chamberlain (2000) and Rose (1996), González Rey (2002, 2005, 2013, 2014, 2019b) was critical to the epistemological problems present in the dominant modern science. He consis-tently challenged (1) the uncritical appropriation of methods and techniques from different fields, (2) the neglect of the qualitative ontological specificity of social sciences and humanities, and (3) research projects sustained by inductive criteria (González Rey & Mitjáns Martínez, 2017a).

González Rey (2019b) argues that the epistemological problems of modern science have had several consequences, which also include current problems in qualitative research. Among them, González Rey highlights the separation between theory, research and practice. Theories are often considered as a set of concepts a priori to be applied both in research and in practice. Still, research, when reduced to its empirical dimension, is considered apart from practice, which is also linked to the dissociation between application of instruments, a stage that is still known as "data collection", and the interpretation of results, often considered as "data analysis" within the research process. In this context, González Rey defended, throughout his work, the need to revitalize the epistemological discussion in scientific research and in practice as a unit, instead of promoting a mere innovation from the methodological point of view. He states:

> The revitalization of the epistemological is, therefore, a necessity in face of the attempt to monopolize the scientific based on the relationship of data with the validity and reliability of the instruments that produce them. This instrumentalism corrupted the objective of science and led to the reification of the empirical, causing profound distortions when using the theory. For this reason, talking about qualitative methodology implies a theoretical-epistemological debate, without which it is impossible to overcome the instrumental cult derived from hypertrophy that considers the instruments as ways of direct production of research results. (González Rey, 2005, p. 03)

González Rey (2013) argues that empiricism, which ended up being one of the hallmarks of positivist research, is one of the central factors that have prevented qualitative researchers from seeing that the strength of an alternative methodological representation lies in the recognition of the status of ideas, that is, of the theoretical production as an essential attribute of the construction of knowledge. He said: "Qualitative methodology very often ignores the epistemological principles that underlie scientific production, and this leads to producing alternatives that are within the epistemological limits of the options it intends to overcome" (González Rey, 2002, p. 26).

More specifically, in the boom of qualitative research in psychology in the 1980s and 1990s, despite the important contributions in the first half of the twentieth century—exemplified by the innovations undertaken by Psychoanalysis, by Vygotsky and, especially, by the group of K. Lewin—as well as the criticism of S. Koch and G. Allport in the second half of the twentieth century, there was a relatively uncritical import of methodological references from the social sciences (González Rey & Mitjáns Martínez, 2017a). This process, according to González Rey and Mitjáns Martínez (2017a), represented an orientation towards qualitative research in methodological terms, rather than the construction of epistemological bases and consistent ontological definitions about the phenomena that demanded new methodologies to be studied. The result of this was the frequent superficial appropriation of Phenomenology as a reference, marked by little depth of this broad and heterogeneous philosophical perspective.

As discussed in other publications (Goulart, 2018; Patiño & Goulart, 2016, 2020; Patiño, 2016) based on the contributions of authors such as González Rey, Koch and Danziger, qualitative research in humanities and social sciences, in an effort to distance itself from dominant quantitative perspectives, ended up crossed by historical deadlocks of modern science, with emphasis on the hegemony of the empirical, the emphasis on supposedly exact descriptions, theoretical apriorism and researcher's neutrality. In this regard, however, González Rey and Mitjáns Martínez comment:

> The difference between qualitative and quantitative research is not instrumental nor is it defined by the type of results obtained. The essential difference between both types of research is epistemological: both in the processes of obtaining the information as in the construction processes of that information. (2016, p. 9)

From the 1990s, different alternatives in the field of qualitative research were developed and consolidated. Some of them, which had their origin in previous decades, such as Action Research, Cartography and Discourse Analysis, maintained their interdisciplinary traditions, being derived from other disciplines. González Rey and Mitjáns Martínez (2017a) argue that, in different fields, such as Psychology and Education, Hermeneutics has come to be configured as the most used perspective to legitimize the use of interpretation, although it frequently did not delve into its epistemological consequences for the production of knowledge from specific fields. They explain that hermeneutics centralized the text as an object so that all human processes started to be read as text. However, it "(...) is not oriented to the study of the individual as the author of the text" (González Rey & Mitjáns Martínez, 2017a, pp. 20–21).

Based on the unfolding of hermeneutics, different critical aspects began to emphasize discourse, communication, language, deconstruction, social construction, dialogical realities, among others (Harré & Stearns, 1995; Parker, 2015). However, González Rey (2018) argues that, despite the value of these perspectives in the denaturalization of human processes, many of them culminated in the neglect of the individual as an active dimension of these constructions. In this way, all the richness of subjectivity, including imaginative, emotional, motivational and subversive processes, was placed outside the readings of social life and considered mere epiphenomena of hegemonic discourses.

It is in this gap that the epistemological and methodological contribution of González Rey (1997, 2002, 2005, 2017; González Rey & Mitjáns Martínez, 2016, 2017a, 2019) is inserted, when proposing Qualitative Epistemology and the constructive-interpretative methodology as bases for the study of individual and social subjective processes. These contributions will be developed in the following sections of this chapter.

5.3 Qualitative Epistemology and Constructive-Interpretative Methodology for the Study of Subjectivity

As Mitjáns Martínez (2014) explains, Qualitative Epistemology[2] was particularly influenced by French Historical Epistemology and the Epistemology of Complexity, but it emerges in a particular science, i.e. Psychology, as a creative conception of knowledge production oriented towards a specific object: subjectivity. However, due to its scope and unfolding in multiple research projects, Mitjáns Martínez explains

---

[2]The term "Qualitative Epistemology" was coined by González Rey in 1997 in response to the way the majority of psychologists had adhered to qualitative research in the 1980s and 1990s: in an instrumentalist perspective, without epistemological or theoretical consistency (González Rey & Mitjáns Martínez, 2017).

that this perspective is relevant to support the production of knowledge about subjective processes in various fields, such as in health, education, organizations, clinic, politics, communities, among others.

According to González Rey,

Qualitative Epistemology represents the production of knowledge and, with it, research as a subjectively configured process and theoretical production, both by the theories of which they are part, and by the researcher himself/herself. (…) Science is legitimized as a production of intelligibility that can dialogue all the time with the methodological process through the researcher's theoretical production. (González Rey, 2014, p. 32)

This perspective is based on the understanding of scientific knowledge as a constructive-interpretative process (González Rey & Mitjáns Martínez, 2016, 2019). In this sense, we do not have direct access to the studied reality, but we can generate intelligibility about it from relevant theoretical representations to its specificities. In the case of subjectivity, González Rey and Mitjáns Martínez (2017a) argue that its study is only possible indirectly, through a constructive-interpretative methodology.

The constructive-interpretative methodology has as its main characteristic the construction of information process, which is based on a complex system of expressions that are beyond the explicit content of the information generated by the other, articulating gestures, postures, speech and emotionality (González Rey & Mitjáns Martínez, 2019). All this information, which emerges in an unpredictable way throughout the research field, constitutes the raw material for the researcher's intellectual constructions.

González Rey (2019b) explains that this process acquires scientific status because the researcher, based on different partial constructions, i.e. conjectures, indicators and hypotheses, becomes able to articulate them in a developing theoretical model. This theoretical model has no claim to take the place of truth, but rather to represent the best construction to generate intelligibility about the problem studied at a given moment. González Rey and Mitjáns Martínez (2019) point out that it is not the theory itself that offers conditions to assess whether the theoretical model is the best option at that moment, but rather the interrelation between conjectures, indicators and hypotheses articulated in it, becoming the best source of intelligibility about the problem studied, compared to other models. "In this process, previous hypotheses may be integrated within a wider theoretical model or may simply be abandoned, taking into consideration new constructions that will emerge throughout the research" (González Rey & Mitjáns Martínez, 2019, p. 46)

The construction of information represents the process that leads to a theoretical model. The first step of this process, as González Rey and Mitjáns Martínez explain, is the elaboration of conjectures, that is, "(…) reflections, doubts and ideas, in relation to which a well-formulated hypothetical meaning cannot be yet assigned" (González Rey & Mitjáns Martínez, 2019, p. 50). Conjectures represent suspicions, or questions that accompany the researcher in the next steps of his/her research, but that, at the same time, open the way to more consistent meanings about the researched problem, becoming, then, indicators.

Regarding the process of construction of indicators, González Rey explains: "The process of setting indicators is an interpretation process that takes place supported by a multiplicity of information obtained by different instruments and by the constant intellectual intervention of the researcher" (González Rey, 1997, p. 146). This definition has been sustained and developed over the years. In a more recent publication, González Rey and Mitjáns Martínez (2017a, p. 30) affirm that the indicators represent "(…) the meanings that the researcher elaborates about events, expressions or expression systems, which do not appear explicitly, in its meaning, by research participants". The hypothetical character of the indicators, based on the researcher's interpretative construction, is central to this definition. As already mentioned, subjectivity does not appear explicitly and cannot be "apprehended" directly, either by direct observation, by the explicit content of speech or by behaviour. Thus, it becomes essential to pay attention to the most diverse forms of expression of the other and to the researcher's effort, to explain what these forms of expression mean, in relation to the investigated problem. In this sense, several elements may be relevant in the construction of indicators in addition to the content of what is said, such as the adjective or personalized way of narrating experiences, body expressions, speech emotionality, silences, the way in which different moments in the life of its author appear, the excessive emphasis on one aspect of life to the detriment of others, as well as the articulation of these various aspects (González Rey & Mitjáns Martínez, 2017a).

Something fundamental in the construction of information in this perspective, as González Rey and Mitjáns Martínez (2016, 2017a) explain, is that the indicator does not represent an isolated or conclusive definition of the researched problem or an act of knowledge in the face of presented information, but a resource in the course of a theoretical construction. Thus, an indicator is only relevant if it opens the way for the generation of other indicators, or if it is related to other indicators previously constructed. The construction of an indicator represents the principle of a "trail" of thought on the researched topic, a chain of meanings, which becomes more comprehensive as it unfolds in the development of new indicators, which, gradually, will lead to the elaboration of a consistent hypothesis about the problem in question. It is worth mentioning that "indicators that are integrated within a hypothesis are different, their congruence is given by the meaning generated by the researcher" (González Rey & Mitjáns Martínez, 2016, p. 10). Importantly, the concept of hypothesis within this framework differs from the hypothetical-deductive model, according to which the hypothesis is a construction prior to the research itself, so that it has the function of refuting or corroborating that one. According to González Rey and Mitjáns Martínez (2017a, p. 111), within the scope of the constructive-interpretative methodology, the hypotheses represent "(…) the paths in which the theoretical model gains explanatory capacity". Also, hypotheses do not represent the sum or synthesis of the indicators—which would represent, in an epistemological dimension, a remnant of a representational epistemology (González Rey, 2014) that focuses on the accumulation of information and constructions that would serve to describe reality as it is. In this perspective, the theoretical construction, articulated with the network of indicators and hypotheses, is a living process, which permanently represents an act of creation by the researcher.

On the one hand, a hypothesis represents a construction of broader meanings, of an explanatory nature, about the studied topic. On the other hand, based on the articulation of different indicators, the hypothesis itself starts to guide the construction of other indicators, which will expand its generalization capacity. According to González Rey (2014, p. 30), "indicators do not 'validate' theoretical constructions, but they are evidence of their validity within the available presentation system". Thus, the hypothesis is not the conclusive commentary of an investigative process, but the theoretical model itself under development, which can be fed, tensioned and even changed by new different indicators that emerge in the information construction process.

Theoretical models are built based on case studies, which, within this methodology, are configured as general methodological resources. González Rey (2019b) explains that the value of case studies is not empirical. On the contrary, it represents a pillar of research as a theoretical enterprise. A theoretical model emerges with the first case studied, but, once built, the next case study is a continuation of the first, expanding its elements and encompassing its capacity for generating meanings. In this sense, the development of a theoretical model is a process that is always far from completion, since it can be permanently enriched by new case studies, which contribute with new ideas, information, indicators and hypotheses.

This is precisely the value of singularity as a legitimate source to produce scientific knowledge (González Rey, 2005). The epistemological value of singularity does not lie in the uniqueness with which subjective processes occur, but in the possibility that these singular expressions provide information and foster constructions that allow a complex theoretical model in development to be expanded, allowing the phenomenon studied to be thought beyond the uniqueness with that it presents itself (González Rey & Mitjáns Martínez, 2016).

In this sense, González Rey's Qualitative Epistemology is guided by the notion of theoretical generalization, unlike the inductive generalization still dominant in qualitative research (González Rey, 1997, 2005). While the inductive generalization is based on what different case studies have in common, theoretical generalization is based on theoretical models capable of generating different explanations about the studied topic (González Rey, 2019, 2019b). Theoretical generalization represents:

> (…) the capacity that a theoretical model has to produce new meanings and articulate different relationships between them in the research process. Such meanings and relationships, in turn, will have a value to signify new events and situations that, before this construction, were unintelligible. (González Rey, 2014, pp. 18–19)

As previously argued, generalization is not due to what different singular cases have in common, but to the definition of a configuration that allows the articulation of different units, which change the content from case to case and from one situation to another, at the same time that it allows different explanations about the same phenomenon (González Rey, 2019b). In short, we could place the construction of theories as a general objective of the production of scientific knowledge. But as González Rey recalls,

> making theory, however, differs from "applying" theories—a term that only makes sense in a science that defines itself as empirical. Theories in our proposal can never be applied, as the concepts of a theory take new forms and generate specific meanings in view of the

new demands that all research implies. In this sense, the 'use of theories' always implies 'making theory', which represents an active process of the researcher, which permanently presupposes his/her condition as an author. (González Rey, 2014, p. 17)

Indeed, the condition of authorship on the part of the researcher, a fundamental process of the proposal of Qualitative Epistemology and the constructive-interpretative methodology, is one of the great difficulties related to learning and using this approach in research. As González Rey and Mitjáns Martínez (2019) point out, the empirical-instrumental tradition, still dominant in the hegemonic institutionalization of social sciences, emphasizes instruments on dialogue, responses on constructions, collection of information on theoretical constructions and confirmation/refutation on hypothetical paths. However, González Rey's proposal is directed in the opposite direction. It implies the revitalization of science as a living and creative production based on the emergence of the researcher as the subject of knowledge production—an absent principle either in phenomenology, in hermeneutics, or discourse analysis (González Rey & Mitjáns Martínez, 2017a).

The metaphor of configurational logic (González Rey, 2005) expresses precisely the importance of the researcher emerging as a subject in the course of the research, emphasizing his/her responsibility in the construction of the theoretical model under development, which opens new paths of intelligibility, integrating singular expressions of the participants to a set of meanings, which, in their articulation, acquires explanatory capacity over a subjective system. There is no abstract and a priori criterion to be followed, other than that of his/her own theoretical reflection.

This conception represents a shift in the very representation of theory. As discussed in the aforementioned quotation, different from "applying" theories, González Rey (2014) emphasizes "making theory": "Theories are subjective resources used to produce intelligibility on the world and, precisely because of this subjective character, they configure our world, not representing something external to be used in a timely manner and only on certain occasions" (González Rey, 2014, p. 17).

Another fundamental contribution of this proposal is the epistemological dimension of dialogue as a central resource for the production of knowledge. In this perspective, dialogue ceases to be understood as an exclusively linguistic process, to be understood as a differentiated subjective process (González Rey & Mitjáns Martínez, 2019). Dialogue represents a shared social space through the establishment of a relational bond that does not deny the singularities of its protagonists (Goulart, 2017, 2019). Like all realities subjectively configured by the human being, dialogue takes on unpredictable paths, generating multiple processes beyond the control of its participants (González Rey & Mitjáns Martínez, 2019).

In this perspective, dialogue not only marks a different notion of the researcher–participant relationship but is one of the epistemological pillars for a new representation of the research itself. The investigative process comes to be understood as an open social space, which subjectively mobilizes its protagonists (researchers and participants) to take positions and actions in a living relational fabric that can gain relevance for the researched topic. This is why, rather than being oriented to answer questions that are asked by the researcher, the participant is invited to delve into a dialogical process that mobilizes new subjective productions due to the emotional involvement that is developed throughout the research field process. This process is not reduced to the empirical dimension, but it is also based on the options that the researcher assumes in this relational plot from what he is capable of theoretically producing. From this epistemological and methodological standpoint, there is a rupture with the historical dichotomy between "data collection" and "data analysis". The research field itself is considered as a theoretical pathway in permanent development, which feeds and is fed by the construction of conjectures, indicators and hypotheses that are assembled within an ongoing theoretical model. The definition of the research instruments, far from acquiring an abstract, neutral and universal connotation, expresses creative research resources that favour the dialogical process, being also inseparable from the theoretical model under development (González Rey, 2005).

This approach differs from other perspectives that enhance dialogue as a linguistic phenomenon and end up defending the researcher's condition of "not knowing", such as some currents of social constructionism (Gergen, 1994). For González Rey, both the theoretical model constructed, as well as the creation and maintenance of dialogue, is permanently crossed by theoretical production as a differentiated subjective process (González Rey & Mitjáns Martínez, 2017a, 2019).

As previously stated, Qualitative Epistemology and the constructive-interpretative methodology are inseparable from the Theory of Subjectivity. This tripod provides grounds for a new representation of the research/practice unit, which is oriented towards creation, not the instrumental application (González Rey, 2019b).

5.4 Final Remarks

González Rey's Qualitative Epistemology and constructive-interpretative methodology represent new possibilities for the production of knowledge within social sciences and humanities by proposing explicit criteria of a qualitative approach that considers human creativity and emotionality crucial dimensions of scientific construction. On the one hand, this approach overcomes the rationalism of hegemonic scientific representations that have reified the symbolic dimension of social productions through categories such as meaning, language and discourse, to the detriment of emotion as a central field of human productions. In this sense, González Rey's proposal proposes subjectivity as a symbolic-emotional system that generates subjective realities, thereby granting emotion a new theoretical-ontological status that had been historically denied.

The principles of Qualitative Epistemology, which emphasizes knowledge production as a constructive-interpretative and dialogical process, as well as singularity as a legitimate source for scientific knowledge, represent the epistemological ground for constructive-interpretative methodology. In this perspective, research is understood and assumed as a living process in which the researcher and participants are agents of a dialogical experience, mobilized by subjective productions related to the topic studied. This characteristic breaks with the empiricist, positivist and mechanistic visions that assumed science as an arid, rigid and rationalist process in which the participant was a mere object that responded to instruments with a supposedly a priori scientific value.

From this perspective, the researcher is central as the author of theoretical models about the studied topic. This condition breaks with the idea of the researcher as an uncritical reproducer of theories that are intended to be applied to certain realities, without due heuristic value. This instrumentalist view of the dominant investigative methodology is precisely what has led to the pauperization of the production of ideas in the knowledge production process, thereby eliminating any possibility of epistemological novelty.

The constructive-interpretative methodology proposes the indissociable link between research field and theoretical construction. The construction of information is a central aspect of this methodological approach. This process is based on the articulation of conjectures, indicators and hypotheses that gain consistency on the investigative path towards the construction of a theoretical model. It is not, therefore, a matter of postulating isolated or conclusive definitions as acts of knowledge in the face of the studied topic. Conjectures, indicators and hypotheses must present a necessary link both with the singular case study and with the more comprehensive theoretical system that underlies them. The ongoing theoretical model represents the best possible system of intelligibility to understand the studied topic at a certain time and space.

To conclude, we can say that González Rey's epistemological and methodological proposal highlights qualitative research as a theoretical enterprise. Theory is revitalized as a dynamic system, in permanent development, which considers human creativity and emotionality as crucial dimensions of scientific construction. In this sense, theory, epistemology and methodology emerge as an inseparable unit.

References

Chamberlain, K. (2000). Methodolatry and qualitative health research. *Journal of Health Psychology, 5*(3), 285–296. https://doi.org/10.1177/135910530000500306.

Danziger, K. (1990). *Constructing the subject*. New York: Cambridge University Press

Danziger, K. (1997). *Naming the mind: How psychology found its language?* London: Sage Publication.

Gergen, K. (1994). *Realities and relationship*. Cambridge: Cambridge University Press.

González Rey, F. (1997). *Epistemología cualitativa y subjetividad* [Qualitative epistemology and subjectivity]. São Paulo: Educ.

González Rey, F. (2002). *Pesquisa qualitativa em psicologia: caminhos e desafios* [Qualitative research in psychology: paths and challenges]. São Paulo: Thomson Learning.

González Rey, F. (2005). *Pesquisa qualitativa e subjetividade: Os processos de construção da informação* [Qualitative research and subjectivity: The processes of information construction]. São Paulo: Thomson.

González Rey, F. (2009). Epistemología y Ontología: un debate necessário para la Psicología hoy [Epistemology and Ontology: a necessary debate for Psychology today]. *Diversitas, 5*(2), 205–224.

González Rey, F. (2013). O que oculta o silêncio epistemológico da psicologia? [What hides the epistemological silence of psychology]. *Pesquisas e Práticas Psicossociais [Researches and Psychosocial Practices], 8*(1), 20–34.

González Rey, F. (2014). Ideias e modelos teóricos na pesquisa construtivo-interpretativa [Ideas and theoretical models in constructive-interpretive research]. In A. Mitjáns Martínez., M. Neubern, & V. D. Mori (Orgs.), *Subjetividade contemporânea: discussões epistemológicas e metodológicas* [Contemporary subjectivity: epistemological and methodological discussions] (pp. 13–34). Campinas: Alínea.

González Rey, F. (2017). Advances in Subjectivity from a Cultural-Historical Perspective: Unfoldings and consequences for cultural studies today. In M. Fleer, F. González Rey, & N. Veresov (Eds.), *Perezhivanie, emotions and subjectivity. perspectives in cultural-historical research* (Vol. 1, pp. 173–193). Singapore: Springer. https://doi.org/10.1007/978-981-10-4534-9_9.

González Rey, F. (2017). The topic of subjectivity in psychology: Contradictions, paths and new alternatives. *Journal for the Theory of Social Behaviour 47*(4). 502–521. https://doi.org/10.1111/jtsb.12144.

González Rey. (2018). Subjectivity and discourse: Complementary topics for a critical psychology. *Culture & Psychology, 25*(2), 178–194. https://doi.org/10.1177/1354067X18754338.

González Rey, F. (2019a). Subjectivity as a new theoretical, epistemological, and methodological pathway within cultural-historical psychology. In F. González Rey, A. Mitjáns Martínez & D. M. Goulart (Eds.), *Subjectivity within cultural-historical approach. theory, methodology and research* (pp. 21–36). Singapore: Springer.

González Rey, F. (2019b). Methodological and epistemological demands in advancing the study of subjectivity from a cultural-historical standpoint. *Culture & Psychology, 0*(0), 1–16. https://doi.org/10.1177/1354067X19888185.

González Rey, F., & Mitjáns Martínez, A. (2016). Una epistemología para el estudio de la subjetividad: sus implicaciones metodológicas [An epistemology for the study of subjectivity: its methodological implications]. *Psicoperspectivas (Online): Individuo y Sociedad* [Psicoperspectivas (Online): individual and society], *15*(1), 5–16. http://dx.doi.org/10.5027/psicoperspectivas-Vol15-Issue1-fulltext-667.

González Rey, F., & Mitjáns Martínez, A. (2017). *Subjetividade: epistemologia, teoria e método* [Subjectivity: epistemology, theory and method]. Campinas: Alínea.

González Rey, F., & Mitjáns Martínez, A. (2017b). Epistemological and methodological issues related to the new challenges of a cultural–historical-based psychology (pp. 264–296). In: M. Fleer, F. González Rey, N. Veresov (Orgs.). *Perezhivanie, emotions and subjectivity: Advancing Vygotsky's legacy* (pp. 264–296). New York: Springer.

González Rey, F., & Mitjáns Martínez, A. (2019). The constructive-interpretative methodological approach: orienting research and practice on the basis of subjectivity. In F. González Rey, A. Mitjáns Martinez, & D. M. Goulart. *Subjectivity within cultural-historical approach: theory, methodology and research* (pp. 37–60). Singapore: Springer. https://doi.org/10.1007/978-981-13-3155-8_3.

González Rey, F., & Patiño, J. F. (2017). La Epistemología Cualitativa y el estudio de la subjetividad en una perspectiva cultural-histórica. Conversación con Fernando González Rey. *Revista Estudios Sociales, 60*, 120–127. https://doi.org/10.7440/res60.2017.10.

Goulart, D. M. (2017). *Educacão, saúde mental e desenvolvimento subjetivo: da patologização da vida à ética do sujeito* [Education, mental health and subjective development: from the pathologization of life to the ethics of the subject]. Ph.D. thesis, University of Brasília.

Goulart, D. M. (2018). A pesquisa qualitativa em psicologia: contradições, alternativas e desafios [Qualitative research in psychology: contradictions, alternatives and challenges]. *Revista Psicologia, Diversidade e Saúde* [Psychology, Diversity and Health Journal], *7*(1), 1–4. http://dx.doi.org/10.17267/2317-3394rpds.v7i1.1825.

Goulart, D. M. (2019). *Subjectivity and critical mental health: Lessons from Brazil.* London: Routledge. https://doi.org/10.4324/9781351251907.

Harré, H. R., & Stearns, P. (Eds.). (1995). *Discursive psychology.* London, UK & Los Angeles. USA: Sage.

Koch, S. (1999). *Psychology in human context: Essays in dissidence and reconstruction.* In D. Finkelman & F. Kessel, (Eds.), Chicago: The University of Chicago Press.

Mitjáns Martínez, A. (2014). Um dos desafios da Epistemologia Qualitativa: a criatividade do pesquisador [One of the challenges of qualitative epistemology: the researcher's creativity]. In: A. Mitjáns Martínez, M. Neubern, V. D. Mori, (Orgs.). *Subjetividade contemporânea: discussões epistemológicas e metodológicas* (pp. 61–86) [Contemporary subjectivity: epistemological and methodological discussions]. Campinas: Alínea.

Patiño, J. F. (2016). *A formação investigativa de doutorandos em educação e psicologia: um estudo da relação orientador-orientando a partir da Teoria da subjetividade* [The investigative training of doctoral students in education and psychology: a study of the supervisor-student relationship based on the Theory of Subjectivity]. Ph.D. thesis, University of Brasilia.

Parker, I. (2015). *Critical discursive psychology.* London: Palgrave Macmillan.

Patiño, J. F., & Goulart, D. M. (2016). Qualitative epistemology: A scientific platform for the study of subjectivity from a cultural-historical approach. *The Journal of International Research in Early Childhood Education, 7*(1), 161–180.

Patiño, J. F., & Goulart, D. M. (2020). Qualitative epistemology and constructive-interpretative methodology: a proposal for the study of subjectivity. *Studies in Psychology, 41*(1), 53–73. https://doi.org/10.1080/02109395.2019.1710809.

Rose, N. (1996). Power and subjectivity: Critical history and psychology. In Carl F. Graumann & K. J. Gergen (Eds.), *Historical dimensions of psychological discourse* (pp. 103–124). Cambridge: Cambridge University Press. https://doi.org/10.1017/CBO9780511571329.006

Daniel Magalhães Goulart is an Assistant Professor at the Department of Theory and Foundations of the Faculty of Education of the University of Brasilia. He is also a Collaborating Professor at the Master's in Psychology of the University Center of Brasilia. He graduated as a psychologist from the University of São Paulo and completed his Ph.D. at the Faculty of Education of the University of Brasília (CAPES), Brazil. He is the current coordinator of the Reading and Research Group "Subjectivity: Theory, Epistemology and Methodology". His latest books are: (1) Subjectivity within a cultural-historical approach: theory, methodology and research (Ed., Springer, 2019), (2) Subjectivity and critical mental health: lessons from Brazil (Routledge, 2019), and (3) Saúde mental, desenvolvimento e subjetividade: da patologização à ética do sujeito [Mental health, development and subjectivity: from pathologization to the ethics of the subject] (Cortez, 2019).

José Fernando Patino Torres is a Psychologist, holds a Master's in Cultural Psychology from Universidad Del Valle (Colombia), and a Ph.D. in Education from the University of Brasilia (Brasil). He is a Professor of the Psychology Undergraduate Program and a Visiting Professor of the Graduate Program in Communication and Society at the Federal University of Tocantins (Brasil). He is also a Visiting Professor of the Specialization Course in Family and Couples Therapy, Pontifical Catholic University of Goiás (Brasil).

Part II
Dialogue and Contribution for Different Contexts and Fields

Chapter 6
A Theory of Subjectivity in the Context of Critical Currents Trends in the Cultural-Historical Approach

Wanda C. Rodríguez Arocho

Abstract The reception and appropriation of L. S. Vygotsky's work in the West occurred in the context of the cognitive revolution in which his theory of the development of higher psychological functions and its relationship to education were emphasized. The historical and sociocultural context of his life and other works were sometimes ignored and other times simplified or misrepresented. A revisionist revolution is currently taking place that has propelled the recovery of some ignored or overlooked aspects of Vygotsky's legacy and a deeper understanding of the historical, cultural and socio-institutional conditions of his work. As an active participant in that movement, González Rey stated and confronted some of the problems associated with the readings and interpretations of Vygotsky. He constructed a theory of subjectivity within the cultural-historical approach that elaborates upon some of the concepts that were ignored or neglected in the treatment of Vygotsky's legacy, such as sense, social situation of development, *perezhivanie*, emotions, and consciousness as a complex system. The aim of this chapter is to examine his theory as an example of knowledge production realized amid new developments within the cultural-historical approach and simultaneously rooted in the biographical, institutional, and sociocultural contexts that shaped his commitment to critical reflexivity on the history of psychology.

6.1 Introduction

Matusov (2008) has argued that Vygotskian academia has not been reflective regarding the way in which history, culture, social institutions, practices and discourses shape their theoretical and empirical work. He points out the lack of "systematic analysis of the programmatic nature of Vygotskian (and even non-Vygotskian) research as shaped by local cultural, historical, and institutional practices and conditions" (p. 6). It is remarkable that given that history, culture, and society are

W. C. Rodríguez Arocho (✉)
University of Puerto Rico, San Juan, Puerto Rico
e-mail: wandacr@gmail.com

© The Author(s), under exclusive license to Springer Nature Singapore Pte Ltd. 2021
D. M. Goulart et al. (eds.), *Theory of Subjectivity from a Cultural-Historical Standpoint*,
Perspectives in Cultural-Historical Research 9,
https://doi.org/10.1007/978-981-16-1417-0_6

the main themes of the cultural-historical approach which are central to Vygotsky's account of the development of complex mental functions in humans they have not received a central role in understanding the construction of his theory and its subsequent developments nor any other productions in the field. This remarkable fact is striking if we consider that Vygotsky himself reflected on the processes of knowledge production, distribution and use in his essay *The historic meaning of the crisis of psychology: A methodological investigation* (Vygotsky, 1927/1997) and pointed to the complexity of these processes. This text has received renewed attention recently (Dafermos, 2014; Zavershneva, 2012; Zavershneva & Osipov, 2012). In that text there are some clues to approach the problem of the reception of Vygotsky's work in the West that have served to advance the revisionist movement (Dafermos, 2016; Yasnitsky & Van der Veer, 2016).

Vygotsky (1927/1997) argued that to understand the life, death, and transformation of concepts in scientific productions we need to take into account "(1) the general socio-cultural context of the era, (2) the general conditions and laws of scientific knowledge; (3) the objective demands upon scientific knowledge that follow from the nature of the phenomena studied in a given stage of investigation" (p. 241). After discussion of these ideas, Dafermos (2018) reformulated them and made a proposal that includes five interrelated dimensions:

1. the socio-historical context within which the theory is formed,
2. the scientific context, trends in the of field of philosophy and science,
3. the specific characteristics of the subject matter under investigation,
4. the particular subjects involved in the production and application of scientific knowledge and the development of their research programs, and
5. a study of the personal network of these subjects and their relations to the scientific community (p. 5).

Vygotsky's (1927/1997) original statement and Dafermos' (2018) reformulation are compatible with the methodology for the study of the history of psychology proposed by Rosa et al. (1996). These authors argue that there is a critical-reflexive function to the study of the history of psychology. The scrutiny of the discourse of psychological ideas produced in the past will serve the dual purpose of understanding their links to the contexts of their production and using that understanding to a better comprehend current epistemic actions. These actions refer to the practices employed in the production and communication of knowledge. They proposed three interrelated levels of analysis to approach the study of these actions. The first is the discourse analysis of the products of epistemic practices, particularly texts and other forms of communication of the knowledge produced. The second is biographical analysis, which focuses on how and why an author produces a text. This level includes intellectual, motivational, and affective conditions of the producer of the epistemic action. The third is a socio-institutional level of analysis in which the practices, institutions and groups that enable the production of knowledge are considered. The three levels interact generate conditions of possibility for the production process and the subsequent dissemination process. They seem suitable to examine González Rey theory of subjectivity.

The problem of the lack of reflexivity in the history of psychology in general and in the cultural-historical psychology in particular has been stated occasionally during the development of the approach, as well as has been stated the lack of discussion of their ontological and epistemological problems (González Rey, 2009; Rosa & Valsiner, 2018; Valsiner & Rosa, 2007). Recently, these concerns have gained visibility and fostered debate within the Vygotskian academia. Two indicators of this shift are the archival or revisionist revolution in Vygotskian studies (Yasnitsky & Van der Veer, 2016) and a surge on studies of the international reception and appropriation of Vygotsky's ideas (Dafermos, 2016; García, 2019). Some of the issues addressed by these productions have been pointed out before by Vygotskian scholars, such as linguistic problems reflected in the translations of Vygotsky's works (Daniels, 2001), decontextualization (Elhammoumi, 2001), selectivity and omissions in the works published and translated (Veresov, 1999) and interpretations mediated by cultural frames of mind and ideological biases (Ageyev, 2003).

Most of these critical assessments were pointed out and discussed by González Rey (2011a) in his analysis of Vygotsky's legacy. However, the impact was limited because, at the time, they were isolated and sporadic in the cultural-historical field. So, what has changed to make it possible for more coordinated efforts to underline the cultural, historical, and socio-institutional dimensions of the knowledge production and uses in the cultural-historical approach? Cultural and historical transformations have propelled the emergence of new economic and political configurations, the new technologies impacting all orders of social life, the problematization of categories such as age, gender, race, ethnicity, social class, and religion in academia and everyday life are some of the conditions that serve as a context for shifts in many disciplines. Philosophy of science, sociology of knowledge and the affective shift have taken central stage in a community of social and human sciences scholars and their productions. The new cultural-historical context allows opportunities for new explanations in a wide range of nontraditional topics.

6.2 The Theory of Subjectivity as a Creative Process/Product

In the last decade of his life, González Rey intensified his work on the formulation of his theory of subjectivity within the cultural-historical approach (González Rey, 2011b, 2019a). A brief consideration of his discourse in epistemic practices, particularly texts and other forms of communication of the knowledge, are useful to understand his approach. He was committed to communicate that his contribution was based and attached to the cultural-historical approach, while simultaneously represented a new development (González Rey, 2019a), a new path (González Rey, 2017b) and a way to advance an alternative understanding of Vygotsky's legacy. He was successful in his endeavor and lived to see his theoretical and methodological contributions to the study of subjectivity discussed and applied (Fleer et al., 2017; González Rey et al., 2019).

It is beyond the aim of this chapter to conduct a detailed presentation and analysis of González Rey's theory and the methodology he proposed for the study of subjectivity. This has been done already (Fleer et al., 2017; González Rey et al., 2019). However, it is important to point to some aspects of his discourse and to examine its relation to other conceptual and methodological productions. He made it clear that his theory's assumptions and postulates were a refutation of traditional psychology, both in its philosophical grounds and its theoretical and methodological productions. He was critical of the way psychology in general and the cultural-historical approach have paid limited attention to the intricate relationship between ontology, epistemology, theory, and research methodology in the production of psychological knowledge. These issues were discussed several times in his works and were explicitly addressed in the formulation of his theory (González Rey, 2007, 2009, 2019a). His words demonstrate that reflexivity, critical thinking, dialogical inquiry and creative appropriation were essential to the formulation of his theory.

Ample and profound knowledge of theoretical and methodological production in psychology and other social sciences was a useful tool to undertake and accomplished a reflective approach to the history of the discipline. He concluded that the "topic of subjectivity has been overlooked in a psychology mainly grounded in rationalism and empiricism" (Gonzaléz Rey, 2019a, p. 3). This conclusion was the beginning of the development of a new theoretical and methodological approach in psychology that would place subjectivity at its core. By making the history of psychology a ground for reflexivity in the context of a critical historiographic movement in psychology (Dazinger, 1997; Koch, 1999). González Rey became convinced that ontology and epistemology needed to be integrated into the new production. Regarding this issue, he states that "as a new ontological domain shared by all processes and human phenomena, including culture, subjectivity is integrative of processes that historically have been treated separately as thought, motivation, imagination, perception, personality among others" (Fleer et al., 2017, p. 4).

The proposition of a new ontology implies an invitation to reconsider the traditional ontology upon psychology developed. If the definition of what is to be study changes, then a different methodology is needed. To comply with this need, González Rey advocated for a Qualitative Epistemology expressed in a constructive-interpretative methodology to approach the study of subjectivity (González Rey, 2007, Patiño & Goulart, 2016). The reflective process that led to these conceptualizations was embedded within a critical perspective grounded both in the understanding of the cultural and socio-institutional dynamics involved in the production of scientific knowledge and a deep knowledge of paradigms, theories, and research in different contexts. Regarding the former, he emphasized those conditions in comparisons between Soviet and Western approaches to psychology (González Rey, 2011a). Regarding the latter, he made an important contribution by recovering the voices and legacy of Soviet psychologists little known in the West but important for a deeper understanding of Vygotsky's legacy, like Sergei Rubinstein, Lidya Bozhovich and V. E. Chudnovsky (González Rey, 2011a). It is worth noticing that one of his last works focused on the legacy of Bozhovich and the importance of her work in developing some of Vygotsky's ideas (González Rey, 2019b). This critical approach to contexts of scientific productions and the productions themselves served González Rey to recognize their scope and limits, to face some problems and to make a creative proposal to overcome them.

In addition to reflectivity and critical thinking, González Rey's theory of subjectivity evidence a dialogical approach that fosters his creative appropriation and elaboration of previous and current productions in psychology. Dialogicity is present in at least two ways. First, as it is visible in most of his texts, he relied on intertextuality to develop ideas and arguments. Quotes and references are frequently used in his confrontation of ideas expressed by authors from the past or the present. This practice served to avoid one of the limitations Matusov (2008) identified in Vygotskian academia: the need "to identify the tacit opponents to whom our approaches dialogically reply" (p. 8). Second, the dialogical approach is also visible in the interaction, communication and collaboration practices in the learning and practice communities in which he participated (Goulart, 2019).

The outcome of the dynamic process examined constitutes the key in the formulation of González Rey's theory of subjectivity. The role of dialogue and communication is highlighted in the theory (Fleer et al., 2017). He made a creative appropriation and elaboration of themes and concepts that were neglected in the dominant interpretations of Vygotsky in the West that emphasized the development of culturally mediated cognitive functions that reinforced reductionistic or simplistic explanations. In doing so, he recovered Vygotsky's first and latest works where emotions, affect, sense, *perezhivanie*, the social situation of development and consciousness take the central stage (González Rey, 2019a). He also questioned interpretations and positions "that link Vygotsky' cultural-historical theory to Leontiev's activity theory" (González Rey, 2019). He problematized dichotomies such as external/internal realities and interpsychological/intrapsychological processes and claimed they perpetuate reductionistic and simplistic explanations of the psyche. Based on Vygotsky's latest's works (that he considered closer to Rubenstein's ideas than to Leontiev's), he rescued the notions of units and systems and elaborated upon them (González Rey, 2011a). He proposed the idea of the human psyche as a unit of symbolic-emotional processes grounded in culture and social practices, but irreducible to them. The configuration of the processes depends on the sense attributed by the subject to the sociocultural experiences he lives and is always the result of complex symbolic-affective dynamics (González Rey, 2011b).

González Rey's conceptualized subjectivity as "the unit of symbolical and emotional processes that form a new phenomenon" (Fleer et al., 2017, p. 3). He developed the concepts of subjective sense and subjective configuration to represent the processes by which the personal and the social create each other. He elaborates on the reciprocal constitution of individual and social subjectivities in a dynamic process characterized by contradictions, uncertainty, complexity, and uniqueness. That makes it this theme elusive for traditional psychological theories and methods of study. Fleer et al. (2017) propose that the task to advance the concepts of subjectivity, emotions and *perezhivanie* within the cultural-historical approach should be guided by three principles: (1) overcoming social determinism; (2) challenging the understanding of the human mind as the result of internalized operations, and (3) the development of an integrative system. It could be said that these principles were followed in the development of the theory of subjectivity.

González Rey reiterated the inscription of his theory in a cultural-historical approach. He declares that the process of formulation of his theory was enriched by this revisionist movement (González Rey, 2008) as well as through the dialogue with critical Latin American psychology (González Rey, 2004). He also integrates aspects of Moscovici's theory of social representations, Kurt Lewin's and other Gestalt theorists' writings, as well as current discussions on the philosophy and sociology of science and other theories of subjectivity (González Rey, 2008, 2019a).

In the review of González Rey's creative path to the formulation of his theory of subjectivity I have focused on some epistemic practices he carried on in his creative endeavor. These practices are tied to contexts marked by transformations in all orders of human life, including the current trends of critical perspectives in the of fields of philosophy and science. I pointed out his commitment to the development of a new ontological, epistemological, and methodological approach to what he understood should be the object of study of psychology. I also recognized his main interlocutors in a dialogic inquiry that lasted decades as he referred to their knowledge production and research programs. The first section of this book provides details about González Rey's biography. In the next section, I highlight some life experiences that helped to shape his practices in knowledge production.

6.3   The Personal Path to the Theory of Subjectivity

The biographical account of Goulart et al. (2020) present and discuss significant experiences in the life and work of González Rey. They begin with a quote from Spanish philosopher José Ortega y Gasset (1883–1955) expressing the idea that the subject himself is inseparable from his life circumstances. This idea of unity between self and environment was addressed by Vygotsky in this text *The problem of the environment* (1935/1994), to which González Rey referred to several times based on its emphasis in dealing with situated emotional experience (*perzhivane*) "…we are dealing with the unity of personal characteristics and situational characteristics…" (p. 342). His work was generated through historical, relational, affective, motivation, and intellectual experiences that are inseparable from the spaces of social subjectivity where he lived.

Fernando González Rey was born in Cuba in 1949 and died in Brazil in 2019. His childhood, adolescence and early adulthood were marked by the Cuban Revolution. He was part of a generation that was impacted in ways difficult to understand for people who have not experienced rapid and dramatic changes in their ways of life. Although separated in time and sociocultural context, the Cuban Revolution shares some parallel with the Russian Revolution of 1917, in addition to their commitment to Marxism. This parallel refers to individual and social subjectivity.

In his analysis of generational transformations in Soviet psychology, Kozulin (1984) points out that for the first post-revolution generation the experience was signified not merely as "a political turnover that changed the ruling class and economy" (p. 15), but "as a cosmic event that would transform everything from technology to the very nature of people, their conduct, their culture" (p. 15). This appreciation is echoed by Luria (1979) in his autobiography as he states that his entire generation was "infused with the energy of revolutionary change- the liberating energy people feel when they are part of a society that is able to make tremendous progress in a very short time" (p. 17).

For some people those changes were very personal and profoundly transformational. That was the case of a group of young Cuban psychologists that were granted scholarships to undertake graduate studies in Russia in the context of the close relationship that the former USSR and Cuba had at the time. González Rey was part of that group whose members were individually and collectively challenged in many ways. Among the main challenges were (1) moving to a geographically distant country very different from a Caribbean island in climate, social and cultural norms, traditions, and practices, (2) leaving behind family, friends and a known environment, (3) learning and mastering a new language in order to communicate and participate in their new context, (4) completing their postgraduate training with new academic practices and, after that, and (5) returning to Cuba to transfer the knowledge developed to academia and professional practice. The impact of the experience was felt in their academic and professional careers and in the country (Bernal & Rodríguez Arocho, 1990; Calviño & de la Torre, 1997; de la Torre, 2009).

His postgraduate education in the USSR placed González Rey and his Cuban colleagues sharing the experience in a privileged position. They all got access to literature in the original language that was not very well known in the West. He became interested in the concepts of personality and communication. On the former, he recognized the influence of Bozhovich and on the latter the influence of B. F. Lomov. In the process, he initiated a critique of the concept of activity in Soviet psychology that deepened over time (González Rey, 2017a).

After returning to Cuba González Rey and his colleagues assumed leadership in the field of psychology in activities as teaching, researching, and developing and implementing applications in serval areas, mainly education, health, and work. He continued working on the topics of personality and motivation. In his writings at the time, the traits that I pointed to as key to the development of his theory of subjectivity (reflexivity, critical thinking, and a dialogic approach) started to make themselves visible. These traits may well be shared by others because, as Calviño and de la Torre (1997) point out, the transference of what they had learned and practiced in the USSR was confronted by the tensions and contradictions of another reality in their transfer to Cuba. Despite these difficulties, González Rey was able to advance an important research program about personality, motivation and moral development. He was a productive and influential academic. However, his circumstances eventually changed. A historical account of Cuban psychology in the context of the Revolution by de la Torre (2009) may help to put this in perspective.

The account of de la Torre (2009) proposed a periodization of four stages. The first one, in the decade of 1960, was characterized by using psychology as a tool in the great social transformations taking place in the country. The second stage, covering the decade of 1970, was a continuation of the previous decade but characterized by an acritical extrapolation of Soviet models to psychology and its applications. The third stage during the 1980s included a significant development on original national knowledge productions and applications that lasted until the early 1990s. The fourth stage, during the 1990s was marked by the disintegration of the USSR, which had a dramatic impact in the Cuban economy and sociocultural life. This period was a turning point in González Rey's life.

According to Goulart et al. (2020) from 1995 to 1999 González Rey was a visiting professor in Brazil. Their account states that "tensions with more orthodox wings of the Ministry of Higher Education and the Communist Party" (p. 4) set conditions that didn't allow his return to Cuba nor that of Albertina, his professional and life partner. The new circumstances left him in Brazil, speaking a new language, living in a new sociocultural context, and beginning a new career at the Centro Universitario of Brasilia as his main workplace. There and at the University of Brasilia he formed several research groups and advanced his work on the theory of subjectivity. While in Brazil, he was forthcoming expressing his points of view about the Cuban Revolution and its developments (González Rey, 2019a, c).

In sum, González Rey's life placed him in circumstances, some of them extraordinary, that allowed him to develop as an individual and social subject. The changes in his social situation of development placed him in contexts where emotional experiences were intense, and he integrated them into his intellectual production.

6.4   The Socio-Institutional Contexts of the Production and Reception of the Theory

Mitjáns-Martínez's chapter in this book divides the work of González Rey into two main periods characterized by his theoretical and research interests. The first one, from 1973 to 1997, focused on personality and its development. In this period there is an overlapping of socio-institutional contexts of production between academic training and research in Moscow and work and research in Cuba. The second period that covers from 1997 to 2019 was focused on the study of subjectivity and qualitative epistemology. The context for this period were institutions of higher education and research centers in Brazil, mainly in Brasilia. Although these were the specific contexts for face-to-face regular interactions with students and colleagues, it should be kept in mind that there is a broader socio-institutional context in the academic culture that include scientific congresses, publications in specialized journals, media presentations and other forms of exchange.

Mitjáns-Martínez's account of the 23 years González Rey dedicated to the study of personality overlaps with three different moments in de la Torre's (2009) periodization of the development of psychology in Cuba. In her classification for this lapse of time, first, there was a period of irreflective extrapolation of Soviet psychology, then there were original productions with critical perspectives and, finally, a disruption in many dimensions of life in the midst of the disintegration of the USSR. It is difficult to accommodate González Rey's work in the first period because, since his years as a graduate student in Moscow, he was critical of theoretical and methodological approaches to personality. In his early works, his critical perspective was integrated into his research. However, he had to struggle with accepted views of personality as the expression of individuals traits or characteristic that remained relatively stable over time and served to orient human activities, as he was moving to develop a more complex view (González Rey, 1995). In this complex view, the development of personality was linked to the historical, cultural, and social dimensions of its configuration and the unity of affect and intellect was stressed, as was the notion of a systemic dynamic between content and function in human activity. He also underlined the relationship of personality with two other psychological concepts: communication and motivation (González Rey, 1995). In the context of the socio-institutional demands for the application of knowledge to address social issues, his work emphasized the educational implications and applications of the study of personality (González Rey & Mitjáns-Martínez, 1989). His work became very influential and it was frequently cited in the productions of Cuban psychologists in different areas and remained so until the decade of 2000.

Beginning the decade of 1990, the disintegration of the USRR had a severe negative effect on the Cuban economy that affecting the daily life of the population in what was named "the special period" (de la Torre, 2009). In the academic setting, people kept working and providing services, with serious limitations. It is during this period that González Rey went to work in Brazil, where he remained until his death. By then his work was very well known and valued in Latin America, not only because of his contributions to a more complex view of personality from a cultural-historical perspective but also for his active participation in the development of critical social psychology for the region. At that time there was a critical movement in Latin American psychology about the irreflective extrapolation of theories and practices from the United States and Europe. The claim for indigenous perspectives and action research was having an important impact in the region and a cultural-historical perspective was welcomed. Within this movement, social psychology was understood to have political, and ethical ramifications. The personal relations and networks of González Rey with the main protagonists of this movement (Maritza Montero, Ignacio Martín Baró, Ignacio Dobles, and Bernando Jiménez, among others) lasted for many years and influenced (González Rey, 2004) his work.

The shift to subjectivity as the main category of analysis and the development of a qualitative epistemology were in the making when González Rey relocated to Brazil. In what could be considered a prelude to his discussion and critique of the traditional approach to personality in mainstream cultural-historical psychology, González Rey (1999) put forward ideas and notions that would eventually be incorporated in the formulation of his theory. The distinction between meaning and sense, and the emphasis on emotions and feelings as well as motives and needs are the main themes in this work. He points out that the concept of subjectivity is not a substitute for the concept of personality when he states that "the cultural-historical character of subjectivity allows us to integrate the complex dialectical process of personality with social context" (p. 265). In undertaking the elaboration of the concept of subjectivity and the methodology for its study he counted with the collaboration of his wife and colleague and identified and organized persons that were willing to participate in the project.

In shifting the focus from personality to subjectivity one thing remained constant: his ontological and epistemological concern about psychology as a science. Related to that was his critique to empiricism and positivism, which was the foundation of his proposal for a qualitative epistemology for the study of subjectivity as a new ontological domain (González Rey, 1999, 2009, 2019a; Patiño & Goulart, 2016).

The academic institutions where he worked in Brazil were the setting of several research teams focusing on subjectivity related to education, health and creativity. During his time there, he was professor, researcher, and mentor to a new generation of colleagues who, from Brazil and other countries, have moved research forward using his theoretical and methodological contributions. He explicitly said that his theory wasn't a closed system but one open to questioning and new developments (González Rey, 2019a).

The influence of his work gradually transcended Brazil and Latin America. While living and working in Cuba he was already a main exponent in international congresses and his work was recognized. Participation in congresses before and after his relocation to Brazil was consistent, as were publications and invitations as a visiting professor were consistent and boosted his international visibility (Rodríguez Arocho, 2019a). That received a definitive push with publications in English journals and edited books which contributed to expand the scope of his work.

After his death, two special sections in volume 30 of the *Revista Puertorriqueña de Psicología* (Puerto Rican Journal of Psychology) have been dedicated to honor the memory of González Rey and present research that used his theory as a conceptual framework (Rodríguez Arocho, 2019a, 2019b). A special issue of the bilingual journal *Estudios de Psicología/Studies of Psychology* was published in 2020 and several books are in process of edition. The *37 Interamerican Congress of Psychology*, sponsored by the Interamerican Society of Psychology and the Cuban Society of Psychology, held in Havana in July 2019, was dedicated to him. This was followed by a special issue of *Revista Alternativas Cubanas en Psicología* (*Cuban Alternatives in Psychology Journal*) in 2020. These events create opportunities to continue dialogues like the one he held in December 2013 with colleagues in Havana about motivation, personality and subjectivity that is available in YouTube. As whole these activities represent an important recognition of Gonzalez Rey's legacy.

6.5   Conclusion

The analysis of González Rey's written texts mentioned in this chapter shows reflective, critical dialogical thinking and creativity. Ideas are always expressed in an articulate argumentative and passionate way. His written and spoken words were intended to problematize, promote debate and stimulate divergent thinking in his interlocutors. The dramatic circumstances of personal experiences in his lifetime allowed him to be a witness to extraordinary changes, namely more than one political and sociocultural revolution during his life in different contexts. He worked in diverse socio-institutional settings, could communicate in several languages, and became part of an international network that is advancing new understandings of Vygotsky's legacy. These intertwined circumstances are present in his theory of subjectivity. After examining his work, his life and the socio-institutional context in which it was produced, the assessment of Goulart et al. (2020) seems to synthesize his theory of subjectivity. They describe it as "an attempt to understand the complexity of human functioning within the conditions of culture, which implies, among other aspects, supporting the generative, creative, countercultural character of individuals and social groups against the normative status quo of a given institution or social, political, cultural reality" (p. 2). In this quote, they capture the subversive character that González Rey attributed to his conceptualization of subjectivity (González Rey, 2017a).

References

Ageyev, V. S. (2003). Vygotsky in the mirror of cultural interpretations. In A. Kozulin, B. Guindis, V. S. Ageyev, & y S. Miller (Eds.), *Vygotsky's educational theory in cultural context* (pp. 432–449). Cambridge: Cambridge University Press.

Bernal, G., & Rodríguez Arocho, W. (1990). Educación y áreas de trabajo del psicólogo en Cuba. *Revista Puertorriqueña de Psicología, 6*(1), 25–53.

Calviño, M., & de la Torre, C. (1997). La historia después de Vygotsky: Una mirada desde lo vivencial. *Revista Cubana de Psicología, 4*(2), 225–234.

Dafermos, M. (2014). Vygotsky's analysis of the crisis of psychology: Diagnosis, treatment, and relevance. *Theory and Psychology, 24*(2), 145–165.

Dafermos, M. (2016). Critical reflection on the reception of Vygotsky's theory in the international academic community. *Cultural-Historical Psychology, 12*(3), 27–43.

Dafermos, M. (2018). *Rethinking cultural-historical psychology: A dialectical perspective to Vygotsky*. Singapore: Springer.

Daniels, H. (2001). *Vygotsky and pedagogy*. New York: Routledge Falmer.

Dazinger, K. (1997). *Naming the mind: How psychology found its language*. Thousand Oaks: Sage.

de la Torre, C. (2009). Historia de la psicología en Cuba: cincuenta años de Psicología-cincuenta años de revolución. Retrieved from www.psicolatina.org/17/cuba/hml.

Elhammoumi, M. (2001). Lost—Or merely domesticated? The boom in socio-historicocultural theory emphasizes some concepts, overlook others. In S. Chaklin (Ed.), *The theory and practice of cultural-historical psychology* (pp. 200–217). Arhaus: Arhaus University Press.

Fleer, M., González Rey, F., & Veresov, N. (Eds.). (2017). *Perezhivanie, emotions and subjectivity: Advancing Vygotsky's legacy*. Singapore: Springer.

García, N. L. (2019). On Vygotsky's international celebration, or how to critically appropriate authors form the past. In A. Yasnitsky (Ed.), *Questioning Vygotsky's legacy: Scientific psychology or heroic cult* (pp. 161–183). New York: Routledge.

González Rey, F. L. (1999). Personality, subject and human development: The subjective character of human activity. In S. Chaklin, M. Heedegard, & U. F. Jensen (Eds.), *Activity theory and social practice* (pp. 253–275). Aarhus: Aarhus University Press.

González Rey, F. L. (2004). La crítica de la psicología social latinoamericana y su impacto en diferentes campos de la psicología [The critique of Latinamerican social psychology y its impact in different fields of psychology]. *Revista Interamericana de Psicología, 38*(2), 351–360.

González Rey, F. L. (2007). *Investigación cualitativa y subjetividad* [Qualitative research and subjectivity]. México, DF: McGraw Hill.

González Rey, F. L. (2008). Subjetividad social, sujeto y representaciones sociales [Social subjectivity, subject and social representations]. *Diversitas- Perspectivas en Psicología, 4*(2), 225–243.

González Rey, F. L. (2009). Epistemología y ontología: Un debate necesario para la psicología de hoy [Epistemology and ontology: A neccessary debate for today's psychology]. *Diversitas: Perspectivas en Psicología, 5*(2), 205–224.

González Rey, F. L. (2011a). *El pensamiento de Vygotsky: Contradicciones, desdoblamientos y desarrollo* [Vygotsky's thinking: Contradictions, unfoldings and development]. México: Editorial Trillas.

González Rey, F. L. (2011b). The path to subjectivity: Advancing alternative understanding of Vygotsky and the cultural-historical legacy. In P. Portes & S. Salas (Eds.), *Vygotsky in the 21st century society: Advances in cultural-historical theory and praxis with non-dominant communities* (pp. 32–49). New York: Peter Lang.

González Rey, F. L. (2017a). Advances in subjectivity from a cultural-historical perspective: Unfolding and consequences for cultural studies today. In M. Fleer, F. L. González Rey, & N. Veresov (Eds.), *Perezhivanie, emotions and subjectivity: Advancing Vygotsky's legacy* (pp. 173–193). Singapore: Springer.

González Rey, F. L. (2017b). Salpicadas críticas y malabarismos en torno a "hacer psicología en Cuba". *Revista Puertorriqueña de Psicología, 28*(1), 198–211.

González Rey, F. L. (2019a). Subjectivity as new theoretical, epistemological and methodological pathway within cultural-historical psychology. In F. L. González Rey, A. Mitjáns-Martínez, & D. Goulart (Eds.), *Subjectivity within the cultural-historical approach* (pp. 21–36). Singapore: Springer.

González Rey, F. L. (2019b). Fifty years after L. I. Bozhovich's personality and its formation in childhood: Recovering her legacy and her historical role. *Mind, Culture, and Activity, 26*(2), 108–120.

González Rey, F. L. (2019c). Crítica, psicología y ciencias sociales en Cuba. *Teoría y Crítica de la Psicología, 12*(1), 1–9.

González Rey, F. L, & Mitjáns-Martínez, A. (1989). *La personalidad: Su educación y desarrollo* [Personality: Its education and development]. La Habana: Editorial Pueblo y Educación.

González Rey, F. L., Mitjáns-Martínez, A., & Goulart, D. (Eds.). (2019). *Subjectivity within the cultural-historical approach*. Singapore: Springer.

Goulart, D. (2019). Subjectivity and life: In memory of Fernando González Rey. *Mind, Culture, and Activity*. https://doi.org/10.1080/10749039.2019.1619775.

Goulart, D., Mitjáns-Martínez, A., & Esteban-Guitart, M. (2020). The trajectory and work of Fernando González Rey: Paths to his theory of subjectivity. *Studies in Psychology, 41*(1), 9–30.

Koch, S. (1999). *Psychology in human contexts: Essays in dissidence and reconstruction*. Chicago: University of Chicago Press.

Kozulin, A. (1984). *Psychology in utopia*. Cambridge, MA: MIT Press.

Luria, A. R. (1979). *The making of a mind: A personal account of soviet psychology* (M. Cole & S. Cole, Eds.). Cambridge, MA: Harvard University Press.

Matusov, E. (2008). Applying sociocultural approach to Vygotskian academia: Our tzar it is not like yours and yours isn't like ours. *Culture and Psychology, 14*(1), 5–35.

Patiño, J. F., & Goulart, D. (2016). Qualitative epistemology: A scientific platform for the study of subjectivity from a cultural-historical approach. *International Research in Early Education, 7*(1), 162–181.

Rodríguez Arocho, W. C. (2019a). Fernando Luis González Rey (1949–2019). *Revista Puertorriqueña de Psicología, 30*(1), 176–178. http://www.ojs.repsasppr.net/index.php/reps/article/view/564/618.

Rodríguez Arocho, W. C. (2019b). En Memoria de Fernando González Rey (1949–2019): Introducción. *Revista Puertorriqueña de Psicología, 30*(2), 230–232.

Rosa, A., Huertas, J. A., & Blanco, F. (1996). *Metodología para la historia de la psicología* [Methodology for the history of psychology]. Madrid: Alianza Editorial.

Rosa, A., & Valsiner, J. (2018). The human Psyche lives in semiospheres. In. R. Rosa & J. Valsiner (Eds.), *Cambridge handbook of sociocultural psychology* (2nd ed.) (pp. 16–34). New York: Cambridge University Press.

Valsiner, J., & Rosa, A. (2007). The myth and beyond: Ontology of Psyche and epistemology of psychology. In J. Valsiner & R. Rosa (Eds.), *Cambridge handbook of sociocultural psychology* (pp. 23–39). New York: Cambridge University Press.

Veresov, N. (1999). *Undiscovered Vygotsky*. New York: Peter Lang.

Vygotsky, L. S. (1927/1997). The historical meaning of the crisis of psychology. In R. W. Rieber & J. Wollock (Eds.), *The collected works of L. S. Vygotsky: Problems of the theory and history of psychology* (Vol. 3, pp. 233–344). New York, NY: Plenum Press.

Vygotsky, L. S. (1935/1994). The problem of the environment. In R. Van der Veer & J. Valsiner (Eds.), *The Vygotsky reader* (pp. 338–354). New York: Blackwell.

Yasnitsky, A., & Van der Veer, R. (Eds.). (2016). *Revisionist revolution in Vygotsky studies*. New York: Routledge.

Zavershneva, E. (2012). Investigating L. S. Vygotsky's manuscript "The historical meaning of the crisis in psychology". *Journal of Russian & East European Psychology, 50*(4), 42–63.

Zavershneva, E. I., & Osipov, M. E. (2012). Primary changes to the version of "The historical meaning of the crisis in psychology" Published in the collected works of L. S. Vygotsky. *Journal of Russian & East European Psychology, 50*(4), 64–84.

Wanda C. Rodríguez Arocho is retired Full Professor from the University of Puerto Rico, where she received a doctoral degree in Psychology (1989) and a master's degree in Education (1977). She worked for 25 years at the Department of Psychology there after five years of teaching and counseling in public schools in Puerto Rico. Her teaching and research work have focused on cognitive processes, learning and human development from a cultural-historical perspective She has four books and more than fifty articles in professional journals and edited books. She has been a guest lecturer or professor in many Latin American universities and has occupied leadership positions the American Psychological Association, American Counseling Association and the Interamerican Society of Psychology.

Chapter 7
Understanding and Developing Vygotsky's Legacy Through the Work of González Rey

David Subero and Moisès Esteban-Guitart

Abstract Lev Vygotsky (1896–1934) is the most influential and, at the same time, controversial figure in the context of cultural-historical theory. Far from providing a conclusive and homogeneous thought system, what Vygotsky offers us is the chance to explore new understandings on human consciousness and psychological functioning. In our view, the main contribution that González Rey has made to Vygotskian studies is precisely this: he provides us with a new interpretative framework, not only to better understand Vygotsky, but also to go beyond him, and to open up broad horizons of understanding of phenomena that were simply intuited by Vygotsky, such as the notion of sense, or that of *perezhivanie*. This chapter is divided into five sections. First, we briefly contextualize the purpose of the chapter. Second, we put the discussion into context by addressing Vygotsky's life and intellectual development, and take the opportunity to contrast the three stages of Vygotsky proposed by González Rey with other contemporary views. Third, we discuss the importance of the work carried out by Lidia Bozhovich (1908–2004). Fourth, we describe how González Rey arrived at his theory of subjectivity. Finally, we discuss the relevance of a theory of subjectivity within the framework of Vygotskian studies.

7.1 Contextualization

It could be said that all intellectual production is indebted to a biography. In this sense, any effort at intelligibility relies on life experiences from which various conceptualizations and understandings emerge, forged by these experiences. This is especially true in our view in the case of such creative and unique works as those of Fernando Luis González Rey (Goulart et al., 2020). His participation in the Cuban revolution, and his subsequent critical reexamination of it, are interwoven with his resolve

D. Subero (✉) · M. Esteban-Guitart
University of Girona, Girona, Spain
e-mail: davidsubero@gmail.com

M. Esteban-Guitart
e-mail: moises.esteban@udg.edu

© The Author(s), under exclusive license to Springer Nature Singapore Pte Ltd. 2021   105
D. M. Goulart et al. (eds.), *Theory of Subjectivity from a Cultural-Historical Standpoint*,
Perspectives in Cultural-Historical Research 9,
https://doi.org/10.1007/978-981-16-1417-0_7

to proclaim the inherent nature of human decision and creativity, while opposed to any attempt to reduce it to biological, discursive, institutional or environmental processes. This seems to us to be the core of González Rey's contribution and, at the same time, it is what articulates and gives coherence to his proposal, made while fully and honestly engaged in his own life.

We shall not attempt, in this chapter, to summarize the author's extensive work, since his contributions, as can be seen in this book, cover such broad territory as conceptualization and methodology, critical theory, as well as original ontological and psychological conceptions. Instead, our aim, in the form of a tribute to a generous legacy, is to describe the critical role that Vygotsky played in González Rey's theory of subjectivity. It was in some ways an ambivalent relationship between the two authors since although the influence the former had on the latter is well recognized, González Rey critically reexamined Vygotsky's legacy in his pursuit of his own genuine and creative proposal.

We ourselves had the good fortune to meet and exchange views with González Rey on several occasions. The subjective configuration we share never fails to generate happy memories of a very special and unique character, full of vitality and generosity. We had initiated a lively discussion concerning his theory of subjectivity (widely discussed in this book) and our own work linked to the notion of *funds of identity* (Esteban-Guitart, 2016; Subero, 2020). Like any human process, incomplete by definition, the debate continues and will continue to simmer and, although we shall not address the issue in this chapter, it does add a certain color to our personal, affective, and intellectual relationship. In one of his posthumous texts, González Rey made a similar conclusion, saying:

> Bozhovich took an important step toward recognizing that personality is not a reflection of the world, but a production within cultural-social processes that are historically located. In this regard, she made explicit what was implicit in Vygotsky's final concepts, such as sense and perezhivanie. Bozhovich's advances in terms of motivation and personality were an important antecedent for new paths within cultural-historical psychology, such as funds of identity and subjectivity. (González Rey, 2019, p. 118)

We cannot disagree with González Rey. And indeed, the objective we pursue in this chapter is to trace the links in his work with Vygotskian theory, including those based on contributions by Bozhovich, an author who deserves more recognition, and one who we think can stimulate contemporary debates on personality, identity, motivation, meaning, or the notion of *perezhivanie*—all of which are understood, as we shall see, as dynamic "epistemic" processes and generators of psychological and cultural realities.

7.2 Biography and Intellectual Development of Lev Vygotsky

It is the instrumental period of the work of Lev Semyonovich Vygotsky (1896–1934) which made the most impact in the West, beginning, in particular, with the publication of a collection of his essays, *Mind in Society* (Vygotsky, 1978), which brought to light such well-known categories as *higher psychological functions*, the *zone of proximal development*, *internalization*, *mediation* or *inter-* and *intrapsychological processes*, among others. The core idea of this period can be summarized under the *principle of signification*, according to which our species is characterized by the regulation of behavior, our own and others, by means of the creation and use of signs and symbols (Esteban-Guitart, 2010; Vygotsky, 1997): traffic lights tell us when to cross a street; a crucifix on the wall exalts a religious belief; the alarm clock wakes us in the morning, while WhatsApp amplifies and regulates our social interactions beyond the barriers of time and space.

However, far from seeing the study of Vygotsky's work as a regular sequence of categories and harmonious moments with each other, we must understand this as a system that is contradictory, alive, and developing (González Rey, 2011) as well as being subject to all kinds of political and personal vicissitudes, including professional career concerns (Esteban-Guitart, 2018).

The analysis of the different periods of Vygotsky's works has been dealt with by authors in different ways, with various interpretations put forward. Recently, an intellectual biography of Vygotsky reconsidered the various stages of the author's evolution, and distinguished six periods: prophet, Bolshevik, reflexologist, psychologist-reactologist, revisionist, and holistic (Yasnitsky, 2018). Alternatively, Zavershneva and van der Veer (2018) distinguish five periods of Vygotsky's work: a pre-psychological period (1912–1922), the "reactological" period (1923–1925), instrumental psychology (1926–1929), a transitional period in which he introduced the systemic principle: (1930–1931) and, finally, his development of the theory of dynamic semantic systems and the psychology of experience (1932–1934).

In contrast, González Rey (2009, 2011, 2014, 2016)—who highlights some of the contradictions of Vygotskian thought and the sometimes accelerated development of his ideas—concluded that there were just three distinct periods in the life and work of Vygotsky. There is a certain amount of (dis)convergence among the three periods, especially in relation to the first and third, during which notions such as *perezhivanie* appear.

The first of these periods is characterized by the work involved in his doctoral thesis, *Psychology of Art*, as well as his studies on pedagogy and defectology. In *Psychology of Art*, the mind is understood as an active, generative and systemic system that is linked to dynamic processes via the personality. It is in these dynamic processes that Vygotsky began to assign a leading role to emotions and feelings, which are associated with imagination and fantasy, through which the signification of the forms of psychological organization of individuals is highlighted (Vygotsky, 1971). According to González Rey (2009), this sensitivity toward human processes as intellectual-affective production would be shelved as his instrumental period took hold, only to be reexamined more explicitly in the third and final period of his work.

The second period, or *instrumental impasse*, centers on a number of works Vygotsky produced between 1928 and 1931 which highlight the use of cultural tools and semiotic mediation for the development of higher psychological functions. In this period, the ground rules of official scientific Marxism had already been established and a series of guidelines ordained—objectivity, scientism, naturalness, reflection—that would, to a large extent, condition the development of psychology at that time. In this context, Vygotsky proposed that the psyche is configured as the result of the internalization of external operations, which are themselves reduced to operations with objects and signs. The origin of the psyche and human behavior is assumed to be social and cultural. On the other hand, the dichotomy between the internal and the external becomes evident by means of these internalization processes in a direct and linear way. The reflection of external functions in the internal operations implies a passive-assimilative role for the human mind which is understood as a result of the genetically previous, social-material world. At this juncture, there is no trace of the idea of mind as a system and he moves on toward an objective, materialistic, and mechanistic psychology. This change in Vygotsky's criteria are understandable given that his thinking and interests were, at that time, closer to Bekhterev's reflexology and Kornilov's reactology (Esteban-Guitart, 2018).

However, toward the end of this instrumental period, a problem began to emerge that, for Vygotsky, was fundamental in the history of psychology and for which, until then, he had not found a satisfactory solution: *the problem of consciousness* (Yasnitsky, 2018; Zavershneva, 2014). Nevertheless, Vygotsky did not attempt to define consciousness at this stage, much less propose a possible ontological definition of the phenomenon. But we now know that one of his unfinished projects was, precisely, the development of a general theory about consciousness (Zavershneva & van der Veer, 2018). In search of a reciprocity between the external and the internal, consciousness emerged as a fundamental unit to overcome this dichotomy. During his instrumental stage, what was relevant was the sign, the mediating operations, and the passing of inferior psychological functions to the superior ones; but the author now began to change his focus toward the relationships between the functions, or psychological processes, pointing out that it is these relationships that change and are modified, causing new constellations—psychological systems—to emerge in the course of human development. This dynamism, and the emergence of new relationships in consciousness, became incompatible with a construction of the mind based on action, and subject to it. He needed to return to the understanding of the psyche as a complex system in order to find an answer to the dilemma.

Incidentally, according to Zavershneva (2014), Vygotsky's "conceptualization" of consciousness can also be used to distinguish three periods in his work. Between 1924 and 1926, Vygotsky interpreted consciousness as a mechanism for transmitting reflexes, an idea illustrated in his book on pedagogy or educational psychology (Esteban-Guitart, 2018). Subsequently, from 1927 until 1931, he saw consciousness as a secondary system of connections between the higher psychological functions. Finally, in a moment of critical reflection of the ideas developed so far, between 1932 and 1934, consciousness was conceived as a dynamic semantic system (Zavershneva, 2014).

In any case, the third and final stage of Vygotsky—according to Gonzalez Rey (2011)—involves the reexamination and reevaluation of the works relating to a holistic and experiential vision of psychology that explores notions such as those of meaning, social situation of development, dynamic systems, the active nature of the psyche, and the idea of *perezhivanie* as a unit of analysis of human consciousness. Some authors underline the importance and influence, at that time, of gestaltism (especially Kurt Koffka) as well as Kurt Lewin (Yasnitsky & van der Veer, 2016).

Throughout the history of psychology, emotions had been relegated to the study of the psyche or else understood simply as by-products of cognition. However, Vygotsky now proposed that there was a functional unity between affection and intellect. Understanding the psyche as a complex system meant going beyond the idea of emotions as natural regulators and giving them a new psychological quality; emotions now formed part of a whole system comprising the set of human psychological manifestations—thinking, perception, memory, fantasy, or language—which, together with the environment and other contextual forces and situations, would merge into one individual *perezhivanie*. Thus, the concept of *perezhivanie* is understood as the psychological unity between the cognitive and affective that the environment articulates (González Rey, 2016). In this way, the conception of the environment linked to operations with objects was rejected in favor of a conceptualization of the social environment as a process in which there is no separation between the context and the psychological organization of the individual (González Rey & Mitjáns Martínez, 2016).

In the same vein, the concept of *sense* in the conceptual development during this third stage of Vygotsky's thinking is especially noteworthy. Originally, the idea of sense appears in reference to language and is defined as all of the psychological elements that appear in consciousness with the emergence of the word (Vygotsky, 1987). The referential importance of sense derives from an understanding of sense as a psychological unit of consciousness, which is activated through language with others, with an open and flexible disposition. Bearing in mind that the concept of communication had not been developed in the framework of Soviet psychology, this precedent would pave the way for further developments. González Rey, as we will argue below, would take up the concept again in a different ontology linked to the subjective senses within the theory of subjectivity (González Rey, 2019).

7.3 Personality as a Theoretical Resource for Investigating Subjectivity

The prevalence of activity theory during the Soviet period had the effect of sidelining the concepts of *perezhivanie*, sense, and the importance of cognitive-intellectual and affective elements as a generative unit; this, in turn, reduced the influence of Vygotsky to that of his instrumental period. The dogmatic objectivism of Marxist psychology began to give way at the Fifth Congress of the Society of Psychologists of the Soviet Union, with the introduction of new theoretical premises such as the symbolic in its broadest sense, the relevance of communication, and a broader understanding of culture and social reality (González Rey, 2014). Some years before, Bozhovich's laboratory was one of the few that had reexamined the concepts of the social situation of development and *perezhivanie* and, within its experimental activities, resumed work on them, thus making advances in a new conception of personality and motivation that could not be reduced to the tenets of the instrumental approach (Chudnovskii, 2009; González Rey, 2019).

In particular, Bozhovich looked again at the social situation of development and *perezhivanie*, understanding them as part of the same process. In addition, she highlighted a third variable, the chronological periods or stages, when defining psychological development (something Vygotsky had also explored shortly before he died). The importance of the stages of development arose from the idea that those elements of the environment that can influence the child do so in different ways depending on the child's stage of development (Bozhovich, 1968). Thus, the social situation of development is understood as the combination of internal development processes and external conditions that are typical of each stage of development; and this combination shapes both the dynamics of mental development and the new psychological formations that emerge (Bozhovich, 1968). In this way, the unit to be used in studying the social situation of development is the *perezhivanie*, as an active and generative process. Bozhovich took up the concept of *perezhivanie* that Vygotsky had begun to develop but not without making two fundamental criticisms of it. The first involved the intellectualist nature of the concept, and the second was the need to take the concept further, toward self-generative units in the development of personality.

As regards the first, Bozhovich criticized the "intellectualist" nature of the concept in that Vygotsky reduces *perezhivanie* to children's ability to generalize their experience, which implies there is a hierarchy between that which is cognitive above that which is affective, thus undermining the idea of a unitary and equidistant nature of the development process (Bozhovich, 2009).

In relation to the second criticism, Bozhovich suggests emphasizing the self-generative nature of personality and its "independence" from the immediate influences of the environment. In this way, *perezhivanie* no longer responds to specific social influence and is seen instead as an expression of the child's motivation system within which the different motivational processes interrelate with each other, becoming, themselves, something that the individual needs (González Rey & Mitjáns Martínez, 2016). The motivational spaces are formed as areas of production of self-generative units, with the emphasis on the active and dynamic affective/emotional and intellectual processes that emerge in the transactional framework of human actions in particular cultural and historical environments (González Rey, 2019; Bozhovich, 1968). In this way, human development does not arise in the external environment in any immediate way, but rather, it is the self-generating character of personality that is emphasized. However, these positions had certain limitations which subsequently came under the critical eye of González Rey (2014). We will now turn our attention to three of these limitations.

First, one of the explanatory limitations within this theory of the development of personality was how, within the complex cosmos of relationships and social processes, personality acted in a unique way. What was needed, in this case, was the existence of concepts that despite differentiating the individual from the social, allowed the construction of a type of phenomenon whose nature was peculiar to human processes, both social and individual. These reflections gave rise to what would later become configurations of personality which, in a different ontological framework, would subsequently be established as "subjective configurations" (González Rey, 2014).

Second, relating to the concept of the social situation of development, and given the need to define the social environment beyond the immediate external influences, Bozhovich incorporated the concept of *internal position* expressing a complex nucleus of interrelated psychological characteristics associated with the position that the child has within the groups that surround him (González Rey, 2019: Bozhovich, 1968). In this way, a deeper understanding was sought of the child's psychological characteristics in relation to the system of those of their closest social relationships that influence their behavior. However, what was initially an attempt to go further than the immediate social spaces became an immediate understanding of the social relations within spaces that the author, in some of her research, considered to be specific systems of interrelation; such as, for example, school and family.

When a child is in school, not only is he generating *perezhivanie* in the social influence he is receiving—from the teacher, from the classroom, from the school—he also brings with him a subjective world comprising multiple symbolic productions subjectivized by the individual throughout his life story and which also emerge at this time. The criticism of Bozhovich refers to the fact that, in a transactional view, a social space can only be a moment in the child's life. That is to say, the subjective social world of the child—which he himself produces—cannot be left out of the social spaces he moves in. A phenomenon such as, for example, school failure cannot be determined by specific spaces of interrelation, nor to a set of biographical memories which accumulate in children more as a reproduced phenomenon than as generative production. This calls into question the self-generative nature of the units defended by Bozhovich. Therefore, we understand that the accumulation of retrospective experiences from specific social spaces in which these experiences determine the development of the person is incompatible with a vision of development in which life experiences and unique life stories intermingle and emerge as self-generated units.

Thirdly, one of the most innovative components of Bozhovich's proposal regarding personality development was the assertion that certain psychological formations of personality throughout this process are especially sensitive to particular moments of development. However, one of the criticisms of the author concerns the idea of reducing the representation of a child's development to standardized stages based on children, adolescents, and young people who attend school (González Rey, 2019). We understand such universalization in fixed and stable stages is incompatible with a vision of development in which culture and social conditions are dynamic, diverse, and subjectively constructed by the individual. This assertion leads us to the notion of subjective development, inseparable from culture and human agency, as a symbolic-emotional unit, both individual and social, subject to changes and transformations that are not necessarily under regular and standardized stages (González Rey & Mitjáns Martínez, 2017).

In short, the influence of Bozhovich is key to understanding the intellectual production of González Rey, although as occurred with Vygotsky's work, González Rey also made his own genuine and creative developments and contributions. Personality, in this sense, is not conceived as a reflex, a reaction, or a product of biology or the environment, but rather as a dynamic production via sociocultural processes that are historically contingent. This idea is central to González Rey's theory of subjectivity to the extent that what it emphasizes is the possibility of creating new alternatives within normative systems, an idea that we will attempt to put into context in the following section.

7.4   Toward a Concept of Subjectivity from a Cultural-Historical Standpoint

In addition to the influence of Bozhovich's work and Gonzalez Rey's collaboration with the group of researchers she led in Moscow, the inception of the theory of subjectivity can also be traced back to the way Vygotsky and, especially Rubinstein, understood the relationship between consciousness and human actions (González Rey, 2014). Until then, consciousness had been understood as an intrapsychic entity, an aspect still valid in contemporary theories rooted in cognitivism. Rubinstein (1964), in contrast, proposed a unity between consciousness and activity, by saying that all human action involves consciousness, and in turn, all consciousness itself expresses a system of actions. In fact, Vygotsky, Bozhovich, and Rubinstein moved toward an understanding of the psyche as a system of processes that were continuous and related to each other in ways that blurred the boundaries between the external and the internal (González Rey, 2015).

As a precedent, the Leningrad school also had a major impact on the incorporation of highly important concepts such as communication and the value of what is symbolic-relational in culture. Ananiev, a leading figure of the Leningrad school, defended the idea of the social as a system of relationships based on communication, and man as a communicational and relational being who was active and generative in character (González Rey, 2011). Such reflections, in a time when operations with objects and the cognitive replaced consciousness, had an influence on later developments, such as the theory of subjectivity. In addition to the above, the theory of subjectivity goes beyond the dominant ideas in the cultural-historical perspective and incorporates other resources and references such as the contributions of Kurt Lewin, Michel Foucault's later works on the Self and the art of living—in contrast to discourse theory, social constructionism and the theory of social representations, all of which theoretical perspectives were examined and challenged by González Rey (2017).

In fact, the archeology of González Rey's theory runs parallel to the life and work of the man himself. At a time when most Cuban psychologists preferred to further their studies at the laboratory of Leontiev, González Rey, instead, developed his doctoral thesis on "The role of moral ideals in the formation of students' professional intentions" at the laboratory of Bozhovich, with Chudnovskii. The differences between Leontiev and Bozhovich were notorious. While the former understood motive as external activity, the latter understood the study of human motivation as a process that could not be reduced to elements. González Rey's interest in the formation of personality in terms of the motivational discussion and a comprehensive explanation of the psychological nature of motivation that included motive, consciousness and personality via the concept of will, left an indelible mark on the author in the development of his theories (Goulart, 2019a).

Subjectivity is understood as a new quality in human processes configured within the symbolic-emotional existence, which itself is within sociocultural systems. The psyche is understood and integrated into the system by means of subjectivity. This process is not determined by universal stages or principles. Rather, it materializes through subjective senses and configurations. Subjective senses represent symbolic-emotional units. These units can be described as self-dynamic, variable, generative, and self-regulating that transcend the external objective conditions and characterize human experiences in a completely genuine way (González Rey, 2015). The subjective configurations represent the organization of relatively stable subjective senses in relation to a particularly relevant moment for the person, which in turn becomes a source capable of generating new subjective senses. The really novel thing about this process is that, despite being a consequence of people's lived experiences, the subjective senses and configurations emerge as totally new productions that facilitate new moments of human creation that are subject to emotionality, imagination and creativity. Hence, these self-generative traits allow individuals to transform the environment and themselves—an idea that diverges from the psychological approaches that understand the person as a result of a process of adaptation. When the person can generate subjective configurations that allow them to produce new subjective resources to transcend their immediate circumstances, the individual becomes the subject of the situation. The concept of the subject means that the individual takes up the reins of his own subjectivity, actively making decisions that are generated from his own subjective senses (González Rey, 2017).

As we pointed out earlier, in Soviet psychology at the time, the concepts of society and culture were reduced to activity based on instruments/objects. The attempt to transform psychology into a natural and objective science had led to the symbolic being reduced to signs, and limited to a process of internalization and assimilation (Zinchenko, 2009). Social psychology was not relevant in Soviet psychology—Ananiev and the Leningrad School were rare exceptions—as it was considered a matter for the State. Therefore, the positions that identified Soviet psychology as cultural were, in reality, proposing a psychology that was reduced to the individual and to what this individual did in relation to the objects he or she manipulated, understanding the process of development of the person as a linear series of reflexes. In stark contrast, these advances in the symbolic-affective aspects in the theory of subjectivity meant recognizing the subjective character of processes and systems, such as consciousness, society and culture (González Rey, 2017).

Social realities, from this standpoint, were configured as subjective systems of relations and practice, and this broke with the idea of social reality as a given external environment. For example, a discourse on gender equality by a teacher, given as symbolic discourse, is configured in uniquely different subjective ways by students who share the same classroom context, and these configurations, in turn, configure a series of subjectivities that emerge throughout their current life trajectories. Each scenario or social institution is configured by subjective senses which are, in turn, incorporated into other social productions. Thus the senses and the subjective config-urations are not only an individual phenomenon, but also involve social processes, since social life is subjectively configured in the human phenomenon (González Rey, 2015). Therefore, the concept of social subjectivity becomes of fundamental impor-tance in the process of development; social subjectivity and individual subjectivity are two sides of the same coin.

Vygotsky, in the final period of his work, pointed out that psychological functions were functions of the person, and that no psychological functions should be divorced from the experience of "the full vitality of life" (Vygotsky, 1987, p. 50) since it would then no longer be effective as a motive for behavior. However, he could never quite develop this premise beyond some fragmented concepts and without any specific psychological functions. In our view, it is the theory of subjectivity that allows "the full vitality of life" to be taken into account when it comes to understanding the integration of psychological functions (psychological systems) via the symbolic-emotional character in individual subjective configurations (González Rey, 2015).

7.5 The Relevance of a Theory of Subjectivity Within the Framework of Vygotskian Studies

In the end, although human subjectivity has a social, historical and cultural genesis, it cannot simply be reduced to an epiphenomenon of the environment. Instead, and this is, in our view, the most important contribution in Vygotskian studies, human subjectivity is a generative system—open to new creations and cultural alternatives; in short, life options and projects—in normative and institutionalized social spaces. This does not mean we need to assume an individualistic and rationalist perspective, but rather, something which is dynamic and active in which we take on board the permanent capacity for rupture and creation. Goulart (2019a, p. 105) explains a story involving González Rey which we think illustrates this principle perfectly. During the normative and institutional control that González Rey underwent during his illness, he warned: "Please, do not forget that you, doctors, are supporting me in my treatment, but the protagonist of my health is no one but myself." Beyond the norms and social influences (evidently, we mean those to which one subscribes, explicitly or implicitly), subjectivity is organized as a complex dynamic system of configurations of subjective senses with which symbolic and emotional processes build their own realities. These symbolic-emotional units constitute the ontological character of the human experience linked to the permanent possibility of creating new cultural realities, new paths and life projects. Therefore, says González Rey (2017), subjectivity:

"implies continuous resistance to and confrontation with the social hegemonic status quo throughout the history of mankind, opening a theoretical pathway to explain this resistance. At the same time, subjective phenomena are intrinsically polychromatic inside one culture, making impossible any attempt to standardize subjectivity or to submit it to control. Change and development are intrinsic to subjectivity, so any form of resistance is engendered from inside one structure of power, within new subjective productions that may lead to non-predictable changes and consequences, transcending the dominant established rationality". (p. 6)

Applied in the context of a critical approach in mental health, Goulart (2019b) summarized this perspective in what, for us, is its most profound sense:

"The intention is to promote processes of development and change capable of replacing normative and prescriptive dynamics that often dominate the institutional functioning of mental health services. The search is for the promotion of a logic of transformation, to the detriment of a logic based on mental illness and social exclusion". (p. 41)

González Rey was a protagonist of the Cuban revolution, as we said at the beginning of this chapter, but he questioned the diminishment of the individual in favor of an uncritically accepted doctrine that dogmatically governs people's behavior.

"Institutions always develop a set of symbolic resources to exclude the new and anything that threatens the power of their current protagonists. They represent this threat to their power as a threat to the institution and use it to preserve their positions and to keep institutions in their present status quo, blocking any and all possible change". (González Rey, 2012, p. 106)

González Rey personally endured such exclusion, and that is perhaps why his theory tenaciously tries to safeguard the processes of decision, creation, transformation, and production that are subjective, social and cultural. This leads to an associated ethical commitment because this theory presupposes the development of subjective processes of mobilization and transformation of the status quo. But that is yet another aspect of his work worthy of another text, and an example of what makes González Rey's work and legacy so valuable, because, rather than reaching dead ends and conclusions, he stimulates and opens up new roads.

Funding Note This work was supported by the Spanish Ministry of Economy, Industry and Competitiveness (MINECO), the Spanish State Research Agency (AEI) and The European Regional Development Fund (European Union) [grant number EDU2017-83363-R].

References

Bozhovich, L. I. (1968). *La personalidad y su desarrollo en la edad infantil*. La Habana, Cuba: Pueblo y Educación.

Bozhovich, L. I. (2009). The social situation of child development. *Journal of Russian and East European Psychology, 47*(4), 59–86. https://doi.org/10.2753/RPO1061-0405470403.

Chudnovskii, V. E. (2009). L. I. Bozhovic as a person, a personality and a scholar. *Journal of Russian & East European Psychology, 47*(4), 3–27. https://doi.org/10.2753/rpo1061-0405470401.

Esteban-Guitart, M. (2010). Los diez principios de la psicología histórico-cultural. *Fundamentos en Humanidades, 22,* 45–60.

Esteban-Guitart, M. (2016). *Funds of identity: Connecting meaningful learning experiences in and out of school*. New York: Cambridge University Press.

Esteban-Guitart, M. (2018). The biosocial foundation of the early Vygotsky: Educational psychology before the zone of proximal development. *History of Psychology, 21*(4), 384–401. https://doi.org/10.1037/hop0000092.

Gonzalez Rey, F. (2009). Historical relevance of Vygotsky's work: Its significance for a new approach to the problem of subjectivity in psychology. *Outlines. Critical Practice Studies, 11*(1), 59–73.

González Rey, F. (2011). A re-examination of defining moments in Vygotsky's work and their implications for his continuing legacy. *Mind, Culture and Activity, 18*(3), 257–275. https://doi.org/10.1080/10749030903338517.

González Rey, F. (2012). *O social na psicologia e a psicologia social: A emergencia do sujeito* [Social in psychology and social psychology: The emergency of the subject]. Petrópolis: Vozes.

González Rey, F. (2014). Advancing further the history of Soviet psychology: Moving forward from dominant representations in Western and Soviet psychology. *History of Psychology, 17*(1), 60–78. https://doi.org/10.1037/a0035565.

González Rey, F. (2015). A new path for the discussion of social representations: Advancing the topic of subjectivity from a cultural-historical standpoint. *Theory & Psychology, 25*(4), 494–512. https://doi.org/10.1177/0959354315587783.

González Rey, F. (2016). Vygotsky's Concept of *Perezhivanie* in *The Psychology of Art* and at the final moment of his work: Advancing his legacy. *Mind, Culture & Activity, 23*(4), 305–314. https://doi.org/10.1080/10749039.2016.1186196.

González Rey, F. (2017). The topic of subjectivity in psychology: Contradictions, paths and new alternatives. *Journal for the Theory of Social Behaviour, 47*(4), 502–521. https://doi.org/10.1111/jtsb.12144.

González Rey, F. (2019). Fifty years after L. I. Bozhovich's personality and its formation in childhood: Recovering her legacy and her historical role. *Mind, Culture and Activity, 26*(2), 108–120. https://doi.org/10.1080/10749039.2019.1616210.

González Rey, F., & Mitjáns Martínez, A. (2016). Perezhivanie: Advancing on its implication for the cultural-historical approach. *International Journal in Early Childhood Education, 17,* 143–160.

González Rey, F., & Mitjáns Martínez, A. (2017). El desarrollo de la subjetividad: una alternative frente a las teorías del desarrollo psíquico. *Papeles de Trabajo sobre Cultura, Educación y Desarrollo Humano, 13*(2), 3–20.

Goulart, D. M. (2019a). Subjectivity and life: In memory of Fernando González Rey. *Mind, Culture and Activity, 26*(2), 102–107. https://doi.org/10.1080/10749039.2019.1619775.

Goulart, D. M. (2019b). *Subjectivity and critical mental health*. New York, NY: Routledge.

Goulart, D. M., Mitjáns Martínez, A., & Esteban-Guitart, M. (2020). The trajectory and work of Fernando González Rey: Paths to his theory of subjectivity. *Studies in Psychology, 41*(1), 9–30. https://doi.org/10.1080/02109395.2019.1710800.

Rubinstein, S. L. (1964). *El desarrollo de la psicología. Principios y métodos*. Habana: Editora del Consejo Nacional de Universidades.

Subero, D. (2020). Funds of identity and subjectivity: Finding new paths and alternatives for a productive dialogue. *Studies in Psychology, 41*(1), 74–94. https://doi.org/10.1080/02109395. 2019.1710799.

Vygotsky, L. S. (1971). *The psychology of art*. Cambridge, MA: The MIT Press.

Vygotsky, L. S. (1978). *Mind in society: The development of higher psychological processes*. Cambridge, MA: Harvard University Press.

Vygotsky, L. S. (1987). Thinking and speech. In R. Rieber & A. Carton (Eds.), *The collected works of L. S. Vygotsky* (Vol. 1, pp. 43–287). New York: Plenum Press.

Vygotsky, L. S. (1997). *The collected works of L. S. Vygotsky: The history of development of higher mental functions*. New York, NY: Plenum.

Yasnitsky, A. (2018). *Vygotsky: An intellectual biography*. London, UK: Routledge.

Yasnitsky, A., & van der Veer, R. (Eds.). (2016). *Revisionist revolution in Vygotsky studies*. London, UK: Routledge.

Zavershneva, E. (2014). The problem of consciousness in Vygotsky's cultural-historical psychology. In A. Yasnitsky, R. van der Veer, & M. Ferrari (Eds.), *The Cambridge handbook of cultural-historical psychology* (pp. 63–98). New York, NY: Cambridge University Press.

Zavershneva, E., & van der Veer, R. (Eds.). (2018). *Vygotsky's notebooks: A selection*. Singapore: Springer.

Zinchenko, V. P. (2009). Consciousness as the subject matter and task of psychology. *Journal of Russian and East European Psychology, 47*(5), 44–75.

David Subero holds a Ph.D. in psychology and is an Associate Professor in the department of psychology at the University of Girona, Spain. He has expanded post-doctoral studies at the University of Brasilia (Brazil). He has been a visiting professor at the Normal School of Texcoco (Mexico). He has numerous publications on the relationships between school and other learning contexts, as well as the relationship between culture, identity, and education from a Vygotskian perspective.

Moisés Esteban-Guitart is a Professor at the Department of Psychology at the University of Girona and a Professor collaborator at the Open University of Catalonia (Spain). He is the Director of the Institute of Educational Research at the University of Girona, and Editor of the journal Papeles de Trabajo sobre Cultura, Educación y Desarrollo Humano. His research addresses the connections between identity, culture, and education.

Chapter 8
Advancing Vygotsky's Legacy: Interrupted Argument with Fernando González Rey

Nikolai Veresov

Abstract González Rey's significant contribution is rethinking Vygotsky's theoretical legacy through re-examining the most important defining moments of Vygotsky's work, their contemporary relevance, significance and implications. González Rey called these stages "defining moments". In Hegel (and in Vygotsky) the concept of "moment" has a special meaning and value. For González Rey, defining moments were synonymous with "turning points", points of a sharp change in the development path. The merit of González Rey's work is that he perfectly demonstrated the connection of Bozhovich's work with Vygotsky's ideas and through this, revealed serious differences between the theoretical approaches of Vygotsky and Leontiev. This chapter begins with the discussion on González Rey's contribution. The second part provides my disagreements with some of González Rey considerations about the main stages of the development of cultural-historical theory (CHT). My arguments are grounded on refer to as the new reality with Vygotsky's legacy.

8.1 Short and Very Subjective Introduction

The theory of subjectivity is undoubtedly the main contribution of Fernando González Rey in advancing cultural-historical psychology. Following Vygotsky's fundamental claim that every new approach to scientific problems inevitably leads to new methods and ways of research (Vygotsky, 1997b, p. 27), he has developed a constructive-interpretative method as a specific qualitative epistemological method to study human subjectivity.

Another significant contribution is rethinking Vygotsky's theoretical legacy through re-examining the most important defining moments of his work, their contemporary relevance, significance and implications. González Rey considered this as an important task which might help to reconstruct *the internal logic* and

N. Veresov (✉)
Monash University, Clayton, VIC, Australia
e-mail: nikolai.veresov@monash.edu

© The Author(s), under exclusive license to Springer Nature Singapore Pte Ltd. 2021   119
D. M. Goulart et al. (eds.), *Theory of Subjectivity from a Cultural-Historical Standpoint*,
Perspectives in Cultural-Historical Research 9,
https://doi.org/10.1007/978-981-16-1417-0_8

the *moving forces* of development of Vygotsky's theoretical approaches in different periods of his work.

We met for the first time in 1992 at the ISCAR Congress, Fernando and I were in a state of the permanent debate. We were in complete agreement on some important and fundamental points in relation to the key concepts of cultural-historical theory. We agreed that there is a clear tendency of highlighting some periods of Vygotsky's theoretical path, and an underestimating of other periods. Yet, there were areas we disagreed with and argued about. We had fantastic and often very emotional public and private discussions during his stay at Monash University as a visiting scholar. The discussion continued when we visited the University Centre of Brasilia, and some of these dialogues are reflected in a co-edited book and publications (Fleer et al., 2017a, 2017b; Veresov, 2019). My friend Fernando was always open to any new ideas even if they contradicted his interpretations. The tragic news of his death came a day before my flight to Brazil to meet Fernando. This chapter presents the points that I wanted to discuss with Fernando… now this is tragically an interrupted debate.

8.2 González Rey's Interpretation of Stages of Vygotsky's Theoretical Evolution

8.2.1 Defining Moments of Vygotsky's Work

González Rey (2007, 2008, 2009, 2011, 2014, 2016, 2017) gave, and consistently expanded his original interpretation of the main stages of the theoretical evolution of Vygotsky's views, highlighting three main defining moments. These periods and defining moments look as follows:

The first period—early work of Vygotsky. According to González Rey, "throughout this period, Vygotsky focused on a broad representation of a human psyche that led him to a new definition of it" (González Rey, 2007, p. 6). "For this purpose, Vygotsky used categories such as personality and motivation, trying to 'grasp' a person as a whole, as well as the unity between cognitive and affective processes. This was evident in his book 'Psychology of Art' and in his first works regarding defectology" (González Rey, 2007, p. 6).

The second period—"the semiotic moment", or "an instrumental stage",—the most accepted and known part of Vygotsky's production for Western countries. This moment was centred in the study of the process of mediation and relates to the concepts internalisation, signs and tools (González Rey, 2007).

In later publications, he gives a more detailed description of this moment.

This objectivistic, empirical and natural representation of psychology that Vygotsky explicitly defended above was the official position defended by Kornilov and his group as the basis for a Marxist psychology. That position was to some extent responsible for the type of problems related to the official tendencies within Soviet psychology including subjects matters as the study of the neurophysiology of higher forms of neurological processes and reflections and later, the study of cognitive functions, as understood by as internalised operations. (González Rey & Mitjáns Martinez, 2017, p. 198)

The third and the last defining moment was the period when Vygotsky returns to his primary concern regarding the integration of cognitive and affective processes (González Rey, 2007). During this time, he approached this topic through such concepts as sense, perezhivanie, emotions, imagination and the understanding of thinking as inseparable from emotions (González Rey, 2017, p. 2). Summarising this point, González Rey claims:

> …in the last period of his work, Vygotsky followed some of his foundational ideas from "The psychology of Art" and from some of his first works on defectology, which permitted him to overcome the idea of social determinism of the psyche as a process from the outside to the inside, and to emphasise the emotions, the imagination and the creative character of the individual. (Fleer et al., 2017a, p. 250)

However, in González Rey's opinion, these concepts of the last period of Vygotsky—sense, perezhivanie, emotions, imagination, and the unity of thinking and emotions, as the theoretical representation of the understanding of the human mind as the production of the subjectivity—remained unclear and open for further development. It was exactly this system of concepts that became the basis of the theory of subjectivity created by González Rey and which I would call the cultural-historical theory of subjectivity.

8.2.2 Vygotsky, Bozhovich and Beyond

There is another historical (or better to say cultural-historical) line that González Rey spoke about, revealing the origins of the theory of subjectivity. The article of González Rey about Soviet psychologist Bozhovich (González Rey, 2019) seems to be extremely important since it does not only expand the historical and conceptual contexts but presents a serious and critical challenge to some generally accepted perceptions.

One cannot but agree that after Vygotsky's death, there was a lack of attention to the concept of perezhivanie in Soviet psychology, which was "one of the concepts intrinsically associated with Vygotsky's main positions at the end of his life" (González Rey, 2019, p. 116). The ideas of Vygotsky's last period were not accepted by A. Leontiev. Here is how González Rey characterises this shift: "Leontiev, with his group of Kharkov collaborators, did not follow Vygotsky's orientation toward the study of the structure of consciousness and did not recognize the developmental functions of emotions, but remained in a position to study the genesis and development of consciousness in practical activity in terms of research on the structure of their own activity" (González Rey, 2019, p. 116).

Bozhovich, following Vygotsky's course, focused her research on the problem of affectivity, perezhivanie and integral personality and its development.

First, Bozhovich brought to light the last period of Vygotsky's work, devoted to perezhivanie, social situation of development, and the search for units of affective and intellectual process-es...Second, Bozhovich stressed the idea of the psychological system strongly emphasized by Vygotsky and centered on personality as such a system... Third, Bozhovich, like Vygotsky in his final period, between 1931 and 1934, attempted to decipher the nature of psychological processes. (González Rey, 2019, p. 118)

In this way, she advanced Vygotsky's legacy (González Rey, 2019, p. 118). Bozhovich made explicit what was implicit in Vygotsky's concepts of perezhivanie and sense and made theoretical advances to the solution of the problems which are not resolved until today:

...the ontological vacuum in the definition of human psyche as a motivational system, the early emotional relationships between adults and children, the absence of concepts capable of explaining how the human self is formed within the social fabric, and the integrative motivational synthesis from which human behavior emerges, within which the intellectual processes and emotions appear integrated. (González Rey, 2019, p. 118)

In this regard, Bozhovich's work could be considered as one of the "roots" (or a link to Vygotsky) of the theory of subjectivity. I hope González Rey would agree with this, and I have a reason for this hope:

And, perhaps, most crucial for us today, Bozhovich took an important step forward in recog-nizing that personality is not a reflection of the world, but a production within cultural-social processes that are historically located... Bozhovich's advances in terms of motivation and personality were an important antecedent for new paths within cultural-historical psychology, such as funds of identity and subjectivity. (González Rey, 2019, p. 118)

8.3   Summarising González Rey Contribution

González Rey always strove to ensure that cultural-historical psychology did not remain a collection of frozen dogmas. However, in advancing Vygotsky's legacy one must not lose history itself. A tree without roots becomes inadvertently dry and dies. González Rey's undeniable contribution was the appeal to the history (and origins) of Vygotsky's theory. Addressing the history, he did this within the frame-work of an already established exposition of the main stages of Vygotsky's theoretical evolution. According to the commonly accepted opinion, this evolution consisted of three stages: (1) early works (before 1826/1927); (2) so-called "instrumental period" (1928–1931/1932) and (3) last period (1931/1932–1934) (Zavershneva & Van der Veer, 2018). The problem of how exactly these stages are related remains largely unclear and confusing. The existing picture is characterised by the tendency that certain periods of Vygotsky's work are marked out, leaving the rest in a theoretical shadow. That was Fernando's concern, and this is my concern too.

González Rey called these stages "defining moments" and did not use the term as a beautiful metaphor. For him, defining moments were synonymous with "turning points", points of a sharp change in the development path.

Fernando drew attention to the main aspects in Vygotsky's early works—personality as a holistic system, perezhivanie, emotions and art as a social technique of feelings, and self-determinism, that is, human freedom. The third period of Vygotsky's work was interesting for Fernando primarily because in his opinion Vygotsky had returned to his previous ideas, interrupted by the so-called "instrumental period". I completely agree with González Reys' discovery on the concept of sense in Vygotsky. *The sense, not perezhivanie* is the unity of intellect and affect in human consciousness. Here is how Fernando explains this with the reference to Vygotsky:

> Generally speaking, the problem is not the unity of affect and intellect, as such, but the realization of this unity in a form of a "dynamic system of senses", which embraces the "dynamic of thoughts" (intellect) as well as the "dynamic of behavior and the concrete activity of personality". (González Rey, 2007, p. 8)

Later, he formulated this in a short form: "So, sense represents a cognitive-affective unity configured on human action" (González Rey. 2009, p. 68). This directly follows from Vygotsky's statement: "There exists a dynamic meaningful system[1] that constitutes a unity of affective and intellectual processes" (Vygotsky, 1987, p. 50).

The merit of González Rey is that he perfectly demonstrated the connection of Bozhovich's work with Vygotsky's ideas and through this, revealed serious differences between the theoretical approaches of Vygotsky and Leontiev. Indeed, *neither Bozhovich nor some of Vygotsky's other followers were the "second generation of CHAT"*, they were rather the second generation of cultural-historical theory.[2]

8.4 New Reality and New Arguments

This part of the chapter provides my disagreements with some of González Rey considerations about the main stages of the development of the cultural-historical theory (CHT). My arguments are grounded on what I refer to as "the new reality with Vygotsky's legacy". I will shortly present this new reality and my arguments as possible new avenues of a dialogue the new reality brings to the agenda.

I agree that "the overemphasis of selected aspects of Vygotsky's work resulted in an overshadowing of other ideas that have remained relatively "unknown" (González Rey, 2011, p. 257). I also agree that "it is difficult to temporally segment the diverse

---

[1]Smyslovaya systema in Vygotsky's original text (Vygotsky, 1982, p. 22) which is the dynamic system of senses.

[2]Thus, M. Lisina (1986) and her collaborators have developed the cultural-historical theory of communication. N. Morozova (1969) has developed a series of unique research programs in the field of special education, L. Slavina (1979) created a theory of development of child's motivation and personality development. Although the work of these researchers is unknown to a Western audience, this cannot be the basis for excluding them from the "three-generation" model. The fact is that from the beginning of 1930s there were (and still are) two coexisting approaches—the activity theory and cultural-historical theory which can hardly be considered as two generations of a certain third theory.

qualitative moments of Vygotsky's ideas because his ideas overlap in works written in similar periods" (González Rey, 2011, p. 257). And finally, I completely agree that "it is necessary to go beyond the dominant and fashionable interpretations of Vygotsky's legacy to discover and elaborate new paths of his legacy" (González Rey, 2011, p. 273).

8.4.1 New Reality with Vygotsky's Legacy

On one hand, we have a great number of publications exploring and advancing Vygotsky's legacy in many ways and directions. On the other hand, paradoxically, there is no agreement not only about the main stages of the development of Vygotsky's theoretical views but also about what CHT is as a theory, its subject matter, laws, principles and research method. Saying this, I share Gredler's (2012) point that:

> …ultimately, the theory itself is often discredited when the popular view is found wanting. This problem has not yet occurred with Vygotsky's theoretical system. However, his theory is the most recent perspective to be discussed largely in terms of popular misconceptions. (p. 114)

In my opinion, the problem is that the contemporary representation of Vygotsky's theory, the existing picture of the theory so to say, is not a contemporary picture in its origins. This picture arose a long time ago, in the 70–80s of the last century based on a very limited number of Vygotsky's works published and available to researchers. Starting from *Mind in Society* (Vygotsky, 1978) this picture was doomed to be fragmented, superficial and contradictory. At that time, however, there was no other way to introduce Vygotsky to the Western audience. Michael Cole's Prologue to *The Essential Vygotsky* (Rieber & Robinson, 2004) makes clearer why these drastic editorial changes were considered necessary at the time (p. xi). The publication of the *Collected Works* in Russian and in English did not change the situation significantly. In the 80s–90s, due to limited sources of Vygotsky's original texts available, there could be no other, complete and more accurate picture. However, this does not mean that there can be no other picture now. Why? Because over the past 20 years, what I call "the new reality" of the legacy of Vygotsky has emerged.

In the 1980s, when the Russian edition of the *Collected Works* (1982–1984) was published, a significant number of Vygotsky's works remained unknown and were not included in the volumes. Some of them remained unavailable as they were originally published in the 1920s and 1930s in a very limited number of copies; others existed only in the form of manuscripts, diaries, and notes in archives. The situation started to change gradually, as previously unavailable texts began to appear creating a new reality in Vygotsky's legacy. Since I have discussed elsewhere the content of the new reality with Vygotsky's legacy (Veresov, 2020); in this chapter, I will refer only to those sources that are relevant to the topic.

The first and extremely significant step was made in the recently published book (Dafermos, 2018). On the basis of a deep and detailed analysis from a vast number of sources, including those published in Russian, Dafermos suggests that the theoretical evolution of Vygotsky's thought might be divided into three fundamentally important stages: (1) pre-history of cultural-historical theory which includes reflexological/social behaviouristic phases (1918–1926), (2) primary appearance of cultural-historical theory (1927–1930) and (3) formation and systematisation of cultural-historical theory (1930–1934) (Dafermos, 2018, pp. 63–64). These suggestions are in line with the research I am currently involved in (Veresov, 2020), so this is the basis of my disagreements and suggestions.

8.5 Arguments: Redefining the Defining Moments of Vygotsky's Theoretical Evolution

8.5.1 The First Defining Moment: Going Beyond Precarious Limits of Subjectivism

I would agree that *the first period* of Vygotsky's work is characterised by the focus on various aspects of subjectivity—"topics of clear subjective character, such as personality, fantasy, imagination, unconsciousness, emotions, and so on" (González Rey, 2011, p. 273). No doubts, this moment "was characterized by several publications, among which Psychology of Art, Pedagogical Psychology, 'Consciousness as a Problem in the Psychology of Behavior', and his first works concerning defectology are especially relevant" (González Rey, 2011, p. 258).

However, this is something I would argue with. Most of the abovementioned works of Vygotsky belong to the stage of the pre-history of CHT—the reflexological/social behaviourist phase. By stating this I refer to Vygotsky's presentations he did at All-Russian Congress on Pedology, Experimental Pedagogy and Psycho-Neurology on 6 January 1924. The first presentation with the title "Method of reflexolological research in implementation to the study of the psyche" practically coincides with the article "Methods of reflexological and psychological investigation" (Vygotsky, 1926a, 1997a). The second presentation—"How we can teach psychology now?"—is in correspondence with the book Pedagogical Psychology: the short course (Vygotsky, 1926b, 1991) which is the textbook. This allows. me to assert that Pedagogical Psychology (or at least the major part of it) was written before 1924. Another argument in support of this assumption is that Pedagogical Psychology presents reflexological view on psychological processes.

The major part of Psychology of Art (Vygotsky, 1965) was also written in Gomel, before it was presented as Vygotsky's academic dissertation on 5 October 1925. The subtitle of the book is "An analysis of esthetic reaction". By for unknown reasons this subtitle has been omitted in several later editions (Vygotsky, 1968, 1998b) and the English translation (Vygotsky, 1971). However, this book presented the reflexo-logical (and even reactological) approach to investigating the emotions and feelings related to pieces of arts. Thus, these two books and the article reflect the same reflexological phase of the pre-historical stage of CHT (Veresov, 1999).

The task of building psychology as an objective science (and method) for studying the subjective phenomena using reflexilogical and behaviouristic methods were widely discussed in Russian and Western psychology at that time (see for example, Chelpanov, 1925; Bekhterev, 1925; Pavlov, 1927).

Vygotsky's works written at that stage clearly show his approach was in line with the mainstream trend: consciousness was seen as a reflex of reflexes, as "a very complex structure of behaviour" (Vygotsky, 1997a, p. 79) including "a reflex of social contact" (Vygotsky, 1997a, p. 42). The reflexological method, therefore, was considered the objective method of investigating consciousness as a system of reactions, including esthetical reactions (Psychology of Art) claiming psychologists should be "bigger reflexologists than Pavlov" (Vygotsky, 1997a, p. 47).

I do not think Psychology of Art belongs to the works focused on various aspects of subjectivity. On the contrary, it signifies the transition to scientific (materialist-reflexological) objectivism.

> The search for a way out of the precarious confines of subjectivism has equally characterized Russian art scholarship and Russian psychology during the years of my studies. This tendency toward objectivism, toward a precise, materialistic, scientific approach to knowledge in both fields, gave rise to the present volume. (Vygotsky, 1971, p. 3)

In other words, I only partly agree with González Rey that "Psychology of Art to be the most significant work of this moment" (González Rey, 2011, p. 258). The significance of Psychology of Art (together with Pedagogical Psychology) shows **the first defining moment, the radical transition from subjectivism** to the search for the objective methods of studying human subjectivity.

8.5.2 The Second Defining Moment: Crisis of 1926

This is true, that the agenda of the first stage was abandoned in the second period. However, it seems that this cannot be explained by external reasons only (by the fact that Vygotsky "joined Kornilov's group") (González Rey & Mitjáns Martinez, 2017, p. 198). The crisis of 1926, **the second defining moment** was the reason Vygotsky consciously abandoned his reflexological-behaviouristic programme. Elsewhere, I suggested that such a crisis apparently took place, but at that time there was no evidence that could be invoked (see, Veresov, 1999). The new reality with Vygotsky's legacy related to several new and recently published sources not only confirms that there was a crisis but also reveals its causes and the content. Vygotsky's recently published notebooks of 1926 from Zakharino Hospital (Zavershneva, 2009a) along with some other materials (Zavershneva & Van der Veer, 2018) provide rich material for analysis.

Vygotsky's notebooks show he came to the conclusion that neither reflexological method nor behaviourist approaches are relevant to study human consciousness. The crisis did not change the task to psychology as objective science. However, the approach was totally changed. To build an objective psychology means to move *from empirical-naturalistic psychology to the genetical theory* focused on theoretical and experimental study of the very process of cultural-historical development of higher psychological functions.

This makes the published notebooks from Zakharino Hospital, a valuable source to identify the content of the crisis of 1926 as the turning point, the defining moment. However, it does not explain the causes of the crisis, its moving forces and contradictions which have generated the rejection of the reflexological and behaviouristic models. I believe this contradiction was between old theoretical models and new experimental research data and findings, particularly in the field of defectology.[3]

Three key findings from the research and clinical practice in the field of defectology, are of interest in relation to the topic I discuss here.

Secondary disability, and social environment as a source of development: Putting the question "is the underdevelopment of higher functions in a mildly retarded child caused directly by the primary cause or is this a secondary complication?" Vygotsky referred to defectological research saying that "experimental data and clinical investigation helped to find the answer"[4] (Vygotsky, 1984b, p. 129). And the answer is: since a physical handicap in a human being never affects the child directly as "the eye and ear of a human being are not only physical organs but also social organs" (Vygotsky, 1993, p. 77), the underdevelopment of higher functions in a child with disability is connected with cultural underdevelopment, as she is excluded from the cultural environment. "The fate of personality is decided not by the existence of a primary disability in itself, but by its social consequences" (Vygotsky, 1993, p. 55).

In fact, what we can see here is an emergence of one of the key ideas of CHT which was further improved and reconceptualised in Stage 2 and that is the concept of social environment as a source of cultural development of higher psychological functions in human beings.

Roundabout ways of overcoming disability and two lines of development: Vygotsky begins with reference to research evidence: "We have observed the fact that, when coping with difficulties, the child is forced to proceed along a roundabout path in order to overcome them" (Vygotsky, 1993, p. 126). As a result, compensation, the individual's reaction to a disability, "initiates new roundabout developmental processes - it replaces, rebuilds a new structure, and stabilizes psychological functions" (Vygotsky, 1993, p. 34).

---

[3]Defectology was a scientific term of that time widely used in Russia. Nowadays this term is not politically or socially correct. As the Foreword to Vygotsky's Volume 2 (Vygotsky, 1993) editors say: "Defectology is a term not, at present, readily found in English dictionaries and it does not designate a discipline at universities or a specialty at clinics in the English-speaking world. Yet defektologia in the tradition of the Soviet Union is concerned with abnormal psychology, learning disabilities, and what has been called special education in North America" (p. v).

[4]Sadly, in English translation it reads "Experimental data and clinical research could not give the answer" (Vygotsky, 1993, p. 133).

...in as much as these roundabout paths have been acquired by mankind in the course of his cultural and historical development, and inasmuch as the social environment offers the child a series of roundabout paths from the very beginning, quite frequently we do not recognize that development occurs in this way. (Vygotsky, 1993, p. 164)

Here again, we can see an "embryonic bud" of the concept of two (natural and cultural) lines of development. Later, in the *History of development of higher mental functions,* the idea was conceptualised and included into the wider content of cultural-historical theory (Vygotsky, 1997b, p. 107).

Incongruence and the sign as a psychological tool: Elaborating the idea of round-about ways of cultural development, Vygotsky made an important conclusion: the fundamental fact in the process of cultural development of the child with a disability is inadequacy, the incongruence between his psychological structure and the structure of cultural forms.

What remains is the necessity of creating special cultural tools suitable to the psychological structure of such a child, or of mastering common cultural forms with the help of special pedagogical methods, *because the most important and decisive condition of cultural development – precisely the ability to use psychological tools – is preserved in such children.* Their cultural development might go by different way, it is in principle, entirely possible. (Vygotsky, 1984a, pp. 28–29)[5]

Here we can see an obvious indication of continuity with several key ideas developed into theoretical concepts and principles at stage 2, that are: (1) the concept of sign as a psychological tool where the sign was not anymore seen as an external stimulus *(signalisation),* but related to the activity which distinguishes humans from animals, "an activity of *signification* that is creation and use of signs" (Vygotsky, 1997b, p. 55). From this the next step follows: (2) speech was not seen as the "second signal system" or a social reflex, but as a cultural higher psychological function which is different from language, related to cultural meanings and senses, and develops in the unity with thinking (Vygotsky, 1987).

I undertook a lengthy analysis of the defectological works of Vygotsky to show that when taken together with Zakharino's notebooks, a new light could be brought to the theoretical content of the crisis of 1926. From my point of view, the contradiction of the old theoretical approaches and new experimental findings was what generated the crisis of 1926 and, as a result, the rejection of the idea of reflexological programme of studying consciousness as a reflex of reflexes. On the other hand, some key ideas of CHT appeared in an embryonic form (mostly as experimental and clinical findings) only in 1924–1925, when Vygotsky started his work in the field of defectology, but not before.

The main change which happened was an introduction of a new developmental (genetical) dimension, where the development was seen not as a change of reflexes (as it was approached in the Pedagogical Psychology) and not as changes in the

---

[5]I give this quotation from the original Russian source as the English translation (Vygotsky 1993, p. 47) missed some key words, for example "the cultural development might go by different way" were omitted.

structure of reaction (as in Psychology of Art), but as a process of sociocultural genesis of higher psychological functions of a human being. The clearest evidence of this is the fact that some pieces of text from the Zakharino's Hospital diaries were literally incorporated and improved in The Historical Sense of Psychological Crisis, The History of Development of Higher Mental Functions and other key writings of 1928–1934 as Zavershneva (2009b) brilliantly shows.

The crisis of 1926 was **the second defining moment** in the development of Vygotsky's thought. This means that the second stage—that is, the creation of CHT was caused not by external reasons, but by a contradiction in the development of ideas.

8.5.3   After the Crisis: Cultural-Historical Theory and Experimental Genetic Method (1927–1930/31)

According to González Rey, at this stage Vygotsky's work was aimed at the study of the social character of the higher psychological functions and "restricted to analyzing the use of signs, tools, and operations" (González Rey, 2011, p. 273). Here González Rey's approach coincides with the widespread belief that this period may be called "the instrumental period" (Zavershneva & Van der Veer, 2018, pp. xv–xv).

In my opinion, the new reality with Vygotsky's legacy and the new original Vygotsky's texts that have only recently become available in English and Russian, make it possible to see a more complex picture. Yes, Vygotsky's famous text "Instrumental method in psychology" (Vygotsky, 1997a, pp. 85–89) as well as several others (Problem of the cultural development of the child [Vygotsky, 1928/1994]) definitely belong to this period and focused on studying of cultural signs, tools and operations.

However, Vygotsky's programme was not limited to these aspects. Creating psychology as an objective science remained the main task. What was new was an introduction of *the dialectical understanding of the development* of higher psychological functions (Vygotsky, 1997b, pp. 98–99). What psychology needed was "an introduction of the dialectical method" (Vygotsky, 1997b, p. 3). In other words, a new theory should provide the theoretical tools and experimental method to look at higher psychological functions as facts of historical development to overcome "the one-sidedness and erroneousness of the traditional view" (Vygotsky, 1997b, p. 2). This general approach predetermined two main directions of the research programme: (1) studying the process of mastering external cultural tools and (2) studying the process of development of special (separate) higher psychological functions (Vygotsky, 1997b).

The first direction led to the formulation of the concept of the cultural sign as a psychological tool (Vygotsky, 1997b, 1999), the principle of mediation of higher psychological functions, and the concept of mediating activity (Vygotsky, 1997b, pp. 60–63). The second direction made it possible to introduce key theoretical concepts: the social environment as a source of development (Vygotsky,

1997b, p. 249), internalisation (vraschivanie) (Vygotsky, 1999, pp. 10–53), drama (Vygotsky, 1989) and the system of laws of the genesis of psychological functions (Vygotsky, 1928, 1994, 1997b, 1998a).

The new research field required a new experimental method. In Vygotsky's words, "...the method we use may be called an experimental-genetic method in the sense that it artificially elicits and creates a genetic process of mental development..." (Vygotsky, 1997b, p. 68). Importantly, "this kind of experiment attempts to dissolve every congealed and petrified psychological form and to convert it into a moving, flowing flood of separate instances that replace one another" (Vygotsky, 1997b, p. 68), "the experimental unfolding of a higher process...into a small drama" (Vygotsky, 1989, p. 58). The experimental method was developed in 1927–1931 and we can reconstruct the evolution: form "the technic of double stimulation" (1927–1929) (Vygotsky, 1999, p. 60) to "instrumental method" (1930) (Vygotsky, 1997a, p. 108) and then to the "experimental genetic method" (1931) (Vygotsky, 1997b, pp. 65–82).

Stage 2 might be defined as "the instrumental period"; but what should be taken into account is the studies of sign mediation, mediating activity and instrumental acts were only a part of the very complex research programme of the experimental study *of the whole process of the cultural and historical development of higher psychological functions*; *one from two lines of development* which are "inseparably connected, but never merging into one" (Vygotsky, 1997b, p.14).

The third defining moment: changing the focus, not the theory.

In González Rey's opinion, in the third and the last defining moment Vygotsky returns to his primary ideas with the integration of cognitive and affective processes (González Rey, 2007), through such concepts as sense, perezhivanie, emotions, imagination and the understanding of thinking as inseparable from emotions (González Rey, 2017, p. 2). González Rey considers this was the time when Vygotsky returned to some of his foundational ideas from the Psychology of Art and from some of his first works on defectology (Fleer et al., 2017a, p. 250). This is in line with the widespread belief that in the last years of his life Vygotsky abandoned (or even simply rejected) the ideas of the CHT developed in 1927–1930, including the central concept of higher psychological function. However, such an interpretation raises questions. What was the reason for the rejection of the previous theoretical model? Was there any gap between the third and second stages, similar to the crisis of 1926?

A new reality and new sources—the texts of Vygotsky himself—might give some answers and allows us to propose that this view needs substantial refinement.

First of all, there are two previously unknown publications of Vygotsky, both not yet translated in English, but available in Russian. The first is recently published Vygotsky's Preface to Leontiev's book "The Development of Memory" of 1931 (Vygotsky, 2003) and the second is the chapter The Problem of Development and Disintegration of Higher Psychological Functions (Vygotsky, 1960, 2005). The first text refers to the beginning of the third stage of Vygotsky's work, and the second was one of the last speeches a few weeks before his death.

In the Preface to Leontiev's book of 1931[6] we find the clear and complete formulation of the subject of cultural-historical theory:

> The origin and development of the higher psychological functions, their construction and composition, their way of functioning and their mutual connections and interdependencies, the laws that govern their course and fate – all this is constituting the exact content and the true subject matter of these investigations. (Vygotsky, 2003, p. 89)

The subject matter of CHT was clearly defined as the process of development of the higher psychological functions which includes two important aspects: (1) genetical aspect (the origin and the construction of a system of psychological functions and (2) structural/dynamic aspect focused on inter-functional relations (mutual connections and interdependencies through the processes of differentiation and subordination in a course of development).

In my opinion, this explains the change of the focus of analysis. At the second stage (1927–1930/31), the main task was to identify the laws of the origin of higher psychological functions, but at the last stage, the main task was to study the developmental aspects of reorganisation of the system of functions, inter-functional relationships, interdependencies, the internal and external differentiation of subordination. Development, from a dialectical point of view, is not only the origin and the construction of a new system but includes a qualitative reorganisation within the developing system. That was the point Vygotsky insisted on: the process of development "is a complex dialectical process, characterized by disproportion in the development of separate functions, metamorphoses or qualitative transformation of certain forms into others" (Vygotsky, 1997b, p. 99).

The Problem of Development and Disintegration of Higher Psychological Functions (Vygotsky, 1960, 2005) was a report Vygotsky delivered at the conference of the Institute of Experimental Medicine in April 1934 (Vygotsky, 1960, p. 364). Two months before his death, Vygotsky continued to insist that "the problem of higher psychological functions is the central problem of the whole psychology of man" (Vygotsky, 1960, p. 364).

Not a rejection of the cultural-historical theory, but its further development, or as Dafermos puts it "the formation and systematization of cultural-historical theory" (Dafermos, 2018, pp. 63–64). The transition from studying the genetic processes of the emergence of higher functions to studying their development from the point of view of changing inter-functional relationships was **the third decisive moment in Vygotsky's work**. The first results of this new research programme were presented in this report by Vygotsky. However, at all stages of the development of CHT, the process of development of higher psychological functions remained the main subject matter of the theory.

The research programme of the last stage can hardly be reduced to cognitive-emotional unity of the psyche. Yes, the concepts of sense and perezhivanie do relate to cognitive-emotional unity, but they were developed together with other concepts (psychological neoformation, ZPD, social situation of development) strongly related

---

[6]It is important that that book of Leontiev reflects his study of memory, which he conducted in 1928–1930 under the guidance of Vygotsky before he began to develop a theory of activity.

to the concepts of the previous stage and therefore can hardly be understood without this theoretical connection. I would agree that during the last period of 1932–1934 Vygotsky reconsidered many ideas from the first stage; however, I think they were reconsidered on the basis and within the theoretical framework developed in 1927–1931 and in relation to the change of the research programme, not the change of the theory.

Several laws of inter-functional relations (differentiation and subordination) were established and experimentally confirmed during this last stage of Vygotsky's work (Vygotsky, 2001, 2019). That allowed Vygotsky to develop the theory of pedological age, defining ages as cycles of development, which are qualitatively different from each other where various higher psychological functions are the centres of a child's developing personality (Vygotsky, 1998a, pp. 167–168).

And finally, the new direction of research required a new method of analysis. An experimental-genetic method aimed at studying the origin and structure of separate functions could not be used for a new task, that is, studying a system of psychological functions and qualitative reorganisation of the system of functions. For Vygotsky, a new method was the method of analysis by units, in contrast to the analysis into elements. The unit of analysis (in contrast to the analysis by elements) is "a product of analysis which, unlike elements, retains all the basic properties of the whole and which cannot be further divided without losing them" (Vygotsky, 1987, pp. 46–47). This method was applied to study the word meaning as a unit of analysis of the unity of thinking and speech and perezhivanie as a dynamic unit of consciousness (Vygotsky, 1984a, p. 382).[7]

8.6   Some Concluding and Very Subjective Remarks

Fernando's mind is brilliant. I do not say "was brilliant", I say "is brilliant". People pass away, but their spirit remains. The life of a great scientist does not stop with the cessation of his physical existence. His voice continues to sound in books, articles, recordings of speeches—Fernando's unique subjectivity is imprinted there. Scientific texts are not just objects where something, as it is now fashionable to say, is objectivated and through which something is mediated. Human subjectivity is not in what mediates, but in who produces himself, who mediates by cultural means this dramatic process of self-determined self-creation.

As Vygotsky said, thinking is born from arguments and not from complimentary assents. I am sorry Fernando and I could not continue our discussion and arguing, I hope I can do this with Fernando's students and followers. The theory of subjectivity is developed in a constant dialogue with Vygotsky's tradition and the deeper we understand it, the more opportunities we open up for its further development. Fernando

---

[7]I give a reference to the Russian text as in English translation (Vygotsky, 1998a, p. 294) the "unit" (edinitsa) was mistakenly translated as "unity".

did this perfectly well, considering this a very important part in the development of the theory of subjectivity.

In this chapter, I presented a number of arguments I wanted to discuss with Fernando at our meeting. I leave them to his students and hope that they will serve further discussions and dialogues. Buffon said once: "Nothing is more contagious than the error supported by a big name" (Buffon, 2007, p. 47). However, Faulkner responded: "The past is never dead. It's not even past" (Faulkner, 2015, p. 85). At least I will consider my goal achieved if someone simply draws attention to the new reality with Vygotsky's legacy, which I presented here.

References

Buffon, G. C. (2007). Œuvres. Paris: Gallimard.

Bekhterev, V. (1925). Psihologia, reflexologia I Marksizm [Psychology, reflexology and Marxism]. Moscow: GRIM Publishers. (in Russian).

Chelpanov, G. (1925). Obiektivnaya psihologia v Rossii I Amerike (reflexologia I psihologia povedenia [Objective psychology in Russia and America (reflexology and psychology of behavior)]. Moscow: Dumnov Publishers (in Russian).

Dafermos, M. (2018). Rethinking cultural-historical theory: A dialectical perspective to Vygotsky. Singapore: Springer.

Fleer, M., González Rey, F., Veresov, N. (2017a). Perezhivanie, emotions and subjectivity: Setting the stage. In Fleer et al. (Eds.), Perezhivanie, emotions and subjectivity: Advancing Vygotsky legacy (pp 1–15). New York: Springer.

Fleer, M., González Rey, F., Veresov, N. (2017b). Continuing the dialogue: Advancing conceptions of emotions, perezhivanie and subjectivity for the study of human development. In Fleer et al. (Eds.), Perezhivanie, emotions and subjectivity: Advancing Vygotsky legacy (pp. 247–261). New York: Springer.

Faulkner, W. (2015). Requiem for a Nun. London: Random House.

Gredler, M. (2012). Understanding Vygotsky for the classroom: Is it too late? Educational Psychology Review, 24, 113–131.

Gozalez Rey, F. (2007). Social and individual subjectivity from an historical cultural standpoint. Outlines: critical social studies, 2, 3–14.

González Rey, F. (2008). Different periods in Vygotsky's work: Their implications for arguments regarding his legacy. Paper presented at the Annual meeting of the International Society for Cultural and Activity Research. San Diego, California.

González Rey, F. (2009). Historical relevance of Vygotsky's work: Its significance for a new approach to the problem of subjectivity in psychology. Outlines: Critical Social Studies, 1, 59–73.

González Rey, F. (2011). A re-examination of defining moments in Vygotsky's work and their implications for his continuing legacy. Mind, Culture, and Activity, 18, 257–275.

González Rey, F. (2014). Advancing further the history of soviet psychology: Moving forward from dominant representations in western and soviet psychology. History of Psychology, 17, 60–78. https://doi.org/10.1037/a0035565.

González Rey, F. (2016). Advancing on the topics of the social and subjectivity from a cultural-historical approach: Moments, paths and contradictions. Journal of the Theoretical and Philosophical Psychology, 36, 175–189. https://doi.org/10.1017/CCOL0521831040.

González Rey, F. (2017). Advances in subjectivity from a cultural-historical perspective: Unfoldings and consequences for cultural studies today. In M. Fleer, F. González Rey, & N. Veresov (Eds.), Perezhivanie, emotions and subjectivity: Advancing Vygotsky legacy (pp. 173–195). New York: Springer.

González Rey, F. (2019): Fifty years after L. I. Bozhovich's personality and its formation in childhood: Recovering her legacy and her historical role. *Mind, Culture, and Activity, 26*(2), 108–120. https://doi.org/10.1080/10749039.2019.1616210.

González Rey, F., & Mitjáns Martinez, A. (2017). Epistemological and methodological issues related to the new challenges of a cultural-historical based psychology. In M. Fleer, F. González Rey, & N. Veresov (Eds.), *Perezhivanie, emotions and subjectivity: Advancing Vygotsky legacy* (pp. 195–216). New York: Springer.

Lisina, M. (1986). *Problemy ontogeneza obshenia* [Problems of ontogenesis of communication]. Moscow: Pedagogika.

Morozova, N. (1969). *Formirovanie posnavatelnyh interesov u anomalnyh detei* [The formation of cognitive interests in abnormal children]. Moscow: Prosveschenie.

Pavlov, I. (1927). *Conditioned reflexes: An investigation of the physiological activity of the cerebral cortex.* Oxford University Press.

Slavina, L. (1979). *Psihichesloye razvitie shkolnika I ego vospitanie* [Psychological development of a schoolchild and its upbringing]. Moscow: Znanie.

Veresov, N. (1999). *Undiscovered Vygotsky.* Frankfurt am Main and New York: Peter Lang.

Veresov, N. (2019). Subjectivity and perezhivanie: Empirical and methodological challenges and opportunities. In F. González Rey, A. Mitjans Martinez, & D. Goulart (Eds.), *Subjectivity within cultural-historical Approach* (pp. 61–86). Singapore: Springer.

Veresov, N. (2020). Discovering the Great Royal Seal: New reality of Vygotsky's legacy. *Cultural-historical psychology, 6*(2), 107–117. https://doi.org/10.17759/chp.2020160212.

Vygotsky, L. S. (1926a). Metodika refleksologicheskogo i psikhologicheskogo issledovanija. In K. N. Kornilov (Ed.), *Problemy sovremennoj psihhologii* (pp. 26–46). Leningrad: Gosudarstvennoe Izdatel'stvo.

Vygotsky, L. S. (1926b). *Pedagogicheskaya psihologia. Kratkii kurs* [Pedagogical psychology: The short course]. Moscow: Pabotnik prosvescheniya.

Vygotsky, L. S. (1928). Problema kulturnogo razvitia rebenka [The problem of the cultural development of the child]. *Jurnal psihologii, pedologii I psihotehniki, 1,* 58–77.

Vygotsky, L. S. (1960). Razvitie vischih psihicheskih funktsii [*The development of higher psychological functions*]. Moscow: Academy of Pedagogical Sciences RSFSR.

Vygotsky, L. S. (1965). *Psihologiya iskusstva* [The psychology of art]. Moscow: Iskusstvo.

Vygotsky, L. S. (1968). *Psihologiya iskusstva* [The psychology of art]. Moscow: Iskusstvo.

Vygotsky, L. S. (1971). *The psychology of art.* Cambridge: MIT Press.

Vygotsky, L. S. (1978). *Mind in society: The development of higher psychological processes.* Cambridge: Harvard University Press.

Vygotsky, L. S. (1982). *Sobranie sochinenii* [Collected works] (Vol. 2). Moscow: Pedagogika.

Vygotsky, L. S. (1984a). *Sobranie sochinenii* [Collected works] (Vol. 4). Moscow: Pedagogika.

Vygotsky, L. S. (1984b). *Sobranie sochinenii* [Collected works] (Vol. 5). Moscow: Pedagogika.

Vygotsky, L. S. (1987). *The collected works of L.S. Vygotsky* (Vol. 1). New York: Plenum Press.

Vygotsky, L. S. (1989). Concrete human psychology: An unpublished manuscript by Vygotsky. *Journal of Russian and East European psychology, 27*(2), 53–77.

Vygotsky, L. S. (1991). *Pedaggogicheskaya psihologia* [Pedagogical psychology]. Moscow: Pedagogika.

Vygotsky, L. S. (1993). *The collected works of L.S. Vygotsky* (Vol. 2). New York: Plenum Press.

Vygotsky, L. S. (1994). The problem of the cultural development of the child. In R. van der Veer & J. Valsiner (Eds.), *The Vygotsky reader* (pp. 57–72). Oxford: Basil Blackwell.

Vygotsky, L. S. (1997a). *The collected works of L.S. Vygotsky* (Vol. 3). New York: Plenum Press.

Vygotsky, L. S. (1997b). *The collected works of L.S. Vygotsky* (Vol. 4). New York: Plenum Press.

Vygotsky, L. S. (1998a). *The collected works of L.S. Vygotsky* (Vol. 5). New York: Plenum Press.

Vygotsky, L. S. (1998b). *Psihologiya iskusstva* [The psychology of Art]. Rostov-na-Dony: Feniks.

Vygotsky, L. S. (1999). *The collected works of L.S. Vygotsky* (Vol. 6). New York: Plenum Press.

Vygotsky, L. S. (2001). *Lektsii po pedologii.* Izevsk: Izdatelstvo Udmurdskogo Universiteta.

Vygotsky, L. S. (2003). Predislovie k knige A. N. Leontieva "Razitie pamiati" [Preface to the book of A. N. Leontiev "The development of memory"]. In A. N. Leontiev (Ed.), *Stanovlenie teorii deyatelnosti* [The rise of the theory of activity] (pp. 199–206). Moscow: Smysl Publishers.

Vygotsky, L. S. (2005). *Psihologia razvitia cheloveka* [Psychology of the development of man]. Smysl Publishers.

Vygotsky, L. S. (2019). *L.S. Vygotsky's Pedological Works. Volume 1. Foundations of Pedology.* Singapore: Springer Nature.

Zavershneva, E. (2009a). "Kliutch k psihologii cheloveka": kommentarii k bloknotu L.S. Vygotskogo iz bolnitsy Zahairino (1926) ["The key to human psychology": comments to the notebook of Vygotsky from Zakhairino hospital (1026)]. *Voprosy Psihologii, 3,* 123–141.

Zavershneva, E. (2009b). Issledovanie rukopisi Vygotskogo "Istoricheskii smysl psihologicheskogo krizisa" [The investigation of Vygotsky's manuscript "Historical sense of psychological crisis"]. *Voprosy Psihologii, 6,* 119–138.

Zavershneva, E., & Van der Veer, R. (2018). *Vygotsky's notebooks: A selection.* Singapore: Springer.

Nikolai Veresov is an Associate Professor at the Faculty of Education at Monash University, Australia. He has experience as a day care centre and kindergarten teacher (1987–1991) and secondary school teacher (1982–1987). He received his first Ph.D. degree in Moscow in 1990, and started his academic career in Murmansk (Russia) as a senior lecturer (1991–1993) and the Head of Department of Early Childhood (1993–1997). The second Ph.D. was obtained at the University of Oulu (Finland) in 1998. From 1999 to 2011 he was affiliated to Kajaani Teacher Training Department (Finland) as a Senior Researcher and the Scientific Director of the international projects. His areas of interests include development in early years, cultural-historical theory, and research methodology.

Chapter 9
The Impact and Diffusion of Fernando González Rey's Work in Brazil

Maristela Rossato, Albertina Mitjáns Martínez,
and Luiz Roberto Rodrigues Martins

Abstract This chapter aims to present an analytical description of the impact and diffusion of González Rey's academic works in Brazil. We will study how the author's work has appeared in different areas of knowledge (education, health, qualitative research, law, transdisciplinary and organizational studies, etc.) published as book chapters, masters dissertations, doctoral theses, complete works in congresses, etc.) in different regions of the country. To do so, we will look for that in some relevant databases that allow us to understand the multiplicity of his work in Brazil. The impact of González Rey's work in Brazil will be analyzed through Google Scholar that makes it possible to identify "Index H" and the "i10 Index," which aims to quantify the productivity and impact of scientists based on their most cited articles. The diffusion of the work of González Rey in Brazil will be analyzed using three main references: The Bank of Theses of CAPES (Higher Education Personnel Coordination), the Working Group history of ANPEPP (National Association of Research and Post-Graduation in Psychology), and the Annals of the two editions of the National Symposium of Qualitative Epistemology and Subjectivity.

9.1 Introduction

The main objective of this chapter is to present the impact and diffusion of the work of Fernando González Rey in Brazil. Such objective is justified for at least two reasons. The first of them is that it was in this country in which he arrived in 1995, invited as a visiting professor at the University of Brasília. It was there where he developed

M. Rossato (✉) · A. Mitjáns Martínez · L. R. R. Martins
University of Brasilia, Brasilia, Brazil
e-mail: maristelarossato@gmail.com

A. Mitjáns Martínez
e-mail: amitjans49@gmail.com

L. R. R. Martins
e-mail: luizrrmartins@gmail.com

most of his work and established most of the scientific and academic work networks that significantly expanded his international projection. The invitation, made by the University of Brasilia, to act as a foreign visiting professor, was due to the prestige he already had for the scientific-academic work he developed in Cuba, his country of origin, and which was increasingly internationally recognized, especially in Latin America. When he was not allowed, for political reasons, to return to Cuba after his four-year job as a visiting professor, he had to permanently move to Brazil.[1] It was in this scientific-academic location that he developed his work and consolidated the Theory of Subjectivity and Qualitative Epistemology, which are his most significant scientific contributions.

A second reason that justifies this chapter is the importance of giving visibility to the fact that he was a Latin American author, who was able to develop in a Latin American country, theoretical and epistemological conceptions of international significance and projection. This fact, which might be obvious to some, for multiple reasons has not been common in contemporary relevant scientific production, which, in Psychology's case, is mainly concentrated in the United States and Europe.

González Rey was always a critic of the "cultural colonialism" that prevails in most of Latin American scientific and academic spaces, where productions from the knowledge centers of production are assumed and consumed in a non-reflexive way. This practice limits the interest and the ability to regard the possibility of developing one's own thinking and of producing scientific theory in Latin America. González Rey, without ignoring contributions from other contexts, was an example of this, with his audacity, strength, reflexivity, and independence, being Cuba and Brazil the spaces where he carried out his research and developed his theoretical, epistemological, and methodological concepts. Initially, we will present the international impact of his work based on an analysis of the h-index. This general index includes citations of his work in articles written by Brazilian authors, however, due to the way in which the index was conceived, it is extremely difficult to separate the citations that appear in these articles for specific analysis, which would have been interesting for the central purpose of this chapter. Then, we will present the diffusion of his work in Brazil from three sources that we consider representative in order to achieve the proposed objective.

---

[1] In addition to the Universidade de Brasília (University of Brasilia), González Rey, worked as a professor and researcher at the University Center of Brasilia (Centro Universitário de Brasília), at the Higher Education Institute of Brasilia (Instituto de Educação Superior de Brasília), at the Pontifical Catholic University of Campinas (Pontifícia Universidade Católica de Campinas), at the Catholic University of Brasilia (Universidade Católica de Brasília), at the Pontifical Catholic University of Goiás (Pontifícia Católica Universidade de Goiás) and at the Federal University of Ceará (Universidade Federal do Ceará). He was also invited to give lectures and offer courses at several other Brazilian academic institutions.

9.2   The Impact of the Work of Fernando González Rey

Assessing the impact of an author's work is a challenge that can never be fully covered. Although we have some metric parameters already institutionally recognized that can serve as reference, such as the h-index and the 10-index, which we will analyze later, they do not encompass the real extension of how González Rey's work impacted and impacts researchers and professionals from different areas in different countries.

The impact of his publications in academic discussions, in professional training networks and in other researchers' works cannot be measured, either because those who participate in them do not even publish scientific publications with citations of the author's works, or even because many of them do not even publish books or articles, especially in professional training spaces that are not focused on research.

The impact of his work, directly on people's lives due to the opportunity to read, debate, reflect, and develop, cannot be measured either. In addition to discussing his ideas with renowned researchers in several countries, González Rey also always enjoyed to debate with students, as it was with them—due to the simplicity of the questions that often emerged in their discussions—that new ideas, always registered in his pocket notebook, took shape. As he always affirmed, and which continues to be valid even after his decease, his work is alive and in continuous construction through the lines of research that have been consolidated over the years in different academic spaces.

Some internationally recognized means used to measure the impact[2] of an author's work are the h-index and the 10-index, which highlight the productivity and impact of scientists' and researchers' publications. Created in 2005 by Jorge E. Hirsch, the h-index is a quality and notoriety indicator in the scientific segment calculated by the number of published works and their citations. The 10-index portrays publications that have had at least 10 citations.

Analyzing the citations record of González Rey's publications, we currently have an h-index of 59 and a 10-index of 189 (Graph 9.1). We can also observe the record of the actual number of citations of publications with emphasis on the last 5 years, which concentrates more than 40% of citations from the entire period, regardless of the year in which it was published.

In the following graph (Graph 9.2), we can identify the evolution of citations in González Rey's publications since 1998, when the tallying of citations. It includes works published since the 1980s, which continue to be cited, such as: *Algunas cuestiones teóricas y metodológicas sobre el estudio de la personalidad* [Some Theoretical and Methodological Questions on the Study of Personality] (González Rey, 1982), *Psicología, principios y categorías* [Psychology, Principles and Categories] (González Rey, 1989) e *Personalidad y comunicación: su relación teórica y metodológica* [Personality and Communication: Their Theoretical and Methodological Relationship] (González Rey, 1989).

---

[2]All information presented in this section was systematized from data captured between January and April 2020. Considering that the registration of Google Scholar is continuous, the information will present changes when consulted in other periods.

Graph 9.1 González Rey's h-index and 10-index (*Fonte* https://scholar.google.com. br/citations?user=VdF856 0AAAAJ&hl=pt-BR&safe= strict Capturado em 6 de abril de 2020)

	Todos	Desde 2015
Citações	19862	8324
Índice h	59	43
Índice i10	189	136

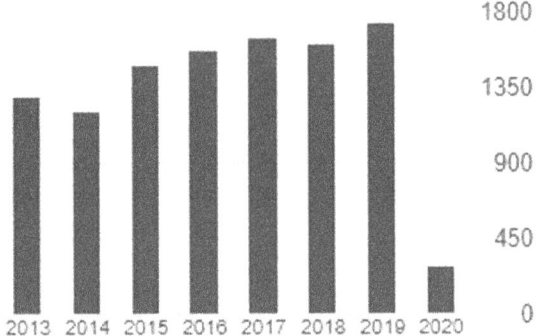

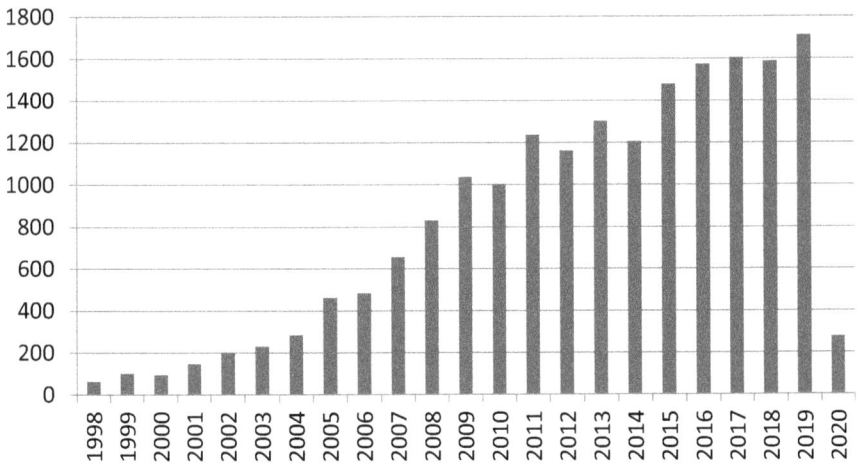

Graph 9.2 Evolution of the record of citations in González Ray's publications (*Source* The authors)

The book *Comunicación, personalidad y desarrollo* [Communication, Personality, and Development], published in 1995, appears in first place with approximately 1,500 citations. In addition to this work, we found three others with more than 1,000 citations, namely: *Pesquisa Qualitativa em Psicologia: caminhos e desafios* [Qualitative Research in Psychology: Paths and Challenges] (2002); *Pesquisa qualitativa e subjetividade: os processos de construção da informação* [Qualitative Research and Subjectivity: The Information Construction Processes] (2005); *Epistemología cualitativa y subjetividade* [Qualitative Epistemology and Subjectivity] (1997). We consider it important to highlight, in a special way, this last publication, where the antecedents, foundations, and essential concepts of the Theory of Subjectivity and Qualitative Epistemology appear in an articulated form for the first time. Since then, this theory has been developed and expanded in all his subsequent scientific research throughout his academic production.

Other three publications appear with citations with numbers between 500 and 1,000, namely: *Investigación cualitativa y subjetividad: los procesos de construcción de la información* [Qualitative Research and Subjectivity: The Processes of Information Construction] (2007); *La investigación cualitativa en psicología: rumbos y desafíos* [Qualitative Research in Psychology: Directions and Challenges] (1990); *Motivación moral en adolescentes y jóvenes* [Moral Motivation in Adolescents and Youth] (1990). When analyzing the number of citations between 100 and 500, we found another 29 works published between 1983 and 2013. We emphasize the fact that, since his first publications, his work already contained innovative ideas that made his publications remain alive in the course of time due to its originality.

González Rey appears in first place in the number of citations when compared to other authors on topics such as "cultural-historical psychology" and "psychological development" with more than 19,000 citations, showing a solid and continually ascending production throughout his life trajectory, fruit of the national and international networks he created, through partnerships and dialogue with different countries, such as Australia, Spain, United States, United Kingdom, Russia, France, in addition to most countries in the Latin American continent such as Argentina, Brazil, Bolivia, Chile, Colombia, Cuba, Ecuador, Guatemala, Mexico, Peru, Puerto Rico, and Venezuela (Graphs 9.3 and 9.4).

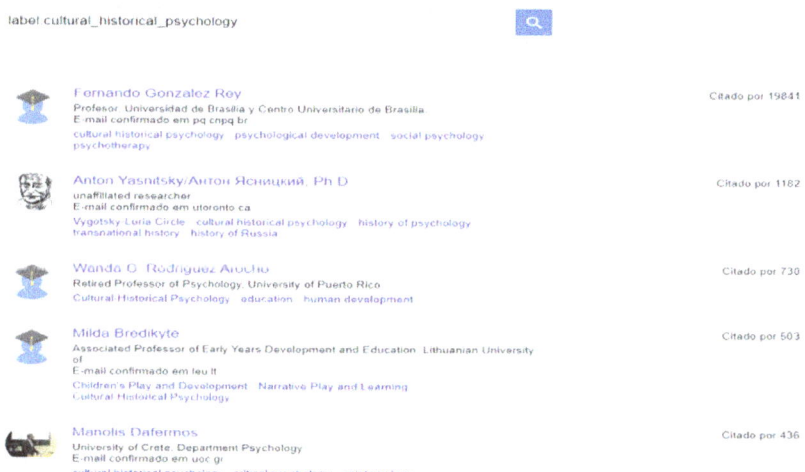

Graph 9.3 Comparison with other authors for cultural historical psychology (*Source* https://sch olar.google.com.br/citations?view_op=search_authors&hl=ptBR&mauthors=label:cultural_histor ical_psychology. Captured on April 3, 2020)

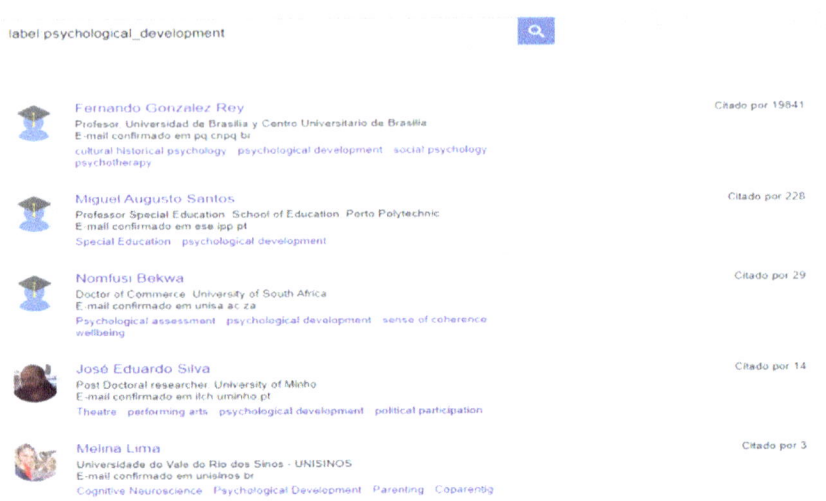

Graph 9.4 Comparison with other authors for the theme psychological development (*Source* https://scholar.google.com.br/citations?view_op=search_authors&hl=pt-BR&mauthors= label:psychological_development. Captured on April 3, 2020)

An important factor that deserves to be highlighted in the author's work and that has contributed a lot to the evolution of his h-index, is the number of publications in different languages that enabled the consolidation of the international network of collaborators in several countries. González Rey has publications in Spanish, English, Portuguese, French, and Russian. Among the publications with more than 100 citations, 22 are in Spanish, 15 in Portuguese, and 2 in English. It is worth noting that the author's investment in English-language publications took place more intensively after 2010, and we believe that is the reason why these publications have not yet emerged among the most cited so far.

To exemplify the linguistic scope of his work, in an excerpt of his most recent productions enrolled in his curriculum considering the last 10 years of his life (2010–2020), 48 articles were published, 21 in English, 16 in Spanish, and 11 in Portuguese. In the same period, he published 12 books either as author or organizer, being 2 in English, 3 in Spanish, and 7 in Portuguese. If you analyze his book chapters' production, there are 19 in English, 5 in Spanish, and 15 in Portuguese. In an integrative analysis of the last 10 years, 44% of the production is in English, 36% in Portuguese, and 25% in Spanish.

Finally, regarding the impact of González Rey's work, we note the impossibility of mapping each source where each of the author's publication was cited, considering the volume of data to be analyzed manually, since the database systems used do not offer a tool for automatic data mining. If it were possible to extract the data automatically it certainly would provide us with a macro overview of the author's insertion in academic circles in different countries and especially in Brazil.

9.3 Dissemination of Fernando González Rey's Work in Brazil

The dissemination of González Rey's work in Brazil will be analyzed through three sources: The Catalog of Theses and Dissertations[3] of the Coordination for the Improvement of Higher Education Personne—CAPES; the history of the "Subjectivity, Learning and Teaching" Work Group of the National Association of Research and Graduate Studies in Psychology—ANPEPP and the Proceedings of the two editions of the National Symposium on Qualitative Epistemology and Subjectivity.[4]

9.3.1 The Catalog of Theses and Dissertations of the Coordination for the Improvement of Higher Education Personnel—CAPES

CAPES, an organization belonging to the Ministry of Education in Brazil, operates evaluating *stricto* sensu Postgraduate Programs, providing access and dissemination of scientific production, promoting investments in the high-level human resources development, both in the country and abroad, promoting scientific international cooperation, inducing and supporting initial and continuing education for basic education teachers working both on-site and in distance learning.[5] CAPES encompasses nine major areas of knowledge, namely: Exact and Earth Sciences, Biological Sciences, Engineering, Health Sciences, Agrarian Sciences, Applied Social Sciences, the Humanities, Linguistics, Letters and Arts, Multidisciplinary Areas.

The CAPES Thesis and Dissertations Catalog was created in 2001 and gathers approximately 500,000 Master's Dissertations' and Doctoral Theses' abstracts from more than 4,500 graduate programs in Brazil in public and private institutions. This database was chosen because it enables the identification of how publications have been disseminated and used in scientific production in graduate programs in the country. All information is recorded in Portuguese and English. In this database, we mapped productions by knowledge sub-area (Master's Dissertations and Doctoral Theses) and geographic region of the university in the country.

---

[3]https://catalogodeteses.capes.gov.br.

[4]We know that choosing these three essential sources leaves out other information that would also express the dissemination of González Rey's work in Brazil, such as the way in which his publications appear in the bibliographic references of doctoral theses, master's dissertations, final works of undergraduate courses, scientific initiation works, abstracts or complete works published in the annals of various national congresses, books that form part of the mandatory or complementary bibliography of university course subjects, among others. However, the search and analysis of this information would imply an archaeological work, impossible to carry out given the number of possible sources and their dispersion.

[5]Fonte. https://www.capes.gov.br. Captured on April 14, 2020.

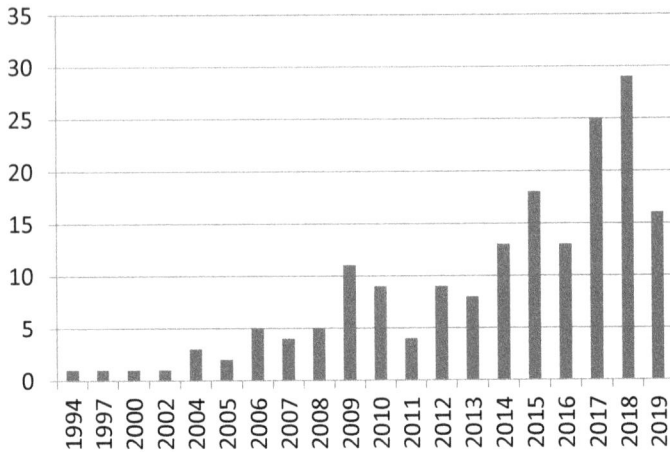

Graph 9.5 Evolution of the number of Ph.D. and Master's researches with the descriptor 'Teoria da Subjetividade' (*Source* The authors)

To identify the dissemination of González Rey's work in the country, we worked with two index descriptors that represent the essence of his work and, consequently, how it has been mostly recognized in Brazil: "Theory of Subjectivity" and "Qualitative Epistemology."[6] In the search criteria utilized the incidence of these two index descriptors in the title, abstract or keyword of each document reference was considered. It is worth mentioning that the search using these descriptors did not enable us to identify the specific nature of how González Rey's theoretical–epistemological framework is used in the publication. Through the complete reading of some of these works, we found that in some of them the author is used as a central reference, in some as guiding the theoretical–epistemological–methodological discussions and, in others, his reference is only part of the set of references used, especially regarding the search carried out with the index descriptor "Qualitative Epistemology".

With the index descriptor "Theory of Subjectivity" 143 searches were found, 59 of which were Ph.D. thesis and 119 of which were Master dissertations, produced between 1994 and 2019.[7] We can see a progressive increase of the works that make use of the Theory of Subjectivity and Qualitative Epistemology as references, with emphasis on the last 10 years, reaching close to 30 searches in 2018. In the graph, below, we can identify the evolution of the productions along this period (Graph 9.5).

Regarding the knowledge subareas in which researches have been carried out, we identified a predominance of Education and Psychology, followed by Teaching and Letters (Graph 9.6).

---

[6]The research was carried out with Portuguese language indexers: Teoria da Subjetividade e Epistemologia Qualitativa.

[7]The 2019 information has not yet been processed in its entirety, since the programs have up to 6 months to inform the agency of the academic evaluations made.

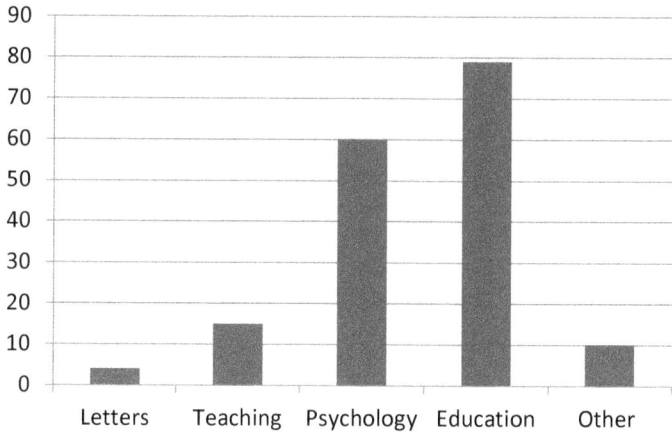

Graph 9.6   Research by Subareas of knowledge using descriptor 'Teoria da Subjetividade' (*Source* The authors)

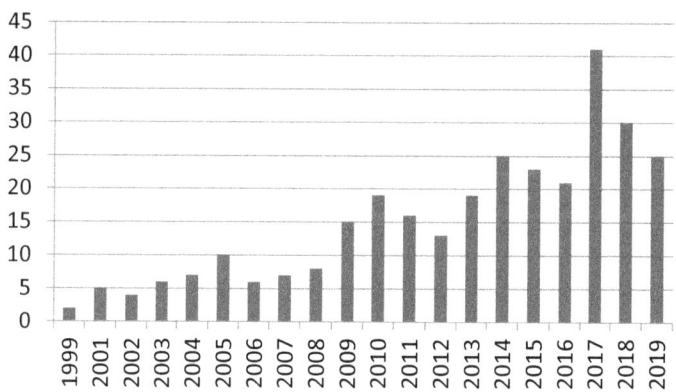

Graph 9.7   Ph.D. and Master's researches using the descriptor 'Epistemologia Qualitativa' (*Source* The authors)

In an analysis of the geographical distribution of the researches carried out, we registered 38 public and private universities, located in the 5 different regions of the country, with a predominance of universities where González Rey had worked as a researcher professor during his stay in Brazil. With the index descriptor 'Qualitative Epistemology', 257 searches were found, 71 of them were for Doctorate Thesis and 186 for Masters Dissertations, produced between 1994 and 2019, and surpassing the number of 40 researches in 2017. In the graph below, we can identify the evolution of the productions during this period (Graph 9.7).

Regarding the knowledge subareas where the researches have been carried out, we identified a predominance of Psychology and Education, followed by Health and Administration (Graph 9.8).

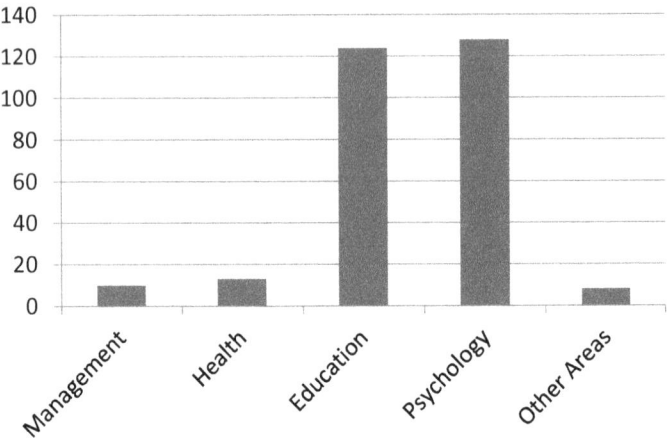

Graph 9.8 Subarea of Knowledge for the index 'Epistemologia Qualitativa' (*Source* The authors)

Regarding "Qualitative Epistemology", we found 52 public and private universities located in the five different regions of the country[8] and predominantly in universities where González Rey had worked as a professor and researcher during his stay in Brazil.

The information presented shows how the work of Gonzalez Rey in the research groups led by him, in the research networks he promoted and in his teaching training in postgraduate programs have enabled doctors, in various academic institutions, to guide doctoral theses and master's dissertations based on the "Theory of Subjectivity" and "Qualitative Epistemology" created by him.

9.3.2   The Subjectivity, Teaching and Learning Work Group

The Work Group—"Subjectivity, Teaching and Learning"[9] GT is part of the National Association of Research and Graduate Studies in Psychology—ANPEPP. The Association was founded in 1983 and aims to bring together graduate programs in Psychology linked to higher education institutions (public and private) to foster and encourage the training of professionals for research and graduate studies in Psychology, observing strict political party, religious and racial neutrality.[10] Since 1988, every two years, the Association has promoted the Brazilian Symposiums on

---

[8]Brazil is a Federative Republic structured in 26 states and the Federal District. It is a country of continental proportions that is divided into 5 geographic regions: south, southeast, north, northeast, and central-west.

[9]Subjetividade, Ensino e Aprendizagem.

[10]Source: https://www.anpepp.org.br/. Captured in April 13, 2020.

Scientific Research and Exchange as a way of consolidating and implementing its objectives together with postgraduate programs.

The Symposiums aim to discuss research, politics, and training within more than 80 post-graduation programs in Psychology in Brazil, affiliated to the Association. In addition to allowing more than 90 GTs (Work groups), the event has several discussion forums in the area of Psychology such as Ethics, Internationalization Policies, Postgraduate Promotion Policies, among others.

For the maintenance of the GTs at the ANPEPP Symposia, at each new edition of the event, the coordinators of each GT need to submit a proposal that is evaluated by the Scientific Committee of the event. This proposal includes information regarding the history of the GT, the profile of its participants, the maintenance of the exchange networks in the last two years, objectives for the next meeting, the schedule of activities to be carried out during the event and the curriculum of the GT coordinator.

The internal dynamics of the task groups are proposed by their coordinators, selected by the members of the group based on criteria established by the Association. During the Symposium, the GT's work simultaneously, each of them with the objective of promoting the exchange of ideas, projects, and productions developed by the researchers working on related topics.

The GT on "Subjectivity, Teaching and Learning" was created in 2010 due to the interest of a group of Brazilian researchers who had been working with the cultural-historical perspective in addressing educational themes and who expressed an interest in knowing and deepening their understating in regard to the Theory of Subjectivity. Since then, this group has been meeting all the necessary requirements, ensuring its approval by the Scientific Committee in the five events that followed. Throughout the six editions of the Symposium in which the GT met, until now, despite members having left and new members coming, more than 70% of the group has remained since its creation, underlying the consolidation of González Rey's work in the members' post-graduation programs, with the development of research and production trajectories anchored in his theoretical–epistemological–methodological foundations. The group has also maintained the criterion of insertion of researchers from more than three of the country's geographic regions and the diversity of institutions of higher education, maintaining the average of ten represented institutions in each event, with a predominance of public institutions from different Brazilian states.

During his life trajectory, the presence of González Rey in the group's meetings has always been very striking, with his active and reflective presence, which has always enabled us exchanges and understanding of his work. His intellectual generosity has always enabled us to live the experience of reflective confrontation of unprecedented ideas, of dialogical tensioning, of the displacement from the commonplace.

The select composition of the group's profile, as previously described, makes the discussions high level, always with the perspective of generating comprehensive advances and greater alignment of the concepts within the group. A concern that always guides the group, in addition comprehensive advances, concerns the misinterpretations of the theoretical, epistemological, and methodological concepts developed by the author. The maintenance of his work involves the commitment of every member of the GT to keep a rigor that minimizes distortions and enlightened

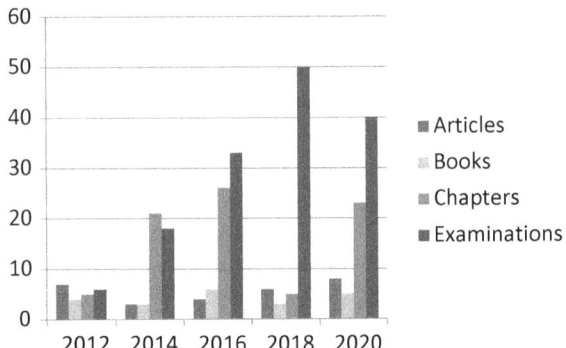

Graph 9.9 Joint production of the members of the GT Subjectivity, Teaching and Learning (*Source* The authors)

the comprehension of his ideas and, in this sense, the shared discussions were, and continue to be, fundamental for the alignment of the reflections around his work.

In graph number 9 we have the registration of the joint production trajectory of the GT members around the theoretical–epistemological–methodological framework developed by González Rey. This production represents the strength and consistency of a network of researchers who have developed a trajectory of investigations, through Master Degree and Doctorate academic guidance as well as other academic activities. It is worth remembering that the production carried out individually by the members of the GT is not included in this graph (Graph 9.9).

In addition to the moments of in-depth discussion that have always been stimulated by González Rey, the group is also organized around several activities: (1) planning joint articles and book publications organized with the GT's identity, (2) the creation of partnerships between the institutions that the members of the GT belong to, (3) and the organization of examining boards, courses, seminars, and support to events like the National Symposium on Qualitative Epistemology and Subjectivity, described in the next section of this chapter.

Among the various joint productions, we highlight the organization of four books that were the result of discussions and productions by the members of the GT, namely: *Ensino e aprendizagem: a subjetividade em foco* [Teaching and Learning: Subjectivity in Focus] (Mitjáns Martínez, et al., 2012); *Subjetividade Contemporânea: discussões epistemológicas e metodológicas* [Contemporary Subjectivity: Epistemological and Methodological Discussions] (Mitjáns Martínez, et al., 2014); Sociedade Contemporânea: subjetividade e educação [Contemporary Society: Subjectivity and Education] (Anache et al., 2015); *Formação de Educadores e Psicólogos: contribuições e desafios da subjetividade na perspectiva cultural-histórica* [Development of Educators and Psychologists: Contributions and Challenges of Subjectivity in the Cultural-Historical Perspective] (Rossato & Peres, 2019).

Up to date in the Brazilian context, for historical, idiomatic, and cultural reasons, among others, books and book chapters are an essential source of information for both scientific production and professional work and academic training. In many contexts, especially in the field of Education, they are comparatively much more used even than scientific articles. For this reason, the books produced by the members of the GT have been widely disseminated and used, constituting an important path that favors knowledge and dissemination of González Rey's work in the country.

9.3.3   National Symposium on Qualitative Epistemology and Subjectivity

Another source of data on the dissemination of González Rey's work in Brazil is the Proceedings of the National Symposium on Qualitative Epistemology and Subjectivity held in Brasilia, Brazil, in 2017[11] and 2019.[12] Due to the increasing use of González Rey's work in various academic institutions, research groups, and by professionals in the fields of education, health, law, and management there was a need to provide broader spaces for the discussion of ideas and concepts regarding the Theory of Subjectivity and Qualitative Epistemology, conditions that allowed the successful organization of the Symposia.

The Symposia aim to promote the debate on the principles and concepts of Qualitative Epistemology and Theory of Subjectivity, as well as their implications for the production of knowledge in the areas of Humanities, Social Sciences, and Health Sciences. The objective is also to encourage the exchange and the formation of national and international research groups networks, as well as promoting a space for discussion among professionals who already have a history of acting guided by the theory's premises, such as: teachers and Education managers, Health psychologists, therapists, social workers, administrators, among others, in addition to undergraduate students who are in an initial professional training process.

The initiative of the first event took place in celebration of the 20th anniversary of the simultaneous publication of the book *Epistemología Cualitativa y Subjectividad* [Qualitative Epistemology and Subjectivity] (González Rey, 1997) in Cuba and in Brazil. As mentioned earlier, this book represented an essential contribution in the foundation of González Rey's ideas. For the celebration of this historic milestone, different researchers and research groups already consolidated in Brazil, such as the Subjectivity, Teaching and Learning GT aforementioned, among others,[13] had the initiative to promote this first national encounter.

The symposia's methodology and the extent of the topics covered,

---

[11] https://simposiosubjetivid.wixsite.com/subjetividade2017.

[12] https://sneqs2019.galoa.com.br/.

[13] Psychology and Health Research Group of the Master Program in Psychology at University Center of Brasília—UniCEUB; Research Groups of the College of Education and Institute of Psychology, from the University of Brasília—UnB; Study and Research Group on Developmental Didactics and Teacher Professionalization—GEPEDI at the Federal University of Uberlândia; Research Groups of the CNPq Research Groups Directory: Study of Subjectivity in Education and Health; Learning, Schooling and Human Development; Subjective Development in school Teaching and Learning Contexts.

   The Symposia have adopted a differentiated format in relation to most events held in Brazil, traditionally focused essentially on giving lectures and socializing scientific works. Since the first edition, the idea has been to bring together people who want to discuss the value and scope of Qualitative Epistemology and Theory of Subjectivity in the production of scientific knowledge, as well as its use in professional practice in different fields. The realization of these events aims to deepen the comprehension regarding the theoretical concepts, question, and value the different ways they have been used. The events also serve to analyze the process of consolidation of this theoretical reference in the academic and professional fields.

   In both editions of the symposium, particular importance has been given to the Round Table Conferences which, in addition to having experts as guests, also have panelists who discuss in-depth the ideas presented by the speakers. The panelists are chosen from among specialists in the subject under discussion, but with other theoretical bases, in order to qualify the debate during the Round Tables. After the Symposia, the texts of the lectures are organized in the form of books aiming at the wide dissemination of the main ideas discussed. As a result of 1st Symposium, the book *Epistemologia Qualitativa e Teoria da Subjetividade: discussões sobre Educação e Saúde* [Qualitative Epistemology and Theory of Subjectivity: Discussions on Education and Health] (Mitjáns Martínez et al., 2019) was published and as a result of the 2nd Symposium the book *Teoria da Subjetividade: discussões teóricas e metodológicas* [Theory of Subjectivity: Theoretical and Methodological Discussions] (Mitjáns Martínez et al., 2020). The Round Tables, due to their content, are central activities during the symposia and also aim to contribute significantly to the work of Thematic Discussion Groups as they constitute privileged spaces for theoretical–epistemological-methodological discussion. The themes of the Round Tables in both editions of the Symposium are presented below in order to provide a broader understanding of how the Theory of Subjectivity and Qualitative Epistemology have been understood and debated.

   Round Tables of the 1st National Symposium on Qualitative Epistemology and Subjectivity, held in 2017:

- Table 1—Subjectivity and Health;
- Table 2—Qualitative Epistemology and Constructive-Interpretive Methodology;
- Table 3—Subjectivity and Education.

Round Tables of the 2nd National Symposium on Qualitative Epistemology and Subjectivity, held in 2019:

- Opening Table—Theory of Subjectivity: contributions in different fields and contexts;
- Table 2—Social subjectivity: meaning and expression in different contexts;
- Table 3—Subjective development: complexity and possibilities;
- Table 4—Methodological challenges of the study of subjectivity: articulation between research and professional practice.

The other differentiated activities of the Symposia are the Thematic Discussion Groups—GDT. They have been constituted as a space aimed toward: (1) clarifying doubts, undoing mistakes, deepening conceptual matters; (2) discussing the contributions of Theory of Subjectivity, of the Qualitative Epistemology and of the Constructive-Interpretative Methodology; (3) providing opportunity to debate conceptual, epistemological and methodological issues in research and professional practice; (4) identifying and discussing problems, difficulties and challenges to be faced (theoretical, epistemological and methodological); (5) proposing ways to advance the development of the Theory of Subjectivity and Qualitative Epistemology.

For the coordination of such groups, qualified people with mastery in each of the themes are chosen and, for approximately ten hours, they discuss in-depth the central concepts of the theory, dialoguing with the researchers and questions brought by the participants. This activity has had a very positive acceptance as it effectively constitutes a space for exchange and great learning for all. The themes that were discussed in the two editions of the Symposium are presented below.

Thematic Discussion Groups of the 1st National Symposium on Qualitative Epistemology and Subjectivity, held in 2017:

- GDT 1—Theory of Subjectivity: discussion of conceptual issues and possible misconceptions;
- GDT 2—Subjective Development and Health;
- GDT 3—Diagnosis, psychotherapy, and subjectivity: discussion of the psychological clinic;
- GDT 4—Training of teachers and education professionals: the subjective constitution of teaching;
- GDT 5—Training of professionals in the health field;
- GDT 6—Pedagogical Work from the perspective of Subjectivity: intervention challenges and didactics in singular pedagogical assistance;
- GDT 7—Subjectivity, inclusion, and disability;
- GDT 8—Research based on Qualitative Epistemology and the constructive-interpretative methodology. Forms of achievement and possible misconceptions;
- GDT 9—Subjective development and learning: the challenge of students who do not learn at school.

Thematic Discussion Groups of the 2nd National Symposium on Qualitative Epistemology and Subjectivity, held in 2019:

- GDT 1—Theory of Subjectivity: conceptual discussions and its relation to other theoretical references;
- GDT 2—Qualitative Epistemology and constructive-interpretive methodology: conceptual discussions and its relation to other epistemological and methodological perspectives;
- GDT 3—The use of qualitative epistemology and the constructive-interpretive methodology in research and professional practice;
- GDT 4—Subjective development;
- GDT 5—Learning and learning difficulties from the perspective of subjectivity;

- GDT 6—Subjectivity in the training of teachers and other professionals;
- GDT 7—Pedagogical work and didactics from the perspective of subjectivity;
- GDT 8—The subjective dimension of disability in the school inclusion process;
- GDT 9—Diagnosis and evaluation from the perspective of the Theory of Subjectivity;
- GDT 10—Psychotherapy and Subjectivity;
- GDT 11—Subjectivity and human health;
- GDT 12—The meaning of subjectivity in several fields: law, organizations, community work, and others.

The events also include other activities such as short courses, conferences, and the launch of books related to the Theory of Subjectivity and Qualitative Epistemology.

Both editions of the symposia promoted the submission of papers by the participants, but not with the aim of presenting them, as traditionally happens, but to favor the GTD thematic discussions. In the 2017 edition we had 108 papers approved, 81 in the form of abstracts and 27 in the form of complete texts, published in the Annals of the event (Anais, 2017). In 2019, we had 144 papers approved, 113 in the form of abstracts and 31 in the form of complete texts, also published in the annals of the event (Anais, 2019). Next, it is possible to see the distribution of works of both events, as identified in Graph 9.10. The subdivision presented was built by the authors of this chapter, taking into account the two central contents of the event— Theory of Subjectivity and Qualitative Epistemology—and the subareas in which these references have appeared with greater recurrence in the Symposia.

Through the Symposiums it has been possible to provide an overview of the interest, use, and dissemination of González Rey's work in Brazil. In both events, we have had researchers, professors, students, and professionals from the five geographic regions of Brazil from more than fifteen public and ten private universities, in addition to more than ten other institutions such as schools and health units. We also recorded the presence of liberal professionals who have sought González Rey's work as a reference for their professional performance (Anais, 2017, 2019).

Graph 9.10 Distribution of the publications (*Source* The authors)

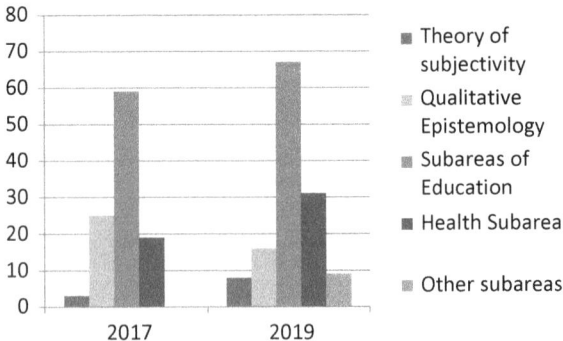

It is important to emphasize that the extent and diversity of the themes addressed in these events, especially as they are national events, show the significance and capillarity of González Rey's work as a theoretical, epistemological, and methodological reference for the work of other researchers and professionals. The networks and research groups derived from his work were present in these events giving visibility to the multiple ways in which the Theory of Subjectivity, Qualitative Epistemology and Constructive-Interpretive Methodology impact scientific research and intellectual production which derive from it. Likewise, in these events, the diversity of ways in which González Rey's work is assumed and used by professionals from different fields in their daily work has become evident. The strength of these national events and their continuity are a clear expression of the legacy of Gonzalez Rey's work in Brazil.

9.4 Final Considerations

At the beginning of this chapter, we discuss the limits of an investigation that aims to measure the impact and diffusion of an author's work. However, the results that we were able to get from the websites and documents allow us to identify how González Rey's work continued to grow, not only in number of publications, but mainly in the consolidation and recognition that he had throughout his academic career.

We emphasize that, possibly, within a few months, the figures presented in this chapter will already be out of date, due to the update of the data systems that were consulted. The speed in change of information especially reveals the importance, the strength, and the liveliness of his work which remains a reference for many students, researchers, and professionals from different areas of knowledge.

In his productive life in Brazil, in the various institutions where he worked as a teacher and researcher, González Rey found the environment essential for his scientific production. The research groups he led and his teaching work, both at the undergraduate and graduate levels in Brazilian academic institutions, were important spaces for conducting research and reflections that significantly contributed to the development and consolidation of the Theory of Subjectivity and Qualitative Epistemology—his most recognized scientific contributions. His scientific production has had a significant diffusion outside the borders of Cuba and Brazil, demonstrating, once again, that scientific knowledge of international impact can be produced in Latin America.

The dissemination and the use of his work in Brazil has been increasing as shown by the sources presented. The knowledge of his work in the five regions in which a country of continental proportions is divided and its presence in 26 states of the Federation and the Federal District shows the capillarity his work has had, given its importance for scientific, professional, and teaching work in different fields, especially in the fields of human development, education, and health. His legacy, without a doubt, constitutes a stimulus for the continuity and advancement of his ideas, a challenge that already undertaken by the main research group that he led in Brazil until his death in March 2019.

References

Anache, A. A., Scoz, B. J. L., & Castanho, M. I. S. (2015). *Sociedade Contemporânea*: subjetividade e educação [Contemporary society: Subjectivity and education]. São Paulo: Memnon.

Anais [do] I Simpósio Nacional de Epistemologia Qualitativa e Subjetividade: programação, resumos e trabalhos completos [Annals [of] I National Symposium on Qualitative Epistemology and Subjectivity: Programming, abstracts and complete papers]. (2017). [online] Brasília. Available at: https://simposiosubjetivid.wixsite.com/subjetividade2017/anais. Accessed 15 Apr 2020.

Anais [do] II Simpósio Nacional de Epistemologia Qualitativa e Subjetividade: programação, resumos e trabalhos completos [Annals [of] II National Symposium on Qualitative Epistemology and Subjectivity: Programming, abstracts and complete papers]. (2019). [online] Brasília. Available at: https://proceedings.science/sneqs-2019. Accessed 15 Apr 2020.

González Rey, F. (1982). *Algunas cuestiones teóricas y metodológicas sobre el estudio de la personalidad* [Some theoretical and methodological questions on the study of personality]. La Habana: Pueblo y Educacion.

González Rey, F. (1989). Personalidad y comunicación: su relación técnica y metodológica. En *Temas sobre la actividad y la comunicación* [Personality and communication: Their technical and methodological relationship]. In *Topics on activity and communication*. Colectivo de autores (pp. 327–347). La Habana: Editorial de Ciencias Sociales.

González Rey, F. (1989). *Psicología, principios y categorías* [Psychology, principles and categories]. La Habana: Editorial de Ciencias Sociales.

González Rey, F. (1990). *La investigación cualitativa en psicología*: rumbos y desafíos [Qualitative research in psychology: Directions and challenges]. São Paulo: EDUC.

González Rey, F. (1990). *Motivación moral en adolescentes y jóvenes* [Moral motivation in adolescents and youth]. La Habana: Editorial Científico-Técnica.

González Rey, F. (1995). *Comunicación, personalidad y desarrollo* [Communication, personality and development]. La Habana: Pueblo y Educacion.

González Rey, F. (1997). *Epistemología cualitativa y subjetividad* [Qualitative epistemology and subjectivity]. São Paulo: EDUC.

González Rey, F. (2002). *Pesquisa Qualitativa em Psicologia*: caminhos e desafio [Qualitative Research in Psychology: Paths and challenge]. São Paulo: Thomson.

González Rey, F. (2005). *Pesquisa qualitativa e subjetividade*: os processos de construção da informação [Qualitative research and subjectivity: The information construction processes]. São Paulo: Thomson.

González Rey, F. (2007). *Investigación cualitativa y subjetividad*: los procesos de construcción de la información [Qualitative research and subjectivity: The processes of information construction]. Guatemala: ODHAG.

Mitjáns Martínez, A., González Rey, F., & Valdés-Puentes, R. (2019). *Epistemologia Qualitativa e Teoria da Subjetividade*: discussões sobre Educação e Saúde [Qualitative epistemology and theory of subjectivity: Discussions on education and health]. Uberlândia: EDUFU.

Mitjáns Martínez, A., Neubern, M. S., & Mori, V. D. (2014). *Subjetividade Contemporânea*: discussões epistemológicas e metodológicas [Contemporary subjectivity: Epistemological and methodological discussions]. Campinas: Alínea.

Mitjáns Martínez, A., Scoz, B. J. L., & Castanho, M. I. S. (2012). *Ensino e aprendizagem*: a subjetividade em foco [Teaching and learning: Subjectivity in focus]. Brasília: Liber Livro.

Mitjáns Martínez, A., Tacca, M. C. R. V., & Valdés-Puentes, R. (2020). *Teoria da Subjetividade*: discussões teóricas, metodológicas e implicações na prática profissional [Theory of Subjectivity: theoretical and methodological discussions and their implications on the professional practice]. Campinas: Alínea.

Rossato, M., & Peres, V. L. A. (2019). *Formação de Educadores e Psicólogos*: contribuições e desafios da subjetividade na perspectiva cultural-histórica [Development of educators and

psychologists: Contributions and challenges of subjectivity in the cultural-historical perspective].
Curitiba: Apris.

Maristela Rossato has a Ph.D. in Education from the University of Brasília. She has more than 25 years of experience in research and teaching in higher education, high, and elementary school. She works in the areas of psychology of learning, developmental psychology, and distance education involving the following topics: development of subjectivity, difficulties in school learning, teacher training, technology impacts on human development, distance learning, and teaching. She is a member of the research group Learning, Schooling and Human Development belonging to the Group Directory of the Lattes Platform. She is currently an Adjunct Professor at the University of Brasília, Institute of Psychology, Department of School and Developmental Psychology, Laboratory of Cultural Psychology, Member of the Postgraduate Program in Human Development Processes.

Albertina Mitjáns Martínez is a Research Professor of the Faculty of Education at the University of Brasilia, Brazil. She obtained her Ph.D. qualification in psychological sciences at the University of Havana, Cuba, and concluded post-doctoral studies at the Faculty of Psychology of the Autonomous University of Madrid. Her research interests focus on education and psychology from a cultural-historical approach in three specific fields: (1) creativity and innovation in education; (2) subjectivity in human development and learning; (3) disabilities and school inclusion. Her latest books are: (1) *Subjectivity Within Cultural-Historical Approach: Theory, Methodology and Research* (Ed., 2019, Springer); (2) *Subjetividade: teoria, epistemologia e método* [Subjectivity: Theory, Epistemology and Method] (Alínea, 2019); (3) *Psicologia, educação e aprendizagem escolar* [Psychology, Education and School Learning] (Cortez, 2019).

Luiz Roberto Rodrigues Martins has a Ph.D. in Education from the University of Brasília and a Master's in Education at the same university, he is a specialist in Public Policy and Government Management. He has conducted research in the area of governmental public policies with a focus on processes related to the social subjectivity in the educational field. He has worked in the planning, implementation, and management of educational policies with the Ministry of Education in different departments for over twenty years.

Chapter 10
Social Relations and Friendships: Pathways to Study Motive, Motivation and Subjectivity

Megan Adams and Gloria Quinones

Abstract This chapter focuses on González Rey's theory of subjectivity in relation to motivation and motives. González Rey's theory of subjectivity provides a framework for the study of friendship, as families with children transition to live in a new country. Analysis explores the subjective productions of children and adults through dialogue and actions, during the process of children becoming friends. Findings indicate that during a playdate, children's shared motives and motivations are subjectively configured through suggesting and agreeing—these processes contribute to emotional engagement of each participant in relation. The social productions of adults, influences children's development of social interactions and possibilities for children to become friends. Adults and teachers create social conditions for children, for example, a mother coaches her child about what to expect when entering new social situations, and a teacher groups children in academic activities to provide opportunities to interact with different class members in different situations. Friendship is a social production and the pathway involves subjectivity, motivations and shared motives, contributing to children's learning and development.

10.1 Introduction

The aim of this chapter is to understand the way motivation is a central dimension of subjectivity in relation to social interactions and friendship in Early Childhood Education (ECE). We focus on the theoretical and epistemological arguments surrounding motive and motivation put forward by González Rey (2008, 2009, 2011, 2012, 2014, 2016, 2017, 2018). We draw examples from our empirical research based on social relations and friendship in early childhood to further theorise motives and motivation in relation to personality development. Theoretically, González Rey

M. Adams (✉) · G. Quinones
Monash University, Melbourne, VIC, Australia
e-mail: megan.adams@monash.edu

G. Quinones
e-mail: gloria.quinones@monash.edu

(2018) highlights subjectivity, as a symbolic-emotional system where individuals are engaged in the generation of subjective productions. We argue the concept of friendship involves subjective senses that are configured in moments of dialogue and action that involve cultural, emotional and symbolic expressions. Children forming social relations and friendships generate subjective senses and configurations that are symbolically produced in a constellation of emotions and motives that are configured in ongoing past, present and future relations.

Motive and motivation are important to subjectivity, and have been developed in fields of mental health and psychotherapy (Mori & Goulart, 2019), however, there has been less attention in early childhood education. Notable exceptions include the identity of young children moving countries with their families (Adams & Fleer, 2016), and teachers living outside their birth country for work purposes and ways they develop a sense of belonging within the international schools (Adams & Fleer, 2019). Quinones (2016) used subjectivity to explore children's affective connections with young peers (babies). Peers subjective senses as moments of action provide an understanding of the children's symbolic and emotional senses as they reciprocally act together (Quinones, 2016). Fleer (2019), used subjectivity and the reciprocal relations generated between students and an early childhood teacher in the teaching of science.

This chapter contributes to furthering the scholarship of González Rey's theoretical construction of subjectivity by outlining motive and motivation as a central dimension for developing social relations in the context of a developing friendship. We put forward the argument that by drawing on empirical examples of two children developing social relations and friendship, theoretically a new path for better understanding subjectivity and motivation is produced.

First, we draw González Rey's theoretical construction of subjectivity and how this is interwoven with motives and motivation. Next, we present empirical research and draw out our interpretation of subjectivity. The case example is part of a larger study on children and families transitioning to a new country (Adams, 2014). The focus is on two children's social interaction during a playdate. A playdate is an invitation for a friend to visit the home of another and build on their friendship (Adams & Quinones, 2020). We argue that playdates are a social space for developing friendships. Subjective configurations and senses of 'making friends' are present through peers' dialogues and actions and are configured through expressions by parents and teachers.

10.2   Subjective Configuration, Motives and Motivation

The quest to understand motivation and personality development was a central component of González Rey's (2004–2014) works. Drawing on studies using Vygotsky's (1994) concepts of sense, perezhivanie and psychological formation, inspired González Rey (2009) to advance the concept of subjectivity. González Rey argued that personality development integrates internal and external psychological processes through 'a complex emotional-cognitive system that produces new realities' (2012 p. 48). Over the last two decades, González Rey, deepened his conceptualisation of personality development through theorising a new understanding of subjectivity (see, González Rey, 2004, 2012, 2019). Here, as with other chapters in this book, we draw on this theorisation to better understand the individual and social dimensions of young children's interactions, which contribute to their personality development. Specifically, the concepts of social subjectivity, subjective sense and configurations in relation to motives and motivation as children form new friendships during transition periods as they move to a new country with their family.

Subjectivity is a self-organising system and is defined ontologically through the formation of symbolic-emotional units (González Rey, 2012). The individual's experience and what the person contributes to the experience form individual subjectivity subjective configurations and subjective senses, which originate from the interweaving of emotions and symbolic processes (González Rey, 2004, 2009, 2012). Subjective configurations are 'flexible, changing forms that are shaped by the context of the situation, the state of mind of the individual during the lived experience, and their participation in various social networks where actions are expressed and undertaken' (Adams & Fleer, 2017, p. 355). Theoretically, subjective senses are interwoven with subjective configurations and are referred to as '... "snapshots" of symbolic-emotional flashes that unfold in a chaotic movement, from which subjective configurations emerge as a self-regulative and self-generative organisation of subjective senses' (González Rey, 2019, p. 28). The generative and regulative organisations of subjective configurations and subjective senses are constantly unfolding and characterise social and individual motives and motivation (González Rey, 2019).

10.2.1   Motives and Motivation

Motives and motivation are contested concepts within cultural-historical literature (see, González Rey, 2011) and rather than entering this discussion, we refine our understanding to using González Rey's (2004, 2014) conceptualisations. Motive and motivation according to González Rey (2014) have been considered as determinants of behaviour, which has led to motives being understood as an individual's actions, leading to reductionism 'such that motives appears to be "motive of learning", "motive of playing"..' (p. 427). This understanding does not allow for the complexity of processes involved with human actions driven by motives. Instead, González Rey (2014) argues that the inseparable moments and generative nature of subjective sense and configurations result in the 'main motive of any human action, but they are not external to the action ... subjective configuration represents the subjective nature of human action...which break down the dichotomies between the external-internal and the social and individual that are currently considered in psychology' (p. 433).

Motive and motivation are inseparable from the complex system and processes that are nestled within social subjectivity, subjective sense and configuration. We argue that the creation of shared motivations, motives, actions and emotions are integral to young children's psychological processes and social interactions as they move countries and enter into social interactions, and form relations with peers and adults new to their social spheres.

10.3 Subjectivity and Motivation—A Constructive-Interpretive Methodology

The constant generative and implicit nature of subjective configuration and subjective sense means they cannot be captured empirically 'by an act of knowledge' (González Rey et al., 2019, p. 31). The processes related to subjective sense and subjective configuration do not appear explicitly through discourse, behaviour or relational processes (González Rey, 2019). For this reason, during empirical studies, subjective configuration and subjective senses are constructed inferentially through a constructive-interpretive methodology (González Rey, 2019). Within this research methodology, the objectives of the research are addressed by theoretical models rather than inductive generalisations. Initially, the researchers are required to make conjectures based on social interactions such as behaviours, actions and discourse. The hypothetical information informs the interpretive constructions and are referred to as indicators, which 'emerge through dialogical processes throughout which different methodological devices are articulated' (González Rey, 2019, p. 32).

The methodology provides an interesting way to examine the social interactions of young children as they are making new friends, particularly their motives and motivation to be together 'configured in action' (González Rey, 2017, p. 516). To add depth to the inferences in the current study, children's, mother's and teacher's dialogues provide different perspectives that when brought together support understanding motives and motivation in relation to children's friendship.

10.3.1 Method

In the current study, video observation and targeted conversations with young children as they went about their everyday life in a new country was a major component of the study. The understanding and interpretation of children's motives and motivation at home, during their school day and in the community, was deepened by semi-structured interviews with the mothers' and teachers of the children.

The researcher and participants were co-constructors of the research project as the teachers provided access to their classrooms, staff and planning meetings. The mothers provided access to their homes from early in the morning until late in the evening and invited the researcher to meals, family excursions to markets, play grounds and sporting fixtures. The children verbally agreed to be in the study. All

Family	Passport country	Focus child's name and age	School attended
Jones	England	Isa 7.3 years	British
King	Australia	Bill 5.3 years	Australian
Schmidt	Holland	Tris 5.2 years	British
Smith	New Zealand England	Zeb 3.9	British
Williams	Australia	Ollie 7.9 years Mish 7.9 years Catt 5.6 years	American

Table 10.1 Family and focus children. This study has its focus on the Jones family

participants actively introduced topics they indicated were of interest to them while living in a new country.

10.3.2 Participants

Ethical procedures from a university ethics committee were followed. In the larger study (see Table 10.1), three principals of international schools, seven teachers and five families were involved (Adams & Fleer, 2015; Adams & Quinones, 2020). The larger study involved seven focus children, ranging in age from 3.9 years to 7.9 years, with a mean age of 5.4 years at the beginning of the study (see Table 10.1).

The data for this chapter originates from one family—the Jones. The video data analysed includes data collected from the family as they move into a new home. The focus child, Isa invites a new friend, Ellie from the neighbourhood to help her rearrange her bedroom. This is followed by a discussion with the mother and the child's teacher. The adults were interviewed to provide different perspectives and understanding of social interaction and the emerging friendship between the children.

10.3.3 Research Tools

The research tools are resources that have a dialogic character, dialogue provides contradictions and openings for subjective configuration from the actual experience (Goulart et al. 2019). The research tools included digital video recorders to complement the field notes and observation of the young children. Informal dialogue between the researcher and the children were captured by video recordings. The dialogue was initiated either by the researcher or the children if one or other required clarification of a point or an activity being entered into. Similarly, the parents and teachers were interviewed through semi-structured means, including formal and informal dialogue. Discussions about situations and resources provided opportunities for the adult participants to co-construct knowledge together and were an avenue for individual expression. The semi-structured interviews offered a socially produced space in which ideas were developed within the research context.

According to González Rey and Mitjáns Martínez's (2019) the tools used in the research support the production of indicators and hypothesis originating from participants dialogue with others and with the researcher. In the case studies presented here, we use this method of analysis to better understand the everyday lives as young children entering into social relations and friendship, with parental and teacher support.

10.3.4   Construction of Information

After ethical permission was gathered by a university ethics committee, the total data gathered consisted of 42 sessions where the researcher participated in the everyday life of the focus children. Dialogue with mothers and teachers occurred at a time and place chosen by them, for example school or home setting and during incidental conversations as time was spent with the family. The construction of information occurred over a six-month-period.

Reviewing and aligning the video data and interviews enabled analysis of the social interactions between the children. Combined with the dialogue from the mother and teacher enabled documentation and construction of the social productions during the process of learning contributing to the children's development. The indicators originated from constructive interpretations of the participants dialogue, outward displays of emotions and actions captured in the video and the dialogues. The subjective senses and configurations of the children were generated by their past and moment-to-moment social interactions, dialogue and the contexts they were situated within.

The interlinking of the children, parents and teacher's individual and subjective productions provided two key social productions. These are central for understanding subjectivity, motives and motivation as the children enter a new social space, and ways they were supported by adults as they engaged in social interactions. The generative and regulative organisations of subjective configurations and subjective senses are constantly unfolding and characterise social and individual motives and motivation:

1. Dialogue and actions are the source of subjective productions that are constantly unfolding and characterise social and individual motives and motivation as children move through the process of learning and development while becoming friends.
2. Social productions of adults influence the conditions created for children's subjectivities, motives and motivation as they create conditions for children to become friends.

10.4   Case Study: Dialogue and Actions as the Source of Social Subjectivities

In this section, we introduce a case study of the Jones family, the focus child is Isa, and the visiting friend is Ellie. The Jones family had been residing in Kuala Lumpur, Malaysia for nine months at the time of the research visit. The family had waited for the house to become vacant and moved into the neighbourhood six-month prior to the research beginning. Isa did not have any friends the same age, who lived in the housing complex.

The family had recently noted that a new family had moved in next door and Ellie requested Isa to be invited for a playdate. The visit involved reconfiguring Isa's bedroom furniture. Isa had requested repeatedly to her mother that they change her bedroom furniture, to make space for a sofa to be placed against the wall. The moving of Isa's bedroom furniture coincided with the first playdate visit by her neighbour, seven-year-old Ellie.

10.5   Observation One—Reconfiguring the Bedroom

The mother, Isa and neighbour Ellie were in the bedroom. The mother took charge of the situation and firmly requested that the children move all of the toys from the bed and floor to the bathroom, so they were out of the way. Ellie was quick to respond and moved a handful of soft toys efficiently to the bathroom. Isa saw a ball, she held it high and let it drop, stating, '*TIMBER!*' As it fell Mother stated, '*Ok that's being silly, darling you're not exactly helping! Ellie and I are doing all the work*'. Isa watched her mother and Ellie pick up more toys.

The three participants discussed the best way to move the bed into the alcove in the room. They discussed whether the sofa that Isa wanted in her room would fit. The mother and Ellie began to push the bed, Isa saw a mattress that was under the bed and when it was uncovered, she began to jump. The mother stated, '*Isa, dear, I don't see you helping—if Ellie wasn't here we would be in trouble!*' Isa continued bouncing on the mattress. Ellie and the mother pushed the bed into the alcove. Isa jumped, shouting '*IT FITS! HORAAY! [the bed] IT FITS! New friends come on over!*' Ellie replies, '*it looks really nice in that space*', and reported that the bed was now in the same position as in her bedroom next door.

Isa continued jumping on the mattress and picked up a toy, '*Isa! What are you doing? If it were not for Ellie this would never be done. Put that down and help, darling!*' Isa placed the toy on the floor and saw another toy, which she picked up and started playing with. Ellie moved all of the toys to the bathroom while Isa played. They all agreed that moving the bed had made the room look bigger. Isa lifted her arms out wide and spun around on the wooden floor in the clear space, and stated, '*Yeah, it is massive! [the bedroom space] I love it!*'.

Isa's, long-term motivation was to change the way her room was configured as she wanted more space to fit in a sofa so her '*new friends from school could all come and play*' (conversation with Isa).

10.5.1 Social Subjectivity: Unfolding Motives and Motivation

From the momentary observation, we interpret the dialogue and the actions as a source of social subjectivity. The observation involved Isa changing her room with her neighbour Ellie and her mother. The motivation in this situation should not be seen as only an intrinsic psychical function but also configured in action (González Rey, 2017). Isa's subjective senses and configuration involved actions directed towards changing her room conceptually, rather than participating, or socially interacting with Isa in the moment. However, her longer term motivation was social as she wanted to invite her friends from school to play.

González Rey (2016) argues 'that intellectual, motor, or any other operation become sources of subjective senses, transforming psychological functions into motives for their own functioning' (p. 15). Once the bedroom furniture was changed to the way she had requested, Isa's emotions were shown through actions and emotive words (jumping up and down and shouting that the bed fits). Isa did not seem to interact with Ellie, there was little acknowledgement of Ellie or recognition that she was in the room. In contrast, Ellie's emerging motive seemed directed towards following the mother's commands and acquiescing to her requests (quickly moved the toys to the bathroom, pushed the bed). The mother directed the conversation as she ordered the children to complete tasks and repeatedly informed Isa that she was not participating and had it not been for Ellie, the furniture would not be moved. It is inferred that the mother's motivation was to move the furniture and return the room to a neat space with the children's help. However, Ellie, not Isa met the mother's immediate demands. The mother's emotions are shown through the tone of voice, which were occasionally softened with terms of endearment (dear, darling) directed towards Isa, and positive comments for Ellie.

On the other hand, reconfiguring Isa's bedroom opens the potential to develop a new social sphere between Isa and Ellie, and potentially other '*new friends from school*'. Even so, in this moment Isa's motivation involved subjective configurations and senses that included emotional enjoyment of playing with toys and then being in her new bedroom space. From Ellie's perspective, she shared her motivation by helping out a new friend and complying with the mother's directions. Social and individual motives are configured as a social production rather than determinants of behaviour (González Rey, 2014), as Isa, her mother and Ellie engage in actions, emotions and dialogue together.

10.5.2   Observation Two—The Reading Corner

The discussion returned to whether or not the sofa would fit against the wall where the bed had previously been positioned. The sofa and cushions were retrieved from downstairs and placed against the wall. There was a gap between the sofa and the wall, in the corner that Isa intended to make into a 'reading corner'. Isa moved to retrieve some cushions and a blanket, restating, '*this is MY private reading corner, MY reading corner*'. Isa looked at the space, then at Ellie and stated: '*Hmm, can you get out please*'. Ellie replied, '*All of us are allowed—only girls are allowed*'.

Ellie seemed to ignore the request to move out of the reading corner, instead, she suggested that Isa place her Barbie stickers on the wall in the reading corner. Ellie was excited and offered to use her own Barbie stickers that matched with Isa's already stuck to the wall. Ellie asked Isa if she wanted some teddy's and ran to fetch one from the bathroom. Ellie retrieved a panda. Isa suggests they only needed a cushion, which Ellie retrieved. Ellie suggested they needed '*a really good book*' in the book corner. Ellie returned from the bookshelf situated outside the room, Isa stated, '*Ellie, it is really good isn't it—only two people are allowed in [the book corner] at the one time and mummy sits on the stool and she reads us a book* (pointed to the stool near the corner)' and pointing to a small stool stated, '*that's called the reading corner stool!*'.

Mother returned and directed the children to move all of the toys from the bathroom back to where they were positioned prior to moving the bed. The children discussed the hidden book corner with great excitement. The mother responded, '*I can't fit in that corner*'. Isa agreed, '*You won't fit [in the corner] but you can sit on the stool and read to us and we sit in the corner*'. Isa's mother nodded her head in an affirmative gesture and stated, '*Ellie, Isa can you help me? I want to finish this today not next week!*'.

10.5.3   Social Subjectivity: Unfolding Shared Motives and Motivation

From this second momentary observation, Isa and Ellie's shared motives and motivation for creating a reading space were integral to becoming friends. Personal and subjective productions were interwoven with shared emotions and symbolic processes while the children acted and participated in the experience. The shared motives involved suggested actions, rather than demanding. The dialogue became part of the subjective space, as children expressed what they wanted, firmly. Each child, self-organised and self-generated creative ideas for the reading space in the corner, and without negotiation silently agreed that the reading corner was for two people, and would be decorated with a cushion, and panda and a special book, with enough room for the mother to sit and read. As Ellie is the invited friend to the playdate it can be inferred that through historical social understanding, it is expected she agreed with Isa' suggestions (fetching a teddy bear, a cushion, a book).

The mother created the conditions for reconfiguring the bedroom and within the new rearranged space, Isa and Ellie created a shared place for reading. Initially, the children's suggestions seemed incongruent. However, after initial suggestions, it seemed there was implicit agreement with each other, which included who was able to enter the space, and the type of decorating and activity that would be undertaken in the corner. The children's individual subjective senses and configurations seemed incongruent in the moment but were not refuted by the other, which contributed to agreement and organising a shared space. The internal/external and the individual/social interactions are unable to be separated (González Rey, 2014) as what each child brings to the situation and the way it is received and acted upon contributes to shared subjective productions. Isa and Ellie are learning about each other and social interaction through, directing, doing, agreeing, ignoring and suggesting alternatives. Through these actions, it is inferred a common bond was formed where their subjective senses and configurations, motives and motivations are brought together and contribute to creating foundations for their friendship to develop.

Entering into a new friendship and a new social space involves the interweaving of each person's subjective configurations and senses. The generative acts of self/social-organising motives and motivations contributed to a silent agreement of ways to participate in the shared space.

10.5.4   The Mother's Subjective Configurations and Motivations About Friends and Friendship

In the following transcript, Isa's mother's subjective sense and configurations in relation to friends and friendships is presented. The mother's experience with her children's friends and friendships provide a perspective of her personal subjectivity and motivation in relation to her family context such as moving countries and the challenges of finding and making new friends.

In order to understand Isa's mother motives and motivations for her children to have friends, we discuss the social space that leads to her behaviours and actions. The mother's main motives are subjectively generated through the living situation of moving countries and supporting her children to make new friends. The mother discussed the positive benefits of moving countries and ways that children are forced to '*adapt, develop, and are pushed to meet with people, and cope with new situations. So, they grow from that and then you consolidate as a family because you are together and have to make new friends together*' (Mother's interview).

The mother also discussed the challenges of moving countries and referred to her own feelings, and how she was, '*really upset that Isa had to leave her friends [in America] and make new friends [in Malaysia]*'. Yet, the mother indicated that she felt '*lucky*' her children were comfortable in new environments. She talked about Isa's *'old best friend, Zoey'* who was a neighbour in America. Zoey was the same age as Isa and attended the same school. According to the mother, Isa talked intermittently about how she missed Zoey but she did not miss living in America or her old school. Zoey and Isa's friendship continued (even though Zoey lived in America and they did not see each other). Isa had not made a best friend in Malaysia. The mother stated, *'She hasn't replaced her, in that sort of way. Zoey, is still sort of in her mind, her best friend. Even now, she talks about Zoey'.*

The mother commented on the transient nature of families involved with the current school Isa attended, and indicated the constant movement of children in and out of the classroom. She stated there had been *'so many people come and go'* in the nine months, Isa had been attending the school. In Isa's classroom, she stated, *'there had been five children leave and five new ones arrive, with a further two departing prior to the end of the school year'*. She then relayed a story about other families who had children between 12 and 13 years of age who requested they attend boarding school so they did not need to continually make new friends and deal with the constant transition of friends in and out of their lives. She compared this to the school that Isa attended in America where the community was stable and most members were *'born and died there'* without moving.

10.5.5   Coaching for School as a Social Motivation for Having Friends

The mother discussed ways she coached both of her children, in advance of situations. Her main technique was to ask open-ended questions such as, *'How do you feel?'*, *'Are you nervous?'* and *'Okay. Maybe what we can do is make sure you smile, be friendly, talk to everybody. You will be nervous. It is normal to be nervous. It would be strange if you weren't, when you're meeting all those people'*. The mother also pre-empted social situations where groups of children had known each other since the beginning of term and suggested it may be challenging for Isa to make friends and to make sure she was, *'nice and friendly'* by smiling, making eye contact helping others. The mother's rationale to coach Isa before experiencing new situations was to initiate Isa's thinking about ways the social situations might unfold, and provide Isa with information that might help her fit in socially.

Coaching is a social production self-generated by the mother in respect to helping out her children with future social interactions. The mother's motive and motivation is subjectively configured through her individual subjectivity (González Rey, 2019), that is her past experience and current situation where she creates conditions for her children to make friends. The interweaving of emotions and symbolic processes experienced with meeting new friends is shaped by the context of moving countries. The personal and subjective productions are expressed in the mother's emotions as she indicated to Isa that 'feeling nervous', 'feeling strange' 'being nice' while meeting new people or friends is not unusual. For the mother to coach her child, as she enters into a new social situation and relations, is an indicator of the generative nature of social subjectivity, where actions, motives and motivations are interwoven. The mother's past experience is subjectively configured and shared with her daughter, so that Isa understood and was provoked to think about what to expect as she entered a new situation.

10.6 Teacher's Subjective Configurations and Sense of Social Interactions

The dialogue and interview with Isa's teacher was in the classroom after school and during class time as the teacher moved from one group of children to another. The teacher discussed the transient nature of families in international schools, and stated, '*even though I have worked in many international schools, I am always shocked by the number of children who move in and out in a given year, it is something that I find really hard to understand!*'.

The teacher commented on how each child was different in the way that they entered the classroom and were equipped (or not) with social skills. In a similar finding to Adams and Quinones (2020), the teacher suggested that many children made friends with neighbours and these friendships were often sustained at a close emotional level, particularly if the children were in the same class and the parents were friends. More specifically, the teacher indicated that Isa quickly became an important member of the classroom, as she was quick to notice if others needed help and was open and friendly to others and often volunteered to do jobs that no one else wanted. According to the teacher, Isa was artistic and drew brightly coloured pictures, which created interest from the other children and initiated conversations.

The teacher helped children's social interactions by organising fluid groups across curriculum activities. The teacher's motivation originated from her past experience as she stated, '...*Initially I let the children choose who they want to sit next to, this seems to help them settle into the classroom better. Then as the time passes, some children will continue to work really well together, whereas others spend more time talking and often this will lead to being silly and disrupting the whole class. Then I step in and choose who they work with*'.

Similar to Isa's mother, the teacher's actions are directed towards children's social skills and fostering opportunities for them to develop social interactions during implementation of the curriculum. The teacher showed sensitivity towards children from families in international schools and placed importance on their social skills. The teacher acknowledged the importance of children making friends and she was attuned to the creation of social networks of neighbours and making sure children have time for social and academic work together in the classroom. The subjective configurations and sense related to understanding social interactions and children's social skills are generated though her past experience working with international families.

10.7   Conclusion

Motives and motivations, subjective configurations and senses unfold in the presence of emotions and symbolical productions of social interaction (González Rey, 2004, 2014). Becoming a friend includes subjective productions where children's congruent motives and motivations of social interactions emerge. Isa and Ellie's individual/shared motives as they subjectively configure their experiences during moments within the playdate, highlight the way playdates are potential social spaces for enacting historical knowledge and learning about current social engagement.

González Rey's, theoretical understanding of subjectivity enabled numerous indicators to be inferred, originating from the children's, mother's and teacher's understanding of social interaction. Similar to Fleer and González Rey (2017) there was a congruent language that emerged in the general discourse expressed as the social subjectivity between the family and school. However different from the 'intellectual deficit and pathologisation associated with instrumental-cognitive representation of learning', (p. 157) the language of the teacher and mother was strength based and placed emphasis on creating conditions for social interaction at both home and school.

Both adults referenced the importance of the children interacting socially when new to a class prior to advances in academic learning were expected '*if they have the social the learning happens really quickly*'. Both indicated that the child's own motivation towards social interactions was to be encouraged, and suggested that creating the conditions for children's autonomy when making friends was important. Indicators from both adults suggested that the child needs support from the adults for new pathways to make friends. These required systematic supports such as organisation of playdates with neighbours and creating social spaces where children can engage during school work and playtime. The interweaving of individual/social subjective sense and configurations directs attention to shared motives and motivations within social interaction. The mother's individual subjectivity was apparent as she suggested that parents need to be open and encourage their child to invite unknown children for play dates, and coach their children in ways to initiate play leading to friendship. The personal subjectivity of the teacher suggests awareness of curricular activities where interactions are fostered.

To study motivation and subjectivity in the context of friendships, subjective configurations and senses from all those involved in the life of children, enriches ways we socially produce conditions that meet aspirations of making friends. Isa's mother drew on her personal subjectivities that included her emotional and symbolical productions as she shared her thoughts that for young children to make a friend includes—being nice, feeling strange, feeling nervous, smiling and talking to everybody. Through observations of Isa and Ellie although some suggestions were ignored or incongruent, moving beyond these to suggest and help, contributes to social engagement. Subjective configurations, senses and productions are generated through motivations and motives that are shared in past, present and future social relations and new pathways for friendship development.

Acknowledgements We would like to thank the families that participate in this study.

References

Adams, M. (2014). Emotions of expatriate children and families transitioning into Malaysia: A cultural-historical perspective. *Asia Pacific Journal of Research in Early Childhood Education, 8*(2), 129–151

Adams, M., & Fleer, M. (2015). Moving countries: Belongings as central for realizing the affective relation between international shifts and localized micro movements. *Learning Culture and Social Interaction, 6*, 56–66.

Adams, M., & Fleer, M. (2016). The relations between a 'push-down and push up curriculum: A cultural-historical study of home-play pedagogy in the context of structured learning in international schools in Malaysia. *Contemporary Issues in Early Childhood, 17*(3), 328–342.

Adams, M., & Fleer, M. (2017). International transitions: Generating subjective sense and subjective configuration in relation to the development of identity. *Mind, Culture, and Activity, 24*(4), 353–367. https://doi.org/10.1080/10749039.2017.1346686.

Adams, M., & Fleer, M. (2019). The role of subjectivity for understanding collaborative dialogue and cultural productions of teachers in international schools. In F. González Rey, A. A. Mitjáns Martínez, & D. M. Goulart (Eds.), *Subjectivity within cultural-historical approach theory, methodology and research* (pp. 165–180). Springer: Singapore.

Adams, M., & Quinones, G. (2020). *Collaborative pathways to friendship in early childhood: A cultural-historical perspective.* Abingdon: Routledge.

Fleer, M. (2019). The role of subjectivity in understanding teacher development in a scientifc playworld: The emotional and symbolic nature of being a teacher of science. In F. González, A. Rey, M. Martinez, & D. Goulart (Eds.), *Theory of subjectivity: New perspectives within social and educational research* (pp. 149–164). Springer: Singapore.

Fleer, M., & González Rey, F. (2017). Beyond pathologizing education: Advancing a Cultural—Historical methodology for the re-positioning of children as successful learners. In M. Fleer, F. González Rey, & N. Veresov (Eds.), *Perezhivanie, emotions and subjectivit,* (pp. 145–172). Springer: Singapore.

González Rey, F. (2004). Subjectivity in communication: Development of personality. In A. U. Branco & J. Valsiner (Eds.), *Communication and metacommnication in human development* (pp. 249–270). Greenwich, CT: Information Age.

González Rey, F. (2008). Subject, subjectivity and development in cultural-historical psychology. In B. Van Oers, W. Wardekker, E. Elbers, & R. Van Der Veer (Eds.), *The transformation of learning: Advances in cultural-historical activity theory* (pp. 137–154). Cambridge, UK: Cambridge University Press.

González Rey, F. (2009). Historical relevance of Vygotsky's work: Its significance for a new approach to the problem of subjectivity in psychology. *Outlines: Critical Practice Studies, 11*, 59–73.

González Rey, F. (2011). A re-examination of defining moments in Vygotsky's work and their implication for his continuing legacy. *Mind, Culture, and Activity, 18*(3). https://doi.org/10.1080/10749030903338517.

González Rey, F. (2012). Advancing on the concept of sense. In M. Hedegaard, A. Edwards, & M. Fleer (Eds.), *Motives in children's development: Cultural-historical approaches* (pp. 45–62). Cambridge, UK: Cambridge University Press.

González Rey, F. (2014). Human motivation in question: Discussing emotions, motives and subjectivity from a cultural-historical standpoint. *Journal for the Theory of Social Behaviour, 45*(4). https://doi.org/10.1111/jtsb.12073.

González Rey, F. (2016). Vygotsky's concept of Perezhivanie in the psychology of art and at the final moment of his work: Advancing his legacy. *Mind, Culture, and Activity, 23*(4), 305–314

González Rey, F. (2017). The topic of subjectivity in psychology: Contradictions, paths and new alternatives. *Journal Theory Social Behaviour, 47*, 502–521. https://doi.org/10.1111/jtsb.12144

González Rey, F. (2018). Subjectivity and discourse: Complementary topics for a critical psychology. *Culture and Psychology.* https://doi.org/10.1177/1354067X18754338.

González Rey, F. (2019). Subjectivity as a new theoretical, epistemological and methodological pathway within Cultural-Historical psychology. In F. González Rey., A Mitjáns Martínez, & D. Goulart (Eds.), *Subjectivity within cultural-historical approach: Theory, methodology and Research* (pp. 21–36). Springer: Singapore.

González Rey, & Mitjáns Martínez. (2019). The constructive-interpretive methodological approach: Orienting research and practice on the basis of subjectivity In F. González Rey, A. Mitjáns Martínez, & D. Goulart (Eds.), *Subjectivity within cultural-historical approach: Theory, methodology and Research* (pp. 37–60). Springer: Singapore.

González Rey, F., Mitjáns Martinez, A., & Goulart. D. (Eds). (2019). Subjectivity as a new theoretical, epistemological, and methodological pathway within Cultural-Historical psychology. In F. González Rey, A. Mitjáns Martinez, & D. Goulart (Eds.), *Theory of subjectivity: New perspectives within social and educational research* (pp. 21–36). Springer: Singapore.

Goulart, D., Rey, G., & Patiño, J. F. (2019). El Estudio de la Subjetividad de Profesionales de la Salud Mental: Una Experencia en Brasilia [The study of the subjectivity of mental health professionals: An experience in Brasilia]. *Athenea Digital, 19*(3), e2548. https://doi.org/10.5565/rev/athenea.2548

Mori, V., & Goulart, D. (2019). Subject and subjectivitiy in psychotherapy: A case study. In F. González Rey, A. Mitjáns Martinez, & D. Goulart (Eds.), *Theory of subjectivity: New perspectives within social and educational research* (pp. 231–244). Springer: Singapore.

Quinones, G. (2016). 'Visual Vivencias' to understand subjectivity and affective connection in young children. *Video Journal of Education and Pedagogy, 1*(3), https://doi.org/10.1186/s40990-016-0004-1.

Vygotsky, L. S. (1994). The problem of the environment. In R. van der Veer & J. Valsiner (Eds.), *The Vygotsky reader* (pp. 338–354). Oxford: Blackwell.

Megan Adams is a Senior Lecturer of Inclusion at Monash University, Melbourne, Australia. She obtained her Ph.D. qualifications in Education at Monash University. Her main research interests are focused on education from a cultural-historical approach using subjectivity to investigate (1) families with young children moving countries (2) identity, curriculum and pedagogy (3) preservice teacher's perceptions about working with students displaying challenging behaviours in classrooms.

Gloria Quinones is a Senior Lecturer in the Faculty of Education, Monash University. Her research interests include early childhood education, affective infant-toddler pedagogies, play pedagogies, peer play, emotions, and visual methodologies.

Chapter 11
Dialogue as a Subjective Process: Impacts on Learning and Development in Schools

Cristina M. Madeira-Coelho

Abstract At the end of the twentieth century, theoretical and methodological issues produced impasses to understand the complexity of human phenomena. Conceptions regarding linguistic-discursive aspects, became center stage, eliminating the role of individuals in their teaching and learning experiences in the context of classrooms, excluding the productive aspect of such processes. These dynamic phenomena were represented with a focus on the instrumental objectivity of "content delivery," without considering individuals' production of those same contents. Criticizing these approaches, this chapter addresses González Rey's Theory of Subjectivity's heuristic contributions, in which the subject's active and complex role in his/her learning and development is re-assumed, both understood as subjective processes constituted through a continuous symbolic-emotional production. In this way, they enable the comprehension of complexities regarding curiosity, interest, and imagination of those involved; communication and dialogue organization in these processes; and the transformations that take place in subjective developments throughout these movements. The concept of dialogue is the conductive thread of the textual organization and educational practices of a field study, which emphasizes the heuristic value of the Theory of Subjectivity for the understanding of these human processes.

11.1 Introduction

This chapter addresses González Rey's contributions to the complex processes of learning and development in education through his Theory of Subjectivity in a Cultural-Historical Perspective (González Rey, 2002, 2011a, 2011b, 2012, 2019). This theoretical approach proposes to reassume the subject's active role in both learning and development processes which are understood as subjective productions. In this perspective, experiences that take place in school settings cease to be just an

C. M. Madeira-Coelho (✉)
Faculty of Education, Universidade de Brasília (UnB), Brasília, Brazil
e-mail: cristina.madeira.coelho@gmail.com

© The Author(s), under exclusive license to Springer Nature Singapore Pte Ltd. 2021   173
D. M. Goulart et al. (eds.), *Theory of Subjectivity from a Cultural-Historical Standpoint*,
Perspectives in Cultural-Historical Research 9,
https://doi.org/10.1007/978-981-16-1417-0_11

intellectual-discursive process to be configured as a continuous process of symbolic-emotional production, i.e., a subjective production. Hence, a strict linguistic approach to the concept of dialogue is considered to narrow this understanding, because it tends to eliminate the role of individuals in their experiences of teaching and/or learning, and mainly exclude the productive character that these persons present in their learning and development processes.

Although the Theory of Subjectivity approach is characterized by the configurative integration of concepts, among them subjective sense, subjective configurations and social subjectivity, subject and agent,[1] the text focuses on the heuristic value of an innovative conception of dialogue, assuming it favors new understandings regarding learning and development processes.

Thus, in addition to the relevance of dialogue as one of the epistemological principles that underlie Qualitative Epistemology, this original dialogical dimension favors the emergence of theoretical productions related to the subjective development of teachers and students in learning contexts in school settings.

The first part of the text seeks to characterize actions and interrelations that organize teaching–learning contexts, emphasizing their complexity and the relational nature that favors learning and development. This complexity confirms the unity of the social and the individual in subjective productions. Then, a brief critical exposition on different theoretical approaches that, at the end of the twentieth century, organized the understanding of human processes based on the centrality of a semiotic and dialogical matrix follows. As a response to the impasses that arise from the presented perspectives, the epistemological and theoretical dimensions that the concept of dialogue assumes in the perspective of the Theory of Subjectivity are underlined, in which its' understanding is expanded, beyond the limits circumscribed to the use of language or into the symbolic competence.

Finally, we address an example of research on educational practices that emphasize the value of the dialogical human encounter at the coexistence in educational daily life. This qualitative human relationship highlights topics about dialogic teaching that favor subjective learning and development (Mitjáns Martínez & González Rey, 2017).

---

[1]The concepts will be addressed and defined throughout the text. At this point we are interested in defining agent and subject. "The agent would be the individual ...- or social group- located in the turn of events in the current field of their experiences; a person who makes everyday decisions, thinks, likes, or dislikes what happens to him, which ... gives him participation in this course of events. In turn, the concept of subject represents that one which opens a path of subjectivity, which transcends the normative social space within which his experiences take place, exercising creative options in the course of such experiences, which may or may not be expressed through action" (González Rey & Mitjáns Martínez, 2017, p. 73).

11.2   A Child Who Learns and a Teacher Who Teaches: A Dialogical Relational Process

Educational contexts bring together groups of people around a procedural and institutionalized task. By involving themselves with knowledge, teachers, and students, in theory, can become protagonists of processes that constitute possibilities for both. In principle, individual's relational experiences, in this context, would organize learning and promote development. The manner in which teachers organize educational contexts, perceive themselves in their action, interpret situations and established relations, evaluate the impact of their actions, in short, how they understand their professional exercise are processes that works in two directions: it is both oriented in relation to the Other, as well as transformative of those who undertake them. Thus, pedagogical practices simultaneously make possible both "outward" changes and "inward" transformative changes. This bidirectionality constitutes the unity of simultaneously social-individual aspects that in turn signal the theoretical challenge for understanding the unity that is established between teaching and learning. The theoretical approach of cultural-historical subjectivity allows us to understand that socially constituted teaching processes are constantly renewed as subjective learning. There is, therefore, a dialectical relationship that is potentially organized in the teacher–student relationship: on the one hand, the reflexive possibility that action brings to its agents, on the other, the possible transmission and effects in which this action can be configured by the relationship partners.

In line with this configuration of the teaching process, learning, considered here as the learner's singular action, is not reduced to intellectual-cognitive functions, but is expanded, in the relationships established, into a symbolic-emotional system constituted throughout each learner's subjective experiences.

When subjectively involved with the production of knowledge, the learner manifests a quality of development that is not simply transferred from the external environment but is the result of this generative character highlighted in the subjective configuration of learning. As González Rey and Mitjáns Martínez clarify:

> Subjective configurations are a moment of self-organization that emerges in the chaotic flow of subjective senses, and that define the course of a life's experience, specifying dominant subjective states of the studied question. These configurations are not the sum of subjective senses, but appear as a subjective formation that generates senses that have a certain convergence among themselves and that present one of the essential elements of the person's hegemonic affective states in the course of an experience. (2017, p. 52)

The teacher–student relationship is, therefore, the basic matter which constitutes both teaching and learning. As a result, it is presumed that these relationships can only be understood and explained if we consider the subjective configurations of individuals and social groups that experience their relations in this social context of development, which is the school. Teaching and learning, therefore, muster evidence of the value that the social-individual unit assumes for understanding such processes.

However, as a socially configured context, the pedagogical encounter takes on, simultaneously, institutional, social, and individual aspects in which affective-emotional relationships and social encounters, different discursive practices, as well as specific forms of language, are involved. Although guided by institutional regularities and maintained by the uses of language, these practices can be organized through unique ways of thinking, feeling, imagining, acting, and expressing themselves from people who can either repeat patterns and prejudices indefinitely or make new subjective configurations emerge, at each different moment provoking unusual situations, imaginative solutions and creative developments.

A reductionist understanding of learning and development processes creates the illusion that patterns of normality stem from the autonomy of a brain that develops itself. This perspective strengthens dichotomizations between normal and pathological, since the same scale homogenizes times and quantities and simultaneously disregards qualitative singularities of people and their relationships, which become ruled by homogeneous and normative standards. The need for a strong review of theoretical models, from which policies, actions, and educational relations unfold within the scope of school education, therefore, becomes evident. The complexity of the matter does not allow for reductionism and requires articulated approaches that 1-enable new intelligibilities regarding human processes experienced in social relations; 2-enable transformations that favor healthy processes, not arising from dichotomous limitations; 3-recognize the subjective functioning integrated to processes of learning and development in the encounters, actions, and relations that bring together the particular individual and the social community in which he is inserted.

11.3 Dialogue and Pedagogical Relationships

In the development of studies in the social and human sciences, the educational context has been recognized for its dialogical characteristic that constitutes itself as a potentiality for developing strategies and promoting learning. This characteristic prevailed throughout the final decades of the twentieth century, aimed at linguistic studies that began to focus on the everyday uses of language, including in school contexts (Madeira-Coelho, 2004). Structural studies of Conversational Analysis (Sacks et al., 1974) were pioneers that addressed the daily rituals of linguistic uses such as the exchange of turns in conversation or the taking the floor from which structural rules are derived which, in the school context, would serve as normative models for the (in)adequacy of educational dialogue. Even before these authors, although restricted to the scope of the former Soviet Union, the definition of dialogue defended by Mikhail Bakhtin (1895–1975) was developed. For the author, in a strict sense, dialogue was the most important form of verbal interaction, but also, in a broad sense, it was considered as all verbal communication, and not only out loud and face-to-face speaking (Bakhtin, 2012). Thus, the Russian philosopher expands the significance possibilities regarding dialogical movement, since, in addition to the idea of isolated transmitters and receivers in dialogue, there is a basic tendency of the active reception of the Other, that is, the incorporation of such other in dialogue, in a way that this other, then, constitutes himself as subject-issuer.

The presence of the words of the Other in the self's voice is one of the first elements that characterize the Bakhtinian concept of dialogism, which, thus, relativizes individual authorship and opens space for a collective subject, as mere recreator of practices present in the discursive context. By relativizing individual authorship, dialogism defends the collective character of dialogical production. In a self-marked by multiple voices derived from the dialogical dimension, in which "responsive interactions between two or more social beings are multivoiced, that is, language and consciousness are dialogic in nature, so, only semiotic process constitute personality" (Madeira-Coelho, 2008, p. 253). In this perspective, possibilities for understanding the productive character of people who relate to each other through the procedural dynamics of school context are erased. Interactional Sociolinguistics is yet another tradition in language studies with a strong impact on the study of classroom dynamics. In the words of its author,

> ... we seek to develop interpretative sociolinguistic approaches to human interaction which account for the role that communicative phenomena play in the exercise of power and control and in the production and reproduction of social identity. Our basic premise is that social processes are symbolic processes but that symbols have meaning only in relation to the forces which control the utilization and allocation of environmental resources. (Gumperz, 1982, p. 1)

In this line of research, the intentions go beyond simple descriptive analysis. The main concern is to interpret aspects of human interaction evidenced in the contextually situated conversation, seeking to associate social, sociocognitive, and linguistic characteristics with the communicative strategies updated by the participants involved in the interaction (Madeira-Coelho, 1988). The interaction, as characterized by Interactional Sociolinguistics, maintains the dichotomy between individual and social, sometimes marking social, sociocognitive values to communicative strategies, sometimes reifying efficient strategies, without, however, indicating the processes that underlie them.

In addition to these perspectives, the different Discourse Analysis approaches assemble language analysis methods derived both from traditional Linguistics and from language studies with social and political reflections approach (Fairclough, 2001). The different tendencies of Discourse Analysis have discursivization as their specific object of study, that is, the explanation of how and why the text/subject says what it/he says, "to explain the system of rules that govern the constitution of meaning, as well as the order of needs to which the text responds" (Fiorin, 1990, pp. 173–174). They seek to study the relation between the production of discourses and their constitution processes. However, they impose upon the people in the dialogical relationship, and subordinate them, to discursive formations.

In Psychology, from the 1980s onwards, there is the development of Social Constructionism in the study of cognitive, affective, and behavioral processes of individuals in processes of social interaction, and not of groups, since these would be the object of sociology. Language, religion, customs, myths, as "collective mental phenomena" would emerge from social interactions between individuals. Considered from Kenneth Gergen's, one of its main authors viewpoint, Social Constructionism incorporates Wittgenstein's (1898–1951) relativistic philosophical and linguistic tendencies favoring "language processes in dialogue and in socially produced and shared discursive practices" (González Rey, 2019, p. 27). Here dialogue is understood as a sequence of speech acts and evaluated based on its adequacy in relation to the previous speech shift as a linguistic act (Gergen, 1992). In this standpoint, the person who speaks is always a respondent, being passive and unable to generate new contributions to the process. Since defined by the other's linguistic turn, he brings nothing new to the dialogic process. When reifying explicit or implicit aspects conveyed in/by the uses of language, the studies mentioned above leave out the human encounter that occurs in the dialogical relationship. Therefore, they fail to capture emotionality, affections, setbacks, desires, motivations and/or imagination as part of the human quality that occurs in these relational contexts, that are not linguistic in nature.

From the perspective of the aforementioned studies, agents of experience and people in dialogue are suppressed, and subjective processes denied. It is not a matter of contradicting the importance of the symbolic-dialogical contexts that characterize individuals and human groups, but these people "cannot be considered neither as copies nor as epiphenomena of these contexts" (González Rey & Mitjáns Martínez, 2017, p. 66). Dialogue implies the emotions of those involved, as well as possible moments of contradiction and tension that are of great value for the development of dialogue itself and of the subjects involved in it. It is this tense and contradictory character that promotes reflexivity that goes beyond moments of face-to-face dialogue and that becomes a powerful tool for change and growth (González Rey, 2019, p. 30). Reducing the human to its semiotic component disregards the emotional aspects that constitute this humanity and that need to be considered if there is the intention of generating intelligibilities regarding the processes that are constituted in human relational contexts.

Although an essential aspect, dialogue's semiotic dimension does not determine such processes, since symbolic systems (language included) and emotionality are present in human relational processes and are simultaneously constituted as the production of subjective senses of the people present in such interrelation. Subjective senses, as the basis for the ontological definition of subjectivity, "are symbolic-emotional units in which the symbolic becomes emotional since its very genesis, just as emotions become symbolic, in a process that defines a new quality of this integration" (González Rey & Mitjáns Martínez, 2017, p. 63). In the Theory of Subjectivity approach, the understanding of dialogue is not reduced to verbal or non-verbal linguistic exchanges, as it seeks intelligibilities regarding the symbolic-emotional involvement that emerges in typically human relational contexts, such as those in which learning and development processes occur.

The definition of subjectivity with which we started has advanced with the definition of Qualitative Epistemology and represents a new ontological definition of human processes and phenomena that make man's cultural existence possible, and which are also responsible for the increasingly accelerated changes in culture itself (González Rey, 2019, p. 33). So, this ontological dimension refers to realities' dependent on human knowledge and subjectivity as an ontological definition differs from language, discourse and so many other categories that try to exhaust the ontology of specifically human processes (González Rey, 2019). Subjectivity is a symbolic-emotional system qualitatively differentiated from human beings in social conditions culturally and historically situated in which we live (González Rey & Mitjáns Martínez, 2017, p. 62). Subjectivity in a Cultural-Historical Perspective' studies associate three dimensions in a complex thinking matrix: one theoretical as the Theory of Subjectivity, one epistemological as the Qualitative Epistemology and one methodological as the Constructive-Interpretative Method.

The emergence of Qualitative Epistemology, configured for the production of knowledge regarding subjective phenomena, articulates a network of theoretical concepts from the Theory of Subjectivity that "do not refer to the notions of linear assimilation of the reality in which they are produced" (Oliveira & Madeira-Coelho, 2020, no page). In the author's historical arguments,

> The new theoretical definition required new methodological resources that led me to a different understanding of knowledge and its production processes: from this stems the relationship between theory and epistemology, defined since the beginning of this line of research on subjectivity. (González Rey & Mitjáns Martínez, 2017, p. 28)

In turn, Qualitative Epistemology is organized based on three principles that combine aspects developed explicitly in the constructive-interpretive methodological proposal. These epistemological principles are: (a) the constructive-interpretative character of knowledge production; (b) the legitimation of the singular as differentiated information that "even though based on a specific case, takes on meaning in a theoretical model that transcends it" (González Rey & Mitjáns Martínez, 2017, p. 29); and (c) the relevance of dialogue in the research process, which highlights the value of communicative-dialogical aspects to the emergence of subjective processes. Here, "every dialogue is a constructive process for those who participate in it, and dialogue implies contradictions, ruptures, opening paths, where new relationship processes appear associated with new subjective productions by the individuals in dialogue" (González Rey & Mitjáns Martínez, 2017, p. 29). Thus, in relation to the concept of dialogue, the theoretical-epistemological-methodological articulation is evident, in a configurational logic that considers the subjective complexity of people in dialogue. The configurational logic excludes determinism and paves the way to explanatory processes at the individual level, something that had disappeared with the discursive symbolic dimension in which individual agents appear only as moments of discursive games of a social nature (González Rey & Mitjáns Martínez, 2017, p. 42). For González Rey (2019), only as agents or subjects of the dialogical process, individuals or groups are able to overcome descriptive positions associated with everyday normative language, engaging in subjectively configured reflections without which dialogue itself will not happen, for every dialogue is a constructive process for those who participate in it.

The pedagogical relationship, therefore, cannot be reduced to the linguistic exchanges that people produce in the educational context. Reifying language uses as the only constructive and constitutive domain of people in a pedagogical relationship, becomes a reductionism in the face of the recognition of the complexity that integrates heterogeneous and conflicting realms that, even though result from macro-social processes, are uniquely subjectively experienced by each of the people in relation.

Thus, for school contexts, it remains a challenge to point out a more appropriate place for the complex relationship of people who operate with and through language in the construction of meanings and senses. A look at the speaker's relationship with the language he uses, which admits both ideological-unconscious dependence as well as the production of creative and singular subjective processes, and/or even, the ethical-cooperative integrality with the other. These are all uses established in the human dynamic of dialogical relations, and, therefore, traversed by subjectively configured senses. In this process, the singularities of the dialogue established between interlocutors of the relational dynamics in the school are essential. Dialogicity is thus understood as,

> A process that always involves individuals as active agents in dialogue, which characterizes them as subjective production and not as an ontological definition that reduces human processes to dialogical realities, omitting the presence of subjectivity as differentiated production by the subjects or dialogue agent's. (Mitjáns Martínez & González Rey, 2017, p. 87)

11.4 Evidence from a Field of Study

In this topic, I present extracts[2] from the interpretative construction of Vaz's master's dissertation (2017), supervised by me. However, something different from the original work's objective is sought, for here, in addition to highlighting the value of the human relationship in that school educational context I mean to put in evidence the relevance of a new conceptualization of dialogue, that results from the theoretical development of González Rey's Theory of Subjectivity. I believe that this new point of view about dialogue as a subjective production allows us to understand the singularity of the relationship teacher-group of children's, and also between the children themselves'. In this way, it seeks to transcend interpretations that consider the constitution of the human as a mere dialogical-discursive dimension, highlighting the heuristic value of this conception of dialogue for understanding the learning and development processes that characterize this school context.

Coordinated as ramifications from this information-construction fragment are the dynamics of pedagogical strategies with favorable impact on learning as a subjective process, as well as principles that may guide the processes of teacher professional formation, understood as subjective development.

This construction of information's excerpt addresses a pedagogical activity, characteristic of the educational routine of the social space of a group of six-year olds,

---

[2]The four examples in this chapter correspond to transcriptions of Vaz's (2017) text, and appear in her dissertation in the respective following pages: FRAME 1, pag. 75; FRAME 2, pag. 96; FRAME 3, pag. 96; FRAME 4: pag. 97.

in which multiple and unexpected communication processes emerge both spontaneously and planned by the teacher, placing the dialogue partners in a rich process in novel and unforeseen options that have the potential to become relevant in the dialogue partners' unique productions.

Frame 1: Presenting the Activity

One of the activities that guided the pedagogical work with the class was the project "People have a name and a surname". The aim of the project was to work on the students' identity based on their names and their life stories.

In addition to that, based on each student's name, contents related to the learning of reading and writing were worked upon, such as understanding how the alphabetical writing system functions. Each week the focus was on one or two students and several activities were developed from their names.

At first, the class needed to find out who the "names of the day" were and teacher Alice used several strategies of games and playing for that moment, such as: hangman game, objects that reminded that child, magic box with objects that started with the same letter as the child's name, hidden students' photos, etc. This moment generated a lot of curiosity in the students and the expectative anticipation of being the next ones drawn.

After the discovery, the chosen students were interviewed by their colleagues. There was no pre-defined interview script, and the children could ask any question in order to get to know that student better.

Then, various written activities were carried out with the names of the students of the day, in addition to the collective production of a poster representing a portrait of those children, of which all students participated. At the end, the posters were displayed on the classroom walls.

The manner in which the interview was organized ensured that students became the protagonists of that activity, in which not only the child interviewed had a voice, but all other students as far as they could ask any questions or comments.

In the proposition of the pedagogical activity, the continual dialogical proposal in the teacher's work stands out. Dialogue being understood as a resource that the teacher develops based on otherness ethics, in her pedagogical action. The dialogue that takes place in this pedagogical activity cannot be considered merely as a linguistic exchange. The subjective productions favored by living said activity, characteristic of the classroom's pedagogical routine, are not mere reflexes or epiphenomena of discursive-dialogical realities that convey social symbolic constructions. Here the context of the dialogical relationship enables the partners to assume themselves as active and creative agents of subjective productions. Even the homogenizing institutional standard of the school is relativized by aspects of sharing and respect for everyone's singularities in the classroom's social space. Everyone feels entitled to participate as and when they wish, which favors subjective learning and development. The place occupied by each person in the dialogue involves the elimination of restrictions in communication, which can contribute to differentiated and unique productions of the people involved in the dialogical relation.

Hereinafter is the dialogue of João Carlos' interview, which constitutes one of the indicators of the children's protagonism, which was made possible by the teacher's pedagogical choices, which, in turn, were governed by her own principles that involved her formative processes, her conceptions and subjective productions.

Frame 2: Why Don't You Ever Invite Me?
At this point, the student to be interviewed sits in a low chair in front of the class, while the other classmates are positioned around him, sitting on the floor in a semicircle, which they call "wheel".

Fernando:	Have you ever skateboarded?
João Carlos:	I have!
José:	What do you like to do most?
João Carlos:	To play soccer.
Guilherme:	and why don't you ever invite me or invite everyone else to play football?
Teacher smiles and says:	um, I loved that question. You can speak João Carlos.
João Carlos (thinks a little):	because then there would be too many people there.
Melissa:	But soccer is with a lot of people!
	João Carlos looks away as if he wants to change the subject.
Caio:	What do you like to eat?
João Carlos (thinks a little):	sprinkles and *brigadeiro*.
Guilherme:	And why don't you ever invite me and Gustavo and everyone else when you bring your ball?
Teacher (chuckling):	you can say whatever you want João Carlos, there's no need to be ashamed.
João Carlos:	It's because … sometimes … there are people who play soccer and don't know how to play… and then they kick the ball with the tip of their tennis shoes.
Teacher:	Ahhh ok. But now you can explain to them that they can't kick the ball with the tip of their tennis shoes and you can invite them to play, right?
	João Carlos nods his head, accepting the suggestion for the moment.
Karlos:	Have you ever watched Civil War?
João Carlos:	No, but I already know that Captain America wins.
Karlos:	I've already watched it.
Rita:	Have you ever played with dolls?
João Carlos:	No!
Teacher:	Have you ever played with Maria Flor (his sister)?
João Carlos:	No, when it's like that I get Ken.
Teacher:	I understand, so you use the boy doll, right.
Caio:	and why do men play ball and women are cheerleaders?
	The bell rings for recess and everyone leaves in a rampage.

The teacher behaved as an active participant in the dialogical relation, taking advantage of cues to make interventions, many of them encouraging, others provocative, or even challenging.

Frame 3: Potentiality Derived from the Dialogical Relationship
During the interview, as well as in other moments of collective activities, the teacher would organize speaking turns to ensure the participation of all students and respect for the one who

was speaking. Still, it was the children's own questions that guided the activity. There was no right or wrong question, appropriate or inappropriate question, everything they wanted to know about their colleague could be asked. In this, and in other interviews observed, it was noticed that diverse subjects and distinct dialogue opportunities between the students arose. Sometimes, the teacher would complement a child's question or add others, as was the case in another situation in which she asked the student interviewed: "what is your biggest fear?" and "what is your dream?" Thus, in addition to creating space for students to ask from their perspectives, the teacher also integrated her interest in getting to know that child better.

Both the value that the teacher places on the creation of communicative channels in the classroom's daily activities, as well as her belief in the alternation of collective and individual strategies that organized her pedagogical action, enable the recognition of her orientation toward the construction of opportunities for everyone's expression in the context of this classroom. The way the pedagogical work was planned and carried out made it possible to create relational spaces so as to create several opportunities to get to know her students, become closer to them and allow them to express themselves. The activity assumed a dialogical character because the teacher maintained an active presence in relation to everyone and to the situation itself, sharing opinions, reflections and feelings and encouraging children to act similarly. Dynamics like this, which were part of the educational daily life of this classroom, are linked to the conception that learning is a subjective process, which does not depend only on cognitive functions, but works as a complex system, in which people continuously produce subjective senses articulated, both to others in their life history and to the history of experienced relationships. Thus, each person subjectively configures aspects of their life history coordinated to the production of subjective senses pertaining current experiences.

The value of the different strategies created is not, however, in their instrumental character, but in the way the activity was experienced by the class. Dialogue as the basis of the activities developed and the dynamics of respect, appreciation, and mutual commitments that was established in the social space favored student's expression. In that class, very unique subjective senses were configured and which started to integrate the social subjectivity[3] of that classroom, in which, each child in their own way, allowed themselves to express opinions, ask questions, contribute with reflections, have doubts, express uncertainty and affections.

Frame 4: Challenging Dialogue
In the situation described, questions were asked that referred back to the interviewer's own experiences, as was the case of the question about the movie; questions about the interviewed

---

[3]Individual subjectivity and social subjectivity are two different theoretical concepts that are mutually interrelated. "Social subjectivity represents the complex network of social subjective configurations within which all social performance takes place. These processes happen without the participants that share these social spaces being aware of them. Social subjectivity emerges as part of individual subjectivities in such a disguised way that it is impossible to infer directly from observed behaviors or explicit language" (González Rey, 2015, p. 13).

student's experience, their tastes and interests; and issues involving the interpersonal relationship between children, such as Guilherme's persistence on knowing why he is never invited to play ball.

It becomes clear that, even with João Carlos' first response, Guilherme is not satisfied and continues to insist on the question. At this point, the situation is no longer just an interview, but becomes an opportunity to think about this problem among students. The teacher realizes this and encourages João Carlos to answer sincerely, probably because she considers that Guilherme's question was interesting to instigate that student, in order to provoke reflection. João Carlos was a participative child in class and always took toys on the days they played on the court. However, he usually played with the same classmates, three other boys who were part of a group that called themselves "The vigilantes". At times, the teacher reported easy-going situations regarding this group of students, valuing the friendship between them, however, there were times that situations in which she encouraged students to make new friends and integrate other colleagues in their games were observed.

The reflection and emotionality-provoking dialogue was encouraged by the teacher who recognized the singularities of her students. The "People have a name and a surname" project's interview activity presented itself as a rich moment of learning and relationship among students and between students and the teacher due to its open and dialogical character. The course of the dialogues stimulated discussion among children, from which they could develop emotions and reflections through the course of information. From the answers given to the questions, not only the teacher, but the whole class has the possibility to get to know more about the student being interviewed. As the whole class is involved in activities related to that specific student, it creates an opportunity for all students to have a moment of greater visibility. Furthermore, the way the interview was organized can be understood as an indicator that students have a central place in the development of activities (Vaz, 2017, pp. 97–98).

In this way, the activity promoted moments of provocation and questioning that presented themselves as enablers for subjective development, as they favored the production of new reflective stances directed toward a continuous process of new subjective elaborations in the actual moment of the dialogue, but also in times to come. It is this nature of dialogue that projects dialogue beyond a linguistic-dialogical reality, since subjectivity is assumed as a differentiated production of those involved in the dialogue and time is no longer just related to its current dimension, but gains the consistency of lived life, with its constant comings back and goings forward. In González Rey's words,

> From the perspective of subjectivity, an act of expression, whether gestural, postural, emotional or even contradictory in regards to other's expression, occurs as a dialogic act when it generates commitment that allows a new qualitative moment in this communication, fostering the subjective configuration of the dialogical space. (González Rey, 2019, p. 29)

11.5 Final Considerations

The critical analysis of approaches regarding the concept of dialogue posed challenging questions for the understanding of human processes that emerge in situations of dialogical relations such as the human processes of learning and development in school contexts. By opting for the explicit or implicit aspects of dialogue or discourse, the human encounter that occurs in the dialogical relationship is disregarded, and the approaches fail to capture much of the human production that occurs in these contexts, such as emotionality, affections, setbacks, anxieties, motivations, or imagination. We look to answer such questions based on the quality that the concept of dialogue assumes in the cultural-historical perspective of subjectivity. For this purpose, fragments of the construction of information that addresses a singular pedagogical activity were presented. A pedagogical activity interpreted as favoring of imaginative and creative relational processes, in which moving through uncertainty, considering doubt, error, diversity, and the singularities of the learning and development processes of partners in educational contexts it was possible considering the openness of the dialogic-communicative context to the everyone's participation as active agents in dialogue. Thus, we sought to highlight the epistemological and theoretical dimensions that the concept of dialogue assumes from the perspective of the Theory of Subjectivity and the heuristic value that this conception expanded beyond the limits circumscribed to the use of language and symbolic performance.

We claim that processes of learning and development are dynamic and continuous, in which singular emotional experiences are integrated by human dialogical relationships and actions that favor subjective learning and development in which operational-intellectual processes and imaginative-creative adventures are not dissociated. The evidences of the field work made it possible to weave implications regarding the learning and development processes also of those who teach in their encounter with those who learn. Therefore, it is worth listening to class teacher's words about being a teacher, in which she expresses critical and curious concerns, and her ethical interest in encountering the Other as a constitutive aspect of her profession as a teacher:

> Being a teacher, …, requires breaking with crystallizations, with determinisms, assuming stances and being available to join the continuous flow of spaces and people we meet in the journey. (Silva, 2019)

References

Bakhtin, M. (Volochínov). (2012). *Marxismo e filosofia da linguagem: Marxism and philosophy of language*. 13 (Eds.), Trad. M. Lahud & Y. F. Vieira. São Paulo: Hucitec.

Fairclough, N. (2001). *Discurso e Mudança Social: Discourse and social change*. Brasília, DF: Editora da Universidade de Brasília.

Fiorin, J. L. (1990, jul/dez). Tendências da Análise do Discurso. Trends in Discourse Analysis. Em *Cadernos de Estudos Linguísticos, 19*, 173–179. Campinas: Unicamp.

Gergen, K. (1992). Toward a postmodern psychology. In S. Kvale (Ed.), *Psychology and postmodernism*. London: Sage.

González Rey, F. (2002). *Sujeto y subjetividad—Una aproximación Histórico Cultural: Subject and subjectivity—A cultural historical approach*. México: Thomson Eds.

González Rey, F. (2011a). Sentidos subjetivos, lenguaje y sujeto: avanzando en una perspectiva postracionalista en psicoterapia. Subjective senses, language and subject: Advancing in a post-tractional perspective in psychotherapy. *Riv Psichiatr, 46*(5), 310–314. https://doi.org/10.1708/1009.10978. http://www.rivistadipsichiatria.it/r.php?v=1009&a=10978&l=14979&f=allegati/01009_2011_05/fulltext/8-Gonzalez%20Rey(310-314).pdf.

González Rey, F. (2011b). Lenguaje, sentido y subjetividad: yendo más allá del lenguaje y el comportamiento. Language, sense and subjectivity: Going beyond language and behavior. *Estudios de Psicología, 32*(3), 345–357. https://doi.org/10.1174/021093911797898538.

González Rey, F. (2012). Configuração subjetiva dos processos psíquicos: avançando na compreensão da aprendizagem como produção subjetiva. Subjective configuration of psychic processes: Advancing the understanding of learning as subjective production. In A. Mitjáns Martínez, B. Scoz Lima, & Castaño Siquiera (Org.). *Ensino e aprendizagem: a subjetividade em foco: Teaching and learning: Subjectivity in focus* (Vol. 1, pp. 21–41). Brasília, DF: Líber Livro.

González Rey, F. (2015). A new path for discussion of social representation: Advancing the topic of subjectivity from a cultural-historical standpoint. *Theory & Psychology*. https://journals.sag epub.com/doi/abs/10.1177/0959354315587783.

González Rey, F. (2019). A Epistemologia Qualitativa vinte anos depois. Qualitative epistemology twenty years later. Em Mitjáns Martínez, A. González, F. Rey, & R. Valdés Puentes. *Epistemologia Qualitativa e Teoria da Subjetividade Discussões sobre Educação e Saúde: Qualitative epistemology and theory of subjectivity discussions on education and health*. Uberlândia, MG: EDUFU.

González Rey, F. L., & Mitjáns Martínez, A. (2017). *Subjetividade: Teoria, Epistemologia e Método: Subjectivity: Theory, epistemology and method*. Campinas, SP: Ed. Alínea.

Gumperz, J. J. (1982). *Language and social identity*. Cambridge: Cambridge University Press.

Madeira-Coelho, C. M. (1988). *A Interação Discursiva da Primeira Entrevista Terapêutica: reflexões para a anamnese fonoaudiológica. The discursive interaction of the first therapeutic interview: Reflections for the speech-language anamnesis*. Master dissertation in Linguistics, University of Brasilia, Brasília, non-published.

Madeira-Coelho, C. M. (2004). *Um olhar sobre a relação sujeito-linguagem: a subjetividade e os transtornos de comunicação. A look at the subject-language relationship: Subjectivity and communication disorders*. Doctoral Thesis in Psychology, Brasilia University, Brasília, non-published.

Madeira-Coelho, C. M. (2008). Language, sense and intersubjectivity. In Marios Pourkos (Org.), *Perspectives and limits of dialogism in Mikhail Bahktin: Applications in psychology, art, education and culture*. 1ªed (Vol. 2, pp. 251–265). Rethymnon: University of Crete.

Mitjáns Martínez, A., & González Rey, F. L. (2017). *Psicologia, educação e aprendizagem escolar: Psychology, education and school learning*. São Paulo: Cortez Editora.

Oliveira, A. M. do C. de, & Madeira-Coelho, C. M. (2020). Subjective development process as a path to school learning: The classroom as a dialogic relational contexto. *Studies in Psychology, 41*(1), 115–137. https://doi.org/10.1080/02109395.2019.1710803.

Sacks, H., Schegloff, E., & Jefferson, G. (1974). A simplest systematics for the organization of turn-taking for conversation. *Language, 50*(4), 696–735. https://doi.org/10.2307/412243.

Silva, K. O. (2019). *O Desenvolvimento Subjetivo na Infância: histórias, brincadeiras, peraltagens. Subjective development in childhood: Stories, games, and journeys*. Master's dissertation in Education, Brasília University, Brasília, Brasília. https://repositorio.unb.br/handle/10482/35784.

Vaz, L. (2017). *A sala de aula como espaço relacional: o olhar do professor para as singularidades dos alunos. The classroom as a relational space: The teacher's view of the students' singularities*. Master's dissertation in Education, Brasília University, Brasília. https://repositorio.unb.br/handle/10482/24233?mode=full.

Cristina M. Madeira-Coelho is currently a professor and researcher at the Faculty of Education, University of Brasilia. She has an undergraduate degree in Speech-Language Pathology, a master's degree in Linguistics and a Ph.D. in Psychology, all at the University of Brasilia. The breadth of her education stems from her academic interest in the subject-language learning relationship, which is beyond the scope of the disciplinary areas in her training. Her studies and research are aligned with themes that reflect how these areas intersect with education based on the theoretical framework of subjectivity from a cultural-historical perspective. She primarily researches and works with the following themes: teaching-learning processes, subject and subjectivity, child education, teacher training, language and communication development and atypical development.

Chapter 12
Theory of Subjectivity and Learning: Possibilities and Perspectives

Maria Carmen Villela Rosa Tacca

Abstract The chapter highlights the scope of González Rey's Theory of Subjectivity regarding its thoughts, actions, and practices in the educational field. The focus will fall upon the identification of the learning processes that gain a new understanding when addressed in the context of and links with the processes of subjectification of the person involved with the learning experience. We shall argue that the learning process goes far beyond what happens in the classroom, as events go follow a historical timeline, that is inserted in a culture, in a network of experiences that need to be observed and understood in its constitutive complexity. It is important to indicate that the teaching–learning process must be structured by pedagogical strategies that include listening and giving voice to students, considering that they are continuously producing subjective senses based on the experiences they undergo. The constructive-interpretative analysis of a case indicates the close articulation between individual and social subjectivity and seeks to unravel the subjective productions in the learning process, enabling recognition of continuous movements in the learners who begin to coordinate their own learning, which leads them unto new possibilities in their subjective development process.

12.1 Introduction

To highlight the scope of González Rey's Theory of Subjectivity (1997, 2003, 2004, 2005a) regarding its thoughts, actions, and practices in the educational field is the purpose of this chapter. We intend to focus on the subjectivation processes of the person involved with learning. This implies considering that this process is not merely a practice that is established with the objective of obtaining curricular knowledge or generating previously idealized changes. Learning reaches far beyond what is prescribed in a planned action, insofar as events tread along a historical line, which includes the students' experiences, who are, in turn, in interaction with and rooted in

M. C. V. R. Tacca (✉)
University of Brasília, Brasília, Brazil
e-mail: mctacca@yahoo.com.br

a culture that must be observed and understood in all its complexity. The Theory of Subjectivity gains prominence in education in so far as the importance of student's protagonism in the experiences he/she undergoes. It means considering that changes only happen with commitment, for learning is an act of will, of choice, which requires subjective involvement.

12.2 Theory of Subjectivity

For González Rey (2003) subjectivity is considered a complex symbolic-emotional system, impossible to be divided. A dialogic-dialectic system that is constantly developing,

> Subjectivity (...) represents a symbolic-emotional system oriented to the creation of a particularly human reality, i.e. culture, of which subjectivity itself is a condition for its development and within which it has its own genesis, socially institutionalized and historically situated. (González Rey & Mitjáns Martínez, 2017, p. 27)

In this perspective, a person when learning will have to be subjectively involved, generating a unique configuration that projects them to new experiences. Engaging with learning activities spontaneously or in those that are continuously offered in society, for example, by schools, will happen through a subjective configuration that becomes more and more complex, in the constant process of producing subjective senses, which are the essence of such configurations.

Subjective senses emerge in the course of experience, defining what the person thinks and generates in this process, defining the subjective nature of human experiences.

> [...] It is a fundamental attribute of the subjective configuration, which is a self-generating formation that arises from the diverse flow of subjective senses, producing, considering its generative character, converging groups of subjective senses that are expressed in the most stable subjective states of individuals in the course of experience. (González Rey & Mitjáns Martínez, 2017, p. 63)

In this theoretical approach, we attribute relevant implications of the subjective senses produced in the learning processes. It is a mistake to consider that the student who participates in a learning experience together with a group of colleagues and his/her teacher, is in that space or situation devoid of the value he/she attributes to him/herself; of the manner he/she produces or does not produce subject senses his/her previous school experiences; of the experiences he/she has with his/her family and with members of his/her community; of the social position he occupies in such groups; of the relationships he establishes with colleagues and teachers, for example. It is because of the past and present implications of both the individual, as well as the social group to which he belongs, that the subjective senses produce both individual and social subjectivity.[1] One same life situation can generate subjective senses that

---

[1] Individual subjectivity is constituted by the person's different subjective senses. Social subjectivity implies the presence of subjective senses shared at the social level. Both have a configurational

hinder or create conditions for a learning process. What matters is not the situation in itself, but the subjective senses that the learner produces in experiencing it. It is through this complex path that subjectivity manifests itself.

Inside or outside school, the subjective senses that are produced are integrated with others present in his/her own history constituting the individual subjectivity that is nourished by and nourishes social subjectivity. Thus, no external influence acts directly upon an individual's action. Any influence will acquire meaning in the action, from the way in which it is subjectified by the individual, group, or institution that lives that experience (Mitjans Martínez & González Rey, 2017, p. 64).

Subjective production generates different implications for action. This is because the production of subjective senses entails singularity and unpredictability. The subjective configurations are organized in the conjunction of continuously produced individual and social subjective senses. Social subjectivity supports itself on people's individual subjectivities, but differs from them at the same very same time in which are articulated with them, making them complementary and recursive, but also often contradictory, which reveals its complexity. Individual subjectivity and social subjectivity take on configurations that have their historicity, with no universal and standardized contents, but rather unique contents, given their dynamic constitution, in continuous movement through which subjective senses from different individual and social experiences converge.

In spaces of institutional relations that handle students, it is a very new conception to think of them in the midst of a cultural and social context in which individual and social subjective productions and processes emerge. The most common is to consider the existence of individual differences that are usually linked to conceptions of aptitude, personality traits, tendencies, or natural gifts. However, these schooling institutional environments could have a considerable advancement in terms of the development of their students if they enabled subjective productions articulated with what is prescribed by the different grades and school levels. The learner, since he is subjectively involved with what he learns, expresses a development in this process that is not given from the outside, but is the result of the generative character itself, expressed in the subjective configuration of learning (Mitjáns Martínez & González Rey, 2017, p. 63).

For the Theory of Subjectivity, subjective development is largely integrated with the processuality with which the person starts to assume the condition of subject in his action. This theoretical category is defined considering,

[…] the individual or group that is capable of generating an alternative path of subjectivation within the institutional normative space in which it operates. Being a subject is not a general quality of individuals or groups. One can be a subject in one domain of life and not in another or in a determined situation and not in another […] the subject can express himself or not in

character in continuous movement and interdependence. "Individual and social subjectivity are two levels of development of the same process that are inseparable for both social and individual development" (González Rey, 1997, p. 135).

the action of learning, a matter that results significant for understanding the type and quality of learning. (Mitjásn Martínez & González Rey, 2017, p. 58)

Hence, learning processes are profoundly articulated with the possibility of subjective development. The expectation is that the educational process can move its focus away from the reproduction of selected contents, and move toward an advance for creative and innovative productions. To create possibilities for development, it is to create situations for,

> [...] the emergence of new subjective configurations capable of generating the development of new subjective resources that allow the individual qualitative changes in different areas of life and that generate an increasingly deep personal involvement in the area where the subjective configuration of development is organized. (Mitjáns Martínez & González Rey, 2019, p. 17)

The school favors subjective development when activities, actions, and relationships are directed toward the emergence of new subjective configurations that enable the manifestation of the quality of subject of learning, mainly through the countless challenges and conflicts that are part of the school's routine. As González Rey theorizes: "the subject always exists in the tension between rupture and creation. Moments re characterized by a procedurality that challenges what is constituted, both at the level of individual subjectivity as well as in terms of the social" (González Rey, 2004, p. 22).

An important aspect for this expectation to be fulfilled is the value given to communication and dialogue. The perspective of the person's development is not in isolation, in personal investment, or in cultivating individualities, but precisely in the perspective that are constituted in the relations between people, that is, in social relations.

We get to know people by establishing relationships with and relating to them We can help people in their processes of being and learning, if we get involved with them and spend time with them because we are interested in getting to know them and promoting their development. We will be equipped with practices and ways of dealing with the challenges that arise if we understand the implications of the subjective dimension that are configured in the spaces of relationships between people. Thinking in the Theory of Subjectivity's perspective implies that we become more human as it challenges us to seek to be subjects of our own actions, reflecting upon the limits and possibilities in the context of our experiences and coexistence with others.

In institutions that deal with learning, teaching, and the actions pertaining to said learning and teaching, to take a stance and opt for choices that focus on the subjective dimension calls for necessary changes. We want to highlight in this scenario the teacher and student relationships, in their communicative processes (González Rey, 1995) and the possibilities of creating dialogical approaches in the classroom. Dialogues that entail a conversation instituted by the reciprocity between the actors present in each moment, and aimed at the joint reflection placed as a result of a participative and questioning atmosphere regarding the activities and challenges that present themselves. Open and flexible dialogue becomes possible when teachers and students compose a relational space whose atmosphere represents commitment and responsibility, with the possibility of negotiation without conflict becoming disruptive. For this, an analysis of the motivational aspects that implicate the production of subjective senses is important, as well as the investigation of complexity of such subjective senses.

The communicative and dialogic processes expand, develop and become generators of subjective development in the permanent search for understanding the aspects that become relevant and revealing in the teaching–learning process and that are linked to subjective senses that emerge continuously. In this sense, the teacher must seek to understand the intricate network of individual and social subjective productions that mobilize his pedagogical action. This means observing students in their interaction with the social group, interpreting the flow and relevance of the aspects that constitute their actions and that express the individual and social subjectivity of the group to which they belong.

There is a complex network of social, individual, cultural, and historical conditions that participate in learning situations, bearing in mind the goals to be achieved. In the midst of all these conditions, in all its emotional load, the student's protagonism emerges, which shows that learning, in its complexity, is much more than a cognitive act. In the social relationship resides a system which generates subjective senses in the course of activities that bring unexpected revelations and manifestations. For example, it is worth mentioning a 14-year-old student (7th grade), who, when asked to participate in a survey, is interested in unraveling the reason why she was included in the group of participants that she identified as not being good students. Upon learning which teacher had appointed her name, she reveals her subjective production when she says:

> She thinks of me today the same way she did when I was in fifth grade ... She can't see me without comparing me to my brother, who was her student. He was a very good student and I don't want to be compared to my brother. And I know that I've improved a lot, I've improved a lot, but she doesn't see that. (Tacca, 2006—conversation recorded in a research journal)

On both sides, subjective senses are generated with strong implications to teaching and learning processes. This teacher is remembered by the student within the history of her relationships and the subjective senses produced do not lead to a proximity between them.

To be aware of the subjective manifestations that can reveal emotionalities that permeate learning moments, whether people are aware or not of the impact they cause, is an aspect that should participate in pedagogical choices and practices. There are often queries, questions, and superficial evaluations that hide the reasons behind situations seen as maladjusted and unproductive, resulting in misinterpretations of students and social groups. From the perspective of showing the complexity of the production of subjective senses in learning, we replicate below the interpretative analysis of a student's manifestations in his educational experience, which enabled us to bring concreteness to the theoretical aspects highlighted so far.

12.3 Theory of Subjectivity and Learning: Interpretative Construction of a Case

For the study of subjectivity González Rey (1997, 2002, 2003, 2005b) developed an epistemological conception that aimed to overcome the dominant instrumentalism in Psychology. In this sense, he developed a distinctive Qualitative Epistemology, directed toward the construction of theoretical models,[2] with the idea of generating intelligibility or comprehension focuses regarding that which is being investigated. The empirical and the theoretical are merged in the interpretive construction that takes place in the research process. The approach emphasizes the communicative and dialogical process between researcher and participants, in which the theoretical model evolves according to the development of the interpretative process. An epistemological basis is created that values singularity, in a process that assimilates and produces an articulation that is based on the subjective manifestations that arise, express themselves, and are stimulated in the field of research. Unpredictability is a component to be captured, which demands a constant tensioning from the researcher in his interpretative possibilities as he will be the one to create the explanatory network in the composition with which the participant expresses himself in other moments and situations of the research. In the game of theoretical productions and of fieldwork the hypotheses are constructed process guides, not to be proven, but in the perspective of having explanatory value due to the indicators that support it.

It is with these theoretical–epistemological–methodological principles that we involved ourselves in a study with the purpose of retrieving the value that adolescent students gave to school and the perspectives they had of the future based on the way they dedicated themselves to learning. Based on the advances of the Theory of Subjectivity, we return here to the case study that we developed (Tacca, 2006), which allowed us to understand various aspects of the subjective productions of a 15-year-old student in relation to school and their own learning.

The case study is a methodological option that has allowed the study of subjective configurations, creating conditions for the study of the tension and articulation between individual and social subjectivity in social contexts such as that of the school. It is according to this perspective that we have been investigating subjective manifestations, with a focus of interest in situations that generate conflict or in students that exhibit poor educational performance. The interest in these situations came from the hypothesis that it is in these circumstances that the production of subjective senses is intensified by the level of emotionality they involve and to the extent that there is a divergence between the school and students in relation to what the goals are or what is expected as an outcome of schooling. In the study, we had the intention of creating situations that allowed for the manifestation of these students who belonged

---

[2]"The theoretical model is involved with the decisions and stances taken by the researcher who becomes an interlocutor of the new ideas and hypotheses that he is generating, which lead him to enhance the hypotheses that characterize this model at the present moment or to modify it, supporting himself in new constructions that articulate better with the new emerging hypotheses" (González Rey & Mitjáns Martínez, 2017, p. 90).

to a public school in the state of São Paulo-Brazil and were in the second phase of elementary school—5th to 8th grade (between 12 and 15 years of age).

As teenagers, they were in a phase of life in which they envisioned new possibilities for social participation, aiming at greater independence and autonomy in their actions. We were able to observe, due to the manner in which we introduce ourselves in the school environment, a restlessness, as well as an urgent need to belong to a social group, in which they tested their acceptance and sought identifications. Continually capturing their attention, they launched themselves impetuously, and filled with insecurities, into friendships, groups, going out, and online social networks. This is the feasible interpretation regarding the students from that school, which was observed in a group of students selected for a more in-depth study, from which the case study was designed. The research strategy consisted of first getting to know the school's relational space, participating in teacher's moments of pedagogical coordination, in observing classrooms regarding the way teachers and students interacted, but mainly focusing on the students' subjectivity and what they had to say in terms of learning moments and how they expressed the subjective senses produced in such moments.

Hence, by sharing experiences, interacting and observing stances taken, cooperation and resistance, we were able to discover socially shared subjective productions, as well as perceive a social subjectivity that generated contradictory emotions, making rooted conflicts visible, which, in turn, demanded the observation and investigation such conflicts' origin. We were able to understand that in this social subjectivity the representation of the student that does not comply with the efforts of his teachers and of the school, who intend to make them acquire an important and necessary knowledge organized in the different curricular subjects, stands out. In an interview, the teacher says: *"I invest in them in the same way that I have invested in my own children, who today have already taken their doctoral courses."* It was possible to observe there was a set goal for the pedagogical action, set according to what was perceived as a virtue, as well as a feeling of non-conformity in relation to the students.

Thus, in any place where teachers met, unsurprisingly, subjective senses were expressed in complaints and attempts to explain why students, or a large number of them, did not produce as they could or should, considering all teachers were effort. The explanatory analysis would focus on the existing or non-existing support and family structure, on undeveloped cognitive abilities and skills, on the lack of interest/motivation, inappropriate attitudes such as indiscipline, impoliteness, or on the type way the education system was organized, among others. Considering that they could not go against the flow, they continued their professional activity doing the best they could, but in constant battle for better work conditions. In fact, each one in their own way, tried to spark the students' attention and fulfill their teaching objectives.

In the social subjectivity this challenge was expressed alongside many other frustrations. Moreover, in the daily confrontation of the classroom, in the everyday settled, unsettled, or poorly settled activities, the subjective senses produced were expressed in demands and complaints, and moments of confrontation and conflicts were not uncommon. The way in which the communicative processes were expressed, indicated that in the social subjectivity teachers took one side and the students the other, and that such spaces were often in antagonism.

The classroom observations showed a lot of what the teachers had highlighted, because in fact, the most common attitudes were teachers standing in front of a classroom of very unfocused students, displaying sloppy attitudes, clearly communicating that they did not care what the teacher wanted to explain to them. They were attitudes of explicit confrontation, of defiance in which both sides were tested in their resistance. Interrupting class so that one or another student could be contained in his excesses was frequent. Each interruption was the reason for more dispersion and joking, for in each classroom there was a student who took advantage of the situation to remark ironic comments, prompting the group to laughter, generating yet another situation to be contained so class could continue.

Our attitude as a context observer/observant was always to seek to know origins, for which, basic questions arised: Why do they act like this? What makes learning no longer interesting and valuable? What would they like to learn? In these inquiries, we realized that being attentive to the manifestations of subjective senses could show us the needs, motives and how the articulation between individual and social subjectivity in school was constituted.

In the course of the research, subjective senses in regard to school experiences arose, but mainly in relation to teachers, because in each session the discussions focused on situations in which the relationships between them were the focus. This showed us that in the students' social subjectivity there was an appreciation of learning or of being able to learn closely linked to subjective senses related to teachers, that is, they showed that the teacher's figure and the relationship established with them, was the first link, the channel through which the learning stream could flow. They recounted situations in which the teacher's help, or a time when they received more attention, enabled interest and openness to learning. However, they also reported many other everyday classroom situations where their differences and conflicts stood out. In these circumstances, the subjective senses produced could not support productive learning.

In the varied research situations, the students' singularities became evident, guiding the development of the research's final stage, in which we sought to comprehend aspects of the students' subjectivity. For these interpretative constructions, we were supported by methodological procedures such as: discussions in a small group of selected students; sentence completion instrument that aimed at introducing themes and questions that enabled the development of subjective production indicators; essay writing about school and learning and semi-structured individual interviews with some of them, developing upon what had been discussed throughout the research, expanding and clarifying situations. We performed the interpretative analysis of the production of subjective senses that accompanied and were involved in the learning process of a student that will be disclosed as follows.

12.4 Artur's Case Study

Artur was a 15-year-old 8th grade elementary school student, and introduced himself as being "polite and moody," which already reveals a subjective self-evaluative production. His school records revealed he had never been held back, in to which he points out that he had been a private school student (or paid school in his expression) up to the 5th grade, when, due to his family's move back to São Paulo, his parent's separation and their financial condition at that time, he became a student at the state public school where the research was conducted. He comments that in his educational life, he had initially been a good student, but from the sixth grade forward, when he began at the new school, he changed and his school performance began to decline. He registers as he begins his essay:

> *My learning is a bit outdated because until the fifth grade I studied at a paid school, that is, until the fifth grade I had a good education, then I moved to this public school and it is kind of bad and that's why I think my learning is out of date.* (writing about school and learning)

He considers himself a student of medium–high level results, arguing that he has learning gaps, especially in some Mathematics and Portuguese topics. He recognizes that this is also linked to his lack of interest and even some irresponsibility, which leads him to feel remorseful when he gets a low grade because of his mother who tries hard to give him the very best. When he faces a learning situation, whose challenge he cannot solve, he says that becomes angry, mad, nervous, and that he feels a certain despair. This emotionality is undoubtedly at the base of his learning process.

In the comparisons that Artur makes between the schools he has attended, he assesses that the teachers at the private school paid more attention to students in class and explained the content of the subject better and more often, which allowed him to learn more. However, he managed to make friends at the public school, which he says he would not give up, and analyzes that his teachers are also more laid-back, talking about other matters outside the classroom, but reaffirms that teaching there is poor. Thus, he considers that although teaching is poor or delayed in regard to his private school and that he learns less, everyone is more equal to one another and relations are more friendly between students there.

He states:

> *The paid teachers paid more attention and explained the subject to us, and at the public school they don't, because they are not paid. They say things once and if you understand it, great, otherwise they won't explain it again. The subject of the paid college is much more advanced, things that I am seeing today in the 8th grade I had already seen in the 5th grade.*
>
> *Well, what I didn't learn and should learn, I haven't really learned, but I learned something much better and I also gained much better things, I learned to make and have friends and I have the best friends I could ever want. (writing about school and learning)*

These statements allow the identification of situations and people that represent important subjective senses production focuses for Artur: his mother—with whom he seems to have a commitment; teachers—who can give him access to knowledge and with whom he yearns to be close; friends—an achievement that he values; and knowledge—which he wants to achieve, but toward which he also has contradictory attitudes, for he wants to learn, but not that the school has to offer him.

Arthur seems to go back and forth between a school in which he thinks he had access to knowledge, but in which he did not relate to people ("everyone is stuck up there, nobody talks to anyone"), and another school, in which he regrets the poor teaching, but where he has friends and friendly relations. In this conflicted situation, he seeks a way out and turns to other interests, discovering and dedicating himself to knowledge that does not correspond to any of the school contents—legends, myths, and magic. The interest in esoteric subjects makes him look for this knowledge in books, since he has no one to teach him, either at school or outside. The uncle who shares the same interests lives far away, so he becomes self-taught in the study of the subject, to which he dedicates himself with concentration, as he has read several books and regularly exchanges information on the subject with people via the internet. This interest, and the fact that he remains home alone when he is not at school and while his mother is at work, renders his long hours of reading, which expresses an important motivational configuration. Reading becomes his source of knowledge and guarantees emotional balance, based on what he registers: **Reading** ... *calms me down*; **I'm better** ... *when I'm reading*; **My greatest pleasure** ... *reading*; **When I'm alone** ... *I take the opportunity to read*; **To learn** .... *I prefer to read* (sentence completion). There is no doubt that Arthur's world takes on another dimension when he is involved with matters that interest him, when he surrenders to the possibility of conduct himself in his own learning process.

We can interpret, based on what he says, writes and assembles as a scenario of his experiences that, motivated by a family situation that moved his life, a certain restlessness is manifested in him, an acute critical spirit, even if not always articulated and coherent and, also, some suffering is noticed. Yearning to experience a different situation, he takes alternative paths, integrating an emotionality that awakens him to new areas of interest that organize and constituting themselves subjectively.

The pleasure of being alone, or in the company of his books, which he enjoys and is moved by, and that does not always represent sadness in the scope of his reflections, all configurate Artur subjectively. This interpretive possibility is also based upon a famous phrase by Blaise Pascal (French philosopher) which he repeated twice during the research: *"The more I know people, the more I prefer my dog."* His need for seclusion through reading, the themes he chooses, the fact that he still does not have a special someone with whom to share his emotions becomes a bit clearer, *"No, I don't have anyone, I still prefer reading"* (interview).

The need to know that is being structured in Arthur's subjectivity distances him from school subjects, as he affirms that he has nothing more to learn at this school, because what is taught may be good for those who will follow certain careers, but it does not correspond to what he wants to study in the future. However, concurrently, he recognizes that he has learning gaps, which indicates that this has some value to him. It seems that Artur seeks to live the two realities related to knowing and learning. One being that that aroused in him reflexive emotion and the other, that of the school, standardized and with fixed contents, whose logic does not strike his emotion, but from which he knows he cannot distance himself. Not making a complete break, as he understands that society would not forgive him, he tries to carry the burden of responsibility on one side, while he delights in navigating the other. This is the complex organization that his subjective configuration assumes. When his reflections approach that side that burdens him, he declares:

> **At school** ... *I am mischievous*; **Studying** ... *tires me*; **The happiest time** ... *that that goes by quickly*; **I try** ... *when I think it's worth it;* **Schooling** ... *in my opinion does not lead to many places*; **My opinion** .... *doesn't count*; **I feel** ... *incapable*; **I get depressed** ... *when I don't finish things*; **I cannot** ... *disappoint others*; **My main ambition** .... *my diploma.* (sentence completion)

It is not difficult to notice that, among others, these records reveal a production of subjective senses related to his studying, disclosing a struggle in facing situations that he does not value, but also showing an understanding of the need to honor his commitments, demonstrating a concern as to not disappoint those who placed their trust in him. This is coupled with a feeling of inability and of lesser worth that could be the basis of the difficulty of asserting his own opinion, his point of view, which would explain his withdrawal and the preference for avoiding conflict, which seem to be composed in his subjectivity. They are subjective senses that reveal a certain suffering and conformity. Arthur's alternation between the two realities highlighted above also appears in his ambition to earn a diploma. Would this diploma signify fulfilling a secured family commitment? Is its importance conferred by the achievement of his intellectual autonomy? Or is it the recognition that without it, society would close its doors to him? The latter seems to be the intended scope, as Artur thinks realistically when he says *"I need the diploma to get a decent job."* For this reason, he does not permanently break with school, but is continually peeking at the world that is possible outside of it.

The world outside school that he has learned to peek at and is motivated to know, reveals itself with ample possibilities of exploring what he is willing, motivated, and takes pleasure in seeking. His thinking is allowed many possibilities of concatenation and is revealed in the imagination exercise appears in face of the different realities to be known and learned, which provokes his anxiety and appears in his records as follows:

> **I wanted to** ... *learn everything*; **I wish** ..... *to know*; **It bothers me**... *not to know*; **When I lie down** ... *I think*; **My greatest pleasure** .... *is to know*; **My greatest fear** ..... *the unknown*; **When I have doubts** ... *I look for the answer in books*; **I seek** ... *many things*; **I wish** ... *I could fly*; **I think about** ... *if I will ever reach/find my place.* **The past** .... *brings me memories of the future*; **I can always** ... *get where I want.* (sentence completion)

The number of times that Arthur presents the same elaboration about himself is impressive, his need to know the world and find his place in it, which is also coordinated with what he expressed in other moments of the study, for example when he built learning scenes with objects from scrap or discussed with his colleagues about school and learning. We hypothesize the existence of a complex subjective configuration that is expressed in his anxiety in face of the unknown and also in the strength of the very possibility of getting what he wants, and fighting for it. Perhaps that is why he firmly assumes that, if he could, he would not hesitate to go and live in the countryside with his grandmother, a possibility that would put him in close proximity to his uncle, an intellectual mentor. Artur, at this moment, affirms with conviction what he wants, what he does not want and directs strong criticism to the school and also to his family, but chooses to remain in his own corner, which can be an apparent posture of conformity. In contrast to this apparent conformity, he takes refuge in activities of select interest represents his escape.

Despite his young age, his reflections on life, on himself, as well as the choices he's made, express a very dense production of subjective senses and reveal the existence of a complex, dynamic, and contradictory individual subjectivity, also transversed the by social subjectivity of groups present in his current daily experience. Thus, when completing sentences he reveals:

> **I lament** .... *life*; **I suffer** .... *for everything*; **I have failed** ... *in my ideals*; **In life** ... *things conspire against us*; **Sometimes** ..... *I feel the absence*; **My biggest concern** ... *is with myself*. (sentence completion)

This ability to reflect about himself also tells us of his insecurities, his suffering, his frustrations, his faults, and the choice of having taken over the direction of his own life, placing himself responsible for it, because he cares about himself. In the game of individual and social subjectivity, Arthur takes stances, argues, advances, and retreats. He shows curiosity in understanding the world in its complexity, ambiguity, disparities, and antagonisms (which is present in the themes of his readings) and he directs his concern and motivation toward that. The to anchoring himself in his own strength is revealed, at the same time as confidence, insecurities, and projections for the future are perceived:

> **I love** ... *myself*; **I prefer** ..... *to be who I am than to be someone else;* **I am happy** .... *to be unique.* **My greatest desire** ... *is to be superior to those who are superior to me today.* (sentence completion)

Artur's subjectivity is, therefore, constituted by the complexity of the subjective senses produced in the different contexts and moments of his life. To be able to identify some plots of this configuration was an attempt to show that this configuration is procedural, since it is continuously organized and reorganized in a unique way in the concrete everyday activities (González Rey, 2005a). The subjective senses that are produced in Artur, related to spaces and experiences outside of school, also participate in the context of the classroom and show that they constitute elements of subjective senses that participate in his school learning. Since colleagues and teachers are important elements in his production of meaning, they could also be inserted and highlighted in the relationships established in school contexts, with a view to leveraging his motivational processes toward greater productivity in school learning.

12.5 Conclusive Aspects

This investigation that we undertook from González Rey's Theory of Subjectivity's standpoint, places perspective through introducing a new kind of reflection on students, in understanding them, not based on a behavior, or on a certain moment, or on an influential element or an isolated characteristic, but based on a subjective configuration that is continuously articulated with the social spaces experienced. Learning reveals itself as the production of subjective senses, in which the learner dives completely, in all his historicity, with all the contexts through which he transits, in its various moment. Learning takes on meaning in the articulations that he himself is responsible for making in the context of the intertwining and tension between his individual subjectivity and the spaces of social subjectivity. This articulation always generates new subjective configurations, stemming from the moments of challenge and rupture, of which emerge new formulations and articulations, in a reorganization of the subjective configuration itself. Understanding the history of this articulation and its production is a condition for the possibility of deciphering the processes and manners of learning. At school, this understanding can only be achieved in social relations in which the communication processes, the basis of which is dialogue, establish themselves as an option for both parties—teachers and students.

References

González Rey, F. L. (1995). *Comunicación, Personalidad y Desarrollo*[Communication, personality and development]. La Habana, Cuba: Editorial Pueblo y Educación, Playa.

González Rey, F. L. (1997). *Epistemología cualitativa y subjetividad*[Qualitative epistemology and subjectivity]. La Habana, Cuba: Editorial Pueblo y Educación, Playa.

González Rey, F. L. (2002). *Pesquisa Qualitativa em Psicologia: caminhos e desafios*[Qualitative research in psychology: Paths and challenges]. São Paulo: Pioneira Thomson Learning.

González Rey, F. L. (2003). *Sujeito e Subjetividade*[Subject and subjectivity]. São Paulo: Pioneira Thomson Learning.

González Rey, F. L. (2004). *O social na psicología e a Psicología Social*[The social in psychology and social psychology]. Petrópolis, Vozes.

González Rey, F. L. (2005a). O valor heurístico da subjetividade na investigação psicológica[The heuristic value of subjectivity in psychological research]. In F. L. González Rey (Eds.), *Subjetividade, complexidade e pesquisa em Psicologia*[Subjectivity, complexity and research in psychology] (pp. 27–51). São Paulo: Pioneira Thomson Learning.

González Rey, F. L. (2005b). *Pesquisa Qualitativa e Subjetividade: os processos de construção da informação*[Qualitative research and subjectivity: The processes of information construction]. São Paulo: Pioneira Thomson Learning.

González Rey, F. & Mitjáns Martínez, A. (2017). A. *Subjetividade: teoria, epistemologia e método*[Subjectivity: Theory, epistemology and method]. Campinas, SP: Editora Alínea.

Mitjáns Martínez, A., & González Rey, F. (2017). *Psicologia, Educação e Aprendizagem escolar: avançando na contribuição da leitura cultural-histórica*[Psychology, education and school learning: Advancing the contribution of cultural-historical reading]. São Paulo: Cortez Editora.

Mitjáns Martínez, A., & Gonzalez Rey, F. (2019). A preparação para o exercício da profissão docente: contribuições da Teoria da Subjetividade[Preparation for the exercise of the teaching profession: Contributions from the theory of subjectivity]. In M. Rossato & V. e Peres (Eds.), *Formação de educadores e psicólogos: Contribuições e desafios da subjetividade na perspectiva cultural—histórica*[Formation of educators and psychologists: Contributions and challenges of subjectivity in the cultural-historical perspective]. Curitiba: Appris.

Tacca, M. C. V. R. (2006). Relações Sociais na escola e desenvolvimento da Subjetividade[Social relations at school and development of subjectivity]. In M. I. Maluf (Ed.), *Aprendizagem: tramas do conhecimento, do saber e da subjetividade*[Learning: Plots of knowledge, knowledge and subjectivity]. Petrópolis, RJ: Vozes: SP.

Maria Carmen Villela Rosa Tacca has an undergraduate degree in Pedagogy, a Ph.D. in Psychology from University of Brasília (UnB) and has conducted postgraduate studies with Prof Fernando González Rey at the Pontifical Catholic University of Campinas (PUC-Campinas), where she examined learning and subjectivity. She is currently a full-time researcher at the UnB School of Education. Her studies and research focus on themes that are generated in the intersection between education and psychology, from a cultural-historical approach, with interests in the following topics: teacher-student relationships, the meaning of learning, the process of schooling and school failure, daily life in the classroom, teacher action and the development of subjectivity in education. These topics have been examined at different educational levels.

Chapter 13
Subjectivity, Psychology, Marxism and Critical Realism: Eleven Theses

Ian Parker

Abstract This paper traces through the fraught relationship between psychology and Marxism through a reading of current critical debates in the discipline through Marx's 1845 eleven 'Theses on Feuerbach'. These theses enable us to grasp how Marxism tackles questions ranging from the relation between the individual and the social to social constructionism and discourse and then, crucially, to 'critical realism' in relation to psychology. Questions of behaviour, cognition and biology, as well as the radical status of psychoanalysis in relation to psychology are explored. These eleven theses radically rework human agency, providing an innovative basis for working inside psychology, but also, most importantly, for appreciating how necessary it is to work against psychology. Psychology as a discipline interprets the world, and we learn through Marx that is necessary to change it, in the process dispensing with psychology as such. We must remember that psychology is not a scientific discipline, and cannot become so. It is, as Fernando González Rey reminds us, a discipline concerned with the nature of subjectivity. What is clear is that any realist approach to human action should be undertaken outside the discipline, not inside it. We approach the task of taking subjectivity seriously through Marx's eleven theses.

13.1 Introduction

There are many forms of psychology, and many forms of Marxism, and juxtaposition of the two strands of work has often resulted in an intensification of miscommunication. This may not be a bad thing. Our task as Marxists should be to intensify contradictions rather than aim for some kind of peaceful coexistence with academic systems of thought (Parker & Spears, 1996). Recent international meetings of psychologists and Marxists have emphasized the question of political practice in their discussions of theoretical differences (Arfken, 2011; Painter et al., 2015). This paper is in line

I. Parker (✉)
University of Manchester, Manchester, UK
e-mail: discourseunit@gmail.com

© The Author(s), under exclusive license to Springer Nature Singapore Pte Ltd. 2021
D. M. Goulart et al. (eds.), *Theory of Subjectivity from a Cultural-Historical Standpoint*,
Perspectives in Cultural-Historical Research 9,
https://doi.org/10.1007/978-981-16-1417-0_13

with that focus on our praxis. One way of demonstrating fidelity to Marxism would be to support characterization of psychology with many quotations from Marx. Instead I have chosen one text, the 'Theses on Feuerbach' (Marx, 1845), as a thread to help us provide an overview of links that have been made between psychology and Marxism, key issues that have emerged and questions that remain open. Most academic work deliberately sabotages the hope of linking Marxism with psychology. Each thesis raises issues about the way psychology has addressed subjectivity (González Rey, 2017, 2018).

13.2   The Individual and the Social

In the first thesis Marx writes about the nature of human subjectivity in relation to the social world configured as if it were an 'objective' realm outside us. Marx writes:

> The chief defect of all hitherto existing materialism (that of Feuerbach included) is that the thing, reality, sensuousness, is conceived only in the form of the *object or of contemplation*, but not as *sensuous human activity, practice*, not subjectively. Hence in contradistinction to materialism, the *active* side was developed abstractly by idealism - which of course, does not know real, sensuous activity as such. Feuerbach wants sensuous objects, really distinct from the thought objects, but he does not conceive human activity itself as *objective* activity. Hence in *Das Wesen des Christentums*, he regards the theoretical attitude as the only genuinely human attitude, while practice is conceived and fixed only in its dirty-judaical manifestation. Hence he does not grasp the significance of 'revolutionary', or 'practical-critical' activity. (Marx, 1845, Thesis 1)

What is the form of the two bits of the jigsaw 'individual' and 'society' that would enable them to lock together? The first thesis draws attention to the way one side of 'practical-critical' activity is prioritized at the expense of the other, and the effect of this is to maintain the distinctness of each side. The thesis also highlights the need, human need for an account of 'behaviour' that is also 'sensuous' as the basis of a theory of practice.

There are further issues that arise from the first thesis, and one is the relation between economic class exploitation and cultural oppression, questions of racism. This first thesis includes reference to 'dirty judaical' manifestations of practice, the 'grubby Jewish form' in another translation (Suchting, 1979). Tempting as it is to strike a blue line through bits of Marx's writings, to pretend that certain things were not said, it is more honest and politically correct to confront the traces of reactionary discourse in the text. Marxism has a legacy of collusion in forms of colonialism and racism. This thesis, and other of Marx's writings (e.g. 1843), express a characterization of capitalism which carries with it discourses of anti-semitism, discourses which continue in the formulations of many contemporary Marxist groups (Billig, 1982; Cohen, 1984), though it should be noted here that Marx is sarcastically repeating a notion of Feuerbach's, not endorsing it.

The individual social split is a recurring theme in Marxist theory and forms the foundation of much psychology. The importance of social structures as material forces which have relational and representational dimensions has implications for method as well as for theory in Marxism. It is when we pretend that there is no conflict that we collude with and nourish that alienating social medium.

13.3 Social Constructionism and Discourse

In the second thesis, Marx raises crucial questions for psychologists about their conceptions of reality, how it is 'social constructed' and how we speak about that reality. He writes:

> The question whether objective truth can be attributed to human thinking is not a question of theory but is a *practical* question. Man must prove the truth, i.e. the reality and power, the this-sidedness of his thinking in practice. The dispute over the reality or non-reality of thinking that is isolated from practice is a purely *scholastic* question. (Marx, 1845, Thesis 2)

Perhaps the social constructionist preoccupation with the arbitrariness of interpretation is largely bound up with the role of this issue in the critique of mainstream psychology (Parker, 1998). Although this may be an effective and useful counter to the paradigmatic ambiguity and artifice of much experimental psychology, the relativism that results is a heavy price to pay. In many real-world situations interpretation may be either less or more ambiguous due to the richness of context, and because of the contradictory socially shared nature of language and rationality.

The intelligibility of both language and rationality is largely premised on a shared identity and understanding which provides a basis for common interpretation. When a class identity that should provide an interpretation is confused by a mass of competing interpretations which all claim to be true, just as true, then ideological processes are clearly at work. There are political consequences of this. It is no accident that ethnomethodologists are among the most rabid anti-Marxists, for they are suspicious of any truth claims that a system of theory might make (Parker, 2015). For Marxist's a further refinement is necessary. Divide and rule is maintained in psychology, in part, through the specification of particular discrete topic areas. It is impossible to address the practice of the human agent as a material body, a product of biology and history engaging in thought and action when we are compelled to work within the categories of 'behaviour', 'cognition', the so-called 'biological bases' of behaviour separate from the meaning we accord to our actions. The next theses enable us to address these issues further.

13.4   Behaviour

Let us turn first to behaviour and behaviourism as a reductive approach to human action inside psychology. Marx writes:

> The materialist doctrine concerning the changing of circumstances and upbringing forgets that circumstances are changed by men and that it is essential to educate the educator himself. This doctrine must, therefore, divide society into two parts, one of which is superior to society. The coincidence of the changing of circumstances and of human activity or self-changing can be conceived and rationally understood only as *revolutionary practice*'. (Marx, 1845, Thesis 3)

In the United States, they promise that behaviourism could mould the lives and careers of children if they were caught at an early enough age (Watson, 1913) captured the spirit of similar claims by Jesuits years before, and fed hopes of social change. There was some radical purchase on this idea, and some attraction to behaviourist notions from those on the left. In the 1920s, for example, the Socialist Rand School was kept afloat financially by ticket sales to its psychology lectures, organized with the assistance of John B. Watson (Harris, 1990).

Nevertheless, Skinner's 'radical behaviourism', which has often been attacked by the anarchist left (e.g. Chomsky, 1959, 1973) is predicated, in contrast to Pavolo-vian reflexologists, on the activity of the person, on 'operant behaviour'. Radical behaviourists can link this account of activity with an analysis of the 'contingencies of reinforcement', and also be devout Christians (e.g. Day, 1976) or good Marxists. Despite detractors' attempts to conjure up images of *Brave New World* or *Nineteen Eighty Four*, not to mention Skinner's own politics (which were decidedly to the right), Skinner's (1948) *Walden Two* describes a communal life in which the contingencies of reinforcement are under the collective control of its members. This has inspired attempts by Marxist-Leninist radical behaviourists to set up such communities themselves, and attempts by others to use such communities therapeutically (Cullen, 1991).

13.5   Cognition

Psychologists typically turn to 'cognitive' processes in order to supplement a behaviourist focus. Marx writes:

> Feuerbach starts out from the fact of the religious self-alienation, of the duplication of the world into a religious world and a secular one. His work consists in resolving the religious world into its secular basis. But that the secular basis detaches itself from itself and establishes itself as an independent realm in the clouds can be explained by the cleavages and self-contradictions within this secular basis. The latter must, therefore, in itself be both understood in its contradiction and revolutionized in practice. Thus for instance, after the earthly family is to be discovered to be the secret of the holy family, the former must then be destroyed in theory and in practice.' (Marx, 1845, Thesis 4)

Bowers (1990) argues that increasing abstraction can intensify alienation. Cognitive models are parasitic on the tools and metaphors available to the discipline, notably the digital computer (e.g. Bowers, 1991; Gigerenzer, 1991). The resulting metatheory of the rational information processer is deeply embedded, and supposed limitations on processing capacity divert attention to salient stimuli (e.g. Kahneman et al., 1982) and where cognition is seen as guiding perception and judgement, this typically proceeds automatically through the cognitive structures of categories or schemata (cf. Billig, 1985). We might then ask to what extent the theoretical language of cognitive psychology actually endows the person with any agency at all. Much of 'black box' cognitive psychology simply redirects the determinism of the environment in behaviourism inwards to a cognitive apparatus, leaving the question of intentionality unresolved and resulting in a mechanistic model (Harré, 1974; Shotter, 1975). Although there have been attempts to locate intentionality within a computational framework (e.g. Dennett, 1978), this fails to escape the infinite regress of the homunculus (Palmer, 1987) or the issue of meaning and interpretation (Bem, 1990; Smythe, 1990).

Cognitivism is idealist because it privileges internal mental representation and neglects the constraint of our embodied and biological natures and the material forces of the physical world which structure forms of consciousness. It is individualistic and ahistorical because it abstracts cognition from its social and historical conditions, and it facilitates social control (Shallice, 1984; Shotter, 1987). The liberal and conservative political practices which are prefigured and prescribed by such a psychology provide perhaps the critical verdict from a Marxist perspective. In a western culture in which individualism and rationalism constrain the possibilities of collective consciousness and action, cognitive approaches play a significant ideological role. The mechanistic and the idealist themes in cognitive psychology also provoke, respectively a flight into humanism or biologism.

13.6 Biology

Marx writes of our relation to our bodily existence:

> Feuerbach, not satisfied with *abstract thinking*, wants *contemplation*; but he does not conceive sensuousness as *practical*, human-sensuous activity. (Marx, 1845, Thesis 5)

Marxists need to take the study of biology seriously. It is of crucial importance to a materialist understanding of the person (Timpanaro, 1976), and it is clear that Marx is being misunderstood if Marx is taken to mean that human nature is not important (Geras, 1983). The thesis raises the issue of the abstraction and reification of a psycholological character wrenched from particular historical conditions and social relations. Essentialism in both explicit and implicit guises informs most psychological theorizing, but the task of a Marxist critique would be to define the nature of human nature as a foundation for political action, not for psychology. The inevitable project of psychology is to theorize the individual. A fundamental question, then, for both psychology and Marxism is how individuality is formed out of human nature? The most explicit and crass form of the biological doctrine in the discipline is the hereditarian notion that our natures are preprogrammed in our genes. The Darwinian lesson that the characteristic nature of different species is biologically defined and produced is twisted here so that biology is not just seen as the basis for species being or for individual variation, but for group differences of race, gender and class. The ethologist Lorenz as well as psychologists such as Jaensch were active in offering Nazi race theories a psychological foundation, and Billig (1979) has charted the historical links between hereditarian psychologist such as Jensen and Eysenck and the extreme right, much as Eysenck (1982) might have hypocritically tried to trace his theoretical approach to Soviet precursors. The political consequences and uses of this approach to psychology in testing and educational policy do not have to be spelt out here. It is true that Marx was clearly influenced and impressed by Darwin, and it should not be forgotten that biology forms an important aspect of the materialism that is Marxism (Timpanaro, 1976). However, it is equally clear that a sociobiology, used to ground, explain or justify social divisions and structures has no place in historical materialism.

Nevertheless, we need to understand how the manifold forms of alienation under capitalism bear on our relationship with our own body. As Kovel (2007) points out, there are four aspects of alienation in Marx: a separation from our own creativity, a competitive separation from others, a separation from our own body and separation from nature as such.

13.7 Humanism

Marx warns us that it would be a mistake to flee from our biology, to separate ourselves from it, and to retreat to a simple humanism, as some psychologists do. Marx writes:

> Feuerbach resolves the religious essence into the *human* essence. But the human essence is no abstraction inherent in each single individual. In its reality it is the ensemble of the social relations. Feuerbach, who does not enter upon a criticism of this real essence, is consequently compelled: (i) to abstract from the historical process and to fix the religious sentiment as something by itself and to presuppose an abstract - *isolated* - individual. (ii) Essence therefore can be comprehended only as 'genus' as an internal, dumb generality which *naturally* unites the many individuals'. (Marx, 1845, Thesis 6)

The shift from a crude biological account of the bases of behaviour to simple humanism has been a crucial part of the argument of radicals working the field of mental health. Phenomenological foundations for alternative accounts of mental distress have been important not only in right-wing individualist attacks on the notion of mental 'illness' (e.g. Szasz) and left-liberal and libertarian 'anti-psychiatry' (e.g. Laing), but also for those who have been too sickened by the institutional violence metered out to the mad to turn to theoretical 'anti-humanism' to defend them. Marxist arguments in the radical mental health movement have deliberately turned to humanism (Brown, 1973) and the tradition of Critical Theory and Lukács, 1919–1923; Ingleby, 1970). This has prompted versions of critique in the same spirit on the fringes of psychology (Ratner, 1971) and psychotherapy (Cohen, 1986) directed at the violence which seems to attend theoretical attacks on notions of agency.

It is nevertheless important to distinguish human nature in the terms outlined above from what Geras (1983) terms the 'nature of man' in a specific social and historical context. In this way, particular forms of behaviour characteristic of particular epochs or social relations (such as competitiveness under capitalism) do not have to be seen as intrinsic to humans, but as features associated with particular social relations. This distinction would seem to cover the traditional Marxist objection to an account of human nature, namely that specific features are reified and used to justify certain social or political forms. This view allows us to argue for a human nature and agency while accepting that the broader form and expression of human characteristics and behaviour may take multifarious forms. Such an approach avoids the lure and traps of simple phenomenology which has driven many Marxist (and post-structuralists) to embrace 'anti-humanism'. It is here that Fernando González Rey offers a quite different way of conceptualizing subjectivity that does justice to the humanist spirit of Marxism while refusing attempts to individualize human experience (2017, 2018).

13.8 Psychologisation

The appeal to 'essence' in psychology, whether through humanism or through false universalisation of human experience is a continual temptation in psychology. Marx writes:

> Feuerbach, consequently, does not see that the 'religious sentiment' is itself a social product, and that the abstract individual whom he analyses belongs to a particular form of society'. (Marx, 1845, Thesis 7)

Alongside the assumption in psychology that the individual and society are two separate parts of an equation to be solved, runs a second assumption which is that this scientific discipline can arrive at a correct account, and that this should be universal. If historical materialism provides a foundation for understanding social and psychological ways of being, the next question is how we can arrive at such an understanding. This question of method is central to both Marxism and psychology and drives to the very heart of the difference between the natural and social worlds. A recurring question has been the extent to which psychology (and social science generally) can use as its model scientific investigation in the natural sciences. The problem is that although psychologists look to the natural sciences for their methods, they simply end up with a caricature of those sciences.

The adoption of a realist understanding of science addresses this by undermining the clear gulf between the natural and the social sciences implied by the hermeneutic anti-naturalist position. At a political or discursive level, methods, experimental or otherwise, can be seen as rhetorical devices to engage and convince sceptical audiences, though if they are nothing more than this then the problems of social constructionism resurface, with the question of ideological abuse that many critical writers inside and outside psychology have described. The danger cannot be ignored of 'experimentalism' being employed in a positivistic crusade against other 'soft' methodologies which allow the 'subject' greater voice and are (therefore) adjudged 'unscientific'.

Science should be measured in terms of its sensitivity and fidelity to its object, not in terms of abstract or universalized notions of 'rigour', and Marxism may draw upon a realist view of science applicable to the social world, this is not applicable to the sphere of psychology. Our concern should be with the way critical realism may or may not help Marxists in psychology understand ideology, and with the way representations of science (here, psychological science) may or may not operate as forms of ideology. It does operate as a form of ideology when psychology globalizes itself, and facilitates the 'psychologisation' of society and of each individual within it (De Vos, 2012).

13.9   Personality

Psychology claims to detect, and in the process it defines different kinds of personality, but it does so on a basis that is closer to astrology than science. Marx writes:

> All social life is essentially *practical*. All mysteries which lead theory to mysticism find their rational solution in human practice and in the comprehension of this practice'. (Marx, 1845, Thesis 8)

This question is of course none other than the perennial dualism of agency versus structure that has plagued academic Marxism, and social theory generally.

It would seem to leave all the issues of the agent predetermined whilef compounding those of a human nature, albeit one determined by historical and social context. Despite the value of his materialist approach Lucien Sève's attempt to construct a (scientific) Marxist theory of personality can be seen as a reflection of this tendency to undervalue the role of human agency and to view this as epiphenomenonal to social structures and relations (Leonard, 1984). There are also deep problems with the 'anti-humanism' of Sève's position, and this has much to do with the political context, including the micro-politics of anti-humanism inside the French Communist Party, a micro-politics which also bears on Althusser's work, in which he was writing (O'Donnell, 1982). Elements of humanism, it is true, seem indispensable to theories of liberation (Lacerda, 2015), but to liberation, not to psychology. The question is how this humanism might be reconfigured in such a way as to take account of that which is not immediately conscious to us. For that, we need something from psychoanalysis, perhaps.

13.10 Psychoanalysis

Psychoanalysis is on the agenda in Marx's ninth thesis, where he writes:

> The highest point reached by contemplative materialism, that is, materialism which does not comprehend sensuousness as practical activity, is the contemplation of single individuals and of civil society'. (Marx, 1845, Thesis 9)

The structure of psychology is founded on repression, the repression of the sensuous nature of the human subject. There are many forms of psychoanalysis and many kinds of relationship between psychoanalysis and Marxism (Pavón Cuéllar, 2017).

History shows us that this conceptual relationship always has a directly political context, as the fate of Wilhelm Reich and 'dialectical materialist' psychoanalysis indicates (Reich, 1929). The expulsion of Reich from the German Communist Party reflected moves in other Stalinised sections of the Comintern to force their intellectuals to recant their sympathies with psychoanalysis. In France, for example, the disapproval of anything other than behaviourism was only broken in the 1960s with Althusser's use of Lacan's work within the structuralist tradition, a tradition that was becoming increasingly popular (and not only among Parisien intellectuals), and which also broke with traditional psychoanalytic pessimism about the inflexibility of 'human nature' (Roudinesco, 1990). In the Soviet Union itself, psychoanalysis had been snuffed out by the 1930s. An important exception to Leftist institutions destroyed by the waves of anti-psychoanalytic Marxism in the 1920s was the Institute of Social Research, later known as the Frankfurt School. The Institute, was founded in 1923, nurtured a strand of psychoanalytic Marxist 'Critical Theory' which included Fromm (1932) and Marcuse (1955). A further legacy of the Frankfurt School—in an uneasy tension now with psychoanalysis—is the Marxist tradition on the margins, but inside the discipline of German 'Critical Psychology' (Tolman & Maiers, 1991).

Partly because the Soviet bureaucracy was busy burning Freud's books itself, and would not provide a place of refuge for psychoanalysts fleeing fascism in central Europe, the connection between psychoanalysis and radical thought was effectively destroyed in the 1930s. Psychoanalysis was then also subject to intense repression in the United States, to which many analysts had fled from central Europe (Jacoby, 1983, 1986). Psychoanalysis is systematically distorted in psychology; it is not psychology, but something entirely different.

13.11 Soviet Developmental Psychology

There were alternatives inside psychology under capitalism, but the possibility for building something new in the Soviet Union was crushed by Stalin. This is a history that is distorted within the Soviet Union and outside it by those who configure the theoretical debates in line with different agendas (González Rey, 2014). Marx anticipates some of the conceptual problems when he writes:

The standpoint of the old materialism is civil society: the standpoint of the new is human society, or social humanity'. (Marx, 1845, Thesis 10)

The tradition of developmental psychology is increasingly recognizing the contribution of Lev Vygotsky as an alternative to Piaget, but the political allegiances of Vygotsky in the early years of the Soviet revolutionary state before Stalinism crushed the creative forces released in 1917, and of Piaget working in an evolutionary but also deeply Christian liberal tradition are often forgotten (Burman, 2017). The shift in developmental psychology that Vygotsky's work represents is a shift from seeing the infant as essentially asocial becoming social, part of 'civil society' (through the mastery of internal cognitive stages), but of the 'social humanity' of the infant becoming asocial, individualized in capitalist culture. It is exactly this that Fernando González Rey contributed so much to (2017, 2018).

Vygotsky's earliest work was not, in fact, on child development, but on art and culture, and his focus on the role of language in the constitution and reproduction of 'cognition' has inspired psychologists attempting to provide non-individualistic accounts of memory (e.g. Middleton & Edwards, 1990). Vygotsky anticipates many of the themes of those using 'post-structuralist' ideas to describe the immersion of individual psychology in the structures of discourse and the ways different linguistic forms hold within them radically different kinds of thought. At the same time Vygotsky was working, Vološinov (1973) was producing an account of language that has also influenced theories of discourse outside and now inside psychology. This opens the way to an understanding of how an 'ensemble of social relations' is made into a person. In this way, Vygotsky's work reinforces the turn to discourse that has been an important part of social constructionism in recent years. As we have noted above, however, this turn to social constructionism and discourse has reactionary implications for radicals in psychology concerned with truth, with a scientific approach of any kind.

Bhaskar (1989) has called this the primal problem of the social sciences, and historically it has resulted in two basic camps. On the one hand there is the scientific or naturalistic tradition deriving from Humean empiricist philosophy, which assumes that social behaviour is law-like, and that such regularities can be revealed by controlled observation according to positivist principles (the so-called deductive-nomological model). On the other hand, the hermeneutic tradition sees radical differences between the social and natural worlds and their subject matter. This school of thought derives from the transcendental idealism of Kant and other rationalist or hermeneutic philosophers, and is the cornerstone of Weberian sociology. On this view, the goal of social sciences is the understanding of the meaning of human action in terms of purposes and reasons so that psychology entails the interpretation of individual meaning. The role of intention and agency would seem to rule out the analysis and explanation of behaviour in terms of general causal laws. Psychology is caught between the two camps, reflecting the worst of each of them.

13.12 Critical Realism

> The philosophers have only *interpreted* the world, in various ways; the point is to *change* it.' (Marx, 1845, Thesis 11)

Increasingly, radical philosophers of science have rejected positivism and argued for a 'realist' and 'critical realist' theory of science (e.g. Bhaskar, 1989; Harré, 1972; Harré & Madden, 1975). Empiricism, as the cornerstone of positivism, only permits of trust in the contents of sense experience and thus when taken to the logical extreme results in idealism and even solipsism.

The question then remains as to whether an experimental social or psychological science can be realized in practice. Although it is possible to create closed systems experimentally in the natural sciences in order to isolate the causal powers or physical properties of interacting molecules and so forth, the possibility of ever creating a closed system in social terms is a moot point (cf. Bhaskar, 1989). An experimental approach would appear to assume a certain level of atomism or methodological individualism rejected by classical Marxist analyses. Agents are also different to molecules in that they can interpret, and see beyond the boundaries of the experimental enclosure (Bhaskar, 1989). In short it is debatable whether it is possible to experimentally bound human representation, or abstract the individual from the social relations in which they are embedded, without altering the identity of these representations and relations. On the other hand, the undeniable individualism of experimental psychology also reflects an individualistic culture and practice as much as being an inherent feature of the experimental method, as the doomed efforts of social identity theorists suggest (e.g. Tajfel & Turner, 1986; Turner et al., 1987).

The point has been well-made by anti-colonial, anti-racist and feminist writers that such 'rigour' is a fantasy, reflecting the particular subjective position of the researcher (Hollway, 1989). This paper, which has dwelt on Marxism, would also, in a fuller more rounded account attentive to the subjectivity of those who suffer and resist, have to attend to the intersection between class, sex and 'race' in the history of psychology (Burman, 2018; Teo, 2005). Psychology is rooted in patriarchy as much as it is in capitalism (Eisenstein, 1979).

13.13 Conclusions

Marxism entails a realist view of science applicable to social world but that this is to be contrasted with empiricism or positivism. As many have pointed out, Marx himself engaged in quantitative research and used social data to advance his arguments. Empirical research is not necessarily empiricist—this depends on how data are conceived, used and theorized (Triesman, 1974). An empirical element is also important if we are to avoid the dangers of abstraction, determinism and historicism within Marxism. A central task for a Marxist approach to science then is to be able to distinguish positivist and realist science.

The realist position opens a space for the study of ideology and 'ideological' science. In this respect we should acknowledge that science produces knowledge which feeds into the conditions being studied, and that scientists are active participants in the processes they try to interpret. For Bhaskar and other critical realists, the process of interpreting the world must, of necessity, involve changing it, not only because our explanations, if they are critical, call upon a moral-political commitment to changing conditions that are unjust, but also because as we become aware of those conditions we position ourselves differently in relation to them; we change. It is this process of change that psychology as a discipline blocks, sabotages. This is something that detailed studies of subjectivity carried out by Fernando González Rey (Fernando González Rey et al., 2019) struggled with and aimed to transcend.

References

Arfken, M. (Ed.). (2011). Marxism and psychology special issue, *Annual Review of Critical Psychology, 9*. https://discourseunit.com/annual-review/9-2011/. Accessed 11 July 2018.

Bem, S. (1990). Cognitive representations and intentionality and the realism-relativism controversy. In W. J. Baker, M. E. Hyland, R. van Hezewijk, & S. Terwee (Eds.), *Recent trends in theoretical psychology* (Vol. II). New York: Springer-Verlag.

Bhaskar, R. (1989). *Reclaiming reality: A critical introduction to contemporary philosophy*. London: Verso.

Billig, M. (1979). *Psychology, racism and fascism*. Birmingham: Searchlight.

Billig, M. (1982). *Ideology and social psychology: Extremism, moderation and contradiction*. Oxford: Blackwell.

Billig, M. (1985). Prejudice, categorization and particularization: From a perceptual to a rhetorical approach. *European Journal of Social Psychology, 15,* 79–103.

Bowers, J. M. (1990). All hail the great abstraction: Star Wars and the politics of cognitive psychology. In I. Parker & J. Shotter (Eds.), *Deconstructing social psychology*. London: Routledge.

Bowers, J. M. (1991). Time, representation and power/knowledge: Towards a critique of cognitive science as a knowledge-producing practice. In I. Parker (Ed.) (2011), *Critical psychology: Critical concepts in psychology, volume 1, dominant models of psychology and their limits*. London and New York: Routledge.

Brown, P. (Ed.). (1973). *Radical psychology*. New York: Harper Colophon.

Burman, E. (2017). *Deconstructing developmental psychology* (3rd ed.). London and New York: Routledge.

Burman, E. (2018). *Fanon, education, action: Child as method*. London and New York: Routledge.

Chomsky, N. (1959). Review of B. F. Skinner's verbal behavior. *Language, 35,* 26–58.

Chomsky, N. (1973). *For reasons of state*. London: Fontana.

Cohen, S. (1984). *That's Funny, you don't look anti-semitic: An anti-racist analysis of left anti-semitism*. Leeds: Beyond the Pale.

Cohen, C. (1986). Marxism and psychotherapy. *Science and Society, 50*(1), 4–24.

Cullen, C. (1991). Experimentation and planning in community care. *Disability, Handicap and Society, 6*(2), 115–126.

Day, W. F. (1976). On the behavioral analysis of self-deception and self-development. In T. Mischel (Ed.), *The self: Psychological and philosophical issues*. Oxford: Blackwell.

Dennett, D. C. (1978). *Brainstorms*. Brighton: Harvester.

De Vos, J. (2012). *Psychologisation in times of globalisation*. London: Routledge.

Eisenstein, Z. (1979). *Capitalist patriarchy and the case for socialist feminism.* New York: Monthly Review Press.

Eysenck, H. J. (1982). The sociology of psychological knowledge, the genetic interpretation of IQ, and Marxist-Leninist ideology. *Bulletin of the British Psychological Society, 35,* 449–451.

Fromm, E. (1932). The method and function of an analytic social psychology: Notes on psychoanalysis and historical materialism. In A. Arato & E. Gebhardt (Eds.) (1978), *The essential Frankfurt school reader.* Oxford: Blackwell.

Geras, N. (1983). *Marx and human nature.* London: Verso.

Gigerenzer, G. (1991). From tools to theories: A heuristic of discovery in cognitive Psychology. *Psychological Review, 98,* 254–267.

González Rey, F. (2014). Advancing further the history of Soviet psychology: Moving forward from dominant representations in Western and Soviet psychology. *History of Psychology, 17*(1), 60–78.

González Rey, F. (2017). The topic of subjectivity in psychology: Contradictions, paths and new alternatives. *Journal for the Theory of Social Behaviour, 47*(4), 502–521.

González Rey, F. (2018). Subjectivity and discourse: Complementary topics for a critical psychology. *Culture and Psychology, Online.* https://doi.org/10.1177/1354067X18754338.

González Rey, F., Mitjáns Martínez, A., & Magalhães Goulart, D. (Eds.). (2019). *Subjectivity within cultural-historical approach: Theory, methodology and research.* New York: Springer.

Harré, R. (1972). *The philosophies of science.* Oxford: Oxford University Press.

Harré, R. (1974). Blueprint for a new science. In N. Armistead (Ed.), *Reconstructing social psychology.* Harmondsworth: Pelican.

Harré, R., & Madden, E. H. (1975). *Causal powers.* Oxford: Blackwell.

Harris, B. (1990). Psychology. In M. J. Buhle, P. Buhle, & D. Georgakas (Eds.), *Encyclopedia of the American left.* New York: Garland Publishing Inc.

Hollway, W. (1989). *Subjectivity and method in psychology: Gender, meaning and science.* London: Sage.

Ingleby, D. (1970). Ideology and the human sciences: Some comments on the role of reification in psychology and psychiatry. *Human Context, 2,* 159–180.

Jacoby, R. (1983). *Social amnesia.* New York: Beacon Press.

Jacoby, R. (1986). *The repression of psychoanalysis: Otto Fenichel and the post-Freudians.* New York: Beacon Press.

Kahneman, D., Slovic, P., & Tversky, A. (1982). *Judgment under uncertainty: Heuristics and biases.* Cambridge: CUP.

Kovel, J. (2007). *The enemy of nature: The end of capitalism or the end of the world?* (2nd Rev ed.). London: Zed Books.

Lacerda, F. (2015). Critical psychology and human emancipation: Identifying catalysts for building critical social theory. In S. Tuleski (Ed.), *Liberation psychology in Brazil* (pp. 41–54). Hauppauge, New York: Nova Science Publishers.

Leonard, P. (1984). *Personality and ideology: Towards a materialist understanding of the individual.* London: Macmillan.

Lukács, G. (1919–1923). *History and class consciousness.* https://www.marxists.org/archive/lukacs/works/history/index.htm. Accessed 11 July 2018.

Marcuse, H. (1955/1974). *Eros and civilization: A philosophical inquiry into Freud.* Boston: Beacon Press.

Marx, K. (1843). *On the Jewish question.* https://www.marxists.org/archive/marx/works/1844/jewish-question/index.htm. Accessed 5 July 2020.

Marx, K. (1845). *Theses on Feuerbach.* Available at www.marxists.org/archive/marx/works/1845/theses/theses.htm. Accessed 5 July 2020.

Middleton, D., & Edwards, D. (Eds.). (1990). *Collective remembering.* London: Sage.

O'Donnell, P. (1982). Lucien Seve, Althusser and the contradictions of the PCF. *Critique, 15,* 7–29.

Painter, D., Pavón-Cuéllar, D., & Moncada, L. (Eds). (2015). Marxism and psychology II Special Issue, *Annual Review of Critical Psychology, 12*. https://discourseunit.com/annual-review/12-2015/. Accessed 11 July 2018

Palmer, A. (1987). Cognitivism and computer simulation. In A. Costall & A. Still (Eds.), *Cognitive psychology in question*. Brighton: Harvester.

Parker, I. (Eds.). (1998). *Social constructionism, discourse and realism*. London: Sage.

Parker, I. (2015). *Critical discursive psychology* (2nd ed.). Basingstoke: Palgrave Macmillan.

Parker, I., & Spears, R. (Eds.). (1996). *Psychology and society: Radical theory and practice*. London: Pluto.

Pavón Cuéllar, D. (2017). *Marxism and psychoanalysis: In or against psychology?* London and New York: Routledge.

Ratner, C. (1971). Totalitarianism and individualism in psychology. *Telos, 7,* 50–72.

Reich, W. (1929). Dialectical materialism and psychoanalysis. In L. Baxandall (Ed.) (1972), *Sex-pol essays 1929–1934*. New York: Random House.

Roudinesco, E. (1990). *Jacques Lacan and Co.: The history of psychoanalysis in France—1936–1986*. London: Free Association Books.

Shallice, T. (1984). Psychology and social control. *Cognition, 17,* 29–48.

Shotter, J. (1975). *Images of man in psychological research*. London: Methuen.

Shotter, J. (1987). Cognitive psychology, "Taylorism" and the manufacture of unemployment. In A. Costall & A. Still (Eds.), *Cognitive psychology in question*. Brighton: Harvester.

Skinner, B. F. (1948/1962). *Walden two*. Toronto: Macmillan.

Smythe, W. E. (1990). Mental representation and meaning: Arguments against the computational view. In W. J. Baker, M. E. Hyland, R. van Hezewijk, & S. Terwee (Eds.), *Recent trends in theoretical psychology* (Vol. II). New York: Springer-Verlag.

Suchting, W. (1979). Marx's "Theses on Feuerbach": A new translation and notes towards a commentary. In J. Mepham & D.-H. Ruben (Eds), *Issues in Marxist philosophy, Vol IV: Materialism*. Hassocks, Sussex: Harvester Press.

Tajfel, H., & Turner, J. C. (1986). The social identity theory of intergroup behavior. In S. Worchel & W. G. Austin (Eds.), *The social psychology of intergroup relations*. Chicago: Nelson-Hall.

Teo, T. (2005). *The critique of psychology: From Kant to postcolonial theory*. New York: Springer.

Timpanaro, S. (1976). *On materialism*. London: Verso.

Tolman, C., & Maiers, W. (Eds.). (1991). *Critical psychology: Contributions to an historical science of the subject*. Cambridge: Cambridge University Press.

Triesman, A. (1974). The radical use of official data. In N. Armistead (Ed.), *Reconstructing social psychology*. Harmondsworth: Pelican.

Turner, J. C., Hogg, M. A., Oakes, P. J., Reicher, S. D., & Wetherell, M. (1987). *Rediscovering the social group: A self-categorization theory*. Oxford: Blackwell.

Vološinov, V. N. (1973). *Marxism and the philosophy of language*. New York: Seminar Press.

Watson, J. B. (1913). Psychology as the behaviorist views it. *Psychological Review, 20,* 158–177.

Ian Parker is an Honorary Professorial Research Fellow at the University of Manchester, where he co-directs the Discourse Unit (www.discourseunit.com) and is Managing Editor of Annual Review of Critical Psychology. His latest books are Psychoanalysis, Clinic and Context: Subjectivity, History and Autobiography (2019, Routledge) and Psychology through Critical Auto-Ethnography: Academic Discipline, Professional Practice and Reflexive History (2020, Routledge).

Chapter 14
Human Health and Subjectivity: History, Development and Unfolding

Daniel Magalhães Goulart

Abstract This chapter discusses González Rey's contribution to the field of human health. Different from dominant perspectives, human health is not understood as the opposite of disease, or as an attribute, but as the quality of life processes. Firstly, González Rey's critiques of dominant approaches to human health are highlighted, especially its instrumental character focused on individual processes and social adaptation. Secondly, González Rey's works in the 1980s and 1990s are highlighted. Over this time, he developed the idea that somatic diseases represent integral disorders of individuals, challenging fragmented, and rationalist approaches. He emphasized the generative character of emotions that could cause damage to health, in an articulated way with his understanding of personality at that time. Finally, the value of González Rey's current Theory of Subjectivity for the field of human health is discussed, by articulating its main concepts in an alternative representation of human health. The Theory of Subjectivity is presented as a non-rationalist critical perspective, oriented to construct simultaneously singular complex representations of human health processes and professional actions. In this perspective, history, culture and politics are articulated without neglecting the value of the individual for social processes.

14.1 Introduction

This chapter discusses González Rey's contribution to the field of human health. Different from dominant perspectives, human health is not understood as the opposite of disease, an attribute, or even as a product, but as the quality of life processes (González Rey, 1993, 2011). From this perspective, human health is a complex qualitative process that defines the integral functioning of the organism. This complex qualitative process integrates systemically somatic, psychic, subjective and cultural dimensions, forming a unit in which they are inseparable (González Rey, 2011, 2015).

D. M. Goulart (✉)
Faculty of Education, University of Brasilia, Brasilia, Brazil
e-mail: danielgoulartbr@gmail.com

217

This definition of human health is evidently critical to the dominant approach in the field, which is sustained by the biomedical model (Costa & Goulart, 2015). Within the biomedical model, a mechanistic conception of organic functions has been cultivated, being highly influenced by positivist science and Cartesian ideas (Canguilhem, 2012; Cooper, 1967). In line with Canguilhem (2012), González Rey (2015) argues that this logic has led health practices to move away from traditional clinical approaches, which was previously centred on a deep and singular examination of the individual, in order to depend more on techniques and increasingly sophisticated diagnosis. In such a process, health professionals have become less prepared to formulate differentiated hypotheses about singular phenomena.

In this way, priority is given to the identification and cure of diseases. Everything else is secondary, including the individual who incidentally carries the disease (Goulart, 2019). However, as González Rey (2015) reminds us, the positivist notion of disease emphasizes measurable and observable classifications. It represents a set of standardized symptoms, neglecting individual, cultural and social differences that are permanently expressed in the face of similar diagnosis. This process conceals the need to develop theoretical resources to explain singular processes of any disease development.

González Rey (2011) argues that the biomedical model is also sustained by a causal, and deterministic perspective, in which the pathology is represented by an external entity that reduces the individual to the condition of a victim. However, in line with Foucault (2006, 2008), he argues that this dominant model is deeply connected to broader social dimensions:

> The biomedical model, like science, does not comprise just knowledge; it is an expression of a complex institutional framework that links its advances and ways of acting with interests of power, values and philosophical positions that define the functioning of health institutions. Thus, in the current moment of capitalism – known by some as financial, but which I prefer to call the perverse moment of corrupt, anti-democratic and authoritarian capitalism – such institutions are closely associated with the great capital of the production of medicines and technologies applied to health care practices. (González Rey, 2015, p. 10)

This current association between health institutions and capitalism is expressed by the economic power of the pharmaceutical industry, which very often defines scientific directions and medical institutions, while contributing strong financial support (Goulart, 2017). González Rey (2015) argues this does not only have a guiding role in the development of the technological-instrumental health care model but has a crucial role in the social representation and in the hegemonic values of health professionals and of the health institution.

González Rey's critical gaze at the biomedical model, however, does not neglect important beneficial achievements of modern medicine to humanity, such as the capacity to diagnose various severe illnesses at an early stage and provide different therapeutic resources, as well as the elimination of several infectious diseases. Nor does it intend to build itself in what González Rey (2015) refers to as "inefficient political discourse loaded with irreflective phraseology" of "socialist demagogic capitalism" (p. 10), which, albeit being ideologically aligned with progressive forces, is a reproducer of practices focused on the maintenance of power.

It is also important to acknowledge different theoretical, practical and institutional movements, which, historically, have proposed alternatives to the biomedical model and led to several health reforms (Breilh, 1999), as well as to psychiatric reforms (Basaglia, 1985; Tosquelles, 2001). In psychology, the topic of health and its social genesis has increasingly been addressed with the emergency of community psychology in the United States in the 1960s (Murray et al., 2004). Simultaneously, strategic psychology and the first versions of family and couple therapy have helped to criticize and to offer alternatives to the intrapsychic notion of mental disorder (Haley, 1963). However, according to González Rey (2011), far from leading to a new theoretical concept of mind, this endeavour opened space for a new dichotomy between the relational and the mental.

Also, since the Ottawa Charter for Health Promotion (1986) and the Primary Health Care Movement, social equity, housing quality and education, among other social aspects, have begun to be considered central elements for the health of the population, which historically represented a step forward in relation to the individualistic view of health promotion (Carvalho, 2005). Nevertheless, González Rey (2011) argues that, despite overcoming individualism, the acknowledgement of social aspects in the field of health has frequently led to different forms of sociological determinism, which combines the focus on macrosocial factors and the neglect of the individual development as a potential subject[1] of his/her own health processes.

In this chapter, I will explore González Rey's theoretical contribution to this discussion by presenting two major aspects. Firstly, his work in the 1980s and in the 1990s, which emphasized personality, emotions and way of life. Finally, I present the heuristic value of Theory of Subjectivity from a cultural-historical to signify human health.

14.2   Personality, Emotions and Way of Life: González Rey's Work in the 1980s and 1990s

In González Rey's works in the 1980s and 1990s, the concepts of personality, emotions and way of life were especially emphasized to develop a different understanding of human health. In the first period of his work (1973–1997), which is named by Mitjáns Martínez (2020) in this book as *the moment of personality*, González Rey moved into a new conception of personality and theoretically developed its expression in different areas of psychology, with an emphasis on health and education.

---

[1]The concept of subject from the las moment of González Rey's work will be presented and discussed in the last topic of this chapter. This concept was introduced in 1989 (González Rey & Mitjáns Martínez, 1989) as a theoretical way to overcome a determinist understanding of personality. Human action is not seen as a result of personality, but as a result of the individual who is immersed in the experience. From this perspective, human action is not configured a priori as a result of a psychological structure.

During the *moment of personality* (Mitjáns Martínez, 2020), González Rey led several research projects in the field of human health, especially working with individuals diagnosed with hypertension, cancer, as well as individuals who had experienced myocardial infarction (González Rey, 1988, 1991). He argued that the analysis of the role of personality in somatic diseases implies considering multiple simultaneous aspects that participate in the pathological process, as well as the articulation between personality, society and the active role of the individual as the subject of his/her activity.

Personality is not understood as a stable intrapsychic structure that defines directly the behaviour of an individual. Therefore, González Rey's conception of personality is not articulated with traditional concepts such as traces and factors. In the mid-nineties, he explained:

> Personality is the systemic, living and relatively stable organization of the different psychological formations, their systems and functional integrations of their contents that actively participate in the regulatory and self-regulatory functions of behaviour, being the subject who exercises these functions. (González Rey, 1993, p. 63)

Personality is crucial for human health, according to González Rey (1993) because it facilitates or hinders individual functions that are part of decisions taken in the face of every life situation. In this way, personality participates in the construction of alternative strategies to daily challenges, and may also be part of harmful habits and relationships. Nevertheless, personality never replaces the potentially active role of the individual as a subject. In his view, on the one hand, the individual synthesizes the historicity of his/her personality and the social moment in which it expresses. On the other hand, the individual is active in changing the course of his/her personality, and therefore, his/her system of actions and relationships. That is why González Rey consistently defended that the singular moment of an individual, with its projects, difficulties, tensions and resources, is crucial to be interpreted and should be the basis of any therapeutic process (González Rey, 1993, 2007, 2011).

The relationship between personality and somatic diseases, due to its complexity, should be explained by a dynamic principle, leading to partial and procedural understanding that is permanently in development, something that was partially advanced by humanist psychology (Jourard & Landsman, 1987). In different texts, González Rey (1991, 1993; González Rey & Mitjáns Martínez, 1989) developed the idea that somatic and physical diseases represent complex processes configured by individuals, not fragmented disfunctions. In fact, the disease is not the symptom, but the systemic alteration of the organism that is expressed in the symptom (González Rey, 1993). "A disease never responds to an 'ultimate cause'" (González Rey, 2011, p. 28).

From this perspective, it is indisputable that any somatic health problem affects mental health, and vice versa. They are both moments of a broader system of the individual who becomes ill (González Rey, 1993). In this sense, González Rey shares Lazarus and Folkman's (1994) idea that the term psychosomatic used to address specific diseases is not pertinent, as all disorders and diseases are psychosomatic (González Rey, 1993). For him, there is no linearity between mental processes and somatic symptoms. The mental affects the somatic by the multiplicity of mechanisms, formations and functional manifestations that may generate insecurity, distress, anxiety and other forms of psychological expressions which, after reaching a certain stability at the personality level, affect the somatic functioning of the organism in different ways (González Rey, 1993).

This is related to González Rey's (1993) conception of distress at that time that is, an emotional state that defines the chronic character of emotions that deregulate certain somatic systems. The vulnerability to these states of tension that affect somatic health is articulated to complex personality mechanisms and systems that in some cases, optimize the individual's ability to deal with them and, in others, facilitate the development of distress (González Rey, 1993).

This theoretical perspective is quite different from the cognitive psychology approach to the notion of stress in relation to different types of disease and health problems (Meichenbaum, 1977; Lazarus & Folkman, 1994). Despite advancing in the relational understanding of the genesis of stress and how lived experiences affect an individual's emotions, cognitive psychology kept sustaining strongly rationalist positions, which are based on the "subject-object" scheme, in such a way that external influences may or may not be stressful in themselves (González Rey, 2015). This psychology has failed to advance in explaining the emotions generative character that may be harmful or beneficial to human health (González Rey, 2003).

González Rey (1988, 1991) emphasized the importance of emotions in the integration between mental and somatic health. For him, emotions are expressed both in the intrapsychic and in the interactive dimension, which does not replace its biological character, but integrates it in another level. Emotions are not seen as epiphenomena of other psychic or social processes. They have a generative character that is crucial either to the development of health or to its deterioration.

Different research projects on human health in the 1980s and 1990s led González Rey to summarize general psychological mechanisms that characterize a "non-healthy personality"[2]:

(a) extreme rigidity;
(b) absence of a future temporal perspective, with a predominance of the past as a reference in the individual's current manifestations;
(c) inability to reconceptualize or reassess the situations that generate emotional states;
(d) extremely low level of self-determination and self-regulation of behaviour (González Rey, 1993, p. 11).

For him, the human capacity to face life in a healthy way is closely articulated with the individual's wealth of interests, ability for self-determination, flexibility to generate suitable alternatives to tense and contradictory situations, as well as a wealth of goals and plans, on which one can be supported to face present and immediate demands (González Rey & Mitjáns Martínez, 1989).

---

[2]In different texts, González Rey use the term "non-healthy personality" and even "neurotic personality" to refer to stable psychologic formations and functions that are articulated to dominant states of distress.

Importantly, this individual processes also integrate the social in a complex way, which is another dimension frequently hidden in hegemonic perspectives on human health. In this sense, an important sociological category that González Rey introduced to address this social dimension is the concept of way of life. In a first moment, his definition for this concept was "the way of organizing life and spending time on people's various life goals" (González Rey & Mitjáns Martínez, 1989, p. 256).

The way of life expresses the central motivation of groups and socially situated individuals in systems of concrete activities. This concept addresses important aspects of social life such as the organization of time, consumption patterns, the way of eating, the types of activities in which individuals engage in daily life and how this involvement happens (González Rey, 1993). The way of life integrates naturalized actions, habits and relationship modes on which the individual loses his/her critical capacity and starts to consider them "normal". These processes often lead to the elimination of one's critical capacity and the ability to reflect on his/her distress in relation to them, which significantly reduces the possibilities of change.

González Rey described this alienated characteristic as "passive orientation" (González Rey, 1993), through which the individual adapts himself/herself to what is imposed by the circumstances. The individual does not get authentically involved with the activities and the relationship systems in which he/she participates. "In general, these are individuals guided by a deep external determinism, they live to achieve the valuation of others, or to assert themselves in the values of others, without developing their own spaces" (González Rey, 1993, p. 22).

In this sense, research and practice in the field of human health should contribute to make these processes intelligible, as well as to generate strategies geared towards development instead of "pulling back to normal", precisely because the normal may be disturbing. Communicative processes may support the individual to get healthier and more active, expressing a greater tendency to get involved in the different relationships and activities in which the individual participates (González Rey, 1993).

Throughout González Rey's work in the 1980s and the 1990s, human health was conceived of as a complex, multidimensional, contradictory and active process. He emphasized multiple ways of producing health, which detached him from any standardized and universal approach. Still, the development of his Theory of Subjectivity allowed greater capacity of explaining complex health processes, along with the development of more specific tools for research and professional actions.

14.3   Theory of Subjectivity and Human Health

According to Mitjáns Martínez (2020) in 1997, González Rey advanced his theorization, inaugurating what she entitles *The Moment of Theory of Subjectivity and Qualitative Epistemology*, which he developed until his passing in 2019. Mitjáns Martínez explains that this second moment represents both a continuity and a rupture with the first one. It is defined by the transit of his central theoretical interest from personality to subjectivity, which implied the definition of a new ontology of human processes in the conditions of culture, as well as a more consistent articulation between theory, epistemology and methodology.

González Rey's (1997) book *Qualitative Epistemology and Subjectivity* was the cornerstone of this second moment (Mitjáns Martínez, 2020) and presented a set of articulated concepts that have been developed throughout his work until that moment (Goulart et al., 2020). The main concepts of this proposal are: (individual and social) subjectivity, subjective sense, subjective configuration and subject. From this theoretical perspective, different research studies have been sustained by this theoretical approach in the field of human health, such as Arrais (2005), Mori (2009), Costa (2016), Silva (2016) and Goulart (2019).

In González Rey's words:

> Subjectivity as an ontological domain specifies a new kind of process, that is qualitatively different from all the processes involved in its genesis. As such, subjectivity is ontologically defined by the integration of emotions and symbolical processes, forming new qualitative units: subjective senses. Such subjective senses are "snapshots" of symbolic emotional flashes that unfold in a chaotic movement, from which subjective configurations emerge as a self-regulative and self-generative organization of subjective senses. (González Rey, 2019, p. 28)

This is different from González Rey's initial concept of personality, which was presented in the previous topic, the concept of subjectivity articulates the symbolic[3] dimension with emotions in a unity that represents a new ontological definition of human phenomena. Within the Theory of Subjectivity, personality becomes understood as the complex organization of subjective configurations, whose expression is differentiated in the individual's actions in different contexts (González Rey, 2011).

Subjective senses and subjective configurations are understood as useful concepts for generating intelligibility on health processes that are not explicit neither in the individual's speech, nor in his/her actions routine (González Rey, 2011). They allow the representation of health processes not as elements or fragmented entities, but as a permanent contradictory and open system of processes (subjective senses) and organizations (subjective configurations): Health and disease are understood as complex systems in development, as configurations of a set of different processes that, at a particular moment, facilitate or prevent the individual from generating healthy alternatives in the face of lived experiences. Subjective processes and configurations are an active moment in the broader configuration of the disease, which includes many other subjective processes (González Rey, 2011, p. 28). This conceptual proposal helped him to redefine distress as an essentially subjective process, which is not conscious, nor controlled by rational intentions. It is not an external nor an internal phenomenon, but a complex and multi-determined process that includes both moments in its subjective definition (González Rey, 2011).

As González Rey (2015) argues, subjective senses and configurations are a production of the individual and social groups that need to be interpretatively constructed

---

[3]"The symbolic refers to all those processes that replace, transform, synthesize, systems of objective realities in human realities that are only intelligible in culture" (Mitjáns Martínez & González Rey, 2017, p. 55).

within a set of vastly different expression of the individual or a social group that we are studying. Their consequences are not immediate since it cannot be deducted from the present moment of the lived experience. He illustrated this theoretical argument:

> For example, a cancer patient who refuses to undergo radiotherapy as a complementary procedure to the mastectomy performed on her, cannot be explained by a universal meaning, such as, for example, the so-called "lack of adherence to treatment" or "denial of the experienced situation"; a case like this should always be analyzed in a singular way, as this behavior can be an indicator of multiple and diverse subjective senses. (González Rey, 2015, p. 24)

Moreover, from this theoretical perspective, mental disorder is not conceived of as an individual pathology (González Rey, 2007), but as the "emergence of a type of subjective configuration that prevents the individual from producing alternative subjective senses that could allow him/her new options for life before the rituals perpetuated by this configuration" (González Rey, 2011, pp. 21–22). Importantly, this does not imply reducing all dimensions of such a complex phenomenon to subjectivity, but emphasizing the subjective dimension embedded while living through the process (Goulart & González Rey, 2016; Goulart, 2019).

The symbolic-emotional unity, represented by the concept of subjective sense, incorporates the understanding that social and individual instances can be articulated as dimensions that share a subjective character, in a contradictory way, without one being engulfed by the other (González Rey & Mitjáns Martínez, 2017a). Individual and social subjectivity emerge as two interrelated levels in their subjective configurations. Whereas individual subjectivity refers to the individual's subjective production, which may incorporate, contradict and confront the social spaces of subjectivation that it integrates (González Rey, 2003), social subjectivity is "the complex network of social subjective configurations within which all social functioning takes place" (González Rey, 2015, p. 13).

From González Rey's point of view, the social is not external to the individual, nor can it become a common reference for everyone in a specific context. The social is dynamic and alive in relationships, actions events and in different subjective configurations that are organized in every particular moment of a social reality (González Rey, 2016). An example of social subjective production is the biomedical model, which is so widespread in various current social spaces (Goulart, 2019). The biomedical model is not limited only to the field of practice of isolated individuals, but exerts pressure on practices in various social spaces, referring to epistemologies and techniques that in turn, are deeply rooted in the integrity of social organization.

The development of Theory of Subjectivity led González Rey (2011) to redefine the concept of way of life as a social subjective production related to actions, relations and preferences that define how we live in society. These actions, relations and preferences are not merely dictated by habits and social norms but are understood as multiple subjective configurations articulate to systems of behaviours, which lead us to look beyond what the appearances indicate. According to him, dominant discourses and social representations highly contribute to the usual concealment of the way of life (González Rey, 2011).

González Rey (2011, 2016) argued that no lived experience has a universal psychological significance due to its objective character. Subjective senses and configurations emerge as side effects of a specific life situation. They are defined not by the situation, but by what individuals and social groups produce in the process of living that situation. Topics like health, disease, gender, race and so forth, which constitute our cultural universe as human beings, emerge not as a mimetic reproduction of dominant discourses, but as differentiated subjective productions that are characterized by the tension between the social and the individual.

In this way, González Rey generates a theoretical alternative both to individualistic approaches to human health and to perspectives that reify the discursive or the interactive dimension, such as the most radical viewpoints of social constructionism (Gergen, 1994). Subjectivity is not a consequence of any external condition, whether a discursive or concrete reality, nor does it represent the so-called internalization of social productions, but is understood as a generative system (González Rey, 2016).

The subjective configuration of any mental disorder, for instance, as any other subjective configuration, involves reciprocal individual and social dimensions. In this regard, "unlike the concept of pathology, the concept of subjective configuration allows us to see the suffering as part of a living and differentiated process, which represents an in-process system, not a condition of the individual" (González Rey, 2011, p. 105). That is why the study of subjectivity not only offers a different theoretical representation of human health processes, but also support different forms of diagnostics and practice geared towards the overcoming of current limitations. Mental disorders or any subjective configuration articulated to human health problems are liable to be transformed through dialogical relations that favour the emergence of the agent or the subject of the process.

González Rey and Mitjáns Martínez (2017a) explain the concepts of agents and subjects to signify individuals or social groups with capacity to position themselves, generating subjective processes that are beyond their control and consciousness. They explain:

> The agent, unlike the subject, would be the individual– or social group– situated in the becoming of events in the current field of his/her experiences; an individual or group that makes daily decisions, thinks, likes or dislikes what happens to him/her, which in fact gives him/her a participation in this process. (González Rey & Mitjáns Martínez, 2017a, p. 73)

According to this definition, the emergence of an agent represents a moment of individual or social differentiation within a normative context, which represents a way of positioning that may open different life pathways. Still, being an agent in a specific situation does not imply alternative avenues of subjectivation to a dominant individual or social subjectivity, although this process may be a step towards it. On the other hand, the concept of subject represents the one that opens a proper path of subjectivation, which overcomes the normative social space within which an individual's experiences happen, exerting creative options in the course of them, which may or may not be expressed in the action (González Rey & Mitjáns Martínez, 2017a, p. 73).

González Rey and Mitjáns Martínez (2017a) argue that the emergence of the subject does not happen as frequently as the emergence of the agent. This does not imply the idea of rational control over the world, but the capacity for option, rupture and generative action, the consequences of which are always beyond any conscious intention of its protagonists. The consideration of the aforementioned concepts for studying and generating different forms of practice in the field of human health does not represent only a theoretical, epistemological and methodological perspective but also an ethical-political standpoint to overcome the objectification of the other in any treatment or institutional procedure. This leads us to consider that diagnostics or any treatment should never be situated outside the individual who lives these processes. As González Rey argues:

> Choosing a treatment is not only a position towards a symptom or a future possibility in relation to the evolution of a disease, but also represents a philosophy of life and death, a position towards ourselves as human beings, an expression of our identity in the face of a new situation that will have definitive implications for our lives, among which, death is not necessarily the worst for many of the people who face this challenge. The identification of a path as "the true" and "the best" represents the lack of knowledge of human subjectivity. (González Rey, 2015, pp. 24–25)

This perspective is critical not because of its declarative discourse but due to its consequences, permanent respect to the singularity of the other and its subversive character to dominant and institutionalized processes (González Rey, 2011). Research and professional actions sustained by this proposal are oriented by an ethics of the subject (González Rey, 2007, 2011), "instead of the individual being framed by the formalization of a reified therapeutic relationship, it is the therapeutic relationship that should be guided by the possibilities of emergence of the subject" (Goulart, 2019, p. 102).

Sustaining an ethics of the subject both in research and practice demands working with social conditions and education[4] of the population, so that their processes of subjective development[5] can be fostered. Opposite to the submission and passivity frequently stimulated by institutional processes, this approach emphasizes the capacity of individuals to defend their criteria, ideas and life projects, as well as to participate in processes of change for which they are central, not obstacles. The emergence of individual and social subjects is a central objective of this proposal for health promotion. They can generate and assume new life alternatives in view

---

[4]From this theoretical perspective, education represents a dialogical process geared towards the creation of new life possibilities that favour new processes of development (Mitjáns Martínez & González Rey, 2017).

[5]Subjective development expresses a motivated process that is emancipated from biological needs and adaption, representing the creative capacity of human beings, which is inseparable from the cultural dimension in which we live. It results from the articulation of different subjective configurations in multiple social spaces from where human actions emerge (González Rey & Mijtáns Martínez, 2017b). "One subjective configuration is a driving force of subjective development when it includes the development of new subjective resources that allow the individual to make relevant changes in the course of a performance, relations or other significant lived experiences leading to changes that define new subjective resources" (González Rey et al., 2017, p. 318).

of the objective individual and social conditions that define the objective limits of human actions. "These limits will always be susceptible to alternative subjective productions" (González Rey, 2011, p. 45).

14.4 Final Remarks

This chapter presented and discussed González Rey's contribution to the field of human health. Although addressing different moments of his legacy, along with different concepts and ideas, his whole body of work represents a valuable proposal for advancing a representation of human health as a culturally and historically organized process affected by (1) the subjective production of individuals and social groups in a certain moment of life, (2) the action of individuals, social groups and institutions, (3) current interactive situations, (4) bio-somatic processes, as well as (5) social and natural ecology in which one lives. These processes are permanently articulated, constituting a configurational definition of human health.

Human health has been thought of as inseparable from other vital processes for several decades. However, González Rey's most substantial contribution to this discussion lies in the ontological definition, and consequently in the study and work, of a symbolic-emotional system, that is subjectivity, which is present in the most diverse human areas, including human health. This ontological definition constitutes the basis for a new domain of research and practice, as well as a new articulation between health, education and human development.

From his theoretical viewpoint, so-called "symptoms" are inseparable from a living life network, which integrates actual contexts and the singular histories of individuals, social groups, institutions and cultures. This living life network emerges not as a reflection of external conditions, but as subjective senses related to specific experience, which are articulated to subjective configurations in development of an individual or a social groups' life, including the configurations of the body in its different expressions (González Rey, 2011).

This theoretical perspective sustains a new approach to therapeutic processes, which articulates treatment of health problems with the more general processes of development and with people's way of life. In this sense, the use of time, the activities developed by individuals, the quality of their relationship systems, as well as the development of new processes of socialization become central aspects for any therapeutic work (González Rey, 2015).

No therapeutic process is understood as conservative or progressive per se. It represents an option for the development of individuals and social groups when it defends an ethics of the subject by recognizing the generative capacity of subjectivity as an essential process of change (González Rey, 2011). This implies moving away from the manipulation of the other as a passive patient based on the therapist's knowledge. According to González Rey: "without the emergence of the other as the subject of the therapeutic process itself, there is no therapeutic change" (González Rey, 2011, p. 22).

As González Rey used to affirm in relation to Vygotsky's legacy (González Rey, 2009), González Rey's work is not only valuable for the ideas, concepts and study projects that he fully elaborated to advance a different representation of human health, but also for the theoretical paths that are still opened to be reflected and developed from his inaugural perspective. Among these open paths to be further developed are the complex articulation between subjectivity and body, corporeality, discursive realities, as well as endocrine and nervous systems. Another fruitful possibility of theoretical advance is the way that new forms of virtual communication and work unfold in subjective productions related to different health aspects.

After more than forty years of research and theoretical development, so many other topics emerge to be studied based on current challenges and new realities. The novelty of González Rey's proposal lies on its capacity to integrate social, cultural, historical and current processes in the living system of subjectivity in the most diverse spheres and problems of human life. As he defended throughout his work:

> Social commitment is always a living and critical process, in which the best contributions do not appear because of the protagonists' intentionality, but because of their ability to generate options that make sense in the lives of others, contributing to the generation of new social subjects and new alternatives in the face of the wear and tear of the dominant ones. (González Rey, 2011, p. 133)

References

Arrais, A. (2005). *A configuração subjetiva da depressão pós-parto: para além da padronização patologizante* [The subjective configuration of postpartum depression: Beyond pathologizing standardization]. PhD Thesis, University of Brasilia.

Basaglia, F. (1985). As instituições da violência [Institutions of violence]. In F. Basaglia (Ed.), *A Instituição Negada: relato de um hospital psiquiátrico* [The denied institution: Report of a psychiatric hospital] (3rd ed., H. Jahn, Trad., pp. 34–72). Rio de Janeiro: Edicoes Graal.

Breilh, J. (1999). *Saúde na sociedade: guia pedagógico sobre um novo enfoque do método epidemiológico* [Health in society: Pedagogical guide on a new approach to the epidemiological method]. Rio de Janeiro: Cortez.

Canguilhem, G. (2012). *Writings on medicine*. New York: Fordham University Press.

Carvalho, S. R. (2005). *Saúde coletiva e promoção da saúde: sujeito e mudança* [Collective health and health promotion: Subject and change]. São Paulo: Hucitec.

Cooper, D. (1967). *Psychiatry and anti-psychiatry*. London: Tavistock Publications Limited.

Costa, J. M. (2016). *Subjetividade, educação física e saúde mental: desdobramentos educativos em face á emergência dos sujeitos nos Centros de Atenção Psicossocial - CAPS* [Subjectivity, physical education and mental health: Educational developments in the emergence of the subjects in the Centers of Psychosocial Attention - CAPS]. Ph.D. Thesis, University of Brasília, Brazil.

Costa, J. M., & Goulart, D. M. (2015). A saúde humana como produção subjetiva: aproximando clínica e cultura [Human health as subjective production: Bringing clinics and culture together]. *Psicologia & Sociedade, 27*, 240–242.

Foucault, M. (2006). *History of madness*. London and New York: Routledge.

Foucault, M. (2008). *The birth of biopolitics: Lectures at the Collège de France, 1978–1979*. UK: Palgrave Macmillan.

Gergen, K. (1994). *Realities and relationship*. Cambridge: Cambridge University Press.

González Rey, F. (1988). La psicología: reflexiones sobre su lugar en el campo de la salud [Psychology: reflections on its place in the field of health]. *Revista Cubana de Psicología, 5*(3), 55–60.

González Rey, F. (1991a). Personalidad y salud humana [Personality and human health]. *Revista Cubana de Psicología, 7*(2), 75–82.

González Rey, F. (1991b). *Problemas epistemológicos de la Psicología* [Epistemological problems of Psychology]. México: Colefio de Ciencias y Humanidades/Plantel Sur/Unam.

González Rey, F. (1993). *Personalidad, salud y modo de vida* [Personality, health and way of life]. Mexico: UNAM Iztacala.

González Rey, F. (1997). *Epistemología Cualitativa y Subjetividad* [Qualitative epistemology and subjectivity]. Sao Paulo: Educ.

González Rey, F. L. (2003). *Sujeito e subjetividade: uma aproximação histórico-cultural* [Subject and subjectivity: A cultural-historical approach]. São Paulo: Pioneira Thomson Learning.

González Rey, F. (2007). *Psicoterapia, subjetividade e pós-modernidade: uma aproximação histórico-cultural* [Psychotherapy, subjectivity and post modernity: A cultural-historical approach]. Sao Paulo: Pioneira Thomson Learning.

González Rey, F. (2009). Historical relevance of Vygotsky's work: Its significance for a new approach to the problem of subjectivity in psychology. *Outlines: Critical Practice Studies, 11*, 59–73.

González Rey, F. (2011). *Subjetividade e saúde: superando a clínica da patologia* [Subjectivity and health: Overcoming the clinic of pathology]. Sao Paulo: Cortez.

González Rey, F. (2015). A saúde na trama complexa da cultura, das instituições e da subjetividade [Health in the complex web of culture, institutions and subjectivity]. In F. González Rey & J. Bizerril (Eds.), *Saúde, cultura e subjetividade: uma referencia interdisciplinary* [Health, culture and subjectivity: An interdisciplinary reference] (pp. 9–34). Brasília: UniCEUB.

González Rey, F. (2016). Advancing on the topics of the social and subjectivity from a cultural-historical approach: Moments, paths and contradictions. *Journal of the Theoretical and Philosophical Psychology, 36*, 175–189. https://doi.org/10.1017/CCOL0521831040.

González Rey, F. (2019). Subjectivity as a new theoretical, epistemological, and methodological pathway within cultural-historical psychology. In F. L. González Rey, A. Mitjáns Martínez, & D. Goulart (Eds.), *Subjectivity within cultural-historical approach: Theory, methodology and research* (pp. 21–36). Singapore: Springer.

González Rey, F., & Mitjáns Martinez, A. (1989). *La personalidad: su educación y desarrollo*. Habana: Editorial Pueblo y Educación.

González Rey, F., & Mitjáns Martínez, A. (2017a). *Subjetividade: epistemologia, teoria e método* [Subjectivity: Epistemology, theory and method]. Campinas: Alínea.

González Rey, F., & Mitjáns Martínez, A. (2017b). El desarrollo de la subjetividade: una alternativa frente a las teorias del desarrollo psíquico [The development of subjectivity: An alternative to the theories of psychic development]. *Papeles de Trabajo sobre Cultura, Educación y Desarrollo Humano, 12*(2), 3–20.

González Rey, F., Mitjans Martinez, A., Rossato, M., & Goulart, D. M. (2017). The relevance of subjective configurations for discussing human development. In M. Fleer, F. González Rey, & N. Veresov (Eds.), *Perezhivanie, emotions and subjectivity: Advancing Vygotsky's legacy* (pp. 217–243). Singapore: Springer.

Goulart, D. M. (2017). The psychiatrization of human practices worldwide: Discussing new chains and cages. *Pedagogy, Culture & Society, 25*(1), 151–156. https://doi.org/10.1080/14681366.2016.1160673.

Goulart, D. M. (2019). *Subjectivity and critical mental health: Lessons from Brazil*. London: Routledge.

Goulart, D. M., & González Rey, F. (2016). Mental health care and educational actions: From institutional exclusion to subjective development. *European Journal of Psychotherapy & Counselling, 18*(4), 367–383. https://doi.org/10.1080/13642537.2016.1260617.

Goulart, D., Mitjáns-Martínez, A., & Esteban-Guitart, M. (2020). The trajectory and work of Fernando González Rey: Paths to his theory of subjectivity. *Studies in Psychology, 41*(1), 9–30.

Haley, J. (1963). Marriage therapy. *Archives of General Psychiatry, 8,* 213–234.

Jourard, S., & Landsman, T. (1987). *La personalidad saludable* [The healthy personality]. Mexico: Trillas.

Lazarus, R., & Folkman, S. (1994). *Stress, appraisal, and coping.* New York: Springer.

Meichenbaum, D. (1977). *Cognitive-behaviour modification: An integrative approach.* New York: Plenum.

Mitjáns Martínez, A. (2020). Fernando González Rey's work: Its genesis and development. In D. M. Goulart, A. Mitjáns Martínez, & M. Adams (Eds.), *Theory of subjectivity within a cultural-historical perspective: González Rey's legacy.* Singapore: Springer.

Mitjáns Martínez, A., & González Rey, F. (2017). *Psicologia, educação e aprendizagem escolar: avançando na contribuição da leitura cutural-histórica* [Psychology, education and school learning: Advancing the contribution of cultural-historical Reading]. São Paulo: Cortez.

Mori, V. D. (2009). *Estudio de las configuraciones subjetivas en pacientes con cancer e hipertensión: una aproximación a la salud en una perspectiva histórico-cultural* [Study of subjective configurations in patients with cancer and hypertension: an approach to health from a historical-cultural perspective]. Ph.D. Thesis, Universidad de San Carlos de Guatemala.

Murray, M., Nelson, G., Poland, B., Maticka-Tindale, E., & Ferris, L. (2004). Assumptions and values of community health psychology. *Journal of Health Psychology, 9*(2), 323–333.

Silva, G. F. (2016). *Cuidados Paliativos e subjetividade: ações educativas sobre a vida e o morrer* [Palliative Care and subjectivity: educational actions on life and dying]. Ph.D. Thesis, University of Brasília, Brazil.

Tosquelles, F. (2001). *Las enseñanzas de la locura* [The teachings of madness]. Madrid: Alianza.

Daniel Magalhães Goulart is an assistant professor at the Department of Theory and Foundations of the Faculty of Education of the University of Brasilia. He is also a Collaborating Professor at the Masters in Psychology of the University Center of Brasilia. He graduated as a psychologist from the University of São Paulo and completed his Ph.D. at the Faculty of Education of the University of Brasilia (CAPES), Brazil. He is the current coordinator of the Reading and Research Group "Subjectivity: Theory, Epistemology and Methodology". His latest books are: (1) Subjectivity within a cultural-historical approach: theory, methodology and research (Ed., Springer, 2019), (2) Subjectivity and critical mental health: lessons from Brazil (Routledge, 2019), and (3) Saúde mental, desenvolvimento e subjetividade: da patologização à ética do sujeito [Mental health, development and subjectivity: from pathologization to the ethics of the subject] (Cortez, 2019).

Chapter 15
Subjectivity and Psychotherapy: Contributions of Fernando González Rey

Juan Balbi

Abstract This chapter discusses the contributions of Fernando González Rey to the advancements of the study of subjectivity and its consequences in psychotherapy. From an approach of qualitative epistemology, subjectivity must receive a specific ontological status, as a symbolic-emotional production. The category of "subjective sense," proposed by González Rey, consequently becomes a new psychological unit which allows a completely new perspective in the understanding of personal identity. González Rey proposes a clinical psychology in which the therapeutic relationship is oriented, fundamentally, to generate options in the production of new personal senses in the patient, to replace those subjective senses that were at the base of the emotional disorder. Concepts such as subjective sense, subjective configuration, mental health, psychotherapy and the role of the psychotherapist are discussed throughout the chapter.

15.1 Introduction

It is rare to find among the vast corpus of psychological theory an author who brings together the creative capacity and epistemological rigor of Fernando González Rey. In its first one hundred years of history, psychology had tried to understand its object of study, the human mind, borrowing epistemological paradigms from older sciences, such as physics and biology. Noting that these models, developed for the study of such diverse phenomena, were not fit to access the understanding of subjectivity, González Rey innovated in the elaboration of a specific epistemology, from which he proposed an exhaustive revision of the system of conceptual categories of our field.

From a cultural-historical perspective and based on scientific paradigms that are defined as complex, nonlinear, and non-deterministic (Mitjáns Martínez, 2005), González Rey carried out a prolific intellectual work, whose main objective was

J. Balbi (✉)
Cetepo (Post-Rationalist Center of Psychotherapy), Rome, Italy
e-mail: juanjbalbi@gmail.com

© The Author(s), under exclusive license to Springer Nature Singapore Pte Ltd. 2021
D. M. Goulart et al. (eds.), *Theory of Subjectivity from a Cultural-Historical Standpoint*,
Perspectives in Cultural-Historical Research 9,
https://doi.org/10.1007/978-981-16-1417-0_15

to rethink the nature of subjectivity, assigning constructs that gave it consistency and recognized its unique nature. González Rey's theory of subjectivity is a critical theoretical framework in relation to dominant psychology, which opens a new avenue to explain individual and social human relations as inseparable from broader social dynamics. From this point of view, subjectivity has a culturally, socially, and historically localized genesis. However, it is a generative system, rather than an epiphenomenon of other dimensions (Goulart, 2019). According to González Rey, subjectivity is not defined by any of its specific attributes (internal, private, conscious, unconscious), which are only spaces of its development, but by its ontological specificity. "Subjectivity is a symbolic-emotional production," he stated. Differentiating himself from both positivism and certain versions of phenomenology he wrote (2009):

> In our work we have developed the theoretical construction of a model of human subjectivity in parallel with a differentiated epistemological position that I have called qualitative epistemology (González Rey, 1997), which has among its founding principles the constructive-interpretative character of knowledge; a principle that contradicts the emphasis on description and induction that both positivism and phenomenology, used in social sciences on behalf of Husserl, defend through different constructions and principles. (p. 94)

The epistemological and theoretical premises of González Rey's psychotherapeutic perspective converge with those of the constructivist and post-rationalist therapeutic models (Balbi, 2008). With the fundamental objective of contributing to the advancement of a psychotherapeutic vision oriented to the study of subjectivity, González Rey dealt in particular with developing the category of "subjective sense": "A psychological unit characterized by the relationship between the symbolic and the emotional, a unit in which one evokes the other reciprocally, without becoming its cause" (2009, p. 36). Subjective senses are not a direct result of the impact of experiences in an objective manner, but are rather a production on the side effects of experience. This production is only possible through the "subjective configuration" of the person and the social space in which the production occurs.

15.2   Comparison with Different Conceptions of Subjectivity

González Rey (1999, 2004, 2009, 2011) conducted a profound analysis of the implications and limitations of the different conceptions of subjectivity (or their absence) elaborated by the psychological models that are at the base of various psychotherapeutic methodologies developed throughout the twentieth century. The rigidity with which this notion has been treated is fundamentally due to the reluctance, typical of psychological models of associationist influence, to grant subjectivity a privileged ontological state. The associationist point of view leads to two possible ways that ultimately ignore the category of subjectivity: one is to grant subjectivity its own status, but to continue to approach it from the epistemological perspective developed for the study of physical or biological phenomena; the other, is simply to deny its existence (Balbi, 2004; González Rey, 2005, 2009). González Rey (2009) pointed out social constructionism as the maximum exponent of the position of denying subjectivity, being characterized, precisely, by its radical negation of the subject and by its "radical relationism" (p. 177).

Social constructionism's biggest flaw consists in completely disregarding a unique ontological category for the personal subjective system. According to this approach, the mind, even scientific knowledge, are mere discourses legitimized by consensus in social practices. Thus, social constructionism would be a new form of associationism that leads to a sociological, relational, and discursive reductionism (Balbi, 2004; González Rey, 2009). This perspective, González Rey (2009) noted, is incapable of dealing with ontological entities that do not refer to linguistic productions; therefore, it is impossible to build any bridges between the universe of language and that of personal subjectivity; in this regard González Rey (2009) wrote:

> The reification of the relational, assumed with dogmatic rigidity, does not allow these authors to consider an alternative way of understanding the organization of the human psyche as an instance differentiated from others, within the very context of social practices. (p. 180)

González Rey severely criticized the inconsistency of authors such as Kenneth Gergen and other constructionists (Gergen, 2006; Gergen & McNamee, 1985; Gergen & Davis, 1996) in their attempt to explain psychological phenomena by studying them exclusively from a relational perspective that ignores those characteristics of subject that do not manifest in communication. In this way, the social constructionists end, despite their apparent conceptual complexity, in a surprising epistemological coincidence with behaviorism and other associationist and environmentalist perspectives (Balbi, 2004; González Rey, 2009). I praise the words of González Rey (2009), when he said, critically: "Social constructionism generates a communicative community without an author. The subject does not think, nor generate, nor build; they are merely a moment of a dialogical space where all production is social" (p. 178). I agree with the view that accepting these principles, or ignoring them as if they were unimportant, could imply serious consequences for the development of theoretical psychology and related disciplines. It is worth asking: what would be the role of psychotherapy in a world where we have accepted the absence of any autonomous personal system? (Balbi, 2004; González Rey, 2009).

The denial made by constructionists is based on the criticism of a discontinued definition of subjectivity, said González Rey. This attitude, said the author, limits the heuristic potential of this category when detached from the specific historical context in which it was theorized. He accused constructionist authors of classifying previous productions of knowledge as either true or false. On the contrary, conceiving them as historically and socially intelligible systems would facilitate the recovery of those broad and useful conceptualizations for the advancement of knowledge. Hence, from a deconstructive perspective, he proposed his notion of "zone of sense," as spaces of intelligibility for the advancement of science, in the context of which certain categories, such as "subjectivity," constitute historical moments of more abstract representations, which facilitate renewed options for development in the face of new concrete knowledge and different theoretical frameworks (González Rey, 1997, 2009). González Rey (2009) wrote:

> Categories represent specific moments of a way of thinking that is expressed through language and the representations that dominate a certain historical period; however, the constructions that appear associated with these categories and their possible replications represent zones of sense that guide and produce intelligibility on new aspects of a problem, or that create a new problem for science. Zones of sense are precisely the spaces of intelligibility that, for the development of a science, bring the most enduring aspects of a theory to the scientific scene. In the case of psychoanalysis, the idea of the unconscious represented a zone of sense that opened a new field of construction for human sciences in general, although the specific categories used by Freud to produce knowledge about his representation of the unconscious will represent only one of the many possible approaches to such a complex problem. (p. 27)

González Rey (2009) acknowledged Freudian psychoanalysis for having inaugurated revolutionary zones of sense for the representation of human beings, the unconscious for example, with consequences of great value for the development of human sciences. However, he criticized the reification of the unconscious as an energetic instance of repressed sexual order, since this conceptual category, typical of an ontology of physics, became an obstacle to understanding sexuality as a component of subjectivity. González Rey was especially critical of the Freudian aspiration to conform to the ideal of science embodied by positivist medicine. González Rey (2009) referred to this:

> Freud, like his predecessor Charcot, tries to legitimize his position within positivism, as is fully explained in his Treatise on Neurology for Psychologists. Freud thus joined the movement that sought to exclude the definition of subjectivity and that was led by the organicist medicine of the time. (p. 25)

I agree with González Rey that Freud's biggest mistake, which has unfortunately spread to the whole field of psychiatry and clinical psychology, was to develop his psychotherapeutic method around a vision of mental pathology, which positions the therapeutic method in an objectivist, rationalist, and associationist perspective, according to which the cure is associated with the discovery and elimination of the first causes (Balbi, 2004; González Rey, 2009). González Rey (2009) chooses another perspective, coinciding with Jung's statement that psychotherapy is a subjective production. González Rey's position implies a serious attempt to avoid the tendency of "medicalization" of psychotherapy that is conducted throughout diverse institutions, not only psychoanalytic but in general. Regarding this, González Rey (2009) wrote:

> The direct relationship that developed in some fields of clinical practice between psychotherapy and pathology, typical of a "pathologizing psycho-medical" model, created an irreconcilable division between psychotherapy and subjectivity, which originated in the field of psychiatry due to the possibility to medicate patients. In clinical psychology, this orientation developed into psychometrics, which allowed the psychological disorder to be measured, excluding it from the context in which it appeared as well as from the subject who expressed it. (p. 39)

The main criticism that González Rey (2009) had for the approach of systemic family therapy is that the founders of this model, in their eagerness to focus on the system of relationships, ignored the subjective complexity of the people who comprise it, as well as their belonging to a broader social system. Once again, the behavioral and atomized mind appears as a direct expression of an external influence. González Rey (2009) wrote:

> Systemic family psychotherapy emerges at a time of boom in the theory of homeostatic cybernetic systems and of normative, hierarchically structured social systems. Human phenomena were explained from here on as a combination of elements which behaviors are explained by their structure. The human being lives its experiences within interactive systems. Conflict begins to be analyzed fundamentally in relational terms, associated with the balance of the system in which people interact. (...) From this perspective, the individual subject will eventually be ignored. (pp. 53–54)

An objectivist position, González Rey claimed, that excludes the generating capacity of the mind. He insisted on affirming his opinion that in none of its forms of organization does society operate directly and linearly on the subjective system. The subjective senses are the result of a personal configuration that expresses an original production concerning what has been lived, in which previous experiences occurred in different contexts and moments of the subject's history are integrated. The family emerges, on the other hand, from the differentiated subjective senses that are organized in the personality (a category dear to the author) of those who compose it, as well as in the differentiated spaces of family subjectivity that are generated by the relationships between its members.

González Rey shared the views of Leslie Greenberg and Juan Pascual-Leone (1995), representatives of the dialectical constructivist model, when they describe the process of meaning construction in therapy as a dialectical synthesis between two main types of processing, conceptual and experiential, that act together to constantly generate explanations of experience. These authors identify three important moments in that process of constructing meaning during the therapeutic session: emotional arousal, symbolization, and reflection. The constructions that generate change are produced in a dialectical combination of emotion and reflection. Therefore, it is worth noting that the meaning occurs as a subjective phenomenon that integrates emotion and cognition in a dynamic process. The dynamic synthesis of Greenberg and Pascual-Leone, says González Rey, is a construct that gives a particular ontological status to the experience of meaning.

Our author also supported the critical constructivists, such as Mahoney (1991) and Guidano (1991), when they recognized the importance of hypothesis building in the construction of the therapeutic process. Both Mahoney and Guidano, he said (2009), take an ontological perspective and, unlike constructionists, differentiate hypotheses from the discursive nature of the knowledge that expresses them. That is why it seems plausible to recognize a personal identity, represented as a developing self, which is organized around a continuous process of signifying the subject's experience. He González Rey (2009) considered the concept of dynamic organization of mental disorders offered by Guidano as an interesting contribution: The concept of dynamic organization of mental disorders, presented by Guidano, is interesting in offering an alternative possibility of intelligibility regarding these disorders, differing both from traditional semiological psychopathology and from linguistic discursive reductionism, typical of radical constructivism and social constructionism (p. 68).

González Rey (2009) also valued the concept of Organization of Personal Meaning of Guidano as the opening of a heuristic field, understood as the production of notions that have converging points in the way of representing a phenomenon. In this case, for example, González Rey was particularly interested in the emphasis that Guidano placed on the complexity of an organization, which can manifest itself in various particular ways. Therefore, the etiology of pathological states would not be in its contents, but in its configuration.

González Rey had two objections to Guidano's theory, one referring to the dynamics of therapeutic change and the other of a more epistemological nature. Regarding the first, Guidano (1991) had stated that an increase in clients' comprehension of how their mental processes functioned had a direct correlation with a significant degree of emotional modulation in which new tonalities of feelings were likely to emerge (p. 109).

To which González Rey (2009) replied:

> I think that increasing the patient's understanding of the 'rules for organizing their reality' does not necessarily lead to a significant degree of emotional modulation. Cognition is a subjective process of constructive nature. This is one of the reasons why the change in psychotherapy does not represent access to an unknown reality, but the construction of a new reality. (p. 172)

15.3   Distinction Between "Meaning" and "Sense"

Regarding the coherence between Guidano's theory and its underlying epistemology, in an acute appreciation, González Rey correctly recognized a certain computational tendency in the category of "Organizations of Personal Meaning" that Guidano proposes. "When Guidano defines this category as 'proactive processing', he is confining it, semantically, to the field of the information processing metaphor, from which he tried to differentiate himself," González Rey affirms (2009, p. 170). This is how, through an unfortunate choice of terms, the creator of post-rationalist therapy was unable to fully disembarrass himself of associationist and objectivist connotations. This conceptual ambiguity can be resolved by following the direction proposed by González Rey, and in this way, facilitate the progress of the study of subjectivity as a differentiated ontology.

It is necessary to make a distinction that, although at a first glance may seem to be only of semantic order, carries important consequences of epistemological and theoretical nature. I am referring to the need to differentiate the respective scopes and implications of the notions of "meaning" and "sense" when they are used to describe the specific domain of subjective phenomena. The use of the word "meaning" belongs to a respected tradition of constructivism-based cognitive psychology which began in the middle of the past century. At that time, in a cultural context in which formal linguistics and structuralism began to conquer the human sciences, Jerome Bruner, with the publication of "Acts of Meaning" (1990) challenged the behaviorist principles and the rising computer-based cognitivism stating that "meaning" should be taken as the fundamental concept of psychology. He held that psychology should focus its efforts especially in the study of symbolic activities employed for human beings to give meaning to the world and themselves before anything else (responses to stimuli, observable behavior, bits of information and processing, etc.). Since then and until today, the word "meaning" has been kept at the center of the Constructivist movement, and its translation, "significado" has invaded the world of cognitive psychology in Spanish and Italian speaking countries. Unfortunately, despite wanting to leave behind the connotation associated with information processing, the term "meaning" continues to have a computational cognitive bias that does not include affective experiential and emotional factors.

The category of "sense" has been thoroughly studied by González Rey in his publication "The Social in Psychology and the Social Psychology: The Emergence of the Subject" (2004), and in "Vygotsky's Thought: Contradictions, Splits and Development" (2013), where he takes up a lecture of Vygotsky that has not been widely spread in the West. Vygotsky's best-known work is part of what the author calls his "second period," in which psychological functions, especially consciousness, are described as a direct internalization of the individual's activity. This theory has a clear materialist bias, at the expense of ignoring the dialectical processes of experience, and seems to be overcome in the first and third Vygotskian periods, where his efforts are oriented toward the formulation of a theory of personality (another fundamental category for advancement of psychology). The overcoming of the "objectivist turn," González Rey affirms, occurs when Vygotsky recognizes the systemic character of personality and introduces the concept of "sense." Vygotsky's success was to emphasize the manifestation of sense in meaning, as a singular phenomenon that does not obey the same laws as the latter, but always presents itself with it. Whether he was aware of it or not, says González Rey, Vygotsky introduced a key term that laid the groundwork for the birth of an ontological alternative particularly attentive to the nature of human subjectivity. González Rey, by retaking the concept, deepens and enriches it when, following Vygotsky's thinking, he judges that sense belongs to a different dimension from that of meaning; since it does not imply, like does meaning, a correspondence between the symbol and what the symbol represents, but rather an aggregate of all the psychological facts that arise in consciousness in relation to a meaning (González Rey, 2004, 2009, 2011).

After decades of using the term "meaning" interchangeably, it is necessary to start utilizing the notion of "sense" to refer to a domain of personal experience—where emotions and feelings have a decisive role—and of which meaning is only one aspect. The notion of "meaning" involves a compromise between the subjective world and the world of interactions between individuals; between the symbol and what the symbol represents inside a certain semantic community. The notion of "sense" refers to a totally different dimension, that of the ontology of subjectivity. "Sense," unlike "meaning," does not specify a domain of consensual coordination in a speaking subject's community, but defines a portion of pure experience which exists as a moment of an individual's subjective process. This portion of experience is relevant only in its correspondence with similar intentional states experienced by the person in other instances in which they have felt existentially the same. According to this point of view, "the experience of personal sense" is the result of a dialectical articulation between actual experience and the historically structured psychological world of the subject (Balbi, 2015; González Rey, 2004, 2009). The experience of personal sense not only requires a system with cognitive capabilities and self-conscious experience; the subject should additionally be able to experience the present as a temporary instance between their past and their future, and as a feasible experience in the cycle of life. All this is only possible with the emergence of abstract cognitive structures, which are typical of adolescent development. Hereafter we will use "subjective sense" and "sense of oneself" as key concepts for understanding the experience of personal identity and to refer to domains such as subjectivity, psychopathology, and psychotherapy in a clearer way (Balbi, 2015).

Analyzing Vygotsky's work, our author finds in the concept of "sense" a heuristic value for psychology and the development of an ontological definition of subjectivity (2011, p. 312). Regarding an ontological definition of subjectivity, González Rey (2009) wrote:

> The position that I defend is that subjectivity is the symbolic-emotional plot that is configured in people and in their different social spaces as a result of the multiple experiences they have had. This plot is not the direct and linear result of external experiences, but the result of the multiple collateral effects of experiences that, coming from different fields, are subjectively integrated into each space of social experience defined in terms of culture, which take subjective form through the current subjective configurations of the person, group or institution that lives that experience. The psychological categories that I have developed to account for this process are those of subjective sense and subjective configuration. (p. 36)

González Rey's introduction of the categories of subjective sense and subjective configuration reflect a representation of subjectivity that differs from that of the behavioral objectivist perspective, which maintains that objective influences determine human behavior. This perspective, says González Rey (2009), "ignores that subjective production in the face of these experiences is inseparable from its subjective sense for people" (p. 90).

González Rey proposes a definition of subjectivity as a developing system in which process and organization are integrated. "Configurations and subjective senses express the tension that characterizes subjectivity as a developing system" says González Rey (2009, p. 90). In this developing system, subjective sense, associated with action, appears as a subjectivation process of a field of action of a contextually situated subject. Subjective configurations, composed of different subjective senses and other mental processes that steadily characterize a person's diverse mental productions, constitute a permanent source of the subjective senses that appear in the course of a subject's activity. (González Rey, 2009).

Unlike Vygotsky's definition of "sense," in González Rey's (2011) reformulation, subjective senses are not associated with words, they represent the union of the symbolic and the emotional, they are not an aggregate of elements and they indicate the subjective character of any action or human expression, be it social or individual.

According to this conception, subjective senses are the basic unit of subjectivity (p. 312). González Rey (2011) defines subjective sense as "the unit of symbolic and emotional processes where the emergence of one evokes the other without becoming its cause, forming true chains with very diverse forms of expression according to the context in which the person is involved" (p. 312). Subjective senses are not identical contents, feasible to be replicated in a person's different actions, they are unique, and they emerge as an symbolic-emotional unit in a context that always results from the confluence of various subjective configurations of the personality at a specific moment of the person's life. Historical and social elements, says González Rey (2011), "appear in subjective terms in the person's subjective configurations, these being a more stable unit than subjective senses, but inseparable from the subjective sense of the person" (p. 313). That is to say, subjective senses are the result of a personal configuration concerning previous experiences that occurred in different contexts and moments of a subject's history. The different subjective senses are organized in a personal identity, represented as a self in development, which is organized by the subject around a continuous process of symbolic-emotional significance of their experience. It is only possible to analyze that production of subjective sense considering the individual's subjective configuration and the social space in which it took place (González Rey, 2009, 2011).

15.4 Implications for Clinical Psychology

González Rey proposes a clinical psychology in which the therapeutic relationship is oriented, fundamentally, to generating alternatives toward the production of new subjective senses in the patient, in order to replace those subjective senses that are at the base of emotional disorder. González Rey (2009) is categorical in his definition of psychotherapy:

> Psychotherapy is essentially understood as the subjective productions that take place in a space of dialogue, during which the therapist, supported by hypotheses about the subjective configurations of the problem, induces topics that allow them to converse around areas that may be significant, due to their subjective sense, for the person in therapy. (p. 116)

In González Rey's approach, the psychotherapist is not an objective observer, since they cannot be located outside the relationship; on the contrary, the psychotherapist is an essential part of the symbolic-emotional system produced in the therapeutic space. Another distinctive aspect of this approach is the affirmation that psychotherapy does not consist, as in the medical consultation, in a process of discovery of a certain pathological etiology, nor in solutions centered on the person of the therapist. Psychotherapy is a process of producing new systems of subjectivation. Because of this, González Rey says, "the therapist's hypotheses are not constructed with the objective of accessing the subject's 'truth', but to facilitating the emergence of alternative subjective productions to those associated with the problem for the person who demands the therapeutic space" (p. 116).

González Rey maintains that this facilitation is essential to therapeutic work, since the origin of mental disorders lies in a fixation on a specific type of subjective production; and this happens when a person loses their capacity to actively participate in the production of subjective senses associated with some area of their life, and, thus, they remain at the mercy of those subjective senses associated with mental suffering, in this regard, he maintains:

> Mental disorders represent true recursive systems of subjective senses that, in their develop-ment, become governed by a dominant moment of the configuration that encompasses them, preventing the emergence of new subjective senses. The person is trapped within the limits of a subjective configuration and their productions are dominated by the dominant subjective senses of that configuration. (…) All the subjective resources of the person revolve around the strengthening of that dominant subjective state, that ends up associated with the emergence of psychological symptoms such as depression, anxiety, aggressiveness, etc. (González Rey, 2011, pp. 313–314)

Continuing with the description of the process that leads to mental disorders, González Rey (2011) writes:

> This development is not accessible to the rational processes that support the subject's repre-sentations, nor can it be solved by understanding the causes that determined it, simply because there are no causes, but rather a developing web of symbolic-emotional produc-tions, fed by a multiplicity of elements that converge in the reproduction of the dominant subjective senses. (…) The patient's awareness does not help in that context because it orga-nizes itself within their dominant subjective configuration, becoming just another contributor to the strengthening of the condition. Because of this, a crucial challenge emerges, to redefine psychotherapy in a consequently postrationalist perspective, that does not lead to new and more sophisticated forms of cognition. (pp. 313–314)

Another distinctive aspect of our author's approach is how he conceptualizes ther-apeutic change. According to González Rey (2009), problems are not solved, but instead they cease to exist as such with the appearance of new subjective produc-tions. The dialogical therapeutic constructions that enable change are the product of a dialectical integration of affect and reflection through which a new subjective sense is produced in the patient. The therapist promotes change in the person's experience by facilitating the emergence of new subjective senses, but has no control over the form they take, nor in their future developments. The essential aspect of therapeutic change is associated with the transformation of the person: "from victim of a conflict to subject of a conflict, which represents an alternative that generates new subjective senses and a new identity in relation to the problem that affects them" (p. 117).

15.5   Final Remarks

Given the evident atomization of psychological theory, a critical analysis of the epistemological and theoretical principles of the currents that dominated the field of psychology from its foundation to the present day is necessary, in order to identify the epistemological obstacles that have prevented the development of a universally accepted theory of the human mind that serves as the basis for scientifically based psychopathology and psychotherapeutic practice. González Rey, with his intellectual production, offers us not only a valuable contribution to this essential analysis, but also the foundations for the construction of a theoretical alternative that overcomes these epistemological obstacles. Throughout González Rey's work, there is a severe criticism of the mechanistic, energetic, and environmentalist conceptions of human mental processes; conceptions which share a persistent reluctance to the study of subjectivity, which, as we have seen, our author defended as the distinguished object of study of psychology. The reluctance of these psychological currents to study subjectivity is an inevitable consequence of the incapacity of their explanatory models to fathom something as complex as the subjective system, which cannot be explained, as has been tried in vain for a century, with vicarious models of epistemological paradigms that were effective in explaining physical and biological phenomena of much lower complexity; the black box of behaviorism is the plainest example of the results of this way of thinking (Balbi, 2004). Those paradigms, which had their apogee in positivism, are based on the empiricist-rationalist tradition that is expressed in the field of psychology through associationism, an epistemological premise that is at the base of most psychological models of the twentieth century. I contend that the associationist principles are the main epistemological roadblock for scientific advancements in the study of complex phenomena of the human mind, such as subjectivity, consciousness, and personal identity (Balbi, 2004).

González Rey's most outstanding contribution has been to expose this epistemological obstacle and to propose the elaboration of a specific epistemology and methodology, which, by respecting the ontological particularity of subjectivity, becomes more adequate for its study. It is from this new epistemological foundation that González Rey offers us a different psychotherapeutic theory and practice, which, abandoning the "pathological psycho-medical model" (González Rey, 2009, p. 39), is fundamentally oriented toward generating options in the construction of new subjective senses for the consulting person. González Rey (2011) argues that "mental health is not defined by the absence of conflicts, but by the possibility of generating new processes of subjectivation during these conflicts" (p. 313). From this point of view, all human experience is conflictive, not because of its capacity in itself, but because of the subjective productions generated by a person in the course of their experience. According to González Rey (2011), mental suffering appears "due to the inability to produce new subjective senses in the face of experiences that are fixed as painful and that prevent the emergence of other subjective states different from those dominant experiences" (p. 313). Based on these considerations, González Rey proposes a model of clinical psychology that situates personal subjective sense at the center of its theoretical corpus and a psychotherapeutic method consisting of a complex dialogical process, which aims to facilitate actions and reflections that allow the person to generate new options of subjectivation, in such a way that, in the course of this process, the hegemonic subjective configuration associated with the emergence of symptoms is modified and gives rise to new subjective senses and subjective configurations.

References

Balbi, J. (2004). *La mente narrativa: hacia una concepción posracionalista de la identidad personal.* Buenos Aires: Paidós.

Balbi, J. (2008). Epistemological and theoretical foundations of constructivist cognitive therapies: Post-rationalist developments. *Dial Phil Ment Neuro Cci, 1*(1), 15–27. www.crossingdialogues. com/journal.htm.

Balbi, J. (2015). Adolescence, order through fluctuations and psychopathology. A post-rationalist conception of mental disorders and their treatment on the grounds of chaos theory. *Chaos and Complexity Letters, 9*(2), 85–105. Nova Science Publishers Inc.

Bruner, J. (1990). *The Jerusalem-Harvard lectures: Acts of meaning.* Harvard University Press.

Gergen, K. (2006). *Construir la realidad. El futuro de la psicoterapia.* Barcelona: Paidós.

Gergen, K., & Davis, K. (1996). *Therapy as social construction.* London: Sage.

Gergen, K., & McNamee, S. (1985). *The social construction of the person.* New York: Springer-Verlang.

González Rey, F. L. (1997). *Epistemología cualitativa y subjetividad.* San Pablo: EDUC.

González Rey, F. L. (1999). *La Investigación Cualitativa en Psicología. Rumbos y Desafíos.* San Pablo: EDUC.

González Rey, F. L. (2004). *O Social na Psicología e a Psicología Social. A emergência do sujeito.* Petrópolis: Vozes.

González Rey, F. L. (2005). O valor heurístico da subjetividade na investigação psicológica. In F. L. González Rey (Ed.), *Subjetividade Complexidade e Pesquisa em psicología.* Thomson: San Pablo.

González Rey, F. L. (2009). *Psicoterapia, subjetividad y posmodernidad. Una aproximación desde Vygotsky hacia una perspectiva histórica-cultural.* Buenos Aires: Noveduc.

González Rey, F. L. (2011). Sentidos subjetivos, lenguaje y sujeto: avanzando en una perspectiva posracionalista en psicoterapia. *Rivista di Psichiatria, 46*(5–6), 310–314.

González Rey, F. L. (2013). *O pensamento de Vygotsky: Contradições, desdobramentos e desenvolvimento.* São Paulo: Hucitec.

Goulart, D. M. (2019). Subjectivity and life: In memory of Fernando González Rey. *Mind, Culture, and Activity.* https://doi.org/10.1080/10749039.2019.1619775.

Greenberg, L., & Pascual-Leone, J. (1995). A dialectical constructivist approach to experiential change. In R. A. Neimeyer & M. J. Mahoney (Eds.), *Constructivism in psychotherapy* (pp. 169–191). American Psychological Association.

Guidano, V. F. (1991). *The self in process.* New York: Guilford Press.

Mahoney, M. (1991). *Human change processes: The scientific foundations of psychotherapy.* New York: Basic Books.

Mitjáns Martínez, A. (2005). A teoria da subjetividade de Gonzalez Rey: uma expressão do paradigma da complexidade. In F. L. González Rey (Ed.), *Subjetividade Complexidade e Pesquisa em Psicologia.* Thomson: São Paulo.

Juan Balbi Argentine psychotherapist, Ph.D. in Psychology from the Universidad Autónoma de Madrid. Member of the Italian and Argentine Societies of Cognitive Therapy. Since 1992, he has directed the Cetepo Institute for training and research in psychotherapy. Author of the books: La mente narrativa, Paidós, Buenos Aires (2004); and Terapia Cognitiva Posracionalista. Conversaciones con Vittorio Guidano, Biblos, Buenos Aires (1994); both subsequently published in Italian.

Chapter 16
Reflections on the Challenges of Psychotherapy and the Processes of Social Subjectivity

Valéria Deusdará Mori

Abstract This paper discusses psychotherapy from the perspective of the Theory of Subjectivity and its consequences as a professional practice and its implication to produce knowledge in psychology. The Theory of Subjectivity is centered on understanding the procedural configuration of human phenomena and not on their pathologizing as an entity in the abstract or by criteria external to people. The practice from the perspective defended here is a permanent space of reflection that enables the constructive-interpretative analysis of different phenomena. Construction and interpretation enable the production of knowledge and guide the actions of professional practice in a process in which research and practice mutually constitute each other. In this work, social subjectivity will be discussed as an important process for psychotherapy, as changes in individual subjectivity can constitute changes in social subjectivity. The social subjectivity category is essential in this perspective for understanding the organization of the different configurations that take shape in institutions and groups from the dialogical processes that are organized. The change in psychotherapy cannot be centered only on changing people individually, but also on changing the social subjectivity of the spaces in which people belong to.

16.1 Introduction

Psychotherapy, as a field of research and practice in psychology, has historically been called upon to discuss the way in which human processes are represented and understood in this area. Certainly, there is not only one single understanding of the configuration of human processes in Psychology and this leads to different theoretical and epistemological discussions regarding the type of phenomenon we study, resulting in debates that show the fragmentation of Psychology in different fields and their little interrelation for the significance of what we study. A reflection by

V. D. Mori (✉)
University Center of Brasilia, Brasilia, Brazil
e-mail: morivaleria@gmail.com

© The Author(s), under exclusive license to Springer Nature Singapore Pte Ltd. 2021
D. M. Goulart et al. (eds.), *Theory of Subjectivity from a Cultural-Historical Standpoint*,
Perspectives in Cultural-Historical Research 9,
https://doi.org/10.1007/978-981-16-1417-0_16

Koch (1999) remains relevant even though advances have taken place: "the fractionation of Psychology into insulated areas of study and/or professional interest has continued at an accelerating pace" (p. 115). We continue with the fragmentation that has historically been discussed as a reflection point by different theorists at different times (Danziger, 1997; González Rey, 2016; Koch, 1999) in the sense of advancing in relation to the ideas that human processes can be understood through its separation into parts and the dichotomization of the individual and the social without any articulation with historical processes that constitute the human.

Specifying what psychotherapy means as a practical theoretical field runs through the way human processes are theoretically understood, as well as the idea of what psychotherapy means and its contradictions throughout its constitution as a field of psychology, there is no way to separate these ideas, as expressed in the previous paragraph. The focus on individual processes that guided different theoretical explanations had effects on the practice in psychotherapy (Neubern, 2004; Romagnoli, 2006; Holanda, 2012; Mori, 2019), as the person has long been recognized for attributes that were either pathologized or did not allow explanations at a level that facilitated the understanding of its systemic and procedural configuration. The consequences of this situation were the lack of clarity in the definition of psychotherapy and how to study its phenomena without universalizing or simplifying them. Various theoretical movements have been engaged in deepening this debate.

In this paper, I discuss González Rey's Theory of Subjectivity (1997, 2002, 2003, 2007, 2011, 2016, 2019a) as a promising possibility to advance the understanding of psychotherapy and its relationship with social processes, which are constituents of individual processes, through the subjectivity category developed by the author.

16.2   Psychotherapy and Subjectivity

The separation of Psychology in different fields of study resulted in the representation of theories as related to a type of practice and of different human processes as understood in relation to the specific context in which they express themselves without articulation with other people's living spaces. We have already made great progress in this regard in the contemporary context, even though the constitution of Psychology as a field of science is constituted by contradictions that mark its history, just like any theoretical field, on the other hand, scientific research has made it possible to advance in relation to these dominant representations to overcome these contradictions. The different debates related to the aforementioned enabled new ways of understanding psychotherapy as a resource for practice and research, as well as its definition in order to mean it as a process of relationship and dialogue.

The representation of psychotherapy as a space for research and production of ideas has developed over time (Lacan, 1998; D'Allone, 2004; Vaisberg, 2004; González Rey, 2007, 2011, 2015a; Neubern, 2012; Mori, 2012, 2019; Mori & Goulart, 2019) and has made it possible to overcome the dichotomization of research and practice. The separation of these two processes was supported by the idea that the practice is the result of applying the theory produced in scientific research, and what was defined as science moved away from the daily lives of those who were engaged in different psychology practices. Psychotherapy is a privileged space for research, its configuration as a process allows us access to different possibilities of constitution of human processes and challenges in the production of new forms of explanation due to the unpredictability that characterizes these processes. The theoretical production of research enables new representations about the studied phenomena and in the same way new resources for the practice in different areas of professional performance.

It is important to highlight that the relationship between research and practice is based on the theory or theories that guide the different reflections that take shape in the process, because the lack of clarity and theoretical depth does not allow the understanding of the complexity of the processes we study. González Rey (1997) highlights the importance of theoretical reflection to accompany the production of knowledge, emphasizing theory as a tool of thought that highlights its value due to the quality of the configuration of the research/practice space in its relationship with the psychologist's ideas and imagination, as it makes it possible to break away from the dominant instrumentalism that still dominates in the representation of these processes. The author gives a good summary of what was discussed in this paragraph:

> Human theories are fictions capable of producing intelligibility about matters that other theories do not allow. Speculation is inseparable from doing science, even when it is not the end of a scientific enterprise. Nonetheless, without speculation, there is no thinking, and science is above all a process of production from thinking. (González Rey, 2019a, p. 17)

An important contribution by González Rey is expressed in his concern with the way we produce knowledge to study subjectivity, the author developed Qualitative Epistemology (González Rey, 1997, 2002; González Rey & Mitjáns Martínez, 2017) as a resource to guide and produce knowledge regarding the study of subjective processes. Evidently, the epistemology developed by the author is oriented to answer the questions related to the subjectivity category defined by him in the theory of subjectivity and emphasizes, in his works, the inseparability of theory of subjectivity, constructive-interpretative methodology as the methodological development of Qualitative Epistemology.

The subjectivity category proposed by González Rey incites us to follow a theoretical path in which the answers are not ready, as discussed in the previous paragraph when orienting ourselves from this perspective, it is essential to understand what is defined by subjectivity for the author. I think that a central aspect in its definition is recognition of subjectivity as a system that integrates the different experiences of people who are organizing themselves in processes of subjective sense. Subjective senses are the emotional and symbolic organization of the processes of subjectivity and expresses the ontological specificity of subjectivity (González Rey, 2019a). Thus, subjectivity is defined in this perspective:

> Quality of all complex human and social processes and phenomena, representing them not as two different phenomena that maintain relations of externality and determination of one over the other, but as processes that are configured in a reciprocal, permanent way, in which one is part of the nature of the other. (Mitjáns Martinez & González Rey, 2017, p. 53)

As explained in the quote, subjectivity articulates the individual and the social in a way that one constitutes the other, there are two theoretical categories that enable us to understand these systems in process: individual subjectivity and social subjectivity. Individual subjectivity is not dissociated from social subjectivity, both are mutually constituted and configure subjectivity as a system. The value of this category, for the meaning of different human processes, is expressed in the interrelationship between individual and social. Individual subjectivity is not determined by social subjectivity, or vice versa, in this theory these two systems surpass the dichotomized view between individual and social. Due to their form of constitution, these systems show the "contradictory, complementary and recursive character" (Mitjáns Martinez & González Rey, 2017) of the organization of subjectivity as a process.

The idea of social subjectivity subverts the logic of determination, cause and effect, in which the social is a conditioning factor of individual processes and the idea that the social refers to disarticulated processes of the constitution of the person. In psychotherapy, social subjectivity is a process that is implied in the whole life fabric of the people who participate in these contexts and through it we can explain people's different life configurations that would not be possible to signify without this category. Thus González Rey (2015b) defines it: "Social subjectivity is the network of social subjective configurations within which the different social practices, activities, and institutional rules get subjective senses for those involved in the processes within social institutions and informal social organizations" (p. 13).

The category social subjectivity expresses the complex subjective configuration of different human processes. The different subjective productions, related to people's experiences, mark the way in which they are individually organized and similarly constituted by the different processes that take shape in contexts of their life. Subjectivity is organized into emotional and symbolic processes that are defined as subjective senses: "a particular relationship that takes place between symbolic processes and emotions in a culturally delimited space of activity of the individual, in which both processes are involved in a reciprocal manner without one being the cause of the appearance of the other" (Mitjáns Martinez & González Rey, 2017, p. 52). Subjective senses of different experiences in the person's life constitute different subjective configurations that express the inseparability between individual and social.

The idea of configuration for the understanding of subjective processes is fundamental in this theoretical perspective. It allows us to advance in their representation by recognizing them as systemic and procedural, the subjective configurations express the complex organization of the different lived experiences in which the historical and the current mobilize different subjective senses that constitute these same configurations. Different social processes can be subjectivized in different ways by people, the dominant discourses do not have a direct effect on the way we feel the world but are uniquely configured by people. In psychotherapy, we seek through the analysis of subjective processes to understand how they are subjectively configured in the complex constitution between individual and social, González Rey defines subjective configuration as follows:

> Subjective configurations are dynamic but have a relative stability due to the congruency of the subjective senses that they generate. These are different but complementary in their effects on the subjective settings of individuals and groups in their ongoing actions. (González Rey, 2017, p. 514)

For the study of subjectivity, the configurational logic[1] guides us toward the understanding of different human experiences, as it allows us to advance in relation to deterministic conceptions, both social and individual, which make it impossible to recognize the way in which people produce subjectively in relation to different aspects of life. The idea of subjective configuration makes it possible to understand human processes in their multiplicity, as it integrates subjective senses associated with very distinct experiences from people. Subjectivity is organized by the different effects that a situation has, effects that are linked to historical and cultural processes and not by the direct effect of situations on people.

16.3 Social Subjectivity in Psychotherapy

The resources we use for practice are also resources for research, they are not watertight moments of subjective production that are related either to professional action or to the production of knowledge. Theoretical production organizes itself in research and practice:

> Advancing the theoretical challenges of subjectivity without having research as a basic resource of theoretical production is an impossible task, as it is in the construction processes implied in research and professional practice that theories advance and take shape as living bodies in motion. (González Rey & Mitjáns Martínez, 2017, p. 27)

An essential condition for these two moments, from the perspective of the Theory of Subjectivity, is their organization based on the three principles of qualitative epistemology which is the basis of the Constructive-Interpretative Methodology proposed by the author. They are the ones who guide the making and the theoretical production in this regard. One aspect highlighted by González Rey (2002, 2017, 2019b) is the inseparability of the three principles and their value for understanding subjectivity as a process. They are:

(i)   The constructive-interpretative character of knowledge—the knowledge process is not organized by ready-made models a priori, but by the researcher's ability to articulate theory and ideas in the information construction process.

It is the psychotherapist as an investigator commitment to theory that marks the way in which the constructive-interpretative process is organized. The theory comes to life in its articulation with the processes of reflection and imagination that are configured in the interpretation of the different phenomena studied. The production of knowledge in the psychotherapy process, guided by the constructive-interpretative character, allows us to build theoretical models; model that comes to life through the indicators and hypotheses produced along this path. The indicators are conjectures of

---

[1]"The configurational logic… is the organization of a constructive-interpretative process that takes place in the course of the research itself and through countless channels that the researcher does not define a priori, but that are articulated with the in situ model that accompanies and characterizes the development of research" (González Rey, 2005, p. 123).

the psychotherapist, as well as those of an investigator, and represent the beginning of the production of thought about the studied subject. As different indicators are articulated, hypotheses are produced and enable the construction of the theoretical model. For example, if a 20-year-old girl expresses: "my mother is everything to me" and in another moment: "I would like to understand the hurt I feel toward my mother"; in these two excerpts an indicator can be raised of the contradiction in relation to the mother that the young woman feels, more information is needed so that hypotheses can be produced, the constructive interpretive process is organized in a procedural way. As the hypotheses are organized based on the different indicators, the theoretical model comes to life, based on it, the psychotherapist's actions are guided.

The procedurality of the production of indicators, hypotheses and theoretical model does not conform to the reproduction or application of the theory, but to the deepening of the fundamentals of the Theory of Subjectivity in the sense of signifying the various phenomena beyond the direct evidence. This is one of the challenges for practice and research based on the Theory of Subjectivity, it is not an easy path, it demands breaking with a priori categorizations, breaking with linear determinations of cause and effect due to the very contradictory character of subjectivity. Morin (2007) summarizes what a theory clearly means:

> A theory is not knowledge; it allows knowledge. A theory is not an arrival; it is the possibility of a departure. A theory is not a solution; it is the possibility of treating a problem. In other words, a theory only fulfills its cognitive role, it only comes to life with the full use of the subject's mental activity. (p. 335)

(ii)   The legitimacy of the singular—means recognizing the value of the singular case for theoretical production due to its possibility of opening new paths of signification.

Mitjáns Martinez (2019) suggests that the value of singularity rests on the production of knowledge that is made possible by its form of organization. This is an important point to be considered, because in the study of subjectivity, through a constructive-interpretative process, the singular is an information that takes on meaning in the course of research, in theoretical production; and in the course of practice, in guiding professional actions that are not dissociated from theory. Its quality to produce knowledge is expressed in the following quote:

> Singularity acquired epistemological status in Qualitative Epistemology, for which the singular did not represent uniqueness, but differentiated information that is based on the specific case that takes on significance in a theoretical model that transcends it. (González Rey & Mitjáns Martínez, 2017, p. 29)

(iii) The interactive character of the knowledge production process—research/practice is a social space in which dialogue is organized through the engagement of those involved in the process (researcher/psychotherapist and participants/person in psychotherapy).

Dialogue is a point to be highlighted in this proposal for its quality as a human process that can subjectively mobilize the people who participate in it. Dialogue does not mean a hierarchical relationship between people and the psychotherapist, but it is configured by the difference between people that can mobilize different subjective senses. Dialogue, in the Theory of Subjectivity, is a resource to understand how the other subjectively produces in relation to their different life processes. In addition, it implies mobilizing, in the context of psychotherapy or research, the emergence of the other as a subject or agent[2] in relation to different aspects of his life. This mobilization can be a facilitator of the subjective development of the person, which means the production of new subjective resources that enable changes in different areas of life (Mitjáns Martinez & González Rey, 2017). Alternative subjective productions can be organized through dialogue, both in psychotherapy and in research, and can lead to subjective development. It is important to note that "no psychotherapist's action facilitates one's development by the role of the psychotherapist in itself, but by the way the person in psychotherapy produces subjectively in relation to the processes of psychotherapy" (Mori, 2020, p. 174).

Subjectivity is not directly evident in speech, but through dialogue we can understand how speech appears subjectively configured (González Rey, 2019b). Through the constructive-interpretative process, which is the basis of research and practice, we can advance in the understanding of the different subjective processes that are configured in these contexts of dialogical relationship. From the different hypotheses and theoretical models that are produced in this process, the psychotherapist as an investigator mobilizes the other through dialogue with the intention of facilitating new subjective productions in relation to the different life processes. Well expressed by González Rey (2019b): "it is the constructive-interpretative process of the researcher and the professional that converts dialogue into a privileged process of the production of knowledge in the social sciences, as well as knowledge as a dialogical tool" (p. 36).

Psychotherapy based on the Theory of Subjectivity is configured as a dialogical process that implies the engagement of people who participate in it and can mobilize different subjective processes. In psychotherapy work, in this theoretical perspective, our intention is to understand the diverse constitution of subjective processes considering that changing the social subjectivity of the different spaces of experience of the person is a concrete possibility, because the dialogue mobilizes subjectivity as a process not only individually. The new subjective senses produced in the psychotherapeutic process have effects on different subjective configurations that can, for example, be related to the social subjectivity of the person's work. This social subjectivity can be tensioned by new subjective productions, that is, symbolic-emotion processes of another order can be mobilizers of the configuration of the dominant social subjectivity of a space.

---

[2] "The agent and subject proposed by us are not a-historical, they are not static, they are not substantiated in an original subjective condition. It is an individual or group with the capacity to position itself, to generate, with its positionings, processes that are beyond its control and conscience. It is a subjectively configured individual who generates subjective meanings beyond their representations, but who, at the same time, makes decisions, takes positions, has intellectual productions and commitments, which are the source of subjective meanings and open new subjectivation processes" (González Rey & Mitjáns Martínez, 2017, p. 72).

Daily life can be an example of how social subjectivity is expressed and organized and in the same way we can have subsidies to analyze its configuration and its effects on individual subjectivity. In Brasilia (Brazil), we have a "park" open for some years and, at the time of its inauguration, there was a sign at the entrance that prohibited the entrance of people on foot. A sign that reflects a type of society in which people move around by car, as there were also no bus stops near the park; and privileges a social class that has a car and lives near the park. This is a form of exclusion that is naturalized in everyday life and highlights options that we make as a society, its effects are not visible at first sight, but symbolic-emotion translates into different processes that are subjectified by the people who participate in this city. Dialogic spaces are important so that reflection on processes like the one mentioned above can mobilize new subjective productions in relation to the life we share in society. Dialogic spaces are important so that reflection on the processes mentioned above can mobilize new subjective productions in relation to the life we share in society. It is not the individualization of the social, but its understanding based on the subjective production of people in relation to the side effects of social subjectivity in their life experiences that enables us to understand the configuration of that same social subjectivity. In this case in question, the naturalization of inequalities hides important aspects of the configuration of social spaces and psychotherapy can be the dialogical space for its understanding and mobilization for change, states González Rey (2015a):

> Any social subjective production expresses, through a diverse repertoire of different subjective senses, the multiplicity of social and individual configurations that characterize any space or moment of social life. Social subjectivity thus characterizes the multiple and simultaneous social spaces within which society functions. Social subjectivity represents the complex subjective network of subjective social configurations within which every social functioning takes place. (p. 15)

This reading of subjectivity makes it possible to break with easy and reductionist descriptions of social processes, because neither the individual subjectivity nor the social subjectivity is given, but is produced in the diversity and tension of individual and social moments. Both in the study of subjectivity based on the constructive-interpretative process and in the practice of psychotherapy in this framework, it is important to understand the idea of subjectivity in its complexity. In research and in practice, this process can translate into new possibilities of development for the people who participate in it. The psychotherapist as an investigator guides his actions during the research process or psychotherapy from the theoretical reflections that are taking shape along this path. These reflections must be guided by the idea that subjectivity is not static, but it is a contradictory process that is configured by the relationship between different experiences of the person. Thus, the different actions in this process imply both the social subjectivity of the studied contexts and the individual subjectivity of the people who participate in these contexts.

The singular configuration of these processes allows us to understand different subjective senses that are produced individually and socially. Subjective senses are unique productions that concern the way people and contexts are organized symbolically and emotionally, making it impossible to classify them based on universal criteria, because what takes shape in a society does not reproduce in another and in the same way that an event does not have the same value and meaning for different people. The constructive-interpretative process, in practice and in research, allows to advance in the understanding of the information that comes to life through dialogue, and guide us to actions that can be facilitators of alternative subjective productions. Dialogue is a fundamental process as a resource that makes it possible to advance in the understanding of the processes we study, and the commitment we have with the different people and institutions studied.

The practical relationship and research allow us to reflect that psychotherapy is not organized only as clinical practice, but in different contexts, as institutions for example, and are psychotherapeutic for the quality of human relationship and dialogue it establishes. And in the same way they are possibilities to generate change in different processes of both individual and social subjectivity. The dialogical character of this proposal goes beyond the individualized view of psychotherapy as previously discussed, which results in its value for changing aspects of social subjectivity in different spaces. In research carried out with university professors (Ribeiro & Mori, 2020), the work with the group of professors and the monitoring of their daily lives enabled different reflections on the professors' part on how they could make changes related to the division of tasks and the relationship between them. This resulted in new possibilities for configuring the hegemonic social subjectivity of this educational institution. González Rey (2007) states: "These forms of psychotherapy cannot be aimed solely at changing individual people who participate in a social space, but also at changing the hegemonic social subjectivity in such spaces" (p. 94). In this sense, both in practice and in research social subjectivity processes are understood and mobilized through the action of the psychotherapist or of the researcher.

16.4 Final Reflections

Professional practice and research based on the theoretical framework of subjectivity are guided by the assumptions of the constructive-interpretative method proposed by González Rey, based on the dialogical process that is configured in any of these contexts, we can understand how different subjective configurations are organized and how in them the social and the individual are subjectivated singularly in the lived experience. Both in practice and in research, we are committed to the subjective development of people who participate in these processes as well as to the mobilization of diverse subjective processes that make it possible to change the dominant social subjectivity that can be expressed in the institutions or contexts that we take part in.

The emphasis on individual processes to the detriment of other aspects of human experience remains the dominant representation of psychotherapy, a fact that can be attributed to the way that Psychology was constituted as science and the same way to the idea that processes external to the person, whether social or individual symptoms are defined outside the person's experience. I think that the Theory of Subjectivity has been the possibility of a critical reflection in this process and its contributions aim to overcome the dichotomization at different levels and mainly the understanding of subjective processes as contextualized in a culture and constituted by them. Subjectivity is a theoretical model that allows us to overcome the fragmentation of different human processes and to develop new theoretical models to signify different phenomena in practice and in research that facilitate the understanding and change of processes of social subjectivity.

The configuration of subjective processes in the contemporary moment is marked by consumption, individualistic and the weakening of social institutions making it essential for Psychology different reflections on these realities. Answers that show a new way of signifying subjective processes in order to recognize the person in their condition to generate new alternatives and at the same time that they allow to overcome the notion of regularity and universalization that still happens in such a simplistic way. I think that the notion of subjectivity developed by González Rey is a theoretical possibility to overcome the previous, since the qualitative epistemology for its study is central to the understanding of its complex configuration. Just as the definition of subjectivity integrates in a contradictory social and individual way overcoming its dichotomization, showing that the social is not something abstract, but to be expressed in the different relationship systems that individuals take part in.

References

D'Allone, C. (2004). *Os procedimentos clínicos nas ciências humanas: Documentos, métodos e problemas* [Clinical procedures in the humanities: Documents, methods and problems]. São Paulo: Casa do Psicólogo.

Danziger, K. (1997). *Naming the mind—How Psychology found its language*. London: Sage.

González Rey, F. (1997). *Epistemologia cualitativa y subjetividad* [Qualitative epistemology and subjectivity]. Habana: Pueblo y educación.

González Rey, F. (2002). *Pesquisa qualitativa e subjetividade: Caminhos e desafios* [Qualitative research and subjectivity: Paths and challenges]. São Paulo: Thonsom Learning.

González Rey, F. (2003). *Sujeito e subjetividade: Um enfoque histórico cultural* [Subject and subjectivity: A cultural historical approach]. São Paulo: Thonsom.

González Rey, F. (2005). *Pesquisa qualitativa e subjetividade: Os processos de construção de informação* [Qualitative research and subjectivity: The processes of information construction]. São Paulo: Thonsom learning.

González Rey, F. (2007). *Psicoterapia, subjetividade e pós-modernidade. Uma aproximação histórico-cultural* [Psychotherapy, subjectivity and postmodernity: A historical-cultural approach]. São Paulo: Thonsom.

González Rey, F. (2011). *Subjetividade e saúde: superando a clínica da patologia* [Subjectivity and health: Overcoming the clinic of pathology]. São Paulo: Cortez.

González Rey, F. (2015a). A saúde na trama complexa da cultura, das insitituições e da subjetividade [Health in the complex web of culture, institutions and subjectivity]. In F. González Rey & J. Bizerril, *Saúde, cultura e subjetividade: uma referência interdisciplinar* [Health, culture and subjectivity: An interdisciplinary reference] (pp. 9–33). Brasília: Uniceub.

González Rey, F. (2015b). A new path for the discussion of social representations: Advancing the topic of subjectivity from a culturalhistorical standpoint. *Theory & Psychology, 25*(4), 1–19.

González Rey, F. (2016). Advancing the topics of social reality, culture and subjectivity from a cultural-historical standpoint: Moments, paths and contradictions. *Journal of Theoretical and Philosophical Psychology, 36*(3), 175–189.

González Rey, F. (2017). The topic of subjectivity in psychology: Contradictions, paths and new alternatives. *Journal for the Theory of Social Behaviour, 47*(4), 502–521.

González Rey, F. (2019a). Subjectivity in debate: Some reconstructed philosophical premises to advance its discussion in psychology. *Journal for the Theory of Social Behaviour, 49*(2), 212–234.

González Rey, F. (2019b). Epistemologia qualitativa vinte anos depois [Qualitative epistemology twenty years later]. In A. Mitjáns Martinez & F. V. González Rey, *Epistemologia qualitativa e teoria da subjetividade: discussões sobre educação e saúde* [Qualitative epistemology and theory of subjectivity: Discussions on education and health] (pp. 21–45). Uberlândia: EDUFU.

González Rey, F., & Mitjáns Martínez, A. (2017). *Subjetividade: teoria, epistemologia e método* [Subjectivity: Theory, epistemology and method]. Campinas: Alínea.

Holanda, A. F. (2012). Reflexões sobre o campo das psicoterapias: do esquecimento aos desafios contemporâneos [Reflections on the field of psychotherapies: From forgetfulness to contemporary challenges]. In A. F. Holanda, *O campo das psicoterapias: relfexões atuais* [The field of psychotherapies: Current reflections] (pp. 71–100). Curitiba: Juruá.

Koch, S. (1999). *Psychology in human context: Essays in dissidence and reconstruction*. Chicago: The University of Chicago Press.

Lacan, J. (1998). *Escritos* [Writings]. Rio de Janeiro: Zahar.

Mitjáns Martinez, A. (2019). Epistemologia qualitativa: dificuldades, equívocos e contribuições para outras formas de pesquisa qualitativa [Qualitative epistemology: Difficulties, mistakes and contributions to other forms of qualitative research]. In A. Mitjáns Martinez, F. González Rey, & R. Valdes Puentes, *Epistemologia qualitativa e teoria da subjetividade: discussões sobre educação e saúde* [Qualitative epistemology and theory of subjectivity: Discussions on education and health] (pp. 47–69). Uberlândia: EDFU.

Mitjáns Martinez, A., & González Rey, F. (2017). *Psicologia, educação e aprendizagem escolar: Avançanco na contribuição da leitura cultural-histórica* [Psychology, education and school learning: Advancing the contribution of cultural-historical reading]. São Paulo: Cortez.

Mori, V. D. (2012). Os sentidos subjetivos de ser psicoterapeuta: a aprendizagem em um estágio supervisionado [The subjective meanings of being a psychotherapist: Learning in a supervised internship]. In A. M. Martinez & M. I. Betriz Judith Scoz, *Ensino e aprendizagem: subjetividade em foco* [Teaching and learning: Subjectivity in focus] (pp. 203–218). Brasília: Liber Livro.

Mori, V. D. (2019). A psicoterapia na perspectiva da teoria da subjetividade: a prática e a pesquisa como processos que se constituam mutuamente [Psychotherapy from the perspective of subjectivity theory: Practice and research as processes that are mutually constituted]. In A. Mitjáns Martinez, F. González Rey, & R. Puentes Valdés, *Epistemologia qualitativa e teoria da subjetividade: discussões sobre educação e saúde* [Qualitative epistemology and theory of subjectivity: Discussions on education and health] (pp. 183–201). Uberlândia: Edfu.

Mori, V. D. (2020). Reflection on the value of the theory of subjectivity to signify the practice of psychotherapy. *Estudios de Psicología, 41*(1), 182–202.

Mori, V. D., & Goulart, D. (2019). Subject and subjectivity in psychoterapy: A case study. In F. González Rey, A. Mitjáns Martinez, & D. Goulart, *Subjectivity within cultural-historical approach* (pp. 231–244). Singapore: Springer.

Morin, E. (2007). *Ciência com consciência* [Science with conscience]. Rio de Janeiro: Berthrand.

Neubern, M. (2004). *A complexidade da psicologia clínica: desafios epistemológicos* [The complexity of clinical psychology: epistemological challenges]. Brasília: Plana.

Neubern, M. (2012). Ensaio sobre a cegueira de Édipo: sobre psicoterapia, política e conhecimento [Essay on Oedipus blindness: On psychotherapy, politics and knowledge]. In A. Holanda, *O campo das psicoterapias: reflexões atuais* [The field of psychotherapies: Current reflections] (pp. 13–45). Paraná: Juruá.

Ribeiro, L. F., & Mori, V. D. (2020). Análise construtivo interpretativa dos processos de subjetivos da rotina docente universitária [Constructive interpretive analysis of subjective processes of university teaching routine]. *Trabalho (EN)cena, 5*(1), 181–195.

Romagnoli, R. (2006, jul/dez de). Algumas reflexões acerca da clínica social [Some reflections on the social clinic]. *Revista do departamento de Psicologia - UFF, 18*(2), 47–56.

Vaisberg, T. A. (2004). *Ser e fazer: Enquadres diferenciados da clínica Winnicottiana* [Being and doing: Different frameworks of the Winnicottian clinic]. Aparecida-SP: Ideias e Letras.

Valéria Deusdará Mori is Ph.D. in Psychology at the Universidad San Carlos de Guatemala, Master in Psychology at the University of Brasília, graduated in Psychology at the University Center of Brasilia (UniCEUB). Currently, a Professor of the Psychology course at UniCEUB for the undergraduate and master's degrees. Research interests are focused on psychology from the cultural-historical approach of subjectivity, in the fields of subjectivity, psychotherapy, health, and human development.

Chapter 17
Subjectivity and Children's Play: The Conceptual Legacy of Fernando González Rey in Early Childhood

Marilyn Fleer

Abstract González Rey declared in post Ph.D. research that, "My studies on personality and motivation had led me to the topic of subjectivity…" (González Rey, *Journal for the Theory of Social Behaviour* 45:419–439, 2014, p. 432). In Fernando's quest to re-theorise subjectivity and capture the generative character of emotions as the genesis of new psychological systems, he introduced new concepts—*subjective senses and subjective configurations*. As powerful theoretical concepts, he gifted the international community with a legacy (González Rey et al. (Eds.). *Theory of Subjectivity: New Perspectives Within Social and Educational Research*, Springer, The Netherlands, 2019) that has opened up new directions in research. In this chapter, I contribute to the now well-trodden pathway created by Fernando by discussing imagination, emotions and play in relation to early childhood education. In play children make meaning as they move closer to reality, exploring rules and roles (as social and societal reproductions), at the same time as developing their own storylines (as creative and symbolic productions). The theoretical debt to González Rey's work is shown in this chapter through studying how development in play can be conceptualised as a dynamic system of social relations rather than as a collection of psychological functions. It is argued that, play acts as a mirror image of the symbolic processes, social relations and emotionally imaginative (re)configurations of the subjective character of three and four-year-old children's experiences and psychological operations.

17.1 Introduction

Like González Rey (2011), Gunilla Lindqvist (1995) noted a continuity in the early and the final works of Vygotsky. Both allude to the significance of emotions and symbols, but do so, in different ways. Their combined work helps with realising how play creates and develops the emotional imagination of young children (Fleer,

M. Fleer (✉)
Conceptual PlayLab, Monash University, Melbourne, VIC, Australia
e-mail: marilyn.fleer@monash.edu

© The Author(s), under exclusive license to Springer Nature Singapore Pte Ltd. 2021
D. M. Goulart et al. (eds.), *Theory of Subjectivity from a Cultural-Historical Standpoint*,
Perspectives in Cultural-Historical Research 9,
https://doi.org/10.1007/978-981-16-1417-0_17

2017), where emotions are always acting in partnership with symbolic processes (González Rey, 2012). This chapter draws on the theoretical legacy of González Rey (2015) and studies the subjectivity of a group of three and four-year-old children who experience in social relations an emotionally imaginative PlayWorld (Fleer, 2017) of *The Adventures of Alice in Wonderland* (Carroll, 2009). Building on previous research (Fleer, 2020) which focused on teachers' subjectivity (Fleer, 2019), the goal of this chapter is to draw upon the above concepts to better understand the problem of personality development of the preschool child who is at play.

The theoretical debt to González Rey's work is shown in this chapter through studying how development in and through play can be conceptualised as a dynamic system of social relations rather than as a collection of psychological functions. It is through González Rey's (2012) concepts of *subjective senses and subjective configurations* that we can better analyse how play acts as a mirror image of the symbolic processes, social relations, and emotionally imaginative configurations of the subjective character of three and four-year-old children.

This chapter begins with a theoretical discussion of the problem, followed by an elaboration of the central concepts employed, concluding with details of the study and its findings.

17.2 Theoretical Problem

Vygotsky's theoretical vision entailed a system of concepts, which together enabled researchers to study in a holistic way, human development. However, within Vygotsky's theoretical system, many concepts were unable to be fully developed, thus leaving it to the cultural-historical community to continue to develop and refine the concepts. González Rey (1999) holds a special place in history, as one cultural-historical researcher who took forward Vygotsky's work through developing the concept of *subjectivity*. González Rey (1999) in moving beyond individual subjectivity, re-conceptualised *subjectivity* as, "something different to experience". He said it "is the complex system of meanings and subjective senses which are configured in many different ways throughout human development" (p. 257). He argued that humans are subjectively constituted. The complex social networks that exist within social spaces enable a process of subjectivisation to take place. With this lens, González Rey (1999) captured the complexity of personality development as,

> ...the subjective character of a social space [where] not only the expression of the current interactions of its members...is constituted simultaneously by the ongoing interactions of the persons who are part of that social space in the present time and by those subjective trends that historically have configured it as a moment in its own history and at the same as a particular moment of society. (p. 258)

The complexity of this conceptual dynamic quoted above, needs unpacking if its power is to be harnessed. Therefore, we begin by detailing the concepts of emotions in González Rey's work. In González Rey's theoretical writings, he said that the process of subjectivisation embeds and leaves emotional traces. The personal production is both cognitive and affective. González Rey (1999) drew attention to how "emotions only appear after symbolic processes have been encoded in one way or another in individual experience" (p. 260). They represent "clusters of emotions and ideas in process" (p. 266). Emotions become the "cornerstone in the constitution of personality" (pp. 260–261). *Configurations* as a new concept captures the emotional whole of the dynamic interactions during the process of subjectivisation. *Subjective senses* also a new concept, "defines a relatively stable group of emotions experienced by subjects in their different activities and relations" (González Rey, 1999, p. 263). Together, *subjective senses and subjective configurations* in dynamic relations, enable researchers to holistically understand human development as a unity of emotional and symbolic processes.

González Rey (1999) also said that "Subjectivity is a complex system that constantly reconfigures itself throughout its own development, in an endless process that simultaneously involves the historical and current social conditions in which the subject is immersed" (p. 264). But how these concepts of *subjective senses and subjective configurations* explain the leading activity of the preschool child engaged in imaginary play, has not yet been discussed in the literature. Can symbolic processes and emotions, as constituted through the play of the preschool child, be linked with the view that a "child's play is imagination in action" (Lindqvist, 1995, p. 48) where a unity of emotions and cognition (Vygotsky, 1966) is evident? In play children make meaning as they move closer to reality, exploring rules and roles (as social and societal reproductions), at the same time as developing their own storylines (as creative and symbolic productions). The constant flux is emotional, imaginatively symbolic and realised through relations with others. This aligns well with González Rey's dynamic concepts.

Emotions as a theoretical concept has only received minimal attention in the play literature (exceptions include, Elena Kravtsova, Mariane Hedegaard and L.V. Vygotsky). Hedegaard (2010) has argued that in the literature into play and learning that, "the importance of children's imagination and exploration has been promoted *but only indirectly has the emotional part* through motive analyses been implemented; *the excitement and the tension that play may create* has not been in focus" (p. 71, My emphasis). But what is the place of emotions in children's play? Answering this could give a better understanding of how the preschool child is subjectively constituted through play.

17.3 Child's Play Is Imagination in Action

In order to answer the theoretical questions posed in this chapter, it is necessary to introduce other concepts, concepts that have also been discussed by Fernando González Rey when featuring the work of L.I. Bozhovich and her followers in his writings. González Rey (2002) has foregrounded the concept of periodisation as introduced by Vygotsky (1998) through discussing Bozhovich's (1977, 2009a,

2009b) elaboration of social situation of development, perezhivanie, motives, needs and crisis. I add to this system of concepts around periodisation, contemporary play research, and the original conception of play discussed by Vygotsky (1966) to better understand how three and four-year-old children are subjectively constituted through play. A brief overview of some of these concepts are presented because the development of the child and the development of imaginary play are intertwined.

First, it has been reported in many of the papers of González Rey that Bozhovich undertook a theoretical elaboration of many of the original concepts introduced by Vygotsky. In particular she draws attention to periodisation, where motives and needs are studied and further theorised in relation to the concept of the social situation of development. Of importance to the focus of this chapter, is how this unfinished concept of Vygotsky did not feature a societal perspective in the study of periodisation. González Rey (2002) argued that, "The individual subject is not only a result of direct social influences, but rather he/she is part of the complex social system within which people live and develop as part of a developing social system in its completeness" (p. 132). González Rey draws attention to the need for a holistic interpretation of the preschool child, where the child is embedded in contexts shaped by societal values. In line with this, Hedegaard (2010) brings forward how societies shape institutions through their values operationalised in rules and expectations. In the context of this study, there are expectations in many Western societies that preschools will create conditions where young children have opportunities for play. They provide time and resources, but also set expectations in communities that the preschool period and kindergarten is a time and place for children to play. Therefore, play as a social activity creates particular kinds of conditions for the development of the preschool child.

Second, a cultural-historical conception of play development is defined as the creation of an imaginary situation, where the players see one thing, but imagine something else. That is, they change the meaning of the objects in the sense field and give them a new sense—as happens when a stick becomes a hobby horse and the imaginary situation of horse riding is established between play partners. A new sense of the situation is created, which affords new actions by the players. This is not fantasy argued Vygotsky (1966), but rather it is about children moving closer to reality by exploring the roles and rules within society that become, as Elkonin (2005) said, the content of their imaginary play. The child makes conscious through their play, the rules of their society, and the roles of people within it. For example, when two sisters are pretending to be sisters, they explore what it means to be a sister, how to behave as a sister and what to say to a sister. In their play they make conscious what it means to be a sister and establish a concept of sisterhood. Here the imaginary situation dominates. This is an imaginary situation with rules about sisterhood.

Even though Vygotsky (1966) did not explicitly develop a strong link between play with his theory of human development conceptualised through periodisation (Vygotsky, 1998), he did discuss the development of play itself, showing that it becomes evident when children move from an imaginary situation with rules (being sisters), to rules with an imaginary situation, such as when children play games (chase and tag or card games). This development of children's play marks insights into the child's changing relations with their social and material environment. When children spend longer discussing the rules of play, then actually playing, Vygotsky (1966) argued that development had occurred. In his lecture notes on play, Vygotsky (2005) draws out will and consciousness as characteristics in children's play development. But these ideas were never fully developed in his writing, leaving it to his granddaughter to take forward.

Elena Kravtsova said that a double subjectivity emerges during the development of children's play. The child feels herself/himself above the play exploring the rules/roles and within the play being a play partner. Emotions are also expressed, such as being happy to be playing, but also being emotionally expressive in the content of the play, for instance, when playing hospitals and the child pretends to take medicine or receive an injection. This duality of emotions and consciousness (will) in imaginary situations was elaborated into a complex system of play development by Kravstova and Kravtsova (2010). What is important in her work is theorising how emotions and will act in unity during children's imaginary play.

But what appears to be missing is how emotions, as a theoretical concept, contributes to play development. Vygotsky (1966) made mention that the preschool child's leading activity is to play. He set the stage for emotions within play. But he did not show how play contributes to the development of the child, or how the child is subjectively constituted through the process of playing with others. Further theorisation is needed. To understand this better, the process of subjectivation introduced by González Rey (2002) and discussed above, can help because,

> …it is impossible to distinguish between external influences and internal psychological organisation. In a subjective sense, both moments are blended together in a unique new quality of the subjective configuration of experience. *Subjectivation* is actually a condition of subjectivity, and it is a permanently developing process. This process only takes place as a complex subjective process that involves individual needs, which appear as emotions within the construction process of the subject. Both emotions and constructive processes are present in the process of subjectivation as a whole. (p. 133)

González Rey (2002) opens up a theoretical space because *subjective senses and subjective configurations* act as a universal dynamic to theorise the development of human personality. But how it deals with the development from the leading activity of play for the preschool child to the leading activity for learning of the school child in periodisation is less clear, and therefore this demands other concepts.

Finally, and in line with González Rey (2002), Lindqvist said that, "Play does not keep emotion, thought and will separated from one another" (1995, p. 4) and "…the interplay between emotions and intellect gives rise to the development of imagination in play" (p. 49). This suggests that imagination in play is important for the development of the preschool child. Could play be symbolic productions in action, in the same way as Lindqvist (1995) has said that a "child's play is imagination in action" (p. 48)? In play, there is always a relationship between the fiction of the play plot and actions of the players who draw on the rules and roles in society. Play is therefore constantly in motion as a contradiction between reality and imagination. In play children make meaning as they move closer to reality, exploring rules and roles, as social and societal reproductions, at the same time as developing their own storylines as creative and symbolic productions. The constant flux is emotional, imaginatively symbolic and realised through relations with others. This echoes the subjectivisation process introduced by González Rey. Could play as symbolic productions, emotions, actions and social relations, captured and explained as *subjective senses* and *subjective configurations*, expand understandings of the subjectivity of three and four-year-old children's experiences and psychological operations? To explore this, we build upon previous research (Fleer, 2020) and report further results of a study where affective imagination was featured.

17.4 Study Design

Previous research focused on González Rey's work on subjectivity as a powerful theory for studying digital data generated through a dramatic and imaginative STEM PlayWorld (Fleer, 2018, 2019) of Alice in Wonderland (Fleer, 2020). PlayWorlds was originally developed by Lindqvist (1995). It was designed for preschool children and teachers to come together and dramatise stories. It took place through role-playing stories and fairy tales over weeks and months. STEM PlayWorlds (Fleer, 2018, 2019) also draws inspiration from stories and role-playing. There are 5 characteristics of a STEM PlayWorld: (1) Selecting a dramatic and emotionally charged story; (2) Creating an imaginary situation where children and teachers act "as if" if characters in the story (or associated with it); (3) All children and teachers enter the imaginary situation together to re-live the story; (4) Adventures are planned that extend the story and which create conditions where children need concepts to solve the problems that arise and finally, (5) teachers plan their roles to be with the children as play partners. In previous research, it was found that children can experience emotionally charged events (dramatic story) which lead to an emotional self and other awareness. But less attention was paid to how in play children are subjectively constituted. Following the same study design of an educational experiment (Hedegaard, 2008) and analysing the same data set, this chapter takes up the challenge of how play acts as a mirror image of the symbolic processes, social relations and emotionally imaginative configurations of the subjective character of three and four-year-old children.

The study took place in a preschool setting where community members were predominantly of Western heritage, and families constituted a mix of professional and creative self-employed parents. Two teachers agreed to join with researchers to plan and study the results of an educational experiment designed to increase STEM learning through drama and story reading of *The Adventures of Alice in Wonderland*. An educational experiment takes place within a naturalistic setting that is part of the everyday life of teachers and children. It is a planned intervention into practice. The "researcher builds on already formulated conceptual relations within a problem area that were outcomes" of previous research (Hedegaard, 2008, p. 182) and the "intervention is planned in relation to a theoretical system and not simply from agendas of practice" (p. 185).

Important to the focus of the study reported in this chapter, is how the play conditions were theorised in relation to children's development. We were interested to study how the drama of the story and PlayWorld of Alice in Wonderland created new demands and practices within the research context for studying how children were subjectively constituted in social relations. How the play conditions became developmental can be seen when individuals make social representations that become subjective senses within the collective activity of the STEM PlayWorld. The collective productions of the PlayWorld emerge through the subjective senses generated by the collective, and which has its genesis in the story and role-playing of the characters.

In our educational experiment 18 children (3.0–5.8, mean age of 4.8) participated in the PlayWorld. We followed these children over 7 weeks and documented their play using two cameras. We generated a total of 1,725 digital photographs, 153.3 h of digital video observations and 32.5 h of teacher–researcher interviews/professional development. We analysed these data holistically by conceptualising the play practices as a dynamic system of social relations rather than as a collection of psychological functions. In line with González Rey, we also examined how play subjectively constituted the children within the new practices, paying special attention to affective imagination. For the purposes of this chapter, we drew out of digitally analysed data set, video clips that had been tagged in relation to affective imagination and then examined if and how play acts as a mirror image of the symbolic processes, social relations and emotionally imaginative (re)configurations of the subjective character of three and four-year-old children's PlayWorld experiences and psychological operations.

17.5 Data Presentation and Discussion

In line with Fernando González Rey's theoretical contributions, the results of our study show empirical detail of the subjectivisation process in and through play development. It is through studying children's actions in play that a mirror of the thoughts and emotions of children becomes visible.

Building on previous findings (Fleer, 2020), in this chapter we introduce the first moments when children explore the contractions within the story of Alice in Wonderland in relation to real world practices and the subjectivities that they bring. In our analysis, we determined that contradictions in the story that created emotionally charged moments where children's imagination was being affectively ignited as they expressed their reactions during storytelling and when role-playing in the PlayWorld of Alice in Wonderland. In the set of transcripts that follow we begin with the story telling of Alice in Wonderland, followed by segments of data that show how children express their emotions and thinking through:

- Experiencing the imaginary situation collectively through storytelling
- Imagining and discussing the contradictions as part of the storytelling
- Embodying the contradictions in action through role-play.

17.6   Scene 1: Experiencing the Imaginary Situation Collectively Through Storytelling

In the vignette that follows, the children have previously had the first chapter of story of *The Adventures of Alice in Wonderland* read to them. It is now the first time the children experience the story through the narrative of storytelling, where the two teachers (Olivia and Ruth) sit with the children in a circle on a mat amplifying the emotions associated with the story and generating moments of wondering and problem solving.

> Olivia is telling the story of *The adventures of Alice in Wonderland*. She expressively introduces the moment when Alice has gone down the rabbit hole and has drunk the "Drink me, drink me potion" and has shrunk to fit through the row of small doors inside the rabbit hole. Alice realises she cannot open the small door because it is locked. But the key is on the table, which now in comparison to Alice, is huge and out of reach. Olivia says as she looks up and makes dramatic climbing actions with her hands.
>
> Olivia pauses and then continues with the story, pointing forward as she says, "I really want to get through that door".

In this example, emotions, imagining and thinking are intertwined. The storytelling is emotionally charged, the problem situation that arise creates a dramatic tension for the children, and this appears to amplify a collective orientation to solving the problem of how to get the key down from the table so that Alice can go through the locked door. The children bring to the problem their working theories of shrinking, drawn from the story plot to consider further shrinking so they can go under the door. This example, and the one that follows in Scene 2, ilustrate that for some children, such as Jack, he is trying to make sense of the idea of shrinking as part of the dream that he appears to think must be the reason why Alice was able to shrink after drinking the "Drink me potion". There is a dynamic of imagining "as if" they are with Alice down the rabbit hole, but also imagining "for real" these first moments of storytelling where emotions, thinking and imagining are being configured within the subjectivities of the children. A sense of collective imagining and collective emotional engagement is realised through the PlayWorld of Alice in Wonderland.

17.7   Scene 2: Imagining and Discussing the Contradictions as Part of the Storytelling

In the second example, Olivia is telling the part of the story where Alice is trying to solve the problem of getting the key from the table. The engagement of the children in the drama of the story is now amplified cognitively by the teachers, but only in relation to emotional tension associated with the problem scenario and the collective imaginary situation of Alice down the rabbit hole.

Olivia continues the story by drawing upon the children's suggestions to invite possible imagined solutions, "I wonder if I could eat this cake, and get big or small, and go underneath the door or go get the key to open the door. Ruth says, I wonder what is on the other side of the door. Jack announces, "Yes that is what I am wondering". Olivia says, "Ummm" and then continues with the story, "So she ate the cake". She pauses, "Nothing changed". Jack holds his head, and says, "But it had. She [Alice] touches her head". Ruth repeats and extends Jack's suggestion, "She had to touch her head to feel if she was bigger or smaller or the same". A flurry of children gesture actions that appear as though they are imagining themselves shrinking/growing, most are holding their heads and different children say at the same time "Bigger", "Smaller". The teacher looks to them intently and asks if they are getting bigger or smaller? The children continue to respond, "Smaller", whilst others say "bigger". A singsong cadence and repetition of, "smaller, bigger" is heard from the children.

Next Olivia asks, "I wonder what it would be like to go through the tunnel...." Mary responds firmly, "I would not like to do that at all", as Olivia is saying, "...deep down into the well". Mary repeats, "I would not like to do that actually, at all". Ruth responds to Mary and to the other children saying, "I noticed when Olivia was telling the story, that Alice was feeling brave and courageous. She wasn't feeling scared so much, was she?". Ruth responds, "No" shaking her head. Olivia follows this up with a quizzical facial expression and says, "She kept wondering". Ruth says, "She was curious".

The teachers nod and say in unison, "She was very curious".

The drama of the story and the invitations of the teachers to wonder about shrinking or growing was in response to the story plot of drinking the "Drink me potion". This appeared to add to the dramatic tension. Interestingly, it also appeared to stimulate children's thinking. Children seemed to collectively be imagining solutions, drawing upon the story plot.

The different subjectivities of the children were being brought together, risk taking, problem solving, remembering the story plot, and emotions associated with fear, bravery, curiosity and wonder. The individual and collective subjectivities were not only intertwining through the story plot, but as will be shown progressively in this chapter, were constantly being subjectively re-configured. In line with González Rey (2015), emotions, imagining and thinking appeared to be acting in unison.

17.8   Scene 3: Embodying the Contradictions in Action Through Role-Play

Over the entire period that is the focus of the analysis for this chapter, it was only in the last five minutes that the children actually performed the role-play of Alice going down the rabbit hole. It was the period before this, where a movement from storytelling to role-play, appeared to change the developmental conditions for the children, as the following 3 changes in the observation illustrate.

Change 1: Ruth says to Olivia in a manner that suggests her question is intended for the children, "Do you think because the children are so interested in the story, we could act it out?". This is met with an enthusiastic response by the children: "I would".

As Ruth begins asking, "Who would like to be..." the children put suggestions forward about what they would like to be, "I want to be Alice"; "I would like to be the door"; "We want to be the rabbits" (group of 5 children form); "I'm the white rabbit". The teachers respond positively to the enthusiasm of the children who are now standing up and beginning to position themselves to role-play the story.

Change 2: The children self organise, "I want to be the White Rabbit" "Yeah, I am going to the door. You can go through the door". Jack stands tall whilst Mary points to his legs. Jack spreads his legs as Mary in role as White Rabbit goes between Jack's legs. As she goes through, Jack closes his legs, announcing "And when she goes through, I close the door". At the same time as Mary and Jack are enacting their characters, there are now groups of children enacting other or similar parts of the story. Small groups children simultaneously discuss at length the characters and their action with each other, especially in how to bring the collective narrative of 'as if' they are down the rabbit hole. Towards the end, Mary says to Jack, "Let's practice".

Throughout this period of discussion and short role-play practice, the teachers support the children's play by asking about "What other important roles/things are there in the story?". Only two children move to other parts of the centre, but they stay in close enough proximity to follow the play activity/discussion, and later re-join the PlayWorld when the actual collective performance begins.

Change 3: Now most of the children are together with the teachers, and it is a collective response to role-playing the PlayWorld of Alice in Wonderland. The teachers and children narrate the story, with the teachers filling in the storylines when they appear to need support.

In keeping with Vygotsky's (1966) conception of play development where children spend longer discussing the rules of the play, then actually playing, the children spend most of their time discussing the roles with each other and with the teachers. Some children discuss or practice their actions, and others spend time working out what objects could represent important parts of the story, such as the tick-tock pocket watch, the drink me potion and the eat me cake.

17.9   Conclusion

Vygotsky (1971) argued that Art is not simply a reproduction of reality, but rather it is a productive and generative emotional and creative endeavour. The story of Alice in Wonderland began with story reading, followed by storytelling, and finally a collective PlayWorld emerged. Collectively playing "as if" was not simply a reproduction of reality of the story plot, but rather it was productive and emotional and imaginatively generative. This aligns with González Rey's subjectivisation process, and nuances how the play of four-year-old children can create conditions for the development of subjectivity, but also how play gives the space in which the subjectivities of children come together. This is different to what is normally reported in the play literature, where the focus is usually on dyads. In this study the focus was on all of the children playing within the same collective imaginary situation.

In the study reported in this chapter, it was found that dramatic contradiction emerged in children's play. There was always a dramatic relationship between the fiction of the play plot, such as being Alice in Wonderland, and actions of the players who drew upon the rules and roles in society, where it is impossible for a child to shrink and go down a rabbit hole in reality. That is, the imaginary play of Alice in

Wonderland, created conditions where children were constantly in a contradiction between reality and imagination. This contradiction generated an emotional tension which acted as an important source of children's play development. We especially noted that this social relations and dynamic moments for and between children were configured and re-configured during the many moments of the drama of being in the PlayWorld of Alice in Wonderland. Play gave time and space for these subjective processes.

Building on González Rey (2014), the emotional tension identified in this study was found to be a central driving force in children's play. The study found that emotions are always present in the drama of the play—as a dynamic of raw expressions and consciously realised feeling states. Play is more than imagining, it is imagining with great emotional connection, enthusiasm, expression and tension. This finding speaks directly to what Hedegaard (2010) noted as missing in research into play. Further, this aligns with the Cinderella phenomenon, where emotions appear as the Cinderella to the other two stepsisters, thinking and will (cited in Zaporozhets, 2003). Conceptualising emotions and cognitive processes as dynamic and interlacing within the collective imaginary play gives new ways of understanding children's play. In line with González Rey (2015), this represents a dynamic system of social relations, rather than a collection of psychological functions.

But to understand fully the play of preschool children, we build upon González Rey's conception, by advancing the concept of *collective subjectivitiy* to capture and explain the "group of children in the same imaginary situation" emotionally imagining and experiencing the story of Alice in Wonderland. Collective productions of imagining together, are integrated social productions that emerge through the subjective senses generated by the collective, but with their origins in the story. Without the concepts of subjective senses and subjective reconfigurations it would be difficult to realise these understandings of the emotional and imaginatively generative nature of PlayWorlds for preschool children.

Finally, in answering the theoretical problem posed in this chapter, we argue that the PlayWorld of Alice in Wonderland created unique psychological conditions that could productively contribute to the children's development. The children were emotionally engaged and living through paradoxical situations they encountered. Some contradictions were resolved through a form of magical metamorphosis (drink me potion and then shrinking) and some were discussed morally (I would think before I act and go down the rabbit hole). Therefore, play creates an emotional tension through the contradiction between children's reality and the imaginary situation of the PlayWorld. Consequently, the outcomes of this study show the significance of *affective imagination* of play for realising symbolic processes, social relations, emotionally charged configurations and reconfigurations. This conceptualisation helps explain how emotions in imaginary play, act as the motivating conditions between thinking, will and imagination, which together are an important source of cultural development for three and four-year-old children. Therefore, *affective imagination* and *collective subjectivity* as concepts for explaining play as a leading activity of the preschool child, not only aligns and elaborates González Rey's conception of subjectivity, but it solves the theoretical problem raised in this chapter, giving new possibilities to researchers who are interested in studying children's play.

Acknowledgements I would like to acknowledge the research assistance of Sue March (Team Leader), Yijun (Selena) Hao, Hasnat Jahan, Carolina Lorentz Beltrão, the teachers in the educational experiment and funds from the Australian Research Council for data collection [DP140101131] and for the write up of the results [FL180100161]. Special mention of the expertise of the teachers who collaborated in the educational experiment is also made, as their active and intellectual involvement in the theoretical problem contributed to new understandings.

References

Bozhovich, L. I. (1977). The concept of the cultural-historical development of the mind and it prospects. *Voprosy Psikhologii, 2,* 29–39. https://doi.org/10.2753/RPO1061-040516015.

Bozhovich, L. I. (2009a). L.S. Vygotsky's historical and cultural theory and its significance for the contemporary studies of the psychology of personality. *Journal of Russian and East European Psychology, 42*(4), 20–34. https://doi.org/10.1080/10610405.2004.11059226.

Bozhovich, L. I. (2009b). The social situation of child development. *Journal of Russian and East European Psychology, 47*(4), 59–86. https://doi.org/10.2753/RPO1061-0405470403.

Carroll, L. (2009). *The adventures of Alice in Wonderland.* Herts, UK: Wordsworth Editions.

Elkonin, D. B. (2005). The psychology of play. *Journal of Russian and East European Psychology, 43*(1), 11–21. https://doi.org/10.1080/10610405.2005.11059245.

Fleer, M. (2017). Scientific playworlds: A model of teaching science in play-based settings. *Research in Science Education, 49*(5), 1257–1278. https://doi.org/10.1007/s11165-017-9653.

Fleer, M. (2018). Digital animation: New conditions for children's development in play-based setting. *British Journal of Technology Education, 49*(5), 943–958. https://doi.org/10.1111/bjet. 12637.

Fleer, M. (2019). The role of subjectivity in understanding teacher development in a Scientific Playworld: The emotional and symbolic nature of being a teacher of science. In F. González Rey, A. M. Martinez, & D. M. Goulart (Eds.), *Theory of subjectivity: New perspectives within social and educational research* (pp. 149–164). Dordrecht, The Netherlands: Springer.

Fleer, M. (2020, in press). The legacy of Gonzalez Rey's concept of subjectivity continues to inform and inspire: A study of imagination in STEM and imagination in play. *Studies in Psychology, 41*(1), 203–214. https://doi.org/10.1080/02109395.2019.1710986.

González Rey, F. (1999). Personality, subject and human development: The subjective character of human activity. In S. Chaiklin, M. Hedegaard, & U. J. Jensen (Eds.), *Activity theory and social practice* (pp. 253–275). Aarhus, Denmark: Aarhus University Press.

González Rey, F. (2002). L.S. Vygotsky and the question of personality in the cultural-historical approach. In D. Robbins & A. Stetsenko (Eds.), *Voices within Vygotsky's non-classical psychology: Past, present, future* (pp. 129–142). New York: Nova Science Publishers.

González Rey, F. (2011). A re-examination of defining moments in Vygotsky's work and their implications for his continuing legacy. *Mind, Culture, and Activity, 18*(3), 257–275. https://doi. org/10.1080/10749030903338517.

González Rey, F. (2012). Advancing on the concept of sense: Subjective sense and subjective configurations in human development. In M. Hedegaard, A. Edwards, & M. Fleer (Eds.), *Motives in children's development: Cultural-historical approaches* (pp. 45–62). Cambridge: Cambridge University Press.

González Rey, F. (2014). Human motivation in question: Discussing emotions, motives, and subjectivity from a cultural-historical standpoint. *Journal for the Theory of Social Behaviour, 45*(4), 419–439. https://doi.org/10.1111/jtsb.12073.

González Rey, F. (2015). A new path for the discussion of social representations: Advancing the topic of subjectivity from a cultural-historical standpoint. *Theory & Psychology, 25*(4), 494–512. https://doi.org/10.1177/0959354315587783.

González Rey, F. (2017). The topic of subjectivity in psychology: Contradictions, paths and new alternatives. *Journal of Theory and Social Behaviour, 47*(4), 502–521. https://doi.org/10.1111/jtsb.12144.

González Rey, F. Mitjáns Martinez, A., & Goulart, D. M. (Eds.). (2019). *Theory of subjectivity: New perspectives within social and educational research.* Dordrecht, The Netherlands: Springer.

Hedegaard, M. (2008). The educational experiment. In M. Hedegaard & M. Fleer (Eds.), *Studying children: A cultural historical perspective.* (pp. 181–201). New York, NY: Open University Press.

Hedegaard, M. (2010). Imagination and emotion in children's play: A cultural-historical approach. *International Research in Early Childhood Education, 7*(2), 59–74. Retrieved from https://files.eric.ed.gov/fulltext/EJ1138863.pdf.

Kravtsov, G. G., & Kravtsova, E. E. (2010). Play in L.S. Vygotsky's nonclassical psychology. *Journal of Russian and East European Psychology, 48*(4), 25–41. https://doi.org/10.2753/RPO 1061-0405480403.

Lindqvist, G. (1995). *The aesthetics of play: A didactic study of play and culture in preschools.* Stockholm, Sweden: Gotab.

Vygotsky, L. S. (1966). Play and its role in the mental development of the child. *Voprosy Psikhologii, 12*(6), 62–76.

Vygotsky, L. S. (1971). *The psychology of art.* Cambridge, MA: MIT Press.

Vygotsky, L. S. (1998). *The collected works of L.S. Vygotsky* (Vol. 5). New York: Kluwer Academic and Plenum Publishers.

Vygotsky, L. S. (2005). Appendix. From the notes of L.S. Vygotsky for lectures on the psychology of preschool children. *Journal of Russian and East European Psychology, 43*(2), 90–97. https://doi.org/10.4324/9781315746043.ch3.

Zaporozhets, A. V. (2003). Toward the question of the genesis, function, and structure of emotional processes in the child. *Journal of Russian and East European Psychology, 40*(2), 45–66. https://doi.org/10.2753/RPO1061-0405400345.

Marilyn Fleer Foundation Chair, Monash University, Australia, Australian Research Council 2018 Kathleen Fitzpatrick Laureate Fellowship, honorary Research Fellow, Department of Education, University of Oxford, and 2nd professor position in the KINDKNOW Centre, Western Norway University of Applied Sciences. She was a former President of the International Society of Cultural-historical Activity Research and recipient of the Ashley Goldsworthy Award.